*Making More Milk is an incredible accomplishment, an... ... ...
time. Today, the #1 concern of nursing families is: "How do I know if I have enough milk,
and what do I do if I don't?" The answers are here, but there is so much more. Lisa and Diana
make the complex easy to understand, and their nuanced approach enhances your relationship
with your baby while giving you the tools you need to better plan and understand your own
nursing experience. This book is a treasure!*

—Nancy Mohrbacher, IBCLC, FILCA, author of *Breastfeeding Solutions,
Working and Breastfeeding Made Simple,* and co-author of *Breastfeeding
Made Simple: Seven Natural Laws for Nursing Mothers*

*Making More Milk will become the go-to resource for lactation consultants and parents with
low milk supply. Although written for parents, every IBCLC should have this excellent book
in their library.*

—Jan Barger RN, MA, IBCLC, FILCA, Executive and Program Director for
Lactation Education Consultants

*What an outstanding book! Comprehensive, yet easy to read and understand. This book is
required reading for all of my families who worry about milk supply.*

—Jarold "Tom" Johnston DNP, Midwife, Assistant Professor of Nursing at
Methodist University, Fayetteville, NC

*The second edition of* Making More Milk *is as informative as the first, and even more
thorough. It follows a logical, systematic trail from the most common and solvable difficulties,
through the rare and into the frontiers of new research. I especially liked the anticipatory
guidance for the next baby, these strategies have helped my own clients. Even as an IBCLC
for almost three decades, I learned from this book. I highly recommend it to parents and
professionals.*

—Catherine Watson Genna BS, IBCLC, author of *Supporting Sucking
Skills in Breastfeeding Infants* and *Selecting and Using Breastfeeding Tools*

Making More Milk *is the essential handbook for any mother who is concerned about her
milk production! Lisa and Diana's decades of combined experience, along with their passion
for helping mothers, helps to bring a wealth bring a wealth of information and encouragement
to exhausted, discouraged breastfeeding moms.*

—Bekki Hill, CLC (and low milk supply mom)

# making more *milk*

## Second Edition

## The Breastfeeding Guide to Increasing Your Milk Production

**Lisa Marasco**, MA, IBCLC, FILCA
**Diana West**, BA, IBCLC

New York   Chicago   San Francisco   Athens   London   Madrid
Mexico City   Milan   New Delhi   Singapore   Sydney   Toronto

1 2 3 4 5 6 7 8 9  LCR  24 23 22 21 20 19

ISBN      978-1-260-03115-7
MHID      1-260-03115-2

e-ISBN    978-1-260-03114-0
e-MHID    1-260-03114-4

Cartoons on pages 3, 25, and 169 by Neil Matterson, used with permission.
Illustrations on pages 5, 6,  135, 140, 141, 142, 143, by Taina Litwak, used with permission.
"Lact-Aid" photo on page 44, courtesy of Tricia Phillips, used with permission
"Bra strap" on page 44, "Finger-feeding with Hazelbaker" page 53, "Nipple flip" page 117, "Dancer hold" page 122, by Margaret Wills, used with permission.
"Breast Sandwich" on page 129 is copyright © Diane Lewis Photography, used with permission.
"Oxytocin Nasal Spray for Letdown" on page 184 by Frank Nice, RPh, DPA, CPHP, used with permission
"Pumping and bottle-feeding" on page 205, photos by Alexandra Lloyd, used with permission

McGraw-Hill Education books are available at special quantity discounts to use as premiums and sales promotions or for use in corporate training programs. To contact a representative, please visit the Contact Us pages at www.mhprofessional.com.

*To all the mothers and parents who courageously pursue the journey of nursing with low milk supply out of love for their babies and to the members of the IGT and Low Milk Supply, BFAR, and MOBI communities who generously share their experiences and innovative ideas in order to teach their lactation helpers and assist the parents who come after them.*

# Contents

Foreword     xi

Acknowledgments     xiii

Introduction     xv

PART I     1

## Investigating Your Milk Supply

CHAPTER 1     3

### Understanding Your Milk Factory

The Milk Supply Equation • Seasons of Breast Development: Growing a Milk Factory • Hormones and the Milk-Making Process • The Letdown Reflex: Nature's Delivery System • Reaching Milk Production Equilibrium • Baby Calls the Shots • The Resource-Efficient Breast • The Role of Storage Capacity • Does Milk Production Have an Upper Limit? • Milk Production is Designed to Succeed

CHAPTER 2     15

### What's Normal and What's Not

Commonly Misinterpreted Baby Behaviors • Reading Body Language to Guesstimate Milk Intake • Commonly Misinterpreted Maternal Indicators • Do You Have Enough Milk?

CHAPTER 3     25

### How Do I Know if There Really is a Problem?

How Can I Tell if My Baby is Getting Enough Milk? • Can't I Just Pump to See How Much I'm Making? • The Final Results • Three Rules to Live By

PART II                                                                                    35

## Making the Most of What You Have

CHAPTER 4                                                                                  37

## Supplementing Made Simple

How Do I Know When to Start Supplementing? • How Much is Right and Where
Do I Start? • What's the Best Supplement for My Baby? • What's the Best Way to
Supplement? • What About Weaning from Supplements? • Solids as Supplements

CHAPTER 5                                                                                  57

## Blasting Off to a Great Start

The Lactation Curve • Learn to Hand Express Before Birth • Shop for a Breastfeeding-
Friendly Pediatrician • Plan for a Breastfeeding-Friendly Birth • Start Nursing in the
Golden First Hour After Birth • An Optimal Latch is Key to Optimal Milk Production
• Optimizing Milk Removal • Beware of Tight Bras • Putting it All Together: The
Essential Elements

PART III                                                                                   71

## Investigating Causes of Low Milk Production

CHAPTER 6                                                                                  73

## Is it Something I'm Doing?

Pinpointing the Reasons for Your Low Supply • Latch Problems • Feeding
Management • When Milk Seems to Dry Up Overnight • Sneaky Saboteurs:
Common Substances That Inhibit Milk Production • Pregnancy

CHAPTER 7                                                                                  87

## Is it My Diet?

Calories and Dieting • Nutrients • Conditions That Can Affect Nutrient Intake • Fluids:
The Old Wives' Tale • What About Eating Your Placenta? • Your Nutritional Profile
• Good Food Sources of Lactation-Critical Nutrients

CHAPTER 8                                                                                  99

## Is it Something About My Pregnancy or Birth?

Pregnancy Issues That Can Affect Lactation • Birth Issues • Essential Self-Care

## CHAPTER 9      109
### Is it Something My Baby is Doing?

Suck Problems • The Large, Small, Early, or Meds-Affected Baby • Torticollis • Tongue Mobility Restriction • Palatal Variations • Facial Abnormalities and Jaw Problems • Airway Problems • Cardiac Problems • Nervous System Issues • Infections • Reflux • The Self-Limiting Feeder • When Nothing Seems to Fit

## CHAPTER 10      127
### Is it Something About My Breasts?

Anatomical Variations • Breast Structure • Breast Surgeries • Infections • Injuries

## CHAPTER 11      147
### Is it My Hormones?

Hormonal Issues: The Big Spider Web • Prolactin • Your Metabolic Profile • Infertility • Thyroid Dysfunction • Autoimmune Issues • Menstruation • The Age Factor • Lactation Labs • What do I do Now?

## CHAPTER 12      169
### Is My Letdown Reflex Letting Me Down?

Letdown Reflex Under the Looking Glass • Physical Techniques to Help Trigger Letdown • Mind vs Matter • Matter Over Mind: Organic Problems with Letdown • Lactogenic Substances for Letdown • Moving Ahead

## PART IV      187
### Increasing Milk Production

## CHAPTER 13      189
### *Move That Milk!* Pump It Up!

Breastfeed More Frequently • Express to Plug the Gap • Hand Expression • Pumps • Milk Storage and Leftover Milk • How Long Do I Keep This Up?

## CHAPTER 14      209
### *What the Galactogogue?* Milk-Boosting Medications, Foods, and Herbs

Targeting: Choosing the Best Galactogogue for Your Needs • Pharmaceutical Galactogogues • Lactogenic Foods: Can You Really Eat Your Way to Making

More Milk?  •  Navigating the World of Herbal Galactogogues  •  Homeopathic Galactogogues  •  When Can I Stop Taking a Galactogogue?  •  Galactogogues Tables

CHAPTER 15                                                                                           247

### Making More Milk When You Return to Work or School

Develop Your Game Plan  •  Common Pitfalls  •  Increasing Your Supply While Working  •  Solids Take the Pressure Off

CHAPTER 16                                                                                           257

### Making More Milk in Special Situations

Exclusive Pumping  •  Premature Babies  •  Multiples  •  Relactation  •  Induced Lactation  •  LGBTQ Lactation and Co-Nursing

CHAPTER 17                                                                                           273

### Thinking Outside the Box: Complementary and Alternative Therapies

Chiropractics  •  Traditional Chinese Medicine, Acupuncture, and Acupressure  •  Breast Massage  •  Kinesio Tape  •  Yoga  •  How About a Little Romance?  •  Harnessing the Mind  •  Further Out There  •  Pursuing a Complementary Therapy

PART V                                                                                              279

### Surviving the Present and Planning for the Future

CHAPTER 18                                                                                           281

### Coping with Low Milk Supply

You ARE Successful  •  The Many Emotions of Low Supply  •  Coping Ideas from Real Parents  •  Take it One Day at a Time  •  Be Kind to Yourself  •  Making Peace with Low Milk Supply  •  To the Partners and Families of Those with Low Milk Supply

CHAPTER 19                                                                                           295

### What About Next Time?

A Proactive Approach  •  Planning for the Next Pregnancy  •  Strategies for a Current Pregnancy  •  What About Hypoplasia?  •  Hope Is on the Horizon

References                                                                                          305

Index                                                                                              353

# Foreword

"I wasn't making enough milk, so I had to switch to formula."

I often hear these words or something similar. In so many of these cases, the parents had no one available with the experience and knowledge to evaluate and help remedy the situation. And many times, when supplementation is needed, it is done in a manner to guarantee that supply will drop even further.

I've been working and talking with breastfeeding parents for more than 20 years, and of the many concerns that new parents face, increasing milk supply dominates. On my website KellyMom.com, articles about milk supply, how much milk babies need, how to know if baby is getting enough milk, and pumping output decreases are among the ten most-visited webpages. A quick survey of this month's questions from mothers in the online KellyMom support group show almost a third of all questions are related to how to make more milk.

Milk supply concerns affect parents and babies in big ways. So many of the comments are of this nature:

"I'm in a panic because I won't be able to feed my son."

"My heart is breaking because I can't nurse my baby."

"I'm always stressed about whether I can pump enough."

And while the concerns are all about making more milk, there are so many variations:

"I want to stop supplementing, but I don't make enough milk."

"Is there some medication, herb, or food that will increase my milk supply?"

"What is the best way to feed baby supplements while continuing to breastfeed?"

"My baby is nursing less at night, and it is affecting my supply."

"My baby is drinking more milk than I can pump!"

"I had mastitis, and now my supply has decreased."

"Is it possible to return to breastfeeding after stopping for a few weeks?"

"I didn't make enough milk for my last baby. What can I do to improve supply this time?"

"WHY am I not making enough milk?"

This book is the helpline for these parents. The authors are your sympathetic guides through the often-complicated maze of milk production issues, helping you to understand the latest research while determining how (and when) it applies to you, telling stories of how other parents worked through similar issues, and pointing out useful resources along the way. The authors discuss how milk production works, then lay out the information needed to diagnose a supply problem, the causes of low supply, how to supplement without decreasing your existing supply, the best ways to maximize your supply, and, as the title says, what you can do to start "making more milk."

Many find that their breastfeeding experience is not what they originally expected or planned for. But even if your journey takes an unexpected detour, *you are still a breastfeeding parent*. Every drop of breastmilk that your child gets is beneficial. Every moment at the breast that your child gets is beneficial. Breastfeeding is not all or nothing. Everyone has a different breastfeeding journey. Even if your breastfeeding reality is different than that of another person or what you had envisioned for yourself, this book will be your guide to help you create your own best-case picture of how breastfeeding looks in your life.

When you find yourself in an unfamiliar land, you'll want to make sure that you choose first-class guides. Lisa Marasco and Diana West are professionals in the field of lactation, have decades of experience working with breastfeeding families, and have written books and articles too numerous to mention. I've heard them speak many times, have read their books and articles, and can guarantee that this book contains accurate, fully researched information that is aimed at helping parents with the myriad of supply issues they face.

When I was asked to write this foreword, the previous edition of this book was on my desk, in the first line of books I go to when researching accurate information for breastfeeding families. This updated edition is even better—I hope you enjoy and learn as much from the book as I have!

Kelly Bonyata, BS, IBCLC
KellyMom.com
St. Petersburg, FL
USA

# Acknowledgments

Updating *Making More Milk* required us to lean on the help, experience, and expertise of many colleagues, friends, and clients to make it the best possible. We are indebted to Jan Barger, Cathy Genna, Nancy Mohrbacher, Barbara Robertson, and Diane Wiessinger for their wisdom and practical help in nailing the important issues. We also extend our deep gratitude to Maya Bolman, Melissa Cole, Laurie Nommsen-Rivers, Shannon Kelleher, Russ Hovey, Donna Geddes, Jackie Kent, Peter Hartmann, Sharon Perella, Kay Hoover, Robin Glass, Lynn Wolf, Sheila Kingsbury, Hilary Jacobsen, Sheila Humphrey, Zoe Gardner, Patricia Hatherly, Tom Johnston, Pamela Berens, Anne Eglash, Jane Morton, Tina Smillie, Tom Hale, Frank Nice, Charles Glueck, Diana Cassar-Uhl, Michelle Emanuel, Nancy Williams, Cynthia Good, Stephanie Casemore, Robyn Roche-Paul, Karen Gromada, Alyssa Schnell, Lenore Goldfarb, BreAnne Marcucci, Jennifer Millich, Victoria Nesterova, and Trevor MacDonald for their expert input; Taina Litwak for her beautiful illustrations; Neil Matterson for his insightful and humorous cartoons; Larry Berger for his expert help with photos; Kelly Bonyata for writing our foreword and sharing her lactation curve graphic; Jan Ferraro for her expertise in pumps; and Holly McSpadden for research assistance. A special thanks is owed to our reviewers, especially Kristin Cavuto, Bekki Hill, Hannah Luedtke, Ellen Rubin, Bridget Sundt, Alexis Lombardi, Ibolya Rozsa, Judy Schneider, Kim Rusthoven, and Kelli Fornow, who helped sharpen the final draft; to our focus group for their feedback and stories; and to our agent, Maura Kye-Cassella and our publisher, Christopher Brown, for their patience and support in making this second edition a reality. We are also grateful to Jessica Janoff for generously sharing her beautiful photo for the cover of this new edition. Finally, a big debt of gratitude is owed to Lisa's daughter Stephanie Carroll, who took on the role of organizing, editing, and generally seeing to all the details needed in finishing the manuscript.

# Introduction

When the first edition of *Making More Milk* was written ten years ago, some publishing houses thought there weren't enough parents with low milk supply to need a book like this. If only that were true! A quick glance at online breastfeeding support groups is enough to show the real picture. Although most mothers *should* be able to make enough milk, these online groups are full of mothers who truly *aren't* making enough milk for a variety of reasons. The reality is that 60% aren't nursing as long as they originally wanted, and milk production concerns are high on the list of why.[1] The good news is that, regardless of what's going on, you *can* be a successful breastfeeding mother or parent.

## Breastfeeding Myths

Have you heard stories of nursing parents not having enough milk or their milk drying up "just like that"? If there's no explanation, the next question in your mind may be, "Could it happen to me, too?" The fact is there's *always* a reason, and in many cases the supply problem was avoidable or reversible. The important thing is to educate yourself, because otherwise fear can lead to choices that undermine breastfeeding and unwittingly become a self-fulfilling prophecy.[2]

Another common refrain is that breastfeeding has to be "all or nothing"—all breast or all formula—because doing both is too hard and not worth your time and effort. Such short-sighted advice ignores options that offer babies some human milk when exclusive breastfeeding is difficult or impossible. You may also have heard that you're stuck with your "equipment," and there's not much you can do about it. The truth is that there are almost always ways to improve your milk production.

Today's families are pushing back on unfounded beliefs, banding together to create online support groups for low milk supply where they can share information to help others facing the same issues. Great insights and ideas emerge from these grassroot groups where highly motivated nursing parents explore all options on how to provide more milk for their babies. They understand that breastfeeding doesn't have to be all or nothing and have learned how to manage breastfeeding with a partial supply.

We don't presume to have all the answers, let alone the cures for every low milk production problem, but we've learned a lot more in the past decade. Our goal in this edition is to bring you the best and latest discoveries from every corner of the world that we've found, including ideas that parents are finding on their own, the latest research in scientific fields, and promising new ideas, to help you get to the bottom of what's affecting your supply and find effective ways to increase it.

## Why Some Breasts Don't Make Enough Milk

Research shows that there isn't a single answer and getting a handle on all the possibilities requires investigation. We've found it helpful to break them down into *primary* (internal or intrinsic) and *secondary* (external) causes.[3] *Primary milk supply problems* start within your body. With *secondary milk supply problems,* you start with the capacity to make a full supply, but something happens to reduce how much milk is made. The good news is that most production problems are secondary, which means there's a good chance of recovering your supply if the causes are identified and dealt with quickly enough.

Primary causes may be harder to pinpoint and can overlap with secondary causes. We live in a world that's full of chemicals, pesticides, and medications capable of changing hormones that affect breast development and milk production.[4] Technological advances can overcome hormonal infertility problems, yet little attention is paid to the effect of these same hormones on lactation. And because human biology is complex, a solution for one health problem can sometimes create a problem for lactation, now or later on.

You might already have a good idea of the underlying cause of your low supply. Maybe you had breast reduction surgery, so it makes sense to assume the surgery reduced your ability to make milk. But what if you also have nipple pain? Or a latch or sucking issue that further dents an already fragile supply? What if you *also* have a thyroid problem? Years of experience have taught us that some situations have multiple layers that you may need to work through. Optimizing your milk production depends on taking the time to identify and address all potential factors. In this new edition, we've added the latest research on issues that can affect your supply, along with newly identified factors for low milk production.

## The Latest in Cutting-Edge Research

It's striking that there are still so many mysteries about lactation in a scientific world that has figured out how every other part of the human body works.[5] Despite decreasing funding, good progress has been made in lactation research since *Making More Milk* was first published a decade ago. For instance, we've come to understand how critical early milk removal can be for the process of establishing a good milk supply. We've learned that metabolic health impacts lactation and that autoimmune issues can be a hidden culprit for lactation failure in some rare cases. Our knowledge of breastfeeding with hormone problems continues to expand, and we're starting to realize that diet can make a difference for some women. You'll read about the implications of these new insights and more in Part III.

## What's New in *MMM 2*

An important concept introduced in the first edition was the *Milk Supply Equation*, a breakdown of all the factors required to make and deliver milk. Seeing the big picture first may help you home in on your problems faster. We've now added two more factors: *lactation-critical nutrients* and *no other lactation inhibitors*. The first comes from traditional wisdom and emerging research on the role of various nutrients in lactation and is covered in more detail in Chapter 7. The second is different from the others because it represents all the sneaky secondary things that can still sabotage milk production when everything else is good, many of which are detailed in Chapters 6, 8, and 12. The revised equation appears in Chapter 1. We've also added the *Lactation Curve* to Chapter 5, a helpful new concept that illustrates the power of a strong start and why some parents get better results from their efforts than others.

There are three more new chapters expanding on the impact of pregnancy and birth issues on milk production (see Chapter 8), letdown problems (Chapter 12), and out-of-the-box ideas for increasing milk supply (Chapter 17). In Chapter 15, we share Nancy Mohrbacher's innovative *"Magic Number"* concept for working parents, and in Chapter 13, you'll read about Jane Morton's new insights on the most effective ways to remove milk and push production higher. We've updated the overview about pumps to address technological advances and the many new models on the international market. Chapter 14 has been expanded to add updated information about galactogogues, with companion product information available on our website.

Finally, although current information is scarce, we've started the conversation on co-nursing and transgender lactation issues in Chapter 16. And because we know that not all of our readers identify as women and mothers, we've incorporated more inclusive gender-neutral language throughout the book, such as "they" and "parents," in combination with standard female pronouns.

## Navigating the Low Supply Maze

With a slew of information and products targeting parents with low milk supply, it can feel like you're wandering through a maze in search of answers. How do you know what's true and what works when not everything we hear and read (especially online) is accurate? Starting with how breastfeeding works and what's normal, this book is designed to walk you through the process of determining if there's really a problem, ensure that your baby is thriving, identify the underlying cause(s), and develop a strategy to address the problems and increase your supply.

This last step is critical because your strategy needs to *target* the underlying cause(s) of your low supply to have the best chance of succeeding. It means detective work and careful analysis to narrow down the possibilities. If you don't know *why* you're not making enough milk, you can spend a lot of time, effort, and money on solutions that don't address the real problem. Worse, when they don't work, you may wrongly conclude that *nothing* can help, when your situation might actually have responded better to a different approach or strategy.

The reality is that some cases are very complex, and it's common to hit dead ends as you work your way through, forcing you to go back a step or two and reconsider ideas you discarded earlier. But persistent detective work can have pay-offs. When you've uncovered possible answers, you can then decide what's best for your situation. It's important to keep your health care providers in the loop because they may hold pieces to the puzzle that this book can't provide.

One additional factor that must be mentioned is the effects of poverty, racism, and discrimination on breastfeeding. Parents with less income, People of Color, LGBTQ families, and generally anyone who looks or acts different experience more barriers to their health care experiences, which can lead to less frequent and lower quality help and a higher likelihood of problems with breastfeeding. It's harder to meet breastfeeding goals when the health care system doesn't provide the assistance you need.[6-8] Such parents also have less support for nursing in the workplace, another barrier.[9] We want to acknowledge these less tangible yet very real contributors to milk supply problems and encourage affected families to seek out Baby-Friendly health care facilities (Chapter 5) where you're more likely to receive quality help.[10] And if you're a US parent with limited financial resources, consider looking into lactation help through the WIC (Women, Infant and Children) program, which continues to expand their clinical breastfeeding support services.

Whatever the cause, the path through your personal milk production maze can feel lonely. Parent-run forums and social media groups can offer valuable support and feedback when coping with low milk supply. They get what you're going through because they're going through it, too. And it's not just your online peers who are there for you— we've both had to navigate our own unexpected mazes. Lisa had three typical breastfeeding experiences before encountering a mysterious drop in milk supply with her fourth baby. Diana had breast reduction surgery and was unable to produce enough milk for her first son, though later was able to make enough for her second and third babies. Our personal experience is the basis for becoming International Board Certified Lactation Consultants (IBCLCs) and diving deeply into these issues on behalf of parents like you.

## Your Milk Matters

Sometimes parents fall short of their milk supply goal despite giving it their all. The one message we hope you'll take away is this: *every drop of your milk is precious.* Even small amounts have a unique mix of ingredients and immunities that continue to bolster your baby's health in a way that no formula can ever match. Take pride in what you *can* provide for your baby instead of what you *can't.* This is the first stop in your parenting journey, but there will be many more, built on the foundation of your commitment to giving baby your very best. That's the most that anyone can ask, and it *is* enough.

*We want to hear your story! Please visit our website, LowMilkSupply.org, to share your feedback about what has and hasn't worked for you. With your help, we'll have more answers for future parents and babies.*

# PART I

# Investigating Your Milk Supply

## *Sylvia's Story*

With my first baby, Windom, I had preeclampsia and ended up in the ICU, so we were separated for most of the first 24 hours. He was sleepy and not very interested in feeding. The ICU nurse said not to pump because I wouldn't produce much milk at first anyway.

When we were discharged, the pediatrician told me the expected weight gain was 1 to 3oz (30-90ml) per *day*! This seems laughable now, but I didn't know better then, so I really thought something might be wrong with my milk because he wasn't gaining 3oz a day. My mom believed that my milk wasn't rich enough because she had been told this about her milk when I was a baby. The pediatrician kept bringing us back every 2 days for weight checks and said I should nurse Windom every 3 hours, followed by ½ to 1oz (15-30ml) of formula. When I mentioned my nipple soreness, I was told the best treatment was to limit his time at the breast.

My incredibly supportive sister urged me to get help, so when Windom was a week old, we saw a lactation consultant. After a few weeks of improved latch and more frequent feedings, Windom was doing fine, meeting all developmental milestones, and gaining weight at the lower but acceptable end of normal range.

Things were very different with my second baby, Harper, who seemed to want to nurse every time I blinked my eyes for the first 6 weeks. After going through the sleepy baby stuff with Windom, I was glad to have a baby who was ready to nurse, nurse, nurse. I knew I would not revisit any doubts about supply.

## CHAPTER 1

# Understanding Your Milk Factory

"THE MORE HE CRIES THE LESS HE EATS, SO LESS IS MADE,
SO THERE'S LESS FOR HIM TO EAT, SO HE CRIES BECAUSE
HE DIDN'T GET ENOUGH TO EAT. GOT IT?"

Just like the parents in this cartoon, it's easy to feel confused about how breastfeeding works and whether everything is okay or not. But knowledge is power! When you understand how your body builds and runs your milk factory, you'll have a head start on solving your own personal puzzle. Even if you already know a lot, there's new information to deepen your understanding.

## The Milk Supply Equation

Let's start with the big picture first—it's easier to grasp how breastfeeding works when you can see the master plan. The components necessary for good milk production can be summed up in the following equation:

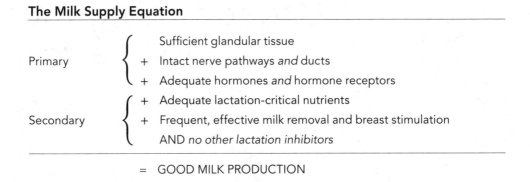

**The Milk Supply Equation**

| | | |
|---|---|---|
| | | Sufficient glandular tissue |
| Primary | { | + Intact nerve pathways *and* ducts |
| | | + Adequate hormones *and* hormone receptors |
| | | + Adequate lactation-critical nutrients |
| Secondary | { | + Frequent, effective milk removal and breast stimulation |
| | | AND *no other lactation inhibitors* |

= GOOD MILK PRODUCTION

When the first 5 components are present *and* there are no saboteurs, the body can produce plenty of milk. Now let's take a closer look at how your milk factory is built and runs.

## Seasons of Breast Development: Growing a Milk Factory

Human milk production—your milk factory—is an amazing process built upon the foundation of mammary gland (breast) development that began before you were born. While most mammals have fully developed mammary glands prior to pregnancy, the human breast develops in stages and doesn't reach full operational maturity until pregnancy and early postpartum. Like a fruit tree in winter with only a few leaves and dormant buds, the nonlactating breast has large and small branches called *ducts* and *ductules*, along with a small number of leaves, the *alveoli*, that contain the milk-making cells. They're clustered in *lobes* that intertwine and sometimes interconnect yet function mostly independently of each other.

During pregnancy, changes on the outside of the breast reflect development of the lactation system within. The *areola* and *nipple* colors deepen, the areola often enlarges, and small bumps called *Montgomery glands* become noticeable on the areola. Veins along the surface of the breast become more prominent, palpable, and bluer, the latter depending on your skin color.[1]

Your breasts may grow larger and become firmer, a sign that the milk-making tissue is growing and maturing, filling out the lobes like a tree leafing out in springtime.

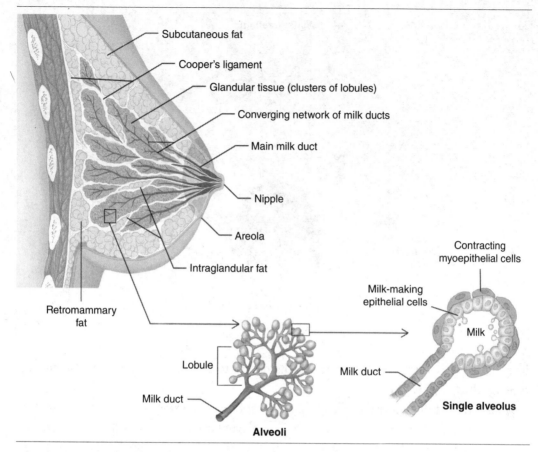

- Subcutaneous fat
- Cooper's ligament
- Glandular tissue (clusters of lobules)
- Converging network of milk ducts
- Main milk duct
- Nipple
- Areola
- Intraglandular fat

Retromammary fat

Lobule

Milk duct

**Alveoli**

Milk-making epithelial cells

Contracting myoepithelial cells

Milk

Milk duct

**Single alveolus**

*Anatomy of the lactating breast*

Breast tenderness is a positive sign that all is proceeding normally. Different parts of your breast can grow at different rates, and some may be more mature than others by the time baby arrives.[2] If growth occurs quickly and extensively, reddish or purplish stretch marks may develop that later fade over time. Breast tissue can continue to grow throughout the first month after birth. It then usually levels off and stays the same until around 6 months, when supplemental foods are introduced and milk production starts to slowly decline.[3]

Once your baby is born, milk production kicks into high gear, and the tree bears its crop of fruit, the milk. The milk-making cells may continue to multiply during the next several weeks in response to frequent milk removal, causing additional breast growth. As your baby grows older and his need for milk gradually diminishes, milk production slows down and unneeded alveoli start to die, just like a fruit tree losing its leaves. This is the autumn season of the breast, when there is still milk-making activity but at a lower

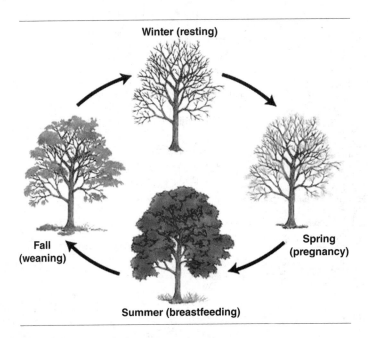

Winter (resting)

Spring
(pregnancy)

Summer (breastfeeding)

Fall
(weaning)

level. During weaning, the breast gradually returns to its resting winter state, the pruned tree, awaiting a new season of pregnancy.

The driving forces of this cycle are hormones. From puberty on, the waxing and waning of *estrogen* and *progesterone* during your menstrual cycle slowly develop the ducts and alveoli over time until around age 35. Pregnancy causes a large spike in both hormones, as well as *prolactin, human placental lactogen* (hPL), *human chorionic gonadotropin* (hCG), and *growth hormone*, which all help to stimulate glandular growth. Of all the hormones, changes in breast size during pregnancy are most closely related to the concentration of human placental lactogen, making it a crucial player in the construction of a good milk factory for your baby. Other key hormones that play a role in mammary development are *insulin, cortisol,* and *thyroid hormones.*

## Hormones and the Milk-Making Process

Understanding how your hormones function helps you know if they're helping or hindering your milk supply. Some hormones are made close to their target, but many are made in one part of the body and travel through blood vessels to reach the place they're needed.

Each hormone has a corresponding *receptor* with a unique shape that interlocks with its hormone like a lock and key. Receptors are located wherever the hormone's influence is needed, such as in the breast. There must be a good match between the amount of hormone and the number of receptors; too much of one and not enough of the other can limit hormone effectiveness. The number of available receptors can change in response to various factors. Their ability to bind together can also be affected; think of how a well-oiled lock turns easily, but a rusty one doesn't. Type 2 diabetes is an example of a rusty lock problem that happens when insulin receptors resist binding to insulin, referred to as *insulin resistance*. Pregnancy and lactation cause many changes in the number and binding ability of hormone receptors important to breast development and milk production.

Many hormones play an important role in the process of making milk. Like ingredients in a cake recipe, some have play minor roles while others are crucial for a good result. *Prolactin*, the major milk-stimulating hormone, comes mostly from the pituitary gland, though a little is made in the breast itself. We normally have a small amount of prolactin in our bodies, but during pregnancy it rises significantly, peaking close to birth. The only reason that the breast doesn't make lots of milk at this point is because the placenta is producing high levels of the hormone *progesterone*, which both stimulates breast growth and interferes with prolactin receptors on the milk-making cells, preventing them from making lots of milk yet. Instead, starting around 10-22 weeks, your first milk *colostrum* is produced.[4] This earliest phase of milk production during the second half of pregnancy is called *lactogenesis I* or *secretory differentiation*.[5]

Since the placenta makes most of the progesterone during pregnancy, progesterone drops quickly once the placenta is delivered, allowing prolactin to start working. With the help of prolactin, insulin, cortisol, and thyroid hormones, milk production

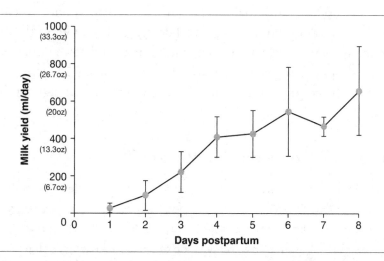

*Milk production normally rises rapidly in the first week, varying among individuals as shown by the vertical lines.[6] Approximately 90% of term parents are producing at least 440ml (~15oz) per day by the end of the 2nd week.[7]* **Copyright: © 2018 Bess et al.**

## Where's the Milk? Delayed vs Incomplete Lactogenesis

When milk production takes longer than 72 hours to increase, it is considered delayed. This is uncommon in traditional societies but happens more frequently in countries such as the United States, where it is common to hear reports of milk not coming in for 4-5 days. Babies may lose a little more weight while waiting for the milk volume to increase. With lots of quality nursing or pumping, milk production usually builds to a full supply. If this doesn't happen despite good management, it is considered *incomplete lactogenesis II* and may indicate a primary problem.[8]

begins ramping up within 30-40 hours.[5] An increase in milk volume is usually noticeable between the 2nd and 4th day after birth, often referred to as the milk "coming in" or "coming to volume." The breasts usually feel warmer, fuller, and heavier, and the milk is lighter in color and more watery than colostrum. This indicates that *lactogenesis II or secretory activation* has begun.[6]

This gradual increase in milk volume is a perfect match for your baby's slowly expanding stomach. *At each feeding*, newborns take on average ½-2 teaspoons (2-10ml) during the first 24 hours, 1-3 teaspoons (5-15ml) on the 2nd day, ½-1oz (15-30ml) on the 3rd day, and 1-2oz (30-60ml) on the 4th day.[9] They eventually settle into an average of 26oz (788ml) per day by the end of the 1st month.[10] A few babies climb a little higher to 30-33oz (900-1000ml) daily[11] by the end of the 2nd to 3rd month. Then the amount plateaus until the start of solids and a gradual decrease in need for milk. *Your baby may take more some days than others*, but he doesn't need more and more milk overall because his growth rate drops in half by 4-6 months and even further by 12 months. The amount he takes in the early months is still enough to fuel his growth throughout the first year.

## How Much Milk Does a Baby Really Need?

Even though most babies take around 26oz (780ml) at the end of the first month and sometimes up to 30oz (900ml) or so from 2-6 months, there are a rare few who grow well with as low as 15oz (440ml) per day or take as much as 40oz (1200ml) per day.[12] What's normal for *your* baby depends on a combination of the calorie content of the milk and your baby's metabolism. You can't compare yourself with your neighbor or best friend!

## The Letdown Reflex: Nature's Delivery System

Every time your baby nurses, nerves in the nipple send messages to the brain that trigger the pituitary to release oxytocin. This hormone causes muscle-like *myoepithelial cells* around the milk sacs to contract and squeeze milk down the ducts for delivery to the baby. The process of releasing milk is called *letdown*, more commonly known as *letdown*. Without this reflex, little milk can be removed, and when not removed well, the breast receives the message to cut back on milk production. This makes your letdown reflex a critical part of the big picture of milk production.[13] Issues that can negatively affect milk release and lead to lower milk production are explored in Chapter 12.

Letdowns are not one-time events but typically happen a few to several times during a nursing or pumping session.[14] They can come with sensations such as tingling, pins-and-needles, warmth, or even sharp feelings as the milk rushes down the ducts, though some parents don't seem to feel it at all. Each individual has their own pattern, and babies learn to anticipate whatever pattern their mothers' reflex follows.[14,15] A hungry baby will continue to suckle off and on when the milk is not flowing strongly, "asking" for another letdown. In the early days, some babies may become upset if this reflex doesn't happen quickly, pulling away in frustration. When milk production and flow are low, they may remain distrustful until the flow is improved, compounding the difficulty in getting breastfeeding going. Over time and with positive experiences, the baby learns to trust the breast, the mother learns to trust that her milk will flow, and both eventually relax into an easier nursing relationship.

The letdown reflex is unique in that it's not controlled exclusively by touch stimulation but can also be triggered by thoughts and feelings. Just seeing or hearing a baby cry can start a letdown, and the next thing you know, there's a wet spot on your shirt. This psychological aspect is the basis for the conditioning of the letdown reflex. As the two of you develop your feeding routine, you subconsciously begin to anticipate the feeding and may start to release milk just at the thought that it's almost time to feed. Pumping parents may have this same response to the sound of the pump turning on—your body has figured out that it is time for the milk to start flowing!

Another interesting aspect is how letdowns affect the appearance of your milk. You may have heard about *foremilk*, the low-fat "skim milk" that first comes out, and *hindmilk*, the high-fat, creamier milk at the end of a feeding. These terms make it sound as if the breast produces two kinds of milk, but that's not the case. As milk is made, the fat globules stick to the sides of the alveoli where the milk is stored and are flushed out gradually by the squeezing of the letdown reflex. The milk your baby receives in the beginning has less fat and a higher percentage of lactose, an important milk sugar, but the longer he feeds on a breast, the more cream he receives, ending up with a nicely balanced meal. If your baby feeds very often, there is less difference in the milk from start to finish.

## Reaching Milk Production Equilibrium

So how do the breasts figure out how much milk to make? Some mothers seem to make enough for twins from the beginning; others start off with a lower volume that gradually increases to meet their baby's needs.

At the same time that the baby's suck triggers the release of oxytocin for letdown, the pituitary gland releases a surge of prolactin to encourage continued resupplying of the breast. This is necessary because the body is constantly clearing out hormones from your system. As a result, your prolactin level gradually decreases in the weeks after birth until it reaches a lower plateau[13]—the more often prolactin surges, the higher the average circulating level, or *baseline prolactin*, will be. Early frequent nursing stimulation also causes prolactin's receptors to multiply, adding laborers to help the assembly line work faster and more efficiently. The more often a baby breastfeeds in the first days and weeks after birth, the more receptors are made.[16,17] *Good receptor development is critical to maintaining long-term milk production.*[18]

While prolactin is dropping and its receptors are being established, the milk-making process changes from being driven largely by hormones (*endocrine*) to more local control in the breast (*autocrine*). It responds to your baby's demand by adjusting

## Second Time Around

You may have heard that you make more milk with the second baby than with the first. Animal research is teaching us that the experiences of your first breastfeeding season cause permanent *epigenetic* changes in your breast, literally changing the behavior of certain genes. With the next pregnancy, the glandular tissue grows more, and the milk volume tends to increase faster and stronger than with your first baby. The work you put in with your firstborn has payoffs![19]

the rate of milk production up or down according to *how much, how well,* and *how often* milk is taken out. The goal of the autocrine process is to fine-tune, or *calibrate,* milk production to meet your baby's actual needs, with a little to spare. Lactation consultant Cathy Genna explains that like the marketing research department for a factory, your body spends the first few weeks after the baby is born determining whether it needs more or fewer assembly lines to meet baby's milk needs. In essence, all the early experiences of how often baby nurses and how much milk he removes is part of the body's "market research phase" for calibrating your milk production. *The more milk that is removed during this time, the higher your milk production will be calibrated.* This is critical in developing the final blueprint for a milk-making factory that will ultimately meet your baby's needs.

## Baby Calls the Shots

Your breast works by a process of *demand-and-supply*: baby suckles when he wants milk, the breast delivers it via multiple letdowns, and then more milk is made to replace what was removed. If your baby has taken all the available milk and keeps asking for more, additional milk will be made.

Your milk factory is designed to have a certain overall rate of milk production but can respond to short-term changes in demand as well. This ability to adjust production according to day-to-day and week-to-week fluctuations in a baby's appetite is referred to as *regulation.* For example, if your sick baby's appetite has dropped off for a few days, you'll first feel full, and then your production will start to cut back to match. Then when baby starts to feel better and his appetite returns, he may want more than you have and ask to nurse frequently, causing your production to regulate back up again.

This infant-driven system of demand-and-supply helps to explain why nursing parents may have very different breastfeeding and milk production experiences from one baby to the next. Each baby provides a new set of cues that triggers production, setting into motion a new and unique experience. Similarly, the larger-producing breast can change from one baby to the next. Interestingly, mothers of baby boys tend to produce more milk than mothers of baby girls because boys grow a little faster and so need a little more milk, thus stimulating a bigger supply.[3] The ability of your body to respond to your baby's milk-making signals depends not only on baby having free access to the breast to send the signals but also on your body having well-functioning nerves to carry the signals from the breast to the brain for processing. It is truly an amazing, coordinated dance between a mother and her baby.

## The Resource-Efficient Breast

Factories don't like to waste precious resources, and neither does your body. It works very hard to find a good balance of milk production that is enough for your baby, plus a safety cushion, by sensitively monitoring the degree of fullness of the breast. The "golden rule of milk production" is that the more often the breast is drained, the harder the body works to restock, and the higher the rate of production. If a factory's warehouse keeps emptying and orders are pouring in, management will hire new workers and speed up the production lines. Your breast tissue may actually grow, adding new machinery.[12] Of course, these adjustments require a little time when baby is asking for more milk than is available. On the other hand, if the breast's warehouse is consistently overflowing, management will slow down the assembly line. And if new orders don't start pouring in, management will eventually downsize the factory by reducing the number of assembly lines and laying off workers. If demand appears to have dropped permanently due to little or no nursing or pumping, management may even close the factory completely. We call this process of the breast permanently getting rid of some or all of the workers and equipment *involution*.[20]

The trigger for these steps is milk sitting around in the breast for extended periods of time, which eventually sends a "time to cut back" message. For a short time, this downward trend of milk production may be reversible, but after a while it is not, depending on individual factors. This is why it's so important to get the milk moving if the breast is very full or engorged. Otherwise, it's possible to swing from too much to very little in a short time. This is also why it isn't a good idea to "fill up" before feeding your baby. More milk might build up in the short-term, but you'll have less next week.[21]

Keeping a baby at the breast may seem counterintuitive when he's taken all the available milk. However, *if he continues to suckle*, he'll get whatever milk is being made and released at that moment while also signaling the factory to step up production.

## The Role of Storage Capacity

The maximum amount of milk that can be stored before the breast says "stop!" is your *storage capacity* and is determined by the amount of fully developed glands inside the breast, rather than outer breast size.[20] Storage capacity, the warehouse for the milk factory, can change and may increase during the first few months depending on your baby's appetite. Storage capacity is also one of the biggest factors in determining how often feedings need to happen. Babies of nursing parents who have smaller warehouses need

## Is it Normal for One Side to Produce More than the Other?

One of the most common observations of nursing parents is that one breast makes more milk than the other. In fact, it's rare for two breasts to be the same size or produce exactly the same amount of milk. More often, one side, usually the right, makes significantly more milk than the other. Although your baby can certainly create a larger supply on one side by his preference, this happens even in women whose breasts are equally stimulated by exclusive pumping. Be sure to alternate starting breasts so that both receive equal stimulation. Or you can try starting on the lower producer every time to even production out. But don't be surprised if one continues to be a "superproducer." It's perfectly normal.

to feed more often, and so the breasts make milk faster to compensate, while babies of nursing parents with large-capacity warehouses have the option of eating larger meals less often, with the breasts making milk more slowly between feedings.[10]

## Does Milk Production Have an Upper Limit?

Unfortunately, we don't have the complete answer on upper limits of human milk production because researchers have not yet explored this subject matter. In theory, according to the demand-and-supply principle of lactation, the more milk that is removed, the more milk should be made. However, ultimately, there are limiting constraints. Some parents' capabilities are limited because their bodies didn't develop a good base of glandular tissue during puberty. Some started with enough, but for some reason that tissue didn't blossom well in response to pregnancy hormones. Others simply don't have enough functional ducts and nerves because of previous breast surgery. Still, why doesn't the functional tissue that *does* exist just produce more milk in response to the demand? Part of the answer may lie in the fact that milk supply is calibrated according to how much and how often your baby removed milk during the early weeks, within the limitations of your overall breast tissue. Some individuals seem to have great flexibility and can easily increase milk production with additional stimulation for quite a while after delivery, but others seem to have a short window of calibration, so that their milk production reaches a plateau and is not as responsive to demands for more milk. These parents' breasts begin losing some of their "leaves" earlier than others do.[22]

13

## Milk Production is Designed to Succeed

Hopefully you now have a better grasp of how your breasts make milk and how you and your baby influence the process. As you continue to read, keep in mind that nature designed lactation to be a robust process with multiple safety nets. If one part of the milk-making factory isn't functioning optimally, another will work harder to compensate. This is why most mothers around the world are able to breastfeed successfully even under less-than-ideal circumstances. It's only when there are numerous breakdowns in the system or one problem is particularly severe that mothers and babies have difficulty breastfeeding. In most cases, keeping mother and baby together as much as possible so that they can respond to each other's cues is key in getting things back on track. But if you're feeling confused about your baby's behavior or what's happening with your breasts, the next chapter will help you understand what's normal and what's not.

## CHAPTER 2

# What's Normal and What's Not

What's "normal" for breastfeeding and what isn't seems to be a common source of confusion. Grandma tells you that the baby is crying after feeding because she ate too much and her stomach is upset. Your neighbor tells you that the baby didn't get enough to eat and is still hungry. Your best friend warns you that the baby may be allergic to your milk. Aunt Suzy thinks the baby is "colicky" and just needs to "cry it out." Which interpretation is true? Which are you more likely to believe if you're already worried about making enough milk?

For better or worse, our first teachers for how to interpret baby behavior are our own circle of family and friends. Unless you have a medical background or formal training in child development, you'll probably rely on their advice as you assess your own baby's behavior for the first time. This can be helpful, but it can also be frustrating because their ideas may be out of date or they may have conflicting opinions. It can also lead you to believe you aren't producing enough milk even if you really are.

The most accurate way to know if your baby is getting enough is by monitoring her weight gain. However, when a scale isn't available, baby's diaper output and behaviors do provide clues. Once you have a good understanding of normal baby and breastfeeding behaviors, misinterpretations and misperceptions are less likely to happen. This chapter will help you sort through the realities and myths of normal breastfeeding.

# Normal Baby Behaviors After Your Milk Comes In

- ☐ Breastfeeds for 10 or more times in 24 hours, often spaced approximately 2-3 hours apart but sometimes clustered closely together.
- ☐ Baby sleeps no more than one 4-5 hour stretch per day until breastfeeding is well established and she is growing appropriately.
- ☐ Baby starts off with a few quick suckles and then transitions to bursts of several sucks with long, drawing jaw movements that pause momentarily so baby can swallow.
- ☐ Baby's swallows can be heard frequently as a whispered "kuh" or a gulping sound in the first 5-10 minutes and then less frequently thereafter.
- ☐ Baby breastfeeds for approximately 15-30 minutes per feeding but sometimes less if milk flow is very fast.
- ☐ Baby seems to drain one breast thoroughly before taking the other side or may not take the second breast at all.

## Commonly Misinterpreted Baby Behaviors

There are many common infant behaviors that can mislead you to believe that your baby isn't getting enough milk.

### Frequent Feedings

It's *normal* for babies to feed frequently, especially during the early weeks. In the first few days, they may nurse as often as hourly; when allowed to do so, mature milk production starts up sooner.[1] Lactation consultant Gini Baker explains that newborn babies "have a job"—to suck, suck, and suck some more to get colostrum so that they'll poop out their meconium, which helps get rid of bilirubin and keep jaundice within normal limits. All this sucking also helps your production increase faster. Once this happens, most new babies settle into feeding every 2-3 hours, typically 10 or more times in 24 hours, and may wake more often to feed at night than in the daytime. Newborns aren't as efficient as they're going to be later on, and they also need to gain weight faster now than they ever will again. How often would *you* need to eat if you were trying to double your weight in 6 months and triple it in a year? Babies need frequent opportunities to feed in order to fuel all that growth.

On the other hand, parents often expect babies to feed at regular intervals around the clock, but some will nurse several times over a period of a few hours and then take an extra-long nap. These "cluster feeds" can occur at any time but happen most often in the late afternoon and evening. Of course, never being satisfied and always wanting to be at the breast can indicate that your baby isn't getting enough. You'll know if frequent nursing is or isn't signaling a problem by keeping an eye on diaper output and weight gain, as explained in the next chapter.

## Feeding Frenzies and Growth Spurts

Parents commonly report days when their babies are extra fussy and seem to embark on a nursing frenzy. You may feel like you're running out of milk because your breasts are soft, when it's actually the reverse: your breasts are soft because your baby is feeding so often that they don't have time to fill up.[2] The positive side is that keeping your breasts emptier is stimulating a higher rate of milk production.

Remember your teenage days? Mom would buy a certain amount of groceries each week. Then one day you started eating ravenously, and before the week was up, the cupboards were bare, and you were searching for more food. Were you starving to death? Nope, you were just extra hungry, and the stockpile of groceries was temporarily depleted. All that was needed was an extra trip to the grocery store to match your appetite. When the growth spurt stopped, your appetite returned to normal. It's the same with babies.

Feeding frenzy days can occur at any time, though they're especially common around 2-3 weeks, 6 weeks, and 3 months, with baby returning to her previous feeding pattern within the week. If milk production has dipped for any reason, it may just be baby's way of building it back up for you. What's most important is to follow her lead.

## The Mother/Parent–Baby Dance

When you're reading a book like this, you're engaging your left brain, the logical part that assesses everything. But breastfeeding is actually a right-brained activity, meant to happen instinctively on both the mother and baby's part. As you go through the process of troubleshooting problems, try to balance your critical left brain with your right-side mama brain, the one that senses the currents below the surface. Don't over-think when to feed your baby; just do it if it seems like that is what's supposed to happen. Dancing with a partner works best when you go with the flow instead of counting steps, and nursing works best in the flow as well. When you live in that place, you will have more confidence in your gut to guide you and tell you if something is amiss.

## Feeding Less Often

Frequent feedings worry some parents, others become concerned that they must not have enough milk when their baby begins to nurse less frequently. If a newborn is feeding fewer than 8 times a day after the first few days of life, it's possible that she's conserving calories because she isn't getting enough milk. But more often, a growing baby is able to take larger feedings, allowing her to go longer between meals. This may especially be true if you have a large storage capacity, allowing your baby to take as much as she can handle in a single feeding. Weight gain will usually tell you which is the case.

## Short Feedings

You may have heard that a baby is supposed to feed for *X* number of minutes per side to get enough milk or to "get to the hindmilk." The problem with this is that babies and breasts vary a lot. Some babies can drink large amounts of milk in as little as 5-10 minutes, particularly if you have a strong milk flow. After the first few weeks, shorter feedings may also be a simple matter of baby becoming more efficient so that she gets the same amount of milk in less time. Or she may be "topping off" in between longer feedings or as part of a cluster feed. Fluctuations in the amount of milk available throughout the day also influence how long a feeding lasts.

On the opposite side of the coin, some newborns stop feeding early out of discouragement or fatigue. They may not be able to get milk out easily due to a latch or suck problem, or they may stop because the milk isn't flowing as fast as they want or expect after having experienced faster flow from a bottle. Babies can also become frustrated by slow milk flow when milk production has decreased for some reason. If you're not sure, have a lactation consultant assess a feeding for you.

## Baby Cries and Takes a Bottle After Nursing

Although an underfed baby may gulp down a bottle after nursing, there are babies who will still take a bottle even after getting enough at the breast. Was the bottle offered because baby truly needed it or because someone else wanted to feed her or thought she needed it? Was baby doing just fine before but watching her down that bottle after a feeding shook your confidence? Or was she crying, and the bottle seemed to calm her down?

Sometimes what's really happening is that baby is being stuffed into a stupor in a very unnatural way. Just because a bottle stops the fussing doesn't *automatically* mean that she needs more to eat. Think about how parents handled this before bottles and formula were invented. Crying can mean things besides hunger; your baby may just need more sucking time, or she may have become upset during or after a feeding because of *allergies, gas,* or *reflux* and finds feeding soothing. Don't be afraid to call your pediatrician if her crying is worrisome, and *be persistent if your gut says that something is wrong and you aren't satisfied with the answers.* It isn't always about your milk supply!

## Baby Chokes, Sputters, and Arches at the Breast

If your baby chokes and sputters while breastfeeding—arching and pulling off, crying, or refusing to nurse for long periods at the breast—it could be an indication of *too much* milk! We once thought that this could be caused by an "overactive letdown reflex," but spraying milk is typically the result of too much built-up pressure in the breast (think of an overfilled water balloon) from overproduction, also called *hyperlactation*.[3] Weight gain may be rapid, or it can be deceptively slow. Gulping, coughing, biting, clamping down, pulling on the nipple, and even screaming are common. Feedings may feel more like battles, with baby having a "love-hate" relationship with the breast and nursing fitfully on and off for only 5 or 10 minutes total. She may also cry a lot and be irritable or restless by the time she's finished. She may burp frequently, spit up after feedings, and be very gassy, and her stools are often green, watery, foamy, or explosive. Your milk may spray forcefully when she comes off the breast, especially early in the feeding. You may feel very full much of the time, even while offering both breasts, and battle plugged ducts that could lead to breast infections. If this sounds familiar, try offering 1 side per feeding for 24 hours as a starting point to see if it helps and visit our website lowmilksupply.org for more information.

An alternate explanation for this behavior is a swallowing problem interfering with the ability to handle normal milk flow. When babies fall behind on their suck-swallow-breathe rhythm, they accidentally start to breathe in milk and will choke and sputter to clear it out. This is sometimes seen with tongue mobility restriction but can also be the result of immature sucking skills or other issues.[4]

## Regular Fussiness in the Late Afternoon or Early Evening

In the first 3 months of life, many breastfed babies fuss in the late afternoon and early evening. Parents often worry that this is a sign that their baby isn't getting enough to eat, especially if the breasts feel deflated. The most likely explanation for this common phenomenon is that your milk reserves have been drained throughout the day and baby is now dredging the bottom of the tank, taking milk as soon as it's made. In fact, this is more likely to happen if you have a larger storage capacity and your baby sleeps longer at night. Feeding more often in the daytime to compensate, she removes milk faster than it is being made in order to get all her meals in.[5]

When there's less accumulated milk in the breasts, the force of the milk flow is reduced. Think of how water in a water balloon squirts out when full but drizzles out when there is less in the balloon. Hungry babies who want their milk *now* may become impatient and irritable when the flow is slower late in the day. This fussy time may also coincide with tiredness and overstimulation, which makes for an impatient, cranky baby who may take a bottle eagerly, reinforcing your fear that she's starving. Most of the time, the reality is that you have plenty of milk over 24 hours, just not a lot right now, *and that's okay.*

Early evening fussiness can also be the result of a frustrated baby whose mother is refusing to offer the breast again "because she just fed." It may be your baby's way of telling you "I need to be held, please." A baby carrier (we love slings) can be your best friend in these moments. Nursing frequently also may be a baby's way of compensating for a temporarily emptier warehouse; if large meals are not available, lots of smaller ones will do. Either way, all that sucking is going to send the breast the "make more milk faster, please" message. Frequent feeding may also be her way of tanking up on calories before a long sleep period. If she calms down right away when put to the breast, the problem more likely is about unrealistic parental expectations.

If you find yourself struggling with this, try breast compressions to increase the force of the flow (see Chapter 5) and then alternate with cuddling movement and singing. Sooner or later, baby will fall into a long, deep sleep. You can also try a lactogenic herbal tea (see Chapter 14) in the late afternoon for a preemptive boost.

## Not Sleeping Through the Night

"Is your baby sleeping through the night?" is one of the first questions new parents hear from friends, relatives, and even health care providers. It stems from a common cultural belief that babies should be sleeping through the night as early as 3 months of age and has become an expectation and measurement of parenting success. However, sleeping for longer than 4 hours more than once or twice per 24 hours in the first month may indicate a baby isn't getting enough milk and sleeps to conserve calories.

It's normal for a baby, especially one who is breastfed, to continue to wake up periodically at night during the first year of life. She may nurse 1-3 times between 10:00 pm and 4:00 am and take more milk at night than in the daytime.[6] How long she can go between feedings is determined by your milk storage capacity and how full the tank is at a given feeding. Infants of parents with larger storage capacity nurse less often overall and eventually go longer between feeds than do infants of parents with smaller storage capacity.[5]

Many parents report that their baby initially started to sleep longer at night, only to have that end after a month or two, leaving them to wonder what went wrong. Actually, it really is what "went normal." Remember, there is more going on in your baby's life than just eating: the discomfort of teething or an illness can awaken her, or she may be mastering developmental milestones such as rolling over, crawling, or standing, causing her to wake up. Life may just be too exciting in the daytime to eat, so she nurses more at night when the world is dark and less stimulating. If you recently went back to work, your baby may also wake more often to make up for missed daytime feedings or even just to touch base and make sure you're still there for her.

There are times when a change in baby's sleep pattern can indicate that she needs more food, but there will be other clues to validate this. If nothing has changed in your life, such as starting on a new medication or heading back to work, and she is still gaining well and putting out lots of diapers, then her sleep pattern is probably related to something other than your milk production.

## Reading Body Language to Guesstimate Milk Intake

Contentment after a feeding can be a good sign. However, babies who aren't getting enough to eat can sometimes fall asleep and initially appear content even though they haven't taken in enough. How do you tell the difference between a baby who is truly full and one who is apparently content but still hungry? Babies may not speak with their mouths, but they sure do speak through their expressions and posture!

A baby who's only getting a little milk out of the breast will quickly slow down to a "flutter" suck and doze off without letting go of the nipple. She may have a puzzled or worried expression, with furrowed eyebrows and a wrinkled forehead as if she's saying, "Something isn't right; why isn't this working?" Her body never fully relaxes while nursing, and her hands may be tightly fisted and close to her face. If she has difficulty latching on to the breast, she may flail her arms about desperately, adding more chaos to the situation. And when taken off the breast, she may immediately wake up or go through a series of "cluster feeds" that never seem to end. A baby looking for more milk may tug and pull at the breast or push and knead it with her hands like a kitten. This instinctive behavior is designed to induce another letdown, which should happen if milk is still available. She may behave in an "antsy" and unsettled manner until milk flows again. Less patient (or fed-up) babies will come off the breast or even refuse to latch after a while, arching stiffly and screaming as if to say, "Not again! I told you this isn't working!" Parents often interpret this to mean that their baby dislikes breastfeeding, when it's more frustration over not being able to figure out how to get more milk faster.

Another nonverbal message is tightly closed lips, which seem to say, "I'm done for now, thank you." Each baby has a limit for how long she's willing to keep trying, and babies born early especially have less stamina. It's important to interpret the messages correctly so that you can change, or help your baby to change, what's not working for her right at this moment. When feedings are stressful or filled with conflict, breastfeeding can become a

## Normal Maternal Breastfeeding Experiences

- ☐ Areolas darken during pregnancy.
- ☐ Breasts felt tender at some point during pregnancy, particularly during the first trimester.
- ☐ Breasts increase in fullness or size.
- ☐ Veins on the breasts become more visible.
- ☐ Breasts feel fuller, firmer, and perhaps warmer as your milk "came in" between the 2nd and 4th day postpartum.
- ☐ Uterine cramping or gushes of blood, called lochia, occur during feeding or pumping sessions the first few days after birth in response to sucking stimulation.
- ☐ Breasts feel softer and lighter after feedings.

trust issue for the baby. Respecting what she's trying to communicate will help rebuild her trust confidence in the breast.

There are also positive baby cues that signal when things are going well. As the milk begins to flow and your baby starts swallowing, her eyes open and the wrinkles and perplexed expression she may have had begin to fade away, as if she's thinking, "Well look at this! I can't believe I'm getting this much! Is it really true?!" And as she begins to fill up, her fists open, her arms relax and drop away from her face, and her eyes slowly close. Parents are often amazed by their baby's "milk-drunk" expression as she releases the nipple and drifts off to sleep.

## Commonly Misinterpreted Maternal Indicators

Some experiences may lead you to believe that you don't have enough milk, yet they're not necessarily reliable signs when taken alone, though several together may indeed be reason to investigate further.

### "I can't pump very much milk"

The amount of milk you can pump may or may not be an accurate measurement of what you're making. Yet some parents decide whether to supplement or continue nursing based solely on what they're able to get out, with sometimes unrealistic expectations.[7] We've seen mothers panic when they weren't able to pump a full bottle after nursing, as if they expected to have an endless fountain of milk!

Effective pumping depends on the quality of the breast pump, the fit of the kit, the density of the breast tissue, and your overall comfort with and response to pumping.[7] Some nursing parents release milk very easily to even a low-quality pump and can drain their breasts quite well, but most respond best to a high-quality consumer- or rental-grade pump. A few individuals don't seem able to effectively extract milk with *any* kind of pump. Pumping can provide some clues to how much milk you have, *but it should not be your only measuring stick*. If you're pumping after nursing, your baby may already have taken most of the available milk. If you've been using a lower-grade or previously used pump and experienced a gradual decrease in milk yield over several weeks or months, it's possible that it may not be your body that is to blame but rather the pump (see Chapter 13).

Hand expressing to see how much milk you can get isn't a very accurate measurement of your milk supply, either. Hand expression is a skill that requires practice to master, and it's still not as effective as a baby who is nursing well.

### "I never got engorged"

If you've been nursing frequently from the start, you may not feel significant discomfort when the milk volume increases, though some feelings of fullness and warmth are common at the start. While you may have been led to expect this experience to be painful, frequent milk removal often helps to avoid or minimize engorgement.

### "My breasts are soft"

In the beginning, your breasts may feel very full before each feeding. After about 6 weeks, though, your milk supply adjusts to baby's needs, and the breasts begin to feel softer and less full (unless it has been an unusually long time between feedings). Most of the time this is normal, but if there's a significant change in softness accompanied by other clues, it could be a sign that the milk factory is cutting back prematurely.

### "I don't feel my letdowns"

Not everyone feels the letdown reflex happening. When you do, you're more likely to feel those in the beginning as a full breast releases; the sensation tends to dampen as the breast drains. Leaking from the opposite breast during a feed usually indicates letdown is occurring, especially when you hear your baby start to swallow at the same time. After several months, letdown sensations often diminish even for those who felt them easily early on.

## Where Did My Milk Go?

Baby just came off the breast and needed a little break, but now she's ready for more. You can feel that your breast has milk, but she's fussing and it isn't flowing. *What happened?* Without any forces continuing to push or pull out the milk out, it will draw back up into the ducts and ductules like a sponge soaking up water. This can be confusing to both you and your baby when the milk isn't coming out the same as before, but if there was milk a few minutes ago, it's still there. Your breast just needs a little more stimulation for another letdown to get things going again.

### "I don't leak"

Leaking between feedings is not by itself an accurate way to gauge your milk supply. It has more to do with the tension of the muscles in your nipples, which differs from person to person, than with milk production. While leaking can be a very positive sign that there is milk in your breasts and some people leak more as their milk production increases, leaking alone does not indicate how much milk you have.

### "My milk looks too thin"

Human milk is often somewhat bluish but can vary in color depending on the foods you eat. These variations don't affect the quality of the milk and are certainly not harmful to your baby. Fluctuations in the amount of fat in your milk depend largely on the degree of fullness of the breasts, the time of day, and the age of your baby; milk at the end is richer than milk at the beginning. There are some factors, such as smoking, that can decrease the fat content of the milk. However, breastfed babies compensate for these changes by regulating the amount of milk they take. If you have milk that is lower in fat overall, your baby may drink more in order to get enough calories for her needs—assuming she has unrestricted opportunities to nurse.[8]

## Do You Have Enough Milk?

Now that you have a good understanding of what's normal for breastfeeding, the next chapter will help you determine if your baby is getting enough milk. If she isn't, the chapters that follow will guide you toward the steps to making more milk for your baby.

## CHAPTER 3

# How Do I Know if There Really is a Problem?

You've probably heard the expression, "Don't put the cart before the horse." Before tackling the question of why your baby isn't getting enough milk or deciding what to do about it, you have to know for sure that there really is a problem. This includes finding out approximately how much milk your baby is getting and whether it is enough for good growth. Mathematical formulas for how much a baby should be taking each day can be misleading because they don't take into account the variations in the calorie content of each mother's milk or a baby's metabolism.[1] The truth is that the amount each baby needs to grow appropriately can vary. One study found a range of 15-40oz (440-1220g) per 24 hours in babies who were growing well![2] When you have the facts, you can build the best strategy for your specific situation.

## How Can I Tell if My Baby is Getting Enough Milk?

Don't you wish the breast had a gauge like that cartoon so you can see exactly how much milk is there and your baby is getting? *When everything is going well it really doesn't matter.* But if you're not sure and are worried, there are two signs to look for.

Doctors look at many things, but baby's *growth* is usually the bottom line. Pediatricians monitor length, head growth, and weight, but for our purposes, weight is the most important. Between doctor visits, *poop* diapers can give you a general idea of how things are going because of the old rule: "What goes in, must come out." If your baby is gaining well, he is likely putting out lots of poop; if he isn't gaining well, the amount will be less. If baby is pooping a lot—*we're talking about the total volume of poop more than the number of diaper changes*—but not gaining well, further medical investigation would be warranted.

### How much should my baby be gaining?

Newborns may lose up to 7-10% of their birth weight in the first days after birth before they begin gaining, with babies born by c-section losing a little more than babies born vaginally.[3,4] Occasionally, excessive weight loss—greater than 10%—occurs rapidly even though the baby appears to be nursing well. In many cases, birth weight may have been artificially inflated by extra water your baby acquired during labor as the result of your IV fluids or medications. After birth, a baby pees out the extra fluid and loses weight. For this reason, it's been suggested that baby's weight at 24 hours should be considered their true birth weight and that weight loss should be calculated from there.[5] When excessive weight loss occurs *along with* lots of wet diapers in the first day or two after birth, this possibility should be considered before hitting the panic button.[6]

If your newborn is less than 4 days old, seems to be feeding well and is healthy, alert, and passing black, tarry meconium stools, chances are good that everything is fine and he'll start gaining once milk production kicks into high gear. This means that if your milk starts to increase on the 2nd day, he'll probably start gaining very early. But if it takes longer to get going, he may lose a little more until your rate of milk production picks up. When milk volume is slow to rise and low intake becomes a problem, temporary supplementation may be needed.

Breastfed babies who are doing well often regain birth weight by the end of the first week. But because some parents and babies may get a slower start, doctors are usually satisfied if a baby regains his birth weight by the end of 2 weeks. A few who have lost excessive weight may not hit their birth weight by 2 weeks, but if they've started gaining *at least* 1oz (30g) a day, they're usually going to be okay. Weighing your baby on an accurate scale every few days or once a week is usually enough, though daily weighing may be necessary in critical cases.

Opinions on what should be considered normal weight gain for exclusively nursing infants are changing.[7] The World Health Organization (WHO) collected information from 6 areas of the world. Of all the groups, babies in the US grew the slowest! Our best guess is that US birth practices have affected the start-up of lactation, and infant growth along with it (see more in Chapter 8). What this means for parents in the US is that their babies may not always reach the WHO standards for weight gain, especially at the start. This does *not* mean supplementation is automatically necessary, but rather that we just need to know that baby has started gaining appropriately.

It also means that we need to be careful not to accept persistent low weight gain without questions. The majority of babies' growth rates will fall between the 25th and the 75th percentiles.[7] Those who continue to grow at *less* than the 25th percentile should be examined closely to make sure that it isn't due to low milk (calories) intake, the most common reason for slower growth. It's important to compare weight gains with diaper output and your baby's body language cues to get a general sense of whether all is okay or not. If he seems relaxed and content after feedings, is being fed on cue *at least* 8 times daily, and is putting out lots of poop, he'll likely be just fine. But a baby who is growing consistently at a slow rate, feeding very frequently, perhaps *sucking on fingers or a pacifier constantly* but otherwise not complaining, may actually not be getting all the milk he would like. Some people try to explain away slow growth as "all the babies in my family are small." But worldwide, infant birth weights in adequately nourished countries are very similar, and genetics don't usually kick in for 6-12 months.

What if your baby was gaining well in the early weeks or months and faltered only later on? A significant drop in percentiles on the growth chart may be cause for concern and further investigation.

## Rate of Weight Gain for Exclusively Nursing Babies in the First Year

**Approximate Weight Gain for Babies in the 25th-75th Percentiles**

| | |
|---|---|
| Week 1 | Initially loses up to 7-10% of birth weight (Note: Weight at 24 hours may be more accurate true birth weight for some babies) |
| Week 2 | Regains to birth weight or has started to gain 1oz (30g) per day |
| Weeks 3-4 | Gains 8-9oz (240-270g) **per week** |
| Month 2 | Gains 7-10oz (210-300g) **per week** |
| Month 3 | Gains 5-7oz (150-210g) **per week** |
| Month 4 | Gains 4-6oz (120-180g) **per week** |
| Month 5 | Gains 3-5oz (90-150g) **per week** or 12-22oz (360-660g) **per month** |
| Month 6 | Gains 2-4oz (60-120g) **per week** or 9-18oz (270-540g) **per month** |
| Months 7-8 | Gains 7-16oz (210-480g) **per month** |
| Months 9-12 | Gains 4-13oz (120-390g) **per month** |

The majority of babies will fall in the 25th-75th percentiles above. Most health care providers are satisfied if a baby is gaining about 1oz (30g) a day during the first 3 months.

**Sources:** WHO Multicentre Growth Reference Study Group. *WHO Child Growth Standards: Growth Velocity Based on Weight, Length and Head Circumference: METHODS and Development. Geneva,* Switzerland: World Health Organization; 2009. Riddle SW, Nommsen-Rivers LA. Low milk supply and the pediatrician. *Curr Opin Pediatr.* 2017;29(2):249-256.

### Weight Gain Tells the Story

*When accurately measured, weight gain over time is the best way to tell that your baby is getting enough milk.* For this reason, getting an accurate weight every time is crucial when your baby's intake is in question. Pay attention to these five factors:

1. **Accurate readings.** Human error in taking weights is surprisingly common. The scale can be used incorrectly, the weight reading can be misread, the numbers can be transposed when written down or typed, the wrong weight can be recorded, or the percentile can be plotted incorrectly. To minimize errors, watch the reading being taken and double-check the figure yourself against what is recorded and plotted in your baby's chart. You can even take a picture of the weight reading for a permanent record. We've seen some crazy mistakes at times!

2. **Use a high-accuracy scale.** Weights on different scales (even in the same office) can yield different results if the scale isn't properly calibrated. Scale type also matters; professional electronic scales are more accurate than spring-loaded scales. Whichever type is used, *comparing weights taken on the exact same scale gives the most accurate results.* Just remember that readings on your scale may differ from those in

your health care provider's office, and readings on different scales in the same office sometimes vary as well.

3. **Lose the clothes.** Be sure to remove all clothing, including hat, socks, booties, and mittens. Either weigh your baby naked or put on a clean diaper each time.

4. **Be consistent.** The more often you weigh, the more important it is to have consistent intervals between weight checks, such as every day at 8 am.

5. **Account for tummy and poop contents.** Measurements can be more accurate by timing the weights for after your baby has pooped and before a feed.

### Poop Diapers Support the Story

In the first 48 hours after birth, exclusively breastfed newborns will pass meconium and 1 or 2 diapers with pale yellow urine. Once the milk volume starts to increase, typically by 72 hours but occasionally a day or two longer, black meconium diapers should start changing to brownish-green and then yellow, and the urine should be nearly colorless and odorless. Reddish "brick dust" urine from uric acid crystals occasionally occurs before the milk increases but should be gone by the 4th to 5th day. If your baby still has black or brown poop after the 4th day, this indicates low intake for whatever reason; be sure to talk to his health care provider.

The number of dirty diapers tend to peak around 2 weeks at approximately 6 per day, then drop to 4 poops at 1 month, 3 poops at 2 months, and 2 poops per day from 3-12 months,[8] though a few continue to poop several times a day. But some babies go once a day, every few days, weekly or even longer, usually after 5 weeks of age.[9] They seem to be fine, though there is some debate about whether to call this normal. Stooling less often is more common if a baby is also receiving some formula.[8] You'll know if this is normal or not by the *size and consistency* of the poop. When a thriving baby's stooling pattern spaces

Typical Number of Poop Diapers During the First 3 Months for Exclusively Nursing Babies[8-10]

| Day 1 | 1 black meconium diaper |
|---|---|
| Day 2 | 2 black meconium diapers |
| Day 3 | 3 transitional brown/green diapers |
| Day 4 | 4 transitional brown/green to yellow diapers, larger than a US quarter |
| 1 week | 4-6 yellow diapers, about the size of a credit card |
| 2 weeks | 5-6 yellow diapers, about the size of a credit card |
| 1 month | 4 yellow diapers, larger |
| 2 months | 2-3 yellow diapers, large |
| 3 months | 2 yellow diapers, large |

out, the poop is still loose but proportionally larger. If you find yourself changing "blow-out" diapers every few days, chances are good that your baby is getting enough to eat.

In the grand scheme of things, **the *amount* of poop is more important than the number of wet diapers** because babies who are not getting enough milk can take in enough to pee frequently but not enough to gain weight and poop. The color of the pee tells its own story, though. While clear urine usually means good hydration, more concentrated yellow or even orange urine can indicate dehydration.

## Feeding Test Weights to Estimate Milk Intake

You can estimate how much milk your baby takes at a given feeding by performing a test weight. This technique is used by many lactation consultants and is especially useful in estimating how much your baby is getting at breast and how much supplement to give (see Chapter 4).

To do a test weight, you'll need access to a high-accuracy (preferably to 2g) electronic scale; a lactation consultant can help you with this. Before you feed, weigh your baby and record the weight, then feed as you normally would. *Don't change baby's diaper or clothing in any way between weights.* (You might want to remove his hat, socks, or mittens beforehand because they often come off with movement and are easily overlooked.) When the feeding is done, weigh the baby again. The difference between the start and ending numbers is the approximate amount of milk taken. Some scales have special functions that automatically calculate the weight difference.

## How Much Should My Baby Be Taking?

It really depends on your baby's age, size, and how often they're feeding. Researchers saw a huge range from zero all the way up to 8oz (240ml) among babies 1 to 6 months of age. A few took up to 6oz (180ml) yet came back an hour later asking for more, while other babies took as little as 1oz (30ml) and then slept 8 hours![11] Below are common amounts, but *keep in mind that these numbers can vary throughout the day and night.*

| Age | Common Amount per Feeding |
| --- | --- |
| First 24 hours | ½-2 tsp (2-10ml) |
| Day 2 | 1-3 tsp (5-15ml) |
| Day 3 | ½-1oz (15-30ml) |
| 4-7 days | 1-1½ oz (30-45ml) |
| 1-2 weeks | 1½-2oz (45-60ml) |
| 2-3 weeks | 2-3oz (60-90ml) |
| 1-6 months | 2-4oz (60-120ml) |

## Note on weight conversions

Ounces can be measured in both weight and liquid volume. 1oz (weight) = 28.3495231g, and 1oz (liquid volume) = 29.35735297ml, close enough to say that 1oz (30g) in weight is equivalent to 1oz (30ml) in milk volume.

Test weights can measure how much milk is transferred during a feeding, but **the information must be interpreted cautiously.** Babies don't eat the same amount each time, *so a single test weight provides only a snapshot of one feeding.* Was it a good feeding, or only so-so? Did the numbers line up with how you thought it went? The best way to get a true and accurate picture is to do test weights of *every* feeding for 24 hours. Always keep in mind that you are measuring what your baby is taking in, *which is not necessarily the same as what you can produce.*

### Is there a device to measure my baby's intake?

More and more new products are hitting the market claiming to measure how much a baby is drinking. One requires the attachment of a small sensor under the baby's ear to detect swallows, then calculates intake with a special algorithm; earphones allow a parent to "eavesdrop" as well. Software is downloaded to your smart phone, which is connected to the device and records the feeding. Background noise can affect results.

Another product uses a battery-operated device to measure the change in your breast size before and after feedings. It's designed to be used together with a car seat hanging scale to calculate milk intake, feeding information into its software.

A third device uses a "standard-sized" nipple shield with an attached sensor to measure milk transfer. Again, it is connected to a smart phone to record and track information per feeding and over time.

Is it worth the money to buy one of these devices? We don't have enough experience to say one way or the other yet, but we're concerned that the technologies may be less accurate in low-supply situations when babies have suck problems or mothers have unusually shaped breasts or nipples. We also wonder how enjoyable breastfeeding will be if you're constantly attaching gadgets and monitoring apps. A thoughtful blog to check out is bit.ly/MMM-Measure. Watch our website lowmilksupply.org for updates on these devices.

## Can't I Just Pump to See How Much I'm Making?

Always remember that *there is no one right amount for everyone; how well a baby gains on the milk he is getting is more important information than just a number.* Also keep in mind that

## 4-Hour Pumping Test

Drain both breasts *thoroughly* once an hour for a total of 4 times using a high-quality pump. The amount of the last expression is your average rate of milk production per hour. Multiply by 24 for your approximate daily milk production.

pumping a couple of times only tells you how much was available and easily extracted from the warehouse at a particular moment, which may differ throughout the day and night. Breast pumps are not babies and may not remove milk as well, though at times they can do a better job. The quality of the pump, its suction and cycling pattern, and how well you respond to it can skew the results.[12] For best accuracy, you'll need to pump for 24 hours or do test weights plus pumping the leftover milk each time.

If the information is really important to you but the thought of measuring for 24 hours is overwhelming, there is another way to estimate your daily milk production in 4 hours instead.[13] This method provides a fair approximation of milk production when a high-quality pump is used *and* you respond well to breast pumps (not all of us do), though it's better applied to research groups than individuals.[14] Because nursing must be interrupted, try this only when the information gained outweighs the disruption and expense.

## The Final Results

Hopefully you now have a better idea of whether there is a problem or not. If your baby is gaining adequately, he should be getting enough milk, and all should be well. But if he still seems miserable or hungry, your doctor may need to rule out a physical problem. *Don't hesitate to seek a second opinion if you're not satisfied with the answer and your gut is saying that something is wrong* even if that means asking the same doctor to reconsider. When no other reasons for your baby's fussiness can be found, erikson.edu/fussy-baby-network and KellyMom.com have good lists of additional resources.

On the other hand, if your baby isn't growing well, the most common reason is simply not taking in enough milk. This may be caused by not feeding often enough, or by a mechanical problem with transferring milk from breast to baby such as latch, suck, letdown, or primary low milk production.[7] As discussed earlier, parents sometimes worry

## Find an IBCLC in Your Area

Diana maintains an international list of IBCLCs specializing in low milk supply at LC4.me and there is a general list on the International Lactation Consultant Association (ILCA) website at ILCA.org. Also, many US Women, Infants, and Children (WIC) offices employ IBCLCs. Often, though, the best way to find an expert IBCLC is word of mouth. Ask your family, friends, obstetrician midwife, and pediatrician.

that the quality of their milk may be the culprit; while this is possible, it is more rare (more in Chapter 7).

If diapers and weight gain suggest that your baby isn't getting sufficient milk yet you feel like you have enough, *your milk supply is at risk*. While you're figuring out the problem, it's a good idea to compress your breasts during feedings and express leftover milk afterward to be fed back. If low production is the source issue, don't be discouraged because production usually can be increased. If the decrease is a result of how nursing has been managed, the information ahead may provide some solutions. But if the problem stems from an issue with your breasts, hormones, or is baby-related, you'd probably benefit from a visit with a lactation consultant skilled in challenging breastfeeding problems. Look for an IBCLC as they have the highest level of training and experience and are required to sit for board exams and recertify every 5 years. For more on why this matters, see bit.ly/MMM-IBCLC.

## Three Rules to Live By

If your baby isn't getting enough milk, you'll need to develop a strategy for improving the situation. A good starting place is lactation consultant Kay Hoover's three rules for solving breastfeeding problems:

**Rule #1—Feed the baby** (see Chapter 4): A baby who is well-fed will feed better at the breast.

**Rule #2—Protect the milk supply** (see Chapter 5): Milk must be removed regularly and thoroughly to keep production as high as possible.

**Rule #3—Find and address the problem** (see Chapters 6-17): After the first 2 have been covered, you can then investigate the problem and develop a strategy to address it.

Even though you may be anxious to begin figuring out what the problem is and boosting milk supply, your first priority is to make sure your baby is well-fed. Supplementary feedings may be necessary, at least for a short time; think of them as transitional tools that keep your baby healthy rather than as a step away from the breast. The next chapter will help you determine the best way to give them in a way that supports breastfeeding.

# PART II

# Making the Most of What You Have

## Emily's Story

Breastfeeding my baby Joshua was challenging. I had sore nipples and engorgement. He became jaundiced, and it was a constant battle to keep him awake. By 3 weeks of age, Joshua weighed nearly a pound (454g) less than when he was born. Not good.

The pediatricians wanted to see him every 3 days to monitor his weight, but their constantly changing advice was frustrating. Finally, when Joshua was 5 weeks old and still under birth weight, I was referred to a lactation consultant, who explained that I had less lactation tissue than normal. She gave me hope that I *could* continue to breastfeed. I started using a Lact-Aid® at-breast supplementer. It felt awkward and silly at first, but Joshua got all the food he needed. I usually nursed on both sides without the supplementer and then nursed with it to "top him off." Once he began eating solids, I nursed him without it. These were my happiest months as a nursing mother. Joshua nursed until he was 11 months old.

My second son, Nathan, was born 2 years after Joshua. I felt much more confident with breastfeeding, but after 10 days of exclusive nursing, Nathan hadn't gained any weight, so I started using the supplementer again. I was frustrated that I couldn't breastfeed exclusively but knew it would be okay. Like his brother, he nursed for close to a year. My sons and I developed our own version of breastfeeding, and I am so grateful that we were persistent. There is something special in putting your child to your breast, even if you need a little bit of help.

## CHAPTER 4

# Supplementing Made Simple

**Rule #1:** While you're figuring out why your milk production is low and what you can do about it, *make sure that your baby has enough to eat.* Supplementation can seem like a step away from breastfeeding, but it's really a step forward because she needs energy to feed to the best of her ability. If your baby needs more milk, this chapter will help you learn how to supplement without reducing supply or interfering with your developing breastfeeding relationship.

## How Do I Know When to Start Supplementing?

The urgency to supplement depends on how much milk your baby is currently getting. The lower the weight gain or feeding test weights, the more critical it is to begin supplementation immediately. On the other hand, if weight gain is just below normal or test weights are only slightly low, you may have more leeway in determining if, when, and how to give supplements. An otherwise healthy baby who is not getting quite enough because of something as simple as not nursing often enough may be able to bring up your supply in a short amount of time without compromising her health.

## How Much is Right and Where Do I Start?

Figuring out how much to supplement means finding the right balance. Per day, your baby needs enough milk to start growing well, and perhaps some extra to catch up if she's been underfeeding for a while. Per feeding, she needs enough to be satisfied but not so much that she feeds less often and understimulates your production. This is important because it isn't uncommon to see a baby over-supplemented by anxious family to the point that she's feeding less than 8 times a day. As much as we may look forward to longer feeding intervals, *right now your breasts need more stimulation, not less*, so frequent feeds are your friend. Aim for at least 9-10 feedings per day. If your baby doesn't want to feed that often, pump or reduce the supplement to encourage more feedings.

The early weeks are a time of rapid growth and building up of your milk production; most full-term babies take around 26oz (780ml) per day by the end of the first month,[1] but sometimes less and sometimes more. That's 3.25oz (98ml) 8 times per day, 2.9oz (87ml) 9 times per day, or 2.6oz (78ml)10 times per day *on average*. They may jump to these amounts quickly in the first 1-2 weeks or work up to them gradually.

**Slow Weight Gain Option 1: No Test Weights**

For a baby who is gaining slowly, adding 4oz (120ml) per day, approximately a ½ oz (15ml) per 8 feedings, can be a good starting point. Your goal is for her to start gaining in the range listed in Chapter 3. If she still seems hungry, bump this up another ½ oz (15ml) at a time while making sure she feeds often.

**Slow Weight Gain Option 2: Using Test Weight Information**

After the first couple of weeks, most full-term exclusively breastfeeding babies take 2-4oz (60-120ml) or so. If you know approximately how much your baby is taking at the breast, subtract that from 3oz and consider this a *starting point* for supplementing. For example, if baby takes 1½ oz (45ml) at the breast, she may need an additional 1½ oz (45ml). Try this amount and see if she's satisfied and how long she seems to go between feedings. Adjust upward by ½ ounce (15ml) (½oz (15ml) increments if she's still hungry or downward if she's going too long between feedings.

**Slow weight gain option 3: using weight gain deficit information**

If you don't have a good idea of what your baby's been getting, lactation consultant Cathy Genna suggests taking baby's weight gain deficit for the previous week and multiplying it by 2 for the ounces or milliliters of total extra milk she may need per 24 hours. That means that if your baby should be gaining 7oz (210g) a week but gained only 2oz (60g) the previous week, she may need 10oz (300ml) of supplement (5oz/150ml × 2) per day to start. Divide this by the number of feedings for a starting point and adjust up if baby is still hungry and down if she starts sleeping longer and feeding less than eight times daily.

Once you've found your starting point, watch carefully to see if your baby wants less or more. Give her whatever she'll take but don't ask her to take more than she really wants. Keep in mind that babies, like adults, vary in how much food they want from one feeding to the next. Estimating the amount of extra milk needed is as much an art as it is a science, and baby herself needs to play a role in this process. If she seems ravenous and wasn't feeding too quickly, don't hesitate to give her a little more than you planned. The key to making adjustments lies in balancing 3 factors: (1) lots of poop, (2) appropriate weight gain, and (3) baby's satisfaction. Adjust the amount you offer up or down a ½ oz (15ml) at a time unless it's obvious that your estimate was really far off. If the change works, stay with it until it isn't working and then adjust again.

## The Significantly Underfed Baby

We can usually trust babies to tell us how much food they need, but some circumstances do require parents to take over for a while. A seriously underfed baby (who may have misled you with her passive behavior) may not show strong hunger cues, sleeping longer and feeding infrequently, and may quit nursing before she has had enough. Poops will be infrequent with poor weight gain, and her feeding behavior may be lethargic. Giving her at least ½ oz (15ml) by bottle or another method before breastfeeding can energize her to feed better—think of it as an appetizer to whet her appetite. *Or she may simply need to be fed in whatever way it takes to get enough milk into her until she is stronger.*[2] During this process, keep in close contact with your baby's health care provider or a lactation consultant to make sure that you're on track. Sometimes the goal of being baby's sole source of nutrition may need to be suspended until she turns the corner on poor weight gain.

Once they start really eating, underweight babies may want more than the typical amount while they catch up on their weight. This usually slows down when a baby reaches the weight she should be based on her birth weight and current age. Supplementing at the breast, as described later in this chapter, is not a good choice until your baby grows stronger. Be sure to pump after nursing to ensure thorough drainage.

## Supplementation at Night

In the beginning, you may need to offer supplements at every feeding, including nighttime. Once your baby has begun gaining well *or* she is older and able to go longer between feedings, it may be possible to forgo supplementing at night.

## What's the Best Supplement for My Baby?

Most people agree that the best supplement is your own expressed milk followed by donor human milk and then commercially synthesized infant formula.[3] If you're making plenty of milk but baby is having difficulty getting it out, you should be able to provide everything she needs by pumping. But if your baby needs more beyond this, first offer whatever you can express—no amount is too small. Then offer the supplement. Giving them separately avoids the risk of baby not finishing it all and some of your milk getting thrown out because it was mixed with the supplement.

*Donor milk* can come from a milk bank or peer donation. Banked milk starts with donors who have been screened medically. Each batch of milk is pooled with milk from three to five donors, pasteurized, and then tested for the highest safety level. Because the need is often greater than the supply, it is prioritized to the sickest and neediest babies and costs around US $3.00-5.00 per ounce, covered by many insurances for medically fragile infants.

Because of the difficulty in obtaining and affording this milk for an otherwise healthy baby, many parents turn to informal "peer" milk-sharing, the modern-day version of the long-revered tradition of wet-nursing. The risks that must be considered include the health status of your donor, any medications or herbs they may be taking, the cleanliness of their environment and collecting equipment, and their milk storage procedures. When a donor is properly screened and risks are minimized, community-based local donor milk can be a good option.[4,5] Although most milk-sharing occurs informally parent-to-parent, the Mother's Milk Alliance in Wisconsin (mothersmilkalliance.org) is an example of a new model of organized community milk-sharing. Donors submit to lab testing before providing milk to a central location, and recipient families can choose to use it as-is or pasteurize it at home.

If you're interested in learning more about milk-sharing, EatsonFeets.org details the pros, cons, and how-to's of milk-sharing, including the option of pasteurization. Human Milk 4 Human Babies (hm4hb.net) is another excellent resource. Mother's Milk Alliance offers easy step-by-step directions for flash pasteurization (bit.ly/MMM-Pasteurize). Be sure to consult with your baby's health care provider when making a decision on donor milk.

If a donor charges for their milk, be wary. There may be an additional risk in what they might do to increase milk volume and profits. One study found higher bacterial counts and another found cow's milk in human milk samples purchased through the internet.[7,8] We've heard stories of babies becoming ill from purchased human milk that was stretched with water, cow's milk, or formula. It's too big a chance to take with your baby's health.

## The 4 Pillars of Safe Milk Sharing

1. **Informed choice**
   - Understanding the options, including risks and benefits, of all infant and child feeding methods
2. **Donor screening**
   - Donor self-exclusion for or declaration of medical or social concerns
   - Communication about lifestyle and habits
   - Screening for HIV I and II, human T-cell leukemia-lymphoma virus (HTLV), hepatitis B virus, hepatitis C virus, syphilis, and rubella
3. **Safe handling**
   - Inspecting and keeping skin, hands, and equipment clean
   - Properly handling, storing, transporting, and shipping of milk
4. **Home pasteurization**
   - Heat treating milk to address infectious pathogens
   - Informed choice of raw milk when donor criteria are met

Source: bit.ly/MMM-Safe and bit.ly/MMM-Pillars[6]

*Infant formula* is the default choice when human milk is not available. Your baby's doctor can help you choose the most appropriate one for your baby. Home-made formula and goat's milk are not recommended because they do not contain all the essential nutrients babies need for optimal growth.

If your baby is close to the age for starting *solids*—usually around 6 months but sometimes earlier—this may be a good option to close the nutritional gap instead of supplemental milk. Choose higher-calorie foods like avocados over standard infant cereals, which contain fewer calories.

## What's the Best Way to Supplement?

There are many devices that can be used to feed supplementary milk to your baby, including nursing supplementers, bottles, finger-feeders, cups, eyedroppers, medicine droppers, and syringes. Each has advantages and disadvantages, and you may decide to use different devices at different stages as circumstances change. Some work best when you have a skilled consultant to teach you the little tricks of the trade that you may need and how to avoid the pitfalls that could sabotage your success. No matter which supplementation device you choose, incorporate as much feeding at the breast as possible to maximize milk removal, minimize flow preference, and maintain baby's familiarity with the breast.

## At-Breast Supplementation

Nursing supplementers use a container or bag and a plastic tube to carry milk to your nipple, where baby can draw from it as she nurses; not a lot has changed technologically in the past decade. They are especially appropriate when low milk production is due to primary causes and provide the double benefits of both feeding your baby and stimulating milk production at the same time. Nursing supplementers can be used for some infant-related situations as long as the baby is able to draw enough milk out in a reasonable amount of time. There are commercial products such as the Lact-Aid® Nursing Trainer System and the Medela SNS™ (Supplemental Nursing System). Or a 3.5- or 5-French gavage tube can also be used by attaching it to a syringe or threading it into a regular baby bottle with a slightly enlarged nipple hole and submerging the end of the tubing in the milk.

## Supplementer Hacks

- Tubing should extend close to the nipple tip; otherwise, the milk flow may become blocked.
- Experiment with tube placement in your baby's mouth. The top middle of the mouth (12 o'clock) is normally suggested, but the 10 or 2 o'clock positions may reduce the risk of the tubing from hitting the top lip on the way in. Or try 6 o'clock by the lower lip.
- Once you've found the best place for the tubing to enter baby's mouth, use 1 or 2 small or medium adhesive bandages to anchor it. They can be left on all day, while paper tape must be replaced each time.
- If you prefer paper tape but putting it on and pulling it off again multiple times a day irritates your skin, try leaving it in place and just layering tape each feeding instead. Wetting it in the shower or with a wet cloth helps remove it painlessly at the end of the day.
- Some parents find it easier to latch their baby first and then sneak the tube in.
- Try tucking the tubing into or under your nursing bra to keep it away from searching fingers.
- Rather than tying a container around your neck, it can be tucked into your bra strap.
- Alternatively, use a rubber band around the container and then pin it to your clothing.
- If the tubing starts to flow less, there may be residual milk build-up. Soak and then flush thoroughly.

Nursing supplementers can be awkward to manage with newborns who have difficulty latching. An alternative is to use a Monoject 412 periodontal syringe commonly used by dentists, which has a nicely curved hard tip (available online through medical, dental, and veterinary supplies). Latch your baby first, then gently sneak the plastic tip of the syringe into the corner of her mouth a ¼ inch (5mm) or so. As she sucks, depress the plunger with short taps to deliver small amounts of milk whenever her jaw drops. Several syringes can be prepared for a feeding so that they can easily be switched out to maintain a constant flow. They only hold a small amount (about ⅓ oz or 10 mL) and last only about a week, so syringes may not be practical for long-term use.

Breast supplementation is ideal for preserving breastfeeding, but it can also be cumbersome and time-consuming, especially during the learning process. More effort is required to prepare, set up, and clean than with regular bottles, and it can take a few days or even weeks to learn the "ins and outs" and feel comfortable using them. Nursing supplementers can leak if not assembled correctly and aren't always as discreet for public nursing. However, parents who overcome these challenges say they enjoy the normalcy and intimacy of an entire feeding at the breast.

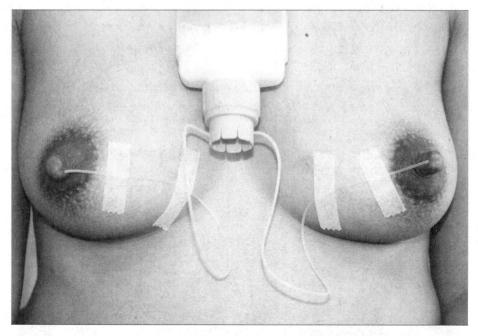

*This nursing supplementer tubing has been placed to enter the lower part of the baby's mouth and stop short of the nipple so baby doesn't use it like a straw.*

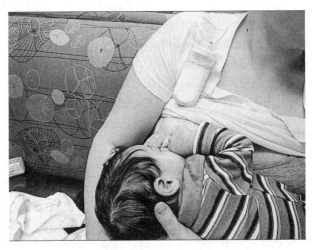

*Using a band-aid to keep tubing in place. Photo courtesy of Sue Stuever*

*Supplementing at the breast with a Hazelbaker feeder. Photo courtesy of Lynn Wolf.*

Bekki had profoundly low milk production and wanted to feed at the breast, but with the steep learning curve and long feeding times, she didn't last long with her first 2 children. Then came her third:

*With my last baby, I challenged myself to supplement at the breast just once a day and increase it by another feeding every week. I gave myself permission to skip it for the day if I was feeling anxious or inadequate. The last feedings to transition to the breast were nighttime feedings. After about 2 months, we were using the Lact–Aid® 100% of the time. This helped take away a lot of the stress and feelings of inadequacy. My older kids quit feeding at all at the breast after mere months, but my third went on until just before her third birthday.*

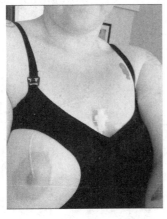

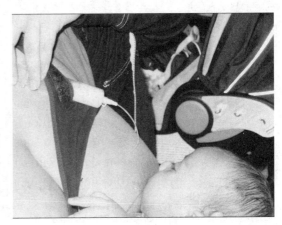

*Positioning a Lact-Aid® tube without taping*

*Using a bra strap to hold a feeding syringe in place*

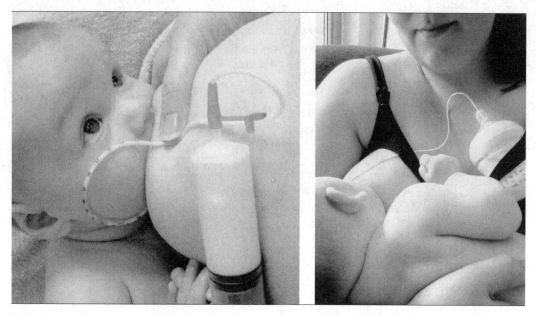

*Supplementing with a feeding tube with syringe combination (left) and a feeding tube with bottle combination (right) courtesy of Rachel Jarlsberg.*

Bekki tried other devices first, but the Lact-Aid® worked best for her: "The Lact-Aid® took more learning on how to set up and clean up, but once I got the hang of it, I could do it with my eyes closed. It was also significantly less messy because it wasn't gravity fed."

For more information, check out bit.ly/MMM-Supplementer and bit.ly/MMM-SNS.

## Bottles

The upside of bottles is that they're easy, convenient, and socially acceptable. The downside is that they must be managed carefully to reinforce good feeding skills and preserve the breastfeeding relationship. Is your baby's suck a factor, or is it mostly a matter of available milk? Lactation consultants and infant feeding experts Lynn Wolf and Robin Glass of Seattle explain that the best bottle for your baby is one that supports moving back to the breast. Here's some of their expert advice.

### Nipple (Teat) Shapes

Despite all the advertising hype, there is no such thing as a nipple that is "most like mother." Breasts and nipples come in a variety of shapes, sizes, and densities. And what's best for one baby may not be good for another. There are certain traits you'll want to look for, though.

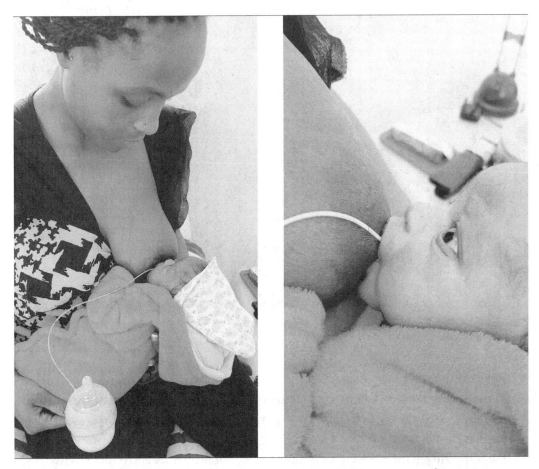

*Supplementing at the breast with a feeding tube and bottle combination. Photo courtesy of Zoe Mataure*

When choosing an artificial nipple for bottle supplementation, look for a shape that supports breastfeeding by encouraging baby to latch deeply, extend her tongue, and cup it around the nipple with relaxed lips. Ultrasound studies show that round nipples with a moderately broad base encourage these motions.[9] Many of today's bottles have bases that are too wide, with skinny nipples that drop steeply before making a sharp 90° turn outward, claiming to imitate breastfeeding. But it can be difficult for a baby to properly grasp and seal on this shape, forcing them to latch more shallowly on the narrower part only. This is especially true for babies with suck problems such as tongue-tie.

Look instead for a bottle nipple that slopes gradually from the tip to base. Can your baby grasp it deeply, extend her tongue, and maintain a good seal with relaxed lips? Does she look comfortable, or does she frequently squirm or readjust her latch? There shouldn't be any leaking of milk or sliding up and down the nipple when a baby is feeding. If she doesn't open wide well, consider a nipple with a bulb that encourages feeding with a wider mouth. While a moderately broad base is preferred, a few babies with suck problems may need a narrower base to be successful.

Another factor is the firmness and texture of the nipple. Some are harder, and some are softer and more flexible. Babies with tight mouths or those who tend to collapse nipples are usually better off with a firmer nipple. If you have very soft breast tissue, consider a bottle nipple that is softer like you.

## Bottle Nipple Shapes

*Top:* Nipples with a wide base and gradual slope from the tip can help support breastfeeding by encouraging baby to suck with a wide mouth.

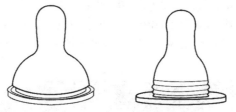

*Middle:* Nipples with a narrower base can be acceptable, but don't encourage baby to suck with a wide open mouth like those in the top row.

*Bottom:* These nipples have a narrow teat and abruptly widen to the base. Most babies will suck on the tip only with very little mouth opening, which undermines the sucking skills they need for breastfeeding.

*Courtesy of Chathuri Sugandhika*

### Bottle Flow Rates

One of the biggest challenges of using a bottle for supplementation is that babies usually prefer to get their milk from whatever flows the fastest. To keep them from preferring the bottle, you'll need to choose a bottle nipple that doesn't flow too quickly and use feeding techniques that mimic breastfeeding patterns.

Unless a baby has a significant sucking problem, a slow-flow nipple is usually best. There are no formal standards for flow rates, and one brand's "slow flow" can flow faster than another regardless of labeling. In fact, nipples from the same package can vary in flow rate, too, so be observant when trying them.[10] Nipples also stretch out over time, and what started out slower may flow faster later on, so keep an eye on this, too. Baby shouldn't take the bottle too quickly or too slowly. Young babies will typically take 2-3oz (60–90ml) in 10-20 minutes, while older ones will take 3-5oz (90-150ml) in 10-15 minutes. In either case, bottle-feeds should not take longer than 30 minutes.

Beyond the bottle itself, how it is offered can also affect the flow. When a baby is positioned lying back with the bottle held up above her, milk flow is fastest due to the downward pull of gravity. But if your baby is held more upright and the bottle is more in front and almost horizontal to the floor, the neutral angle won't flow as fast. Another option for very young babies is to put them "side-lying" on your lap, with the bottle again more horizontal but the nipple tip still filled with milk.

If you can't find a bottle nipple that is both the best shape for your baby's mouth and the right flow, choose the best shape and use techniques to control flow.

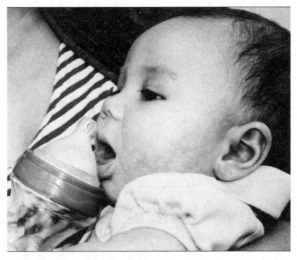

*Latching a bottle deeply. Stroke the nipple across the baby's upper lip first to get her to open wide for a deeper latch.*

### Make the Bottle More Like a Breast

The closer the bottle experience resembles breastfeeding, the more likely your baby is to retain or learn good breastfeeding skills and acceptance of the breast.

As much as possible, try holding your baby against your body and turned inward toward you in an angled position, with her head higher than her legs. If possible, tuck tuck the bottle close to your chest, or you may even be able to tuck it under your arm. Keeping in mind that breastfeeding is normally baby-led, don't "poke" the nipple into her mouth. Instead, lay the bottle nipple across her lips with tip touching just above the upper lip and wait for her to open wide and "ask" for it. Resist the temptation to tap and move the nipple around unless she doesn't respond otherwise. When baby opens wide—you may need to be patient—roll the bottle into her mouth smoothly and deeply.

For babies who exhibit frustration with a breast that doesn't flow right away, try starting the bottle angled so that at first there is no milk in the teat and she must suck for 10 or 15 seconds before it is tipped up enough for milk to start flowing. This imitates the normal short delay to letdown with nursing and teaches her that milk will eventually start coming if she keeps sucking. (On the breast side, be sure to massage first and get some milk flowing before latching so that the breast behaves a little more like the bottle—try to meet baby halfway!)

If your baby tends to start gulping milk rapidly right away, it can be a sign that the nipple flow rate is too fast. You can slow her down by *pacing* the feeding. After several rapid swallows, tip the bottle downward or the baby forward until the milk runs out of the teat, *without removing it from her mouth.* Wait for her to stop sucking. After a short pause, she'll start to suck again, and you can tip the bottle back up. Repeat until baby slows to a more moderate pace (see lowmilksupply.org/paced-feeding.). This technique not only helps to prevent overfeeding due to eating too fast but also imitates the normal flow and ebb of letdowns during breastfeeding, building another bridge back to the breast. Parents often worry about air swallowing, but sucking on an empty nipple is just like sucking on a pacifier; babies won't swallow unless there is something in their mouths to swallow.

### When is the best time to offer the bottle?

Traditional wisdom says that bottles should be given only after offering the breast so that the baby sucks actively to remove the most milk. However, a hungry baby may have less patience for a breast with low supply and may stop trying without taking all the milk that's there. It's as if they know the bottle is coming and are just "paying their dues" at the

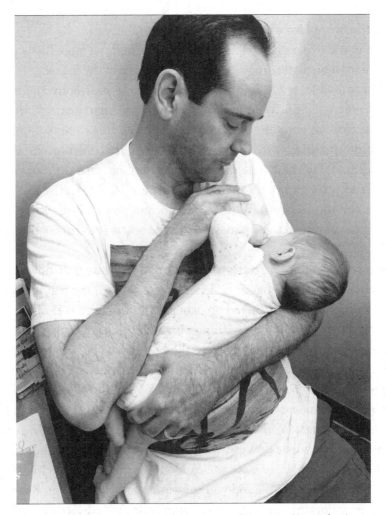

*Offering the bottle with the baby facing you reinforces good breastfeeding skills.*

breast. As a result, they take increasing amounts by bottle, and milk production slows down, requiring even more supplements. This downward spiral effect is the reason that supplementing by bottle has such a poor reputation.

Breastfeeding medicine physician Tina Smillie suggests an alternative that she calls the "Finish at the Breast" method of bottle supplementation. In her practice, she observed that babies who satisfied their initial hunger with a bottle first tended to have more patience feeding at the breast. She began suggesting that parents give a *limited* amount of supplement *before* breastfeeding and discovered that babies would breastfeed longer even if the flow was slow, removing more milk and increasing milk production. For low-supply mom Tiffany, the technique was a turning point: "I felt like it made a positive association with nursing as a place of comfort and full tummy. I also felt like small frequent bottle-feeds followed by nursing reduced my stress level and helped me feel more positive about the nursing experience. It apparently helped my milk supply, too, because we were eventually able to wean off the supplementing."

Another great aspect of the "Finish at the Breast" method is that baby learns to associate the sensation of fullness with the breast rather than the bottle, while you get the satisfaction of a contented baby falling asleep at your breast. Even if your baby just seems to pacify at the breast, it's comforting and builds that bond between you both while providing extra stimulation to your supply. When it happens the other way around, it can be disheartening and undermine your confidence to the point that you end up breastfeeding less and less.

The key to this technique is giving about ¼-½ oz (7-15ml) *less* by bottle than the amount your baby usually needs or takes. If too much is given, baby won't be hungry enough to feed well or long enough at the breast. If too little is given, she may not have the patience to nurse. When she looks relaxed or finishes the bottle, whichever comes first, switch to the breast. If she fusses and seems to want more supplement after breastfeeding, give it to her but be sure to finish at the breast, even if for just a minute or two. It may take a few days of trial and error to determine the best amount.

Be flexible and watch your baby's body language so you can respond to the normal fluctuations in supply throughout the day and night. For example, you may find that you can give fewer supplements (or none!) during the night and before the morning feedings, but in the late afternoon or early evening, you may need to give more. This is fine when it follows the normal fluctuations in your milk supply. As your supply increases, you'll be able to decrease the amount offered up front, little by little. The degree to which this method can increase milk production depends on the reason it is low. If the cause is secondary, it is likely to respond better to this technique than if the cause is primary. But either way, this method can work well to encourage baby to breastfeed longer and more effectively.

### Dealing with Breast Refusal

If your baby is showing signs of breast refusal, try not to take it personally. She isn't rejecting *you*; it just means that conditions need to change to make feeding at the breast more desirable. If the bottle has been easier, she may not trust the breast, even when milk production is improved. From her perspective, she found something that works for her, so why change? Increasing milk production and flow is helpful, but regaining your baby's trust can take time, and efforts to woo her back to the breast can be draining. A gentle approach works better than trying to force the issue. You may have to work slowly and help her make the transition in stages. As described earlier, giving the bottle with the baby turned toward the breast or with a cheek on your bare breast can help build more positive associations. You can also try placing the bottle under your armpit, preferably by a bare breast, so that the baby must face you more fully when she feeds from the bottle as she would at the breast. Offering the breast when she's sleepy and placing her upright skin-to-skin to take advantage of her nursing instincts can also help your baby overcome her resistance.

For Bridget, the bottle-first method was key to reversing their distressing situation: "This is how I got my bottle-preferring baby back to the breast. We had supplemented early with a bottle, and then my baby began to refuse to nurse when hungry. So I would give her about half a feed in a bottle and then let her nurse and finish up with the bottle if needed."

Once your baby starts latching, she'll gradually learn to trust the breast again over several feedings or days, and then feedings will become the enjoyable experience that they were meant to be. A good resource for more on bottle supplementation is *Balancing Breast and Bottle* by Amy Peterson and Mindy Harmer (breastandbottlefeeding.com). If nothing seems to work, don't delay—a lactation consultant may have more ideas using methods that tap into her natural reflexes.

## Finger-Feeding

If your baby must be fed away from the breast and you don't want to use a bottle, finger-feeding is another option. This avoids the use of an artificial nipple and may be especially useful for babies who have certain types of suck problems. A finger-feeder can be made at home using the same gavage tube system described previously. The Hazelbaker FingerFeeder™ (fingerfeeder.com) is a commercial finger-feeding device. You can also use a nursing supplementer clipped to clothing or hung around the neck as usual, with the tubing attached to a finger.

As with using a bottle, it's important to encourage your baby to open her mouth widely before the finger is offered so that she learns the same skills she needs for breastfeeding. Some lactation consultants also recommend using the finger or thumb that is closest to the approximate diameter of your nipple.

Monoject 412 periodontal syringes with a curved, hard tip instead of a needle are another option for finger-feeding. They hold from ⅓-½ oz (10-15ml) of liquid

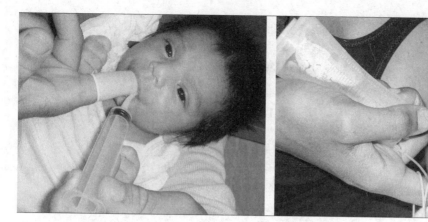

*Finger-feeding with a periodontal syringe and a Hazelbaker feeder (glove optional).*

and are inexpensive (about US $1.00; see the discussion of nursing supplementers). Those with larger barrels usually give too much milk with even a small push, while smaller ones simply may not hold enough milk. Finger-feeding with a syringe is "parent-led" rather than "baby-led," allowing you more control over milk flow. This can be an advantage for babies who have trouble drawing the milk out of feeding tubes. Eye and medicine droppers have also been used to finger-feed but do not offer as much control over how much milk is coming out.

Finger-feeding can be a great in the right circumstances. On the positive side, you can control the flow and it can be used for suck training. On the flip side, babies can develop a preference for it just like for a bottle. For best results, have a skilled lactation consultant teach and observe you; their input is a worthwhile investment.

## Cup-Feeding

Although you might think that drinking from a cup is an advanced skill beyond the capability of infants, babies as young as 30 weeks' gestation have been successfully cup-fed, sometimes before they can effectively breastfeed or bottle-feed. Cup-feeding supports breastfeeding by avoiding nipple or flow preference. However, there also can be significant spillage, which can be frustrating and expensive.

Almost any clean, small plastic or glass cup or bowl can be used to cup-feed, with the exception of disposal paper cups that may contain a plastic coating toxic to infants. There are also cups specially designed for feeding small babies, such as the Medela Soft-Feeder™ and Baby Cup Feeder™, Ameda Baby Cup™, and Foley Cup Feeder. The Soft-Feeder™ and the Foley cup work especially well because they feature a small self-filling

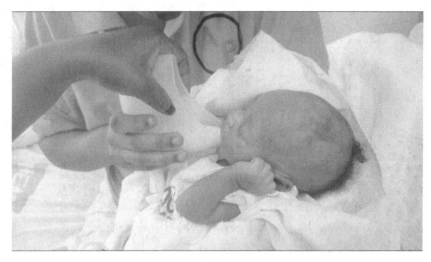

*Cup-feeding with a kindestCup. Photo courtesy of Annie Aloysius*

reservoir that allows control over the flow of supplement. In Europe, the Drickskål Swedish cup is very popular, while the multi-national kindestCup was created to both collect milk and feed back to the baby (kindestcup.com). For more information on how to cup-feed, see bit.ly/MMM-Cup.

## Can I Reuse Leftover Milk?

One issue that can haunt parents is what to do with milk that you've offered to baby but she didn't finish. Nobody wants to throw away their hard-earned milk! The Academy of Breastfeeding Medicine recommends discarding leftover milk in the bottle or any other vessel that baby's mouth touched after a couple of hours.[11] Additional preliminary research suggests that it may be safe beyond that, but further studies are needed before guidelines are changed.[12] Two issues that may influence how long it's good are how clean your pump equipment was as well as how clean the baby's bottle and nipple were, because they're the main sources of bacteria that can accelerate spoilage. Maintaining good cleaning habits will extend the "shelf life" of your milk. Meanwhile, if you find yourself in this dilemma very often, reduce the amount you put in the bottle next time; you can always add more if it's needed!

## What About Weaning from Supplements?

If your milk production increases significantly and your baby begins consistently refusing supplement while continuing to gain well, it may be time to stop supplementing! Test weights can confirm that she is getting the amount she needs, or you can just monitor her diaper output and periodic weight gain.

If baby is not yet refusing supplements but your milk supply seems to be increasing **or** she begins to gain more quickly than necessary, try decreasing the supplement by ¼-½ oz (7-15ml) per feed every few days. You may need to go more slowly, or you may not be able to go lower. Never stop supplementing abruptly if your milk production is not adequate to replace the supplementary feedings.

## Solids as Supplements

The introduction of solids around the middle of your baby's first year is an important milestone. While the first amounts of solid foods babies eat are usually small, about 1 teaspoon (5ml) per meal, starting solids marks the end of your baby's complete nutritional dependence on your milk or formula. It is often at this point that parents are able to gradually replace supplemental feedings with solid foods. However, be sure that solid foods replace supplements, not your milk.

## CHAPTER 5

# Blasting Off to a Great Start

*Courtesy of Manjula Sampath Senaratna*

If you're pregnant, you may be concerned about making enough milk because of previous supply problems, breast surgery, hormonal problems, or a family history of lactation problems. But before diving into how to increase your milk, let's talk about some of the things that help to lay a foundation for the best possible start-up of the milk factory. If you've already had your baby, this chapter may provide insights into where your struggle began.

## The Lactation Curve

In the dairy world, where making lots of milk is a true science, farmers talk about the "lactation curve" of their cows.[1] What they're referring to is how much milk a cow gives over time. Does the cow's production start high and then drop down to a lower plateau? Does it start off lower and slowly increase? Or does it stay the same? Because profits are on the line, farmers pay close attention to all the factors that affect the productivity of their cows.

A great way to understand the curve is to think of your milk production as launching a rocket. You need a rocket with a good-size, well-functioning engine (your breasts) and lots of fuel (hormones and stimulation) to power the rocket off the launch platform against gravity. You set a course that is the right balance of up and out—frequent, quality feeds—to reach orbit. If the rocket levels off too soon, gravity may pull it back to earth sooner than it was supposed to return.

The initial goal for lactation is to reach full production and then sustain it for as long as your baby needs, with gradual reduction. It starts with getting your mature milk production going with good breast tissue, lots of hormones, and lots of stimulation and milk removal. All of these things work together to blast the rocket off the launch pad and into outer space. The rocket has a limited amount of fuel, and it needs to get up high enough into the atmosphere where gravity is lower and less power is needed to keep it going until it completes its mission.

Imagine what would happen if the fuel flow was reduced before the rocket reached its orbit goal. What if the fuel was not flowing fully right from the start? Gravity would pull that rocket back toward the earth, and it might never reach its goal. Further, it would be harder to maintain that lower orbit because gravity is stronger the closer to the ground you get, and the fuel supply is not endless.

Hormones initiate the countdown and lift-off process, and then frequent effective feedings rev up the engines further.[2] Lots of good-quality nursing (or pumping) right after birth stimulates both more prolactin surges and the development of more prolactin receptors for a greater engine response.[1] This combination makes sure your rocket launches off the ground and into orbit quickly. When prolactin levels start their natural decline, having lots of receptors in place ensures that milk production can be maintained to meet your baby's needs.

Launching is the most critical stage of a successful mission. If things go wrong at the start, the potential for a compromised mission is high. That's why we have a whole chapter devoted to getting off to a good start. We understand that for some readers, this stage has passed, and they are in the critical zone. The point is not to panic but to

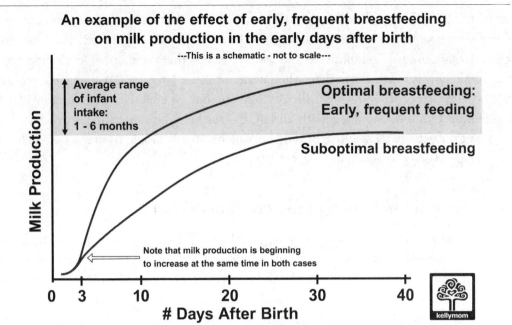

An example of the effect of early, frequent breastfeeding on milk production in the early days after birth (not to scale). Used with permission © KellyMom and Kelly Bonyata.

understand the forces of nature so you can harness them to the best of your ability. Not all rocket launches go as planned, and rocket scientists in the wings may be called on to make quick remote-control adjustments to compensate—otherwise known as "Plan B." If that's where you're at, you may still find helpful ideas in this chapter before moving on to the next.

## Learn to Hand Express Before Birth

Many things about birth are not under your control, but this one is! If ever there are any questions about whether your baby is getting the milk out effectively or adequately, removing colostral milk by hand provides your body with the "go-go-go" message to blast that milk supply rocket off the pad while providing baby with glucose-boosting nutrition.

As long as you are not at high risk of premature labor (sexual relations have been forbidden), this is quite safe and less stimulating than nursing through a pregnancy.[3] Start around 36 weeks; the best time to practice is after a bath or shower, when colostrum is easier to access. The goal isn't necessarily to get lots out but rather *to find your own personal "sweet spot"* for extracting milk effectively. If you're able to express a drop or two, great. If you can easily get more out and want to save it, that's fine, too. Developing your technique now is much easier than when under pressure later on; Chapter 13 covers all the how-to details. If you have difficulty figuring out an effective method, consider a prenatal lactation consultation with an IBCLC for help. Not everyone is good at this right out the gate! Parents with a prior history of low supply problems may want to check out the expanded discussion in Chapter 19 as well.

## Shop for a Breastfeeding-Friendly Pediatrician

When it comes to breastfeeding support, your baby's health care provider can make or break your experience, and you need someone in your corner. Most people choose pediatricians based on feedback from friends, and that's a great place to start. But do they truly support breastfeeding? Many say they do, but their practices may not reflect it. How do they handle weight loss or slow gaining babies? How familiar are they with infant suck problems such as tongue-tie as a cause of breastfeeding problems, and do they support or oppose treatment? Do they work well with and refer to lactation consultants? Do they ever suggest pumping to provide supplement, or is formula their major go-to answer when things aren't going well? What do they recommend for jaundice or vomiting? Do they expect babies to sleep through the night by a certain age? How do they feel about breastfeeding beyond a year of age? Some parents may also want to know how their baby's care provider feels about using donor milk.

Rapport, the level of comfortable communication, is another issue. A health care provider doesn't have to have all the right answers if they are willing to listen to your concerns and consider new information. Stay away from providers who seem to have all the answers and don't have time to listen. Sometimes a provider seems like the right person until you get into that relationship; if you aren't thrilled with how things have gone, don't be afraid to switch.

## Plan for a Breastfeeding-Friendly Birth

The birth experience itself sets the stage for the start of breastfeeding. At the same time, today's parents are more likely to experience multiple interventions than any generation to date—inductions, medications to help labor along, pain medications, surgical births—and these can affect you or your baby's ability to breastfeed after delivery.[4] If your baby hasn't arrived yet, laying the groundwork now to avoid unnecessary procedures such as elective inductions and minimizing the use of labor drugs can help stack the deck in your favor. Lamaze International® has six suggestions for getting birth and breastfeeding off to a good start:[5]

1. Labor begins on its own
2. Freedom of movement throughout labor
3. Continuous labor support
4. No routine interventions
5. Spontaneous pushing in upright or gravity-neutral position
6. No separation of the mother and baby, with unlimited opportunities for breastfeeding and skin-to-skin contact

Research continues to affirm that nature knows best! If you are birthing in a hospital, those designated as Baby-Friendly (bit.ly/MMM-UNICEF) and those with high mPINC (Maternity Practices in Infant Nutrition and Care) scores are more likely to support these policies and have the best breastfeeding rates.[6,7] See lowmilksupply.org/babyfriendly for more resources.

## What if you have a c-section?

Most babies born by cesarean section do well, though some may be sleepier and less interested in nursing if you labored for some time with medications or received general anesthesia. If you know that you'll be having a cesarean birth, being proactive can help get you off to a good start. Find out if it's possible to allow labor to start on its own first so that the baby matures as much as possible, and that intravenous (IV) fluids not be turned on before medically necessary. Ask ahead about having your baby put skin-to-skin on your chest on the other side of the curtain and allowing the umbilical cord to stop pulsing before it's clamped. Newborns are often whisked off to warmers, but research shows that they can be stabilized on their mothers' chests and that this reduces anxiety and the use of postsurgical pain medications and helps launch breastfeeding.[8-10] Don't be afraid to ask someone to help your baby latch if he's ready. Remember, the squeaky wheel gets the grease!

## Start Nursing in the Golden First Hour After Birth

The first hour after birth, called the *Golden Hour* by some, is blast-off time for your milk supply. Ideally, nursing should begin as soon as your baby is ready. Most newborns will

## Should Babies Be Bathed Right After Birth?

Placed naked on their mothers' chests after birth, babies smear amniotic fluid onto the breasts. Later, the smell of the fluid seems to draw them back to the breast like a tracking beacon and trigger their natural latching instincts.[13] When your baby is bathed soon after delivery, the loss of this familiar scent seems to slow his response. Research shows that simply delaying the first bath for at least 12-24 hours increases breastfeeding success.[14] (See this great discussion at bit.ly/MMM-Bath.) If you can wait to wash your own chest as well, these small adjustments in post-delivery routines capitalize on your baby's natural instincts to seek out the breast and feed, nature's way of getting things going!

find the breast and start to suckle within the first hour when placed on their mother's chest.[11] They seem able to get more colostral milk during this golden hour because of the side effects of all that oxytocin from labor pushing the colostrum forward, making it easy to extract. Babies who miss this window may drift into the resting phase, becoming too drowsy to try much for a few to several hours while colostrum may draw back up into the ducts again. Delayed feeding increases their risk for low blood sugar, which may be followed by suggestions to supplement in some manner (and your first opportunity to put that hand expression skill into operation). This is a good reason to delay cord-clamping, keep your baby skin-to-skin, and put off non-urgent tasks like bathing and measuring, which can be done later.[12] As long as your baby is healthy and there aren't any medical concerns, giving him lots of time to suckle right after birth will help get that milk factory going sooner. Smile, be polite, and be firm. It's your baby, not the hospital's!

### What if You Miss the Golden Hour?

What if you don't have that ideal birth? If there are complications, you may not get that first hour together. Even when given the opportunity, not all babies latch well immediately after delivery. Not being able to nurse right after birth does not doom breastfeeding—it just means that it may take a little more work to launch breastfeeding and your milk supply.

If you and your baby are separated after delivery, he hasn't been able to breastfeed, or you suspect that your baby isn't removing colostrum well, *the most important thing that you can do is to express colostrum frequently to jump-start the launch process for milk production.*[15] Try to pump at least every 3 hours as well until baby is able to begin nursing. Dr. Jane Morton of Stanford University Hospital is a passionate advocate of hand expressing in the first 3 days after birth when babies are unable to nurse or nurse well. She works

## Skin-to-Skin Contact: A Powerful Tool

Amazing things happen when your baby is put skin-to-skin on your bare chest. His breathing regulates as he hears your heartbeat. His body temperature stabilizes as he absorbs heat from you. Smelling amniotic fluid from birth (or the milk later on) and feeling your skin triggers the rooting reflex.[17] Even babies who've had bad experiences will search for the breast, and many babies latch for the first time when simply placed on your chest. Skin-to-skin contact, also known as *Kangaroo care*, helps increase milk volume.[17-19] But most important, baby is more likely to nurse when he is "in the restaurant" and smelling your milk.[13,20] So if someone has wrapped your baby, feel free to unwrap him. You can always throw a blanket over both of you if needed.

closely with parents and premature babies, and her research shows that mothers who hand expressed frequently—5 or more times daily—in addition to pumping made the most milk later on.[16] Removing colostral milk is so influential to your start that we hope you'll take the time to view her videos on hand expression and breastfeeding in the first hour; they will make a believer out of you! For more, see bit.ly/MMM-HandExpress and bit.ly/MMM-FirstHour.

## An Optimal Latch is Key to Optimal Milk Production

It's very simple: A good latch gets the most milk from the breast and stimulates the highest production. Ideas about how to achieve the best latch have been evolving in recent years. The basic objective is to get the breast and nipple positioned deeply in the baby's mouth. Not long ago, breastfeeding books were touting the "right way" to breastfeed, complete with step-by-step instructions like a recipe book. We've gotten smarter since then as we've come to understand that there is no single correct way for a baby to latch to the breast, and that latch usually happens better and easier when we give baby more control of the process instead of thinking that we need to do it all. If you haven't tried it yet, a semi-reclining "laid-back" position with the baby on your bare chest triggers his nipple-hunting instincts and gives him the opportunity to find the breast on his own, nature's way. Babies who seemed unwilling to open wide will do their best instinctively when they are initiating the latch. Whatever you do, the most essential measure of a good latch is that *both* of you are comfortable and that milk transfers efficiently.

When your baby latches, pay close attention to how it feels. It's normal to experience some tenderness in the early days, but if it really hurts, he may be attached too shallowly.

## Is Frequent Nursing in the First 3 Days a Bad Sign?

During the first 3 days after birth, many babies will nurse quite voraciously until full milk production starts. Nursing sessions can feel like marathons and last up to several hours off and on, without any clear beginning or end. You may wonder if your baby will ever come up for air! *This doesn't mean he needs more than you are making right now.* Nursing is calming for a baby who is adjusting to his new life outside of the womb. Beyond that, a newborn's stomach is small at birth and stretches out gradually over the first week as your milk comes in. He's just doing his job to hasten the increase in milk volume, and when the milk comes in, he'll likely space out those feedings.

Help him get on deeper by shifting your position or the way he comes to the breast; remember the magic of skin-to-skin and laid-back positioning. If the pain continues, something is wrong no matter how good the latch looks on the outside; seek help from someone who doesn't tell you to "just keep trying."

In the meantime, *get the milk moving.* Don't rely on just your pump quite yet, because hand expression usually gets more out than a pump before the onset of full production.[21] Additionally, pumping can draw fluids forward, making the nipple bigger and latching even harder for your baby. Instead, try hand expressing a few drops of colostrum onto a plastic spoon for someone else to offer the baby while you express into a second spoon. If you can't express much colostrum, *it doesn't mean that you don't have any.* Swollen breast tissue caused by water retention after birth can make expressing colostrum or milk difficult the first few days, and hand expression is a skill that takes some practice. Fortunately, babies don't need a lot. Per feeding, they take on average about ½–2 teaspoons (2–10ml) the first 24 hours, about 1–3 teaspoons (5–15ml) at 24-48 hours, and 1–3 teaspoons (5–15ml) at 48-72 hours.[22] That's a pretty wide range! No matter how much or little, every drop is valuable.

One technique that can soften the areola both to help your baby latch and to make it easier to express colostrum is *Reverse Pressure Softening* (RPS). Simply lean back, put 2 or 3 fingers at the base of the nipple on each side and press in as deeply as you can, holding for about 30 seconds. Then move your fingers to the top and bottom and repeat. The sustained pressure pushes the fluids back, making the area softer and allowing milk to flow. You can read more about RPS at bit.ly/MMM-RPS.

Sometimes the breasts are so swollen from excess fluids or engorgement that you can't get anything out. Lactation consultant Maya Bolman teaches *Therapeutic Breast Massage*

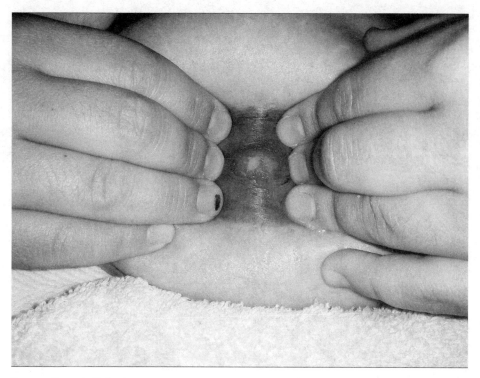

*Reverse Pressure Softening*

*for Lactation* (TBML) to reduce the swelling and trigger letdown.[23] You can learn her techniques at vimeo.com/65196007.

## Optimizing Milk Removal

### Breast Massage and Compression

When your baby is latching well, maximizing drainage helps strengthen the signal to make more milk. Babies remove the most milk when the breast is pushing it toward them during a letdown. One of the difficulties of low milk production, however, is that the letdown reflex is often less effective when it has less volume to work on (lower internal pressure), so milk may not be completely drained by the baby. To help him get the most milk out, gently massage your breasts both before and during feeding.[24,25]

A variation of breast massage called *breast compression* uses external hand pressure to push residual milk closer to the nipple. Grasp your breast with your thumb on one side and your fingers on the other, far back away from the areola. Compress the tissue

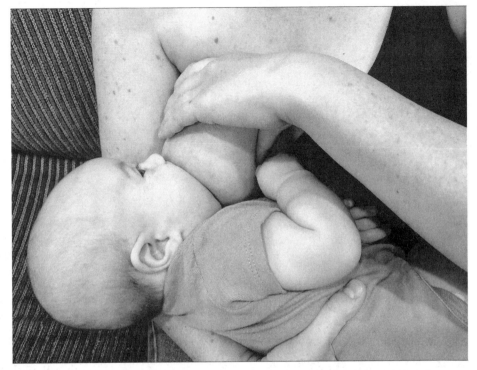

*You can use your free hand to reach over and compress the breast while nursing to help baby get more milk out.*

between your fingers and thumb gently but firmly—it shouldn't hurt or pinch ducts—and hold the compression, pushing forward slightly. If you feel any firm or lumpy areas, focus your efforts there because they may contain pockets of milk. Baby usually will begin swallowing more rapidly; when he slows down, release the pressure and rotate a little to another firm area, repeating the process.

## Stay Close and Feed Often

Research shows that there is no medical reason for healthy mothers and babies to be separated, and in fact, they are less stressed when kept together,[26] which is why rooming-in and couplet care are becoming the standard. Staying in close proximity to your baby after birth stimulates him to feed more often and helps you to learn and respond to his earliest hunger cues. Be sure to nurse often, *at least* 8 times each 24 hours for as long as he baby desires, so long as the latch is comfortable. Remember that frequent feedings in the early days are normal, and for those at risk of low milk production, they may be essential to calibrate the highest milk supply possible. They also help create greater storage

## Worried About Becoming a "Human Pacifier"?

Letting a baby nurse for reasons other than food isn't wrong. It won't cause bad habits or an unhealthy dependence on the breast. *Pacifiers are artificial replacements for your breasts, the original place of comfort.* Babies nurse for many reasons besides hunger: to soothe pain, to calm them when they're scared, to relax and fall asleep, or simply because the world feels right when they're in your arms. There is always a reason! Decades of child development research have shown that a baby whose needs are met learns trust and security. If you suspect it's more than this, though, listen to your instinct and check further. In some cases, a baby may be hanging out on the breast because he truly isn't getting enough to eat.

capacity, which allows you to store more milk at one time for your baby. In general, *the best way to make more milk is to take out more milk.*

### Overcoming the "Visitor Syndrome"

Everyone wants to meet your new baby, but that may come at a cost. Some parents find themselves giving bottles in the hospital because they're uncomfortable nursing or pumping in front of others or asking their company to leave. The visitor syndrome can continue at home as friends and family show up to see your new little one. If they're from out of town, you may feel obligated to stay with them when you really need to sneak off for some privacy to nurse or rest. Worse still, well-meaning friends and relatives may ask to feed your baby a bottle or suggest that the baby isn't hungry yet, he just needs to be held . . . or given a pacifier . . . or walked . . . or burped . . . anything but put back to the breast because it's surely "too soon." By the time everyone leaves, you're exhausted, baby's frazzled, and breastfeeding is off to a slow start.[27] It's hard when you're worried about hurting someone's feelings, but right now launching your milk supply is extremely important. One way you can be proactive is to send a friendly message: "We'd love for you to meet our new baby, but first we need to get to know him ourselves. Thank you for reaching out to us; we'll let you know when we're ready for visitors!"

### Express Milk After Nursing?

The first few weeks after birth are prime time for maximizing milk production, and we are sometimes asked by parents if they should pump after nursing right from the start. If you have a baby who is nursing well and often, and no other reason to suspect your breasts won't make plenty of milk, expressing after breastfeeding is likely more work and stress than benefit for you. If you had problems making milk in the past and are concerned this time around or have other risk factors, however, expressing with a high-quality pump (see Chapter 13) after feedings has increased, or after day 4 if you're not sure, may be beneficial. The idea is to make sure the breasts are well-drained after feedings to calibrate your production to the highest level possible. Be sure to balance this work with getting enough rest; *the process should serve you, not enslave you.* Once you know that you're making enough for your baby, back off of pumping gradually.

## Don't Skip Nighttime Feedings

Most parents feed their babies whenever necessary during the daytime but find themselves longing for an uninterrupted night's sleep. At the same time, newborns often sleep longer during the daytime and eat more at night. Temptation may loom large to have someone else take over the night feeding duties while you sleep. But here's what you need to know: going longer stretches without feeding means less milk removal, and that may send a "slow down the assembly line" message to the breast. Prolactin is also higher at night when you sleep, and the response to your baby's suckling is greater than in the daytime.[28,29] Meanwhile, milk tends to flow more easily at night when you're sleepy and relaxed. This winning combination will go far in maximizing your milk production.

The first key to restful night nursing is to find a lying-down position that works for both of you in bed (not on a reclining chair or sofa because they are a serious risk for infant suffocation). While this comes easily for some, it may take time and experimentation for others. Once you get the hang of night nursing, you may well find yourself dozing right through feedings, especially when your baby is a little older and can easily self-latch. The American Academy of Pediatrics recommends keeping the baby in your room rather than in your bed, but they acknowledge that "sleep happens" when you nurse at night and suggest simply moving the baby to a co-sleeper or crib once you waken.[30] Even if you fall asleep, it's safer to nurse in a bed that you've prepared for night nursing than to fall asleep on a sofa or in an armchair.

Second, take at least 1 or 2 naps during the daytime. They don't have to be long, but close your eyes and let yourself drift off once the baby falls asleep. Roll with your baby's sleep pattern instead of resisting it; you'll be surprised at how much a little extra sleep can help. Even short naps cause prolactin to rise, giving you another hormonal boost. If you find it hard to nap because you have other young children, this is the time to call in favors and ask family and friends for help so you can get some rest.

## How Dangerous is Bedsharing?

Mothers around the world have slept with their babies and nursed throughout the night for thousands of years and higher mammals higher mammals do the same thing. So why do we now hear that what parents and babies naturally do is dangerous? Did nature mess up the blueprint? People worry about sudden infant death syndrome (SIDS) and suffocation with bedsharing, but if you practice the *Safe Sleep Seven* (llli.org/the-safe-sleep-seven), neither is likely to happen. These include:

(1) no smoking in the home or outside;
(2) sober parents (no alcohol or drugs that make you drowsy);
(3) breastfeeding day and night;
(4) healthy, full-term baby;
(5) sleeping on his back;
(6) light clothing and no swaddling; and
(7) a safe sleep surface. This last one means a firmer mattress, no extra pillows, no toys, and no heavy covers; packing any cracks with towels or blankets; and keeping the baby's head outside of the covers.[31,32]

For more about safe bedsharing, we recommend La Leche League International's heavily-researched book, Sweet Sleep: *Nighttime and Naptime Strategies for the Breastfeeding Family*

Perspective is the final ingredient and plays the biggest role in how well-rested parents feel. Those who focus on how stressful the situation is and resent nighttime feedings often wake up tired, grumpy, and irritable. Those who give themselves over to their baby's temporary night needs, however, and who see this as a passing stage or a gift to their baby often find that they feel rested and able to function. In fact, they may not even remember how many times their baby actually fed the night before. A positive perspective, along with any naps you can fit in and an early bedtime, really can make a world of difference in how rested you feel.

Having said this, there are times when a parent may reach a serious point of exhaustion, and this can also take a toll on milk production. There are exceptions to every rule, and it may be necessary and beneficial to take an afternoon or night "off," have someone else watch the baby, and just sleep until you waken naturally. Often the milk that just didn't seem to be there suddenly seems to rebound. As long as this isn't a regular event, you should be okay.

## Beware of Tight Bras

If you wear a bra, it needs to fit; this is one area that you don't want to cheap out on. A tight bra can reduce the warehouse space and limit the amount of milk you can store, ultimately forcing your factory to slow down. Did you know that women who didn't want to breastfeed used to bind their breasts to suppress milk production? Make sure that your bra allows room for expansion so that you can store all the milk your breasts can make.

## Putting it All Together: The Essential Elements

Getting your milk production off to the very best start hinges on frequent and thorough milk removal from birth onward. With an optimal latch, baby will do his part to the best of his ability. Your job is to follow his lead and allow him to breastfeed whenever he asks. Having realistic expectations of new parenthood and a plan to take care of yourself will also help you to cope and even flourish during this time. Preparation and making the baby your first priority will help you to maximize your milk-making potential now and eliminate the most common causes of low milk production.

# PART III

# Investigating Causes of Low Milk Production

## *Rocio's Story*

I suspected I had a milk supply problem at my daughter Sofia's first checkup when she hadn't gained enough. She nursed around the clock and never seemed satisfied. My first intervention was pumping after feedings to empty my breasts. I also took fenugreek and oatmeal daily for a month but saw no change, getting just 1oz (30ml) total. Next I added a tea, and then I tried metoclopramide for a week. At 2 months, a lactation consultant recommended I talk to my doctor about metformin because I had PCOS (polycystic ovary syndrome). Working up to 1500mg of metformin, my supply increased to 1½ oz (45ml) of pumped milk per session. Determined for more, I added 80mg of domperidone and increased to 3½ oz (105ml) per session. But despite all this milk, Sofia wasn't getting it all. After nursing, she was still hungry but leaving milk in my breasts.

At 6 months, we finally discovered that Sofia's tight frenulum was the reason she couldn't remove milk well and I struggled so much. Minor surgery to release her frenulum was a success; my sore nipple problem resolved, and she started emptying my breasts better. I stopped the metformin and then the domperidone, maintaining my supply with just More Milk Special Blend™ tincture. When Sofia turned one, I finally stopped pumping and just nursed. I recall many difficult times, including when well-meaning friends and relatives would suggest I just give up. It was hard to persevere when I was tired from waking at 3:00 am to pump so I could keep my supply stable or when Sofia went on a 2-day nursing strike after her surgery, but with my husband's support, we made it.

# 6

# Is it Something I'm Doing?

In the next 7 chapters, we'll explore various reasons for faltering milk production. This is an important part of the process because the possibility of finding answers provides an explanation (finally!) for what's happening to help you develop a targeted strategy to make the most milk possible. It's easier to hit a target when you can see it clearly.

## Pinpointing the Reasons for Your Low Supply

As you begin this process, start with the question "Was there ever a time that I felt like I had a lot of milk?" If you remember a day in that first week when your breasts felt full, warm, or even hard, your factory likely started up well but then something happened to sabotage your supply. There's a good chance you'll find your problem among the secondary causes in this chapter or the next three. If your milk production seemed low from the start, however, or dropped off despite you and your baby doing everything right, Chapters 10 through 12 about primary problems, those originating with your body, may hold your answers. It's also possible to have more than one thing going on, and that can have a greater impact than a single factor. So try to keep an open mind as you read through these possibilities because there may be unexpected answers.

Secondary problems can be divided into *management, diet, pregnancy/birth,* and *infant.* Low milk supply caused by these issues tends to be easier to reverse than when primary problems are involved. We're going to start with causes that are under your control, such as how often and long you feed your baby, how you bring the baby to your breast, and the possible effects of foods, herbs, and medications on your milk supply. Most of these are relatively easy to fix.

**The Milk Supply Equation**

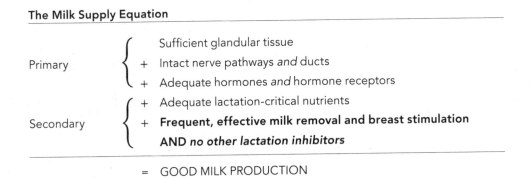

| | | |
|---|---|---|
| Primary | $\left\{\vphantom{\begin{array}{c} a\\b\\c\end{array}}\right.$ | Sufficient glandular tissue |
| | | + Intact nerve pathways *and* ducts |
| | | + Adequate hormones *and* hormone receptors |
| Secondary | $\left\{\vphantom{\begin{array}{c} a\\b\\c\end{array}}\right.$ | + Adequate lactation-critical nutrients |
| | | + **Frequent, effective milk removal and breast stimulation** |
| | | **AND** *no other lactation inhibitors* |

= GOOD MILK PRODUCTION

## Latch Problems

One common cause of low milk production in the early weeks is poor attachment to the breast. When a baby is latched too shallowly, she doesn't have enough breast in her mouth to effectively draw out milk, kind of like chomping on your straw while trying to drink. Less milk is removed, and the breast responds by cutting back on production.

Clues for poor attachment are usually obvious. The breasts will not soften much during nursing because milk is not being drained. Friction to the nipple causes pain and damage (never normal!). As the situation worsens, the baby becomes fussy at breast, pulling off or falling asleep too quickly. Diaper output is scant, weight gain is inadequate, and if she's is jaundiced, the condition doesn't improve after the milk comes in. While initially the breasts were fuller at feeding time, they begin to feel soft and empty all the time.

Some well-intentioned but misinformed health care providers recommend limiting how long a baby breastfeeds on each side to prevent or treat sore nipples. However, it's not how much time your baby spends at breast that causes pain but *the quality of the latch and suck*. Limiting the time at breast without correcting the underlying problem can reduce milk production by limiting milk removal. A much better strategy is to determine why breastfeeding is painful in the first place and fix the problem.

The good news for latch-related supply problems is that correcting the problem is often relatively easy. There are a number of good articles and videos online for getting a deep latch. If you aren't able to fix it on your own, the problem could be related to your baby's ability to suck effectively (see Chapter 9) and may require the help of a lactation consultant.

## Feeding Management

Newborns must feed frequently to fuel their growth and get your milk production up and running. *Your job is to make sure that your baby has all the opportunities she needs.* How feedings are managed is probably the number one cause of faltering milk production. The following can interfere with this process and sabotage your milk factory if they aren't caught early.

### The Sleepy or Nondemanding Baby

There's an old saying, "Let sleeping dogs and babies lie." Sounds like a good idea, especially if you've been told to feed the baby "on cue" and she isn't "asking" at the moment, right? This may be fine for an older baby who is gaining well, but it's not good advice for a newborn who is jaundiced, lethargic, or not gaining weight well.

Excessive sleepiness has several possible causes. A newborn may be drowsy after delivery because of medications given to you during labor. The effects may be brief, or they can linger for several days. Simply not getting enough milk can also cause a baby to sleep too much. She may eventually rouse and show clear hunger cues but fall asleep again within minutes at the breast if the milk isn't flowing quickly or she just doesn't have much energy to feed. This in turn leads to longer naps to conserve energy. Until milk production can be increased, *this baby needs supplementation for energy to feed well at breast.* Tiring out during a feeding and falling asleep too soon can also happen as a result of suck or medical problems on the baby's side, which are discussed in Chapter 9. In the meantime, lots of skin-to-skin contact can help stimulate your baby and trigger her nursing instincts.

Another cause of infant drowsiness is *jaundice*, a temporary yellowing of the skin that often looks like a suntan. Normal *physiologic* jaundice is caused by elevated levels of a blood byproduct called *bilirubin* and is a healthy response to transitioning to life outside the womb. Early and frequent feedings minimize jaundice by stimulating bowel movements, through which bilirubin is eliminated. Water isn't helpful because it produces only urine. If bilirubin levels rise significantly in the early days, enticing your baby to eat is more challenging because bilirubin makes babies sleepy and lethargic. *While babies need to eat to get rid of the bilirubin, sleepy babies can be difficult to feed.* Wake a jaundiced baby to feed at least every 2-3 hours until she starts waking appropriately on her own. Gentle methods such as holding her upright, massaging her body, talking to her, undressing her, or changing her diaper will encourage her to feed. Alternatively, hand-express or pump and feed the milk back to your baby.

Babies usually need more of your milk, not less, to resolve jaundice. Supplementing large amounts of formula is likely to make her sleep too long, reducing your milk production.[1] A better strategy for helping her get enough milk while also keeping your supply strong is to supplement with a small (2-3 tsp/10-15ml) amount of milk before or after each feeding. If baby's bilirubin levels are very high and unresponsive to regular management, she may need larger amounts of supplemental milk or a temporary suspension of breastfeeding (usually 24-48 hours).[1] Make sure to express milk every missed feeding until baby can do the job herself again.

## Watch the Baby, Not the Clock

When do you eat supper? How long does it take? Is it always the same time of day, and do you always eat for the same amount of time? Probably not. Yet it's common for parents to be told that babies should be nursed only every so many hours or for a specific number of minutes on each side.

People in traditional cultures understand that babies should be put to the breast when they ask and nursed as long as they wish, and that how often and how long vary according to each baby's emotional and physical needs at any given time. In our society, however, we tend to believe that babies should breastfeed only for nutrition. Parents are urged to get their babies on a schedule as quickly as possible to instill early discipline, to fit them conveniently into family life, to make life more predictable, or for "sleep training." Whatever a parent's fear or motivation, these are often regarded as important parenting goals. Yet these approaches are risky when it comes to establishing milk supply and ensuring that a baby receives enough calories.

Schedules may seem helpful to parents, but *they don't always meet the needs of nursing mothers and babies.* Rather than allowing milk production to be driven by baby as nature designed, schedules artificially determine when feedings will take place. Individuals with abundant production and vigorously nursing babies may do well, but those with marginal production or babies with difficulties often do not. Even when breastfeeding has gotten off to a great start, feeding schedules can derail an established milk supply, and you could be faced with having to rebuild the milk factory again. Beyond breastfeeding, children who were fed on a schedule as babies had lower IQ scores and didn't do as well academically as those who were fed on cue.[2] Bottom line: Nature knows best! Advice that goes against your instincts on when to feed your baby can undermine your milk supply *and* affect your child's development.

## One-Sided Nursing

Parents with breastfeeding concerns often surf the web looking for all the best tips. You may have read about how not draining the breast well might result in your baby not getting enough of the rich, more satisfying cream at the end of the feeding, sometimes referred to as *foremilk–hindmilk imbalance*. The advice given to counteract this concern is to make sure that the first breast is well-drained before switching sides. Somewhere along the line this information was derailed, and someone started making a blanket recommendation to nurse on only one side per feeding. Mothers with large supplies may be able to get away with this, but most cannot. As a result, a number of babies have not gotten enough to eat and lost weight, and their mother's production down-regulated because each breast was not being drained often enough. Lactation consultants have also reported cases when a baby was routinely fed on one side while milk was pumped from the other side to store for future use, and again the baby was not gaining weight. The solution is simple—offer both breasts every feeding! Use compression to help your baby get as much milk out of the first side before switching to the second. If baby seems full and doesn't want to take the second side, that's okay, too. If you want to collect extra milk, pump the leftovers from the starting breast while feeding your baby on the second side.

Sometimes "block feeding," nursing on the same breast for one or more feedings at a time, is suggested as management for oversupply. This is a valid coping technique but must be managed carefully. The goal is to bring production down a bit and then resume feeding on both breasts. If you find your production swinging from too much to too little, talk to a lactation consultant for help tailored to your situation.

## Pacifiers

Pacifiers can mask the hunger cues of babies who are easily soothed by them. They are often given in the belief that a baby is supposed to be full after so many minutes at the breast and stay content for a certain amount of time. An assertive baby will spit it out and insist on more milk, but an easygoing baby may not be as persistent. This can disrupt the baby-driven milk-making process by forcing inappropriately long feeding intervals that ultimately reduce milk supply.

Of course, there *are* some babies who are uncomfortable and don't settle without extra sucking that you may not have time to give. If this happens a lot, you might want to explore why your baby is so uncomfortable despite being well-fed, and whether there is anything that can be done to help her. Just take care not to let the pacifier take the place of feeding baby when she needs it.

## On the Go, Go, Go

Juggling a baby and the conflicting demands of a busy life is challenging. Feedings can be unconsciously postponed when you're preoccupied with trying to get "just one more thing" done. And if you have older children and are always on the go taking them places, the temptation to put off feedings instead of nursing in the moment may be strong.

In the midst of all the chaos, it's easy to forget how long you used to spend sitting and feeding your first baby. Think back carefully—are there differences that might be contributing to the problem you're experiencing now? Hard as it may feel, it's important to slow down and remember that *this* baby will only be young once, and there is no do-over for meeting today's needs. Carrying her in a soft baby carrier can help you stay connected and aware of early feeding cues (rooting, smacking noises, sucking on a fist) while on the go. In the meantime, don't be afraid to ask for help—if someone else can shuttle a child to practice or pick up an item for you, let them! We weren't meant to do it all alone.

## I Need Sleep!

New parents can become obsessed with sleep simply because it's hard to get enough. Sleep deprivation can drive us to desperation, and the around-the-clock needs of young babies can seem like an impossible demand to meet. Parents in traditional cultures tend to take babies' nighttime needs in stride, but Western living involves clocks, deadlines, schedules, and appointments that don't always suit a baby's way of life. Is it any wonder that we feel stressed over lack of sleep and fear that this stage of life will never end? The hard truth is that babies' needs haven't changed since the stone age, yet they're being asked to adapt to a fast-paced, technologically-driven society rather than us adapting to their needs.[3]

The desire for more sleep is the most common reason given for nighttime bottles. But each skipped feeding decreases milk production by that same amount unless you compensate by pumping, preferably at about the same time, *which defeats the purpose of a relief bottle*. Realistic expectations are important. If your newborn feeds 10 times a day and you want her to sleep 8 hours at night so that you can have a long stretch of uninterrupted sleep, when is she going to get those feedings in? She has just 16 hours, which means she needs to nurse every 1½-2 hours, assuming enough breast storage capacity and that the baby isn't taking milk faster than it is being made after a long night of inactivity. Can you really accommodate this? It's more realistic and normal for a baby to space her feedings throughout the day and night.

Night nursing is easier if the baby is in bed with you or sleeping nearby. Bedsharing is a time-honored tradition that has unfortunately come under fire as newspaper headlines inflame parents' fears of rolling over on their babies. However, Dr. Helen Ball and her research team at the Durham University Infant-Parent Sleep Lab and other infant sleep researchers have shown conclusively that babies and mothers are biologically hardwired to sleep together, affording them more rest and more successful breastfeeding. Not only will your baby nurse easily without having to cry for your attention, but it's also good for your milk supply. Your body functions on a circadian rhythm, a sort of pre-programmed 24-hour clock. Prolactin naturally rises during the night, so nursing at night means higher prolactin surges to help recharge the milk factory.[4] Prolactin also makes you drowsy, nature's way of helping you get back to sleep.

If you choose to bedshare, be sure to do so in a safe manner, just as it's important that a crib be used in a safe manner. A great resource for up-to-date information and a thorough explanation of safety issues is La Leche League's *Sweet Sleep: Nighttime and Naptime Strategies for the Breastfeeding Family.*

## Unnecessary Supplementation

There are legitimate circumstances when a baby isn't getting enough milk and must be supplemented. But there are also times when unnecessary supplements sabotage milk production by reducing milk removal and stretching out feeding intervals. The Santa Barbara County Breastfeeding Coalition surveyed mothers for reasons they stopped breastfeeding before 12 months and found that parents often introduced bottles *before* problems with milk production developed, rarely noticing a connection to their eventual loss of milk supply. Problems often started with "just 1 bottle a day" or "just a few bottles a week," increasing over time because the more supplements given, the more are needed because milk isn't made when it isn't removed. It becomes a slippery slope where bottle feeding eventually seems easier or the baby starts to prefer it. Gratuitous supplementation is the sneakiest cause of management-induced low milk production because it "just sort of happens."

## Are Bottles Really Necessary?

Even when regular separations aren't planned, bottles are often introduced out of concern that baby won't accept them later on. This is realistic in that there does seem to be a window of opportunity in the first 3 months when babies are more willing to take a bottle. But if you won't be away from her on a regular basis, there's really no need to introduce one. In an emergency, she could be fed by cup, spoon, or other devices and will survive. Introducing a bottle just so your baby will take one for an unplanned future event isn't necessary and may undermine your milk supply. It makes more sense for bottle-feeding parents to make sure their babies can breastfeed just in case no formula is available!

Another reason frequently given to use bottles is for others to bond with the baby. This is one of society's great myths. The truth is that a baby bonds to those who hold, touch, and love her, not just the person who feeds her; touch is the magic ingredient to facilitate bonding. Helping family members find other ways—such as burping, baths, and massages—to connect with the baby is a much better alternative than having them compete with you for feeding opportunities. Even pumping milk for the bottle can interrupt the early mother–baby dance and lead to baby preferring the bottle, especially if there have been any difficulties with breastfeeding.

### Outside Interferences

Some nursing parents sail smoothly along until poor advice rocks their boat. This usually happens when they're facing a medical procedure, medications, or hospitalization and are told that they can't nurse for *X* amount of time, usually by staff unfamiliar with current information. To make matters worse, little or no guidance is provided on how to maintain production, and by the time breastfeeding is "allowed" again, milk supply is damaged. Educating yourself on the facts is your best defense, and regular pumping is your backup. Consider whether the person telling you that your milk is not safe is lactation-savvy. *Always get a second opinion from someone with expertise and resources in lactation before following advice to stop breastfeeding.* Hale's *Medications and Mothers' Milk* (updated every 2 years) is an excellent safety reference for both parents and health care professionals. Two others are LactMed (toxnet.nlm.nih.gov/newtoxnet/lactmed.htm), a government-sponsored online resource, and E-Lactancia (e-lactancia.org). Alternatively, Hale's information is also available directly to parents via their mobile app at mommymeds.com or from the InfantRisk Center at infantrisk.com; check the Apple or Android app stores. Arm yourself with information then talk to your baby's health care provider.

## When Milk Seems to Dry Up Overnight

Between 2-4 months postpartum, some nursing parents experience what seems like a sudden drop in milk production. Their babies act hungry all the time, while the breasts feel empty. One possible explanation is that baby's appetite has temporarily increased because of a growth spurt. This isn't a problem unless you start giving supplemental bottles, which reduce milk removal and slow production. The result can be a downward spiral of more fussiness, more bottles, and less milk until one day you feel like you've "just dried up."

A similar "drying up" phenomenon is related to feeding schedules that call for the baby to feed every so many hours (often 3 or longer) by the clock. Everything seems to be working until one day the milk seems to start disappearing. The most likely explanation is inadequate development of prolactin receptors due to chronic, infrequent feeding. Once prolactin levels have dropped, the existing receptors cannot sustain the earlier production level. Milk supply may rebound with renewed stimulation, but other times it can be difficult to resurrect. Feeding more often, possibly coupled with the addition of a galactogogue (see Chapter 14), is usually the best strategy for turning things around.

Another possible reason for the milk seeming to disappear is some kind of inhibiting substance—you'll read more about this next. In rarer cases, this phenomenon occurs despite frequent and effective feedings due to unusual hormonal changes (see Chapter 11). An expert lactation consultant can review your history and the clues you've collected after reading through this book and provide guidance for what steps to take next.

## Sneaky Saboteurs: Common Substances That Inhibit Milk Production

In the same way that a galactogogue stimulates milk production, an *anti-galactogogue* is a substance that *decreases* milk production. Once you've identified and removed the offending item, milk production will often improve on its own. The most common ones are covered next, but if you're interested in the detailed list, you might want to get a copy of pharmacist Phil Anderson's comprehensive 2-part article, "Drugs That Suppress Lactation," through your local library.[5]

### Hormonal Medications
Certain hormones such as estrogen, progesterone, and testosterone can inhibit milk production if their levels are too high or if synthetic versions are introduced at the wrong time during lactation. It has long been recognized that "combination" birth control pills containing forms of both estrogen and progesterone can significantly decrease milk production. The "minipill" is estrogen-free and better for nursing parents, but a small number still experience a drop in supply until the medication is stopped. Research hasn't confirmed it yet, similar problems have been reported with the patch, subdermal implant birth control (Implanon, Nexplanon), and intrauterine devices (IUDs) with hormones.

Removal of the device should help, but many health care providers are reluctant to do this. Depo-Provera, a long-acting injectable type of hormonal birth control, poses a more serious problem because it lasts for 3 months and cannot be reversed; the best option is to try a galactogogue to counter the effect (see Chapter 14).[6-9]

Hormonal birth control has a greater chance of causing problems in the early weeks after birth, when progesterone and estrogen receptors may still be plentiful, than it does later on when they've had a chance to decline, reducing the effect of hormones. Many physicians believe that a safe time to introduce these methods is around the time of your 6-week postpartum checkup, but some individuals are still reactive. Waiting 3 months or longer reduces the risk of trouble; an alternative such as a hormone-free IUD or barrier method can be used for a while.

## Medications and Vitamins

Several medications are known to inhibit milk production. Bromocriptine (Parlodel), once used to dry up the milk of mothers who didn't want to breastfeed, is still used to treat excessive prolactin levels. Cabergoline (Dostinex), another prolactin inhibitor, is used more commonly because it's much safer, but its effects are longer lasting than bromocriptine. Bupropion (Wellbutrin, Zyban), aripiprazole (Abilify),[10] and promethazine have negatively affected some people's supplies.[5] Pseudoephedrine, found in Sudafed (not Sudafed PE) and many other allergy and cold medications, can also be a problem, especially in later lactation.[11] Antihistamines have been under suspicion in past years, but many nursing parents are able to take the newer ones (fexofenadine, loratadine) without noticeable impact.[5]

*Ergot alkaloids* such as methylergonovine maleate (Methergine; see Chapter 8) and dopamine receptor agonists can also lower milk production. Local injection of high-dose corticosteroids (triamcinolone, depot methylprednisolone) reportedly caused dramatic supply drops for three women, starting from 1-3 days after the injections and taking from 1 day to 1 month for the milk to fully return. (Note: This is not a concern for normal doses of oral corticosteroids.)[5]

*Pyridoxine,* more commonly known as vitamin $B_6$, has an inhibiting effect on prolactin and milk production in high dosages (450-600mg per day). Raynaud's disease ran in Zoe's family, and when she developed Raynaud's phenomenon of the nipple (burning sensations), her midwife suggested high doses of $B_6$—200mg taken 3 times per day—to combat it. This treatment brought great improvement to her symptoms, but she felt like her milk was drying up and no amount of extra nursing or galactogogues was making a difference. A chance observation by her partner resulted in some research and the discovery that $B_6$ has been tested for suppressing lactation, including at the dosage she was using.[12] Once Zoe stopped it, her supply returned. While small amounts in multivitamins should not pose a problem,[5] one author of an older commentary nevertheless suggested that nursing parents with normal vitamin levels might be wise to avoid multivitamins with added $B_6$.[13] *You need this vitamin*, just not too much.

## Alcohol

The effects of alcohol (ethanol) on breastfeeding have been widely debated. Nursing parents have long been advised to drink a glass of beer or wine to relax and get their milk flowing. Beer's positive effect on milk supply has indeed been documented, though it's more likely that the barley it's made from is what stimulates milk production since a good nonalcoholic beer has the same effect. Alcohol itself can stimulate prolactin, but it also inhibits oxytocin and the letdown reflex while blood levels are elevated.[14] The immediate effects of alcohol last as long as it's in your system. If you feel "buzzed," your milk is buzzed, too. When you no longer feel intoxicated, the alcohol has left your milk. (There's no need to pump and dump, wasting precious milk, because the alcohol is reabsorbed back into your body at the same rate it leaves your blood.[15,16]) While an occasional *small* glass of beer or wine is unlikely to cause problems, chronic use has the potential to lower milk supply overall.[17]

But here's a twist: women with a *family* history—not personal history—of alcoholism had weaker prolactin responses to pumping than those without this history, and their babies nursed more often, probably to compensate. This difference was exaggerated when pumping after ingesting alcohol.[18] You can't change your family history, but keep in mind that alcohol may negatively affect individuals with a family history of alcoholism more than those without it.

## Cannabis (Marijuana)

Cannabis use has been associated with both higher and lower prolactin levels.[19,20] In a 2018 study, 50% more babies were born underweight when their mothers used cannabis during pregnancy and they were less likely to be breastfeeding at 9 weeks than those whose mothers didn't use cannabis.[21] We don't know how many mothers in that study used it both during pregnancy and breastfeeding, whether other substances often used at the same time (ie, tobacco) might have been a factor, or if breastfeeding ended due to supply problems, but these findings do raise concerns about effects on infant weight and milk production.[19]

## Cigarettes

A comprehensive review confirmed what we've known for a long time: nursing parents who smoke produce less milk and wean earlier. Nicotine reduces prolactin, and oxytocin and letdown may also be affected.[22,23] In one study, those who smoked had 20% less fat in their milk than non-smokers,[24] a concern because less calories to fuel growth means *more* milk would be needed to compensate.[24] And now we've discovered that *second-hand* smoke can be a problem as well: nonsmoking nursing parents living in smoking households didn't breastfeed as long as those living in smoke-free homes, likely due to effects on their milk supply.[25] This is a tough one if family members smoke, but it may help if the individual(s) smoke outside and away from you so that second-hand smoke doesn't undermine your milk production.

## Herbs

Just as there are herbs that may help increase milk production, others seem to decrease it. A lactation consultant once made a home visit to a friend whose milk came in with each baby but disappeared soon after. She watched as her friend was served a steaming bowl of homemade chicken soup heavily seasoned with *sage*, an herb known to reduce milk supply. The mother proudly shared that her helpful partner made it for her after the birth of each baby! When she stopped eating the soup, she was able to breastfeed exclusively for the first time.

*Parsley* is another culinary herb considered to have lactation-suppressing properties in large amounts; a mother who ate several servings of tabbouleh experienced a large drop in production. Similarly, while moderate amounts of oregano in foods is not a concern, lactation consultants have reported cases of milk supply dropping when *oregano oil* was taken to treat a cold. *Jasmine flower* extract decreases prolactin and has been used to suppress lactation.[5]

*Peppermint* is also reputed to decrease production when consumed in larger or concentrated amounts, and the tea has been used to help control some cases of oversupply. Frequent brushing with toothpaste containing real mint oil or even eating potent mint candies has caused trouble for some nursing parents. Lactation consultant Jan Barger tells the story of a mother who called around Christmas complaining that her milk production had abruptly plummeted. It turned out that she had been eating peppermint candy canes "right and left," and her supply rebounded after she stopped.

Most of these herbs don't usually cause problems unless they are consumed regularly or in large amounts. The occasional breath mint, candy cane, or modest serving of Thanksgiving turkey stuffing seasoned with sage should not be a problem.

## Pregnancy

If your production has mysteriously dropped off, especially if your nipples are also newly tender, a new pregnancy could be the culprit. As your body prepares for a new baby, hormones switch gears and lactation is no longer first priority. It's common to begin to notice a decrease in milk production within the first several weeks, and many babies also notice a difference as both volume and taste change.

Nursing through a normal pregnancy will not endanger the new baby or bring on premature labor.[26,27] One factor that does need to be considered is the age of the current nursling when a new baby is conceived because two-thirds of pregnant parents experience a decrease in milk production by mid-pregnancy.[28] In addition, mature milk tends to revert to colostral milk by late pregnancy.[29] If the current baby is still quite young, supplementation may be necessary.

What are your options for increasing production during pregnancy? It really is a case of swimming upstream against nature because your body shifts priority to preparing for the new baby. Nursing more often may help, but many moms can't tolerate it because of nipple tenderness. Herbal galactogogues are another option but must be chosen carefully because some have potentially uterine-stimulating or other properties of concern during pregnancy (see Chapter 14).

The dairy industry has learned that a dry period toward the end of pregnancy helps maximize milk production after the calf is born. Cows with high production in late pregnancy tend to have less milk for the new calf. Might stimulating a higher milk supply during pregnancy cause problems for the next baby's milk supply? While this question hasn't been officially explored, human lactation expert Peter Hartmann suggests that concerned parents consider feeding their current nursling from only one breast starting in the third trimester so that the other returns to pure colostrum production. This is a compromise between continuing to nurse the older baby and maximizing milk production after delivery.[30] Although many mothers successfully use both breasts throughout pregnancy, those who've had past troubles meeting their baby's needs may benefit from this suggestion.

CHAPTER 7

# Is it My Diet?

"Am I doing something wrong?" is probably at the top of your list of whether what you are or are not eating and drinking could be affecting your milk production. If we could teleport back in time a hundred years ago, mothers, midwives, and physicians would all answer yes, of course it's possible! Edward Routh, an English physician, wrote in 1879 that "insufficiency of food must produce insufficiency of milk."[1] It's been cultural wisdom worldwide for hundreds if not thousands of years that diet matters when you're breastfeeding.

Ironically, this wisdom was dismissed during the past few decades. It's often pointed out that mothers in countries with poor food supplies still seem to make enough for their babies to grow. But if you read the research closely, not all of these babies are growing to their potential. And there can be a cost to the mother if she isn't taking in enough nutrients to support both milk-making and her own physical needs because her baby's survival is Nature's priority unless her own survival is threatened.[2] Throughout most of history, steady food sources were not guaranteed. Is there a point where there just aren't enough of all the needed nutrients to reach your full milk-making potential? And can this happen in modern countries where food supplies are plentiful?

While experts were saying that nutrition was only rarely an issue, some families were learning otherwise. The *Mothers Overcoming Breastfeeding Issues* (MOBI Motherhood International) online group has been collecting stories and shared wisdom about foods since 1998. Hilary Jacobson was one member who discovered the importance of certain foods in her diet while struggling to make enough milk for her baby. Her research on traditional food wisdom was eventually compiled in her book, *MotherFood*.[3]

In the dairy world, it's well known that nutrition is critical to milk production. Dairy farmers understand that a cow's diet affects gut health, which in turn affects the ability to absorb necessary nutrients to make milk. And when gut health is poor, the body is also more vulnerable to infections, especially mastitis, a leading cause of reduced milk production. This is why nutrient deficiencies in the feed are at the top of the list of things to investigate when a cow's milk output drops, especially protein, zinc, selenium, iron, copper, and fiber.[4] We're not cows, but some of this science likely applies to humans also, as spelled out in a ground-breaking scientific review that went against the tide in describing how diet might be more important than we've believed.[5]

If you're starting to panic or feel discouraged at the thought of having to worry about your diet on top of everything else, hang on. This information may or may not apply to you, but if it does, your body will probably appreciate the changes you make just as much as your milk supply will. Consider it your wake-up call for taking care of YOU!

**The Milk Supply Equation**

| Primary | { | Sufficient glandular tissue |
|---|---|---|
| | + | Intact nerve pathways *and* ducts |
| | + | Adequate hormones *and* hormone receptors |
| Secondary | + | **Adequate lactation-critical nutrients** |
| | + | Frequent, effective milk removal and breast stimulation |
| | | AND *no other lactation inhibitors* |

= GOOD MILK PRODUCTION

When it comes to nutrition and breastfeeding, there are two issues: calories and nutrients. Let's look at each of these factors. The table at the end of this chapter lists good food sources for your needs.

## Calories and Dieting

Making milk uses calories—you burn calories to make milk, and you give away calories in your milk. Lactation is an expensive process to the body! Throughout most of history, steady food sources were not guaranteed. So Nature wisely programs your body to stockpile energy during pregnancy—that lovely extra fat on the hips—to sustain milk production during scarce food times. If there's enough food, it takes longer to burn off that extra fat. Many moms worry about losing weight after their baby is born, but we've learned that excessive dieting—consuming less than 1500-1800 calories (kcals) on a regular basis—can reduce milk production.[6] If you're hoping to lose weight, be patient and aim for slower, gradual weight loss.

Believe it or not, some nursing parents have discovered that they had to *increase* the calories and fats (healthy ones, of course!) in their diet to satisfy their babies. In a casual online survey, one wrote, "Dropping too many calories too fast negatively affected my milk production," and another commented, "What I found was that on the days when I decided to restrict what I was eating (to lose weight), my output dropped."

Back in 1975, a doctor observing a small group of nursing mothers reported that the "most successful" were eating 50% more than normal, and that one particular mother who was taking in 1950 calories (kcal) per day had to double her intake before she was able to eliminate supplementation.[7,8] A study from Thailand also observed a relationship between a mother's caloric intake and milk volume.[9] Most nursing parents don't need to eat this much extra, but for a few, it's made a big difference.

How you get those calories may matter, too. When two groups of women were fed the *same number of calories* in either a higher-fat, lower-carb diet or a lower-fat, higher-carb diet, the milk of the mothers in the higher-fat diet group had more calories, and their infants gained more even though the babies in both groups were taking close to the same amount of milk.[10] We tend to focus on milk volume, but if you've got high-calorie milk, you shouldn't need as much of it to keep your baby happy and growing well!

## Nutrients

You'll remember from Chapter 1 that hormones direct the process of making milk, like a master baker. There are a number of nutrients that are not only ingredients but also help with the milk-making process as well. Keep in mind that getting these essential nutrients from your daily foods is the goal, but supplements may be helpful in the short term.

### Protein

While it seems like this shouldn't be a problem in developed countries, easy-to-grab high-carbohydrate foods and snacks often replace the protein-rich foods we should be eating. A "weak but significant" association between protein consumption and shorter lactation duration has been observed.[11] Researchers in Thailand tested the effect of supplementing new mothers' diets with eggs, milk, or both and reported that those who received the supplement pumped more milk. This increase was attributed to the protein content of these foods, though it was acknowledged that the added calories may have been needed as well.[12] In Nigeria, milk output in a small group of poorly nourished women climbed as the amount of protein they ate was increased from about 1oz (25g), to 1.8oz (50g), to 3.5oz (100g) per day.[13] Based on these studies, a minimum of 2.3oz (65g) and up to 3.5 oz (100g) seems to be optimal for breastfeeding parents.

## Vitamin B$_{12}$ (Cobalamin)

Specific information on the impact of B$_{12}$ deficiency on milk production is limited. A rat study observed reduced milk volume,[14] and low B$_{12}$ is also known to affect production in cows.[4] Informal stories of parents whose milk production improved when their deficiency was corrected suggest that it is likely essential for human mothers as well. Supporting this idea, Russian mothers given B$_{12}$ injections for the first 2 weeks after birth had higher milk volumes the first week than those who didn't get them.[15] Vegans, some vegetarians, and gastric-bypass patients are at high risk of not getting enough B$_{12}$, as is anyone who has digestion or absorption problems, such as Crohn's disease. Medications such as metformin, certain anti-inflammatories like hydrocortisone, and antibiotic medications such as amoxicillin can deplete your B$_{12}$ stores. Long-term use carries more risk than when the drug is taken for a limited amount of time. B$_{12}$ seems to work best when taken with omega-3 fatty acids, and it stands to reason that eating foods high in both of these nutrients will get faster results. The US recommended daily allowance for lactation is 2.8 µg per day. KellyMom also has a good summary on who needs B$_{12}$ supplements at kellymom.com/nutrition/vitamins/vitamin b12.

## Calcium

Calcium is essential for many processes in the body, including prolactin release.[16] Quite a bit also goes to our babies through the milk, part of which is drawn from our bones. Some scientists theorize that when calcium is low, the body cuts back milk production to protect us from hypocalcemia, too little calcium.[17] One rat study saw lower milk volumes in those fed low-calcium diets,[18] and we know that low-calcium diets can affect milk production in dairy animals, too.[4]

Dairy products are high in calcium, but the body doesn't absorb it well from these foods. Cow's milk protein is both a common allergen and a cause of fussiness for some breastfed infants, leading many mothers to reduce or avoid dairy while breastfeeding. If you're one of these parents, make sure you're eating lots of other high-calcium foods such as nuts, seeds, leafy greens, and bone broths so that you're taking in the recommended amount of 1000mg daily.[19] If you must take a supplement, choose a calcium–magnesium combination because magnesium helps you absorb calcium more completely.

## Vitamin D

Your body requires vitamin D to absorb calcium, which is important for bone health. But emerging research suggests it also plays a role in female fertility[20] as well as our immune system—autoimmune problems happen more often when vitamin D is low.[21] Research in the 1980s observed lower milk production in vitamin D-deficient rats, but this has yet to be explored in human mothers.[5,22] Despite the lack of evidence, some lactation professionals suspicious of a possible connection have started checking levels.

When you spend time in sunshine, your body is able to make its own vitamin D. But many people, especially those with dark skin living in far northern or southern climates with less sun exposure, or who frequently wear long clothing or use sunscreen when outside, are more likely to have inadequate levels. Supplements in the form of $D_3$ and certain foods such as mushrooms, egg yolk, fatty fish, beef liver and fortified foods also provide vitamin D.

It's important that you have enough. According to the Institute of Medicine (IOM), your blood level should be greater than 50nmol/l (20ng/ml) but no higher than 125nmol/l (50ng/ml). New research on vitamin D requirements for pregnancy found better outcomes when the blood level was at least 100nmol/l (40ng/ml), so this may be a good minimum target goal.[23] The IOM recommends that lactating parents take in 600IU (15mcg) daily to support good vitamin D levels,[24] but a study conducted in New York and South Carolina on vitamin D during lactation showed that a much higher amount– 6400IU per day–may be necessary to supply human milk with enough vitamin D to avoid the need to give baby a separate vitamin supplement.[25] The bottom line is that some people may need a much larger supplement than we've believed in order to support both their own needs and that of their baby.

## Iron

Low iron and anemia, a condition that is often—though not always—caused by low iron, are risk factors for low milk production.[26,27] Fatigue and shortness of breath, especially with exercise, are common symptoms. Mild anemia frequently occurs during pregnancy and is rarely a problem, but if there's a large loss of blood during delivery, anemia can develop or worsen. Sleep-deprived new parents may not always realize that anemia may be contributing to their fatigue.[28]

Low hemoglobin was identified in one study as a risk factor for slow onset of milk production after birth,[29] while in another study, nursing mothers with hemoglobin levels below 9.5g/dl did not breastfeed as long as those who had higher levels.[26] Interestingly, researchers discovered that women with poor milk production could have low iron even though their hemoglobin was normal.[30] In rat experiments, iron deficiency caused decreases in both the fat content and quantity of milk produced.[31] One way or another, iron seems to be essential to making a good amount of quality milk. Since many moms become anemic during pregnancy, boosting your high-iron foods is a smart move for your overall health. For best absorption, pair iron-rich foods with those high in vitamin C and avoid eating them with dairy foods, which reduce iron absorption. There are also some galactogogue herbs that are high in iron (see Chapter 14).

## Zinc

This is one of the surprise discoveries of the decade. We now know that zinc is involved at every level of lactation: from the construction of your milk factory during pregnancy, to the start-up of milk production, as an essential ingredient in the milk recipe, to keeping the milk factory open, and to the eventual tear-down of the factory when the journey ends.[32] There must be enough zinc available for all of these processes, or lactation suffers; mildly zinc-deficient rats made less milk,[33] and zinc-deficient human mothers in one study were more likely to have poor milk production than those who had a sufficient amount.[34] Zinc deficiency also adds to oxidative stress (see Antioxidant Foods). Borderline zinc deficiency is more common among women of childbearing age than once thought,[34] and we're finding that some women can have enough zinc but aren't able to use it because of a defect in the system that transports zinc to various places in the breast.[35] There aren't ready tests or fixes for that last one, but at least you have control over taking in enough zinc.

## Iodine

The thyroid gland is a big supporting player to the milk factory, and it needs iodine to function properly.[36] During pregnancy and lactation, iodine requirements almost double, from 150 µg/d to 250-290 µg/d, due to of the increased needs of both the baby and the breast.[37] Yet many mothers are simply not getting enough,[36] which puts them at risk for reduced thyroid function and milk production. You'll want to make sure you're getting enough but beware and don't overcompensate: rats fed excessive iodine also experienced suppression of both thyroid function and prolactin.[38] Japanese adults who gorged on iodine-laden seaweed experienced some suppression of their thyroid function as well.[39]

Iodized salt is a major source of iodine in the Western diet, but if you use natural, non-fortified salt, you may not be getting enough iodine unless you are eating a good amount of other natural sources of iodine. For anyone with borderline low thyroid function, this is definitely something you'll want to consider.

## Omega-3 Fatty Acids and Healthy Fats

Healthy fats provide essential fatty acids and calories. You need a good balance of fats in your diet, and omega-3s are especially important. In one study, giving omega-3 supplements to rats with a diet low in vitamin $B_{12}$ helped to compensate and increase milk volume.[14] On the flip side of fats, unhealthy trans-fatty acids (TFAs) found in hydrogenated oil products such as margarine, shortening, and any foods made from these can reduce total milk fat in lean women.[40] When there is less fat in the milk, a baby needs more milk to get enough calories. As mentioned at the beginning of this chapter, some nursing parents find that they need to eat more healthy fats to make breastfeeding work.

## Fiber

It is well known in the dairy industry that fiber is important to gut health, which in turn is important to a well-functioning immune system and absorption of nutrients. If you can't absorb the nutrients you're eating, that's a problem. And if your immune system is weak, you are more prone to infections. Mastitis is a risk to milk production in cows, and diet tops the list of things to troubleshoot when their milk output drops.[4] Dairy farmers also tinker with the types and amounts of fiber they give their cows to optimize milk production, and they've even experimented with creating low-fat milk right out of the cow by reducing fiber, among other things.

Years ago, a member of an online support list was struggling and trying everything in the book, with little success. She began to notice a pattern in the days when she didn't need to supplement versus those she did. The good days lined up with when she remembered to take her Metamucil® (psyllium) fiber drink for constipation; on the days she forgot, she found herself supplementing. She later noticed that beans worked equally well and became the evangelist of fiber to all newcomers to the group after that. Remember that study showing a "weak but significant" association between protein deficiency and how long mothers breastfed? Well, they found the same association with inadequate fiber in the diet.[11] This isn't going to be everyone's fix, but what do you have to lose?

## Antioxidant Foods

You've probably heard about "free radicals," unstable molecules that can be damaging to our cells in excess and accelerate aging—we call this *oxidative stress*. Breast cancer research is teaching us that oxidative stress can affect the breasts as well,[41] and it also seems to play a role in involution, the process of tearing down the milk factory at the end of breastfeeding.[42,43] *Antioxidants* are the good guys that corner and scavenge free radicals, helping to restore balance and keep cells healthy. Currently there isn't any research connecting oxidative stress and lactation directly. But it makes sense that it could influence how well our milk factory functions, and antioxidants are suggested as part of a nutritional strategy for low milk supply (hypogalactia) in a Ukranian review.[44] Fortunately, nature provides us with foods that are high in antioxidants, such as berries, to help combat oxidative stress. Good for your breast, good for your health!

## Conditions That Can Affect Nutrient Intake

### Vegetarian and Vegan Diets

If you follow a vegetarian or vegan diet, you may be at risk for insufficient amounts of $B_{12}$ because it isn't found in plant sources.[45] This deficiency can affect fetal development during pregnancy and cause a loss of appetite and drowsiness in a breastfeeding baby, with the potential to slow down your milk factory as well. Breastfeeding medicine physician Anne Eglash suggests taking 100-250mcg of $B_{12}$ daily as insurance but also strongly encourages having your levels checked because this may not bring it up fast enough if it's low. Some vegetarian and vegan diets may also be low in protein, calcium, iron, or healthy fats during pregnancy and lactation, so be sure that you're getting enough of all of these important nutrients.[19] Research suggests that you may need 20% more calcium than omnivores for pregnancy and lactation—a total of 1200-1500mg or 8 servings of calcium-rich foods per day to support both your health and milk production. For boosting protein intake, 1½ cups (90g) of cooked lentils or 2½ cups (591ml) of soy milk can provide an additional 25g of protein.[45]

### Special Diets

The diet "du jour" morphs over time. Some call for drastic reductions in calorie intake, while others place emphasis on certain foods while prohibiting others. Diets such as Whole30 and Paleo promote proteins, vegetables, and fruit while avoiding sugars, grains, legumes, dairy, and additives. The Keto diet is similar in emphasizing low carbohydrates. We've heard about milk output doubling for one mother trying the diets but dropping for another, who found that she needed some healthy carbohydrates to maintain production. If supply drops on the keto diet, try adding 1-2 servings of whole grains per meal such as quinoa, brown rice, or 100% whole wheat bread to help bring it back up again. It's likely that the different results are caused by different underlying problems—the diet brought correction for one parent but created a deficit in another. When your baby is young, special diets like these simply to lose weight may not be good for your supply. But if you're aiming to rebalance a metabolic problem such as insulin resistance, they may help. Just do your homework first and make sure that you're getting your critical nutrients and calories.

## Eating Disorders

Nursing parents with a history of eating disorders can breastfeed successfully, but research suggests there is a higher risk of early supplementation and weaning related to concerns about milk supply.[46-49] Anorexia nervosa causes scant fat stores and nutrient intakes, leading to fewer ingredients for making milk. If the disorder started before or during puberty, it's possible that breast development was disrupted if there wasn't enough fat pad for ducts to grow into and form a full foundation for the milk factory.[50] Bulimia with frequent bingeing affects lactation differently, reducing the normal nighttime rise of prolactin along with absorption of necessary nutrients. If you're struggling with an eating disorder while breastfeeding, consider consulting a nutritionist, who can help you maximize your nutritional intake.

## Gastric Bypass

Gastric bypass surgery helps weight loss both by reducing the amount of food that can be eaten and the percentage that can be digested. Nutritional supplements are typically prescribed for life because it is very difficult to absorb all the nutrients the body needs from normal food sources.[19,51]

If you've had gastric bypass surgery, you are at risk of deficiencies that include calcium, vitamins $B_{12}$ and D, iron, zinc, and protein, all important to your milk factory.[51,52] One mother told of significant problems with milk production until she discovered that her zinc was low and her $B_{12}$ was "very low-normal." When she began taking supplements of both nutrients, her milk production stabilized. Blood tests can show if you are absorbing enough nutrients; some experts recommend checking them every 3 months to stay ahead of the game.[49]

Women who have gastric bypass surgery are often encouraged by their doctors to avoid pregnancy in the first 2 years after surgery while they are healing and completing their most rapid period of weight loss. During that time, they are mostly metabolizing fat, and their low caloric intake makes it challenging to consume enough essential nutrients to adequately support pregnancy and lactation. Once past this period, gastric bypass parents who consume at least 65-70g of protein per day[53] along with vitamin supplements–especially $B_{12}$–have a better chance at making enough milk.

One thing to keep in mind: some cases of low milk production may be related to preexisting hormonal conditions associated with obesity rather than the bypass surgery itself (see Chapter 11).

## Fluids: The Old Wives' Tale

A pervasive myth in many cultures is that not drinking enough water causes low milk supply.[54] While it's true that serious dehydration may cause your body to cut back on milk production, the mild dehydration that most of us operate under does not. An old but still valid study from 1940 reported that nursing mothers who were given 1 liter less of water a day than was recommended continued to produce plenty of milk.[55]

The flip side of this belief is that drinking more water makes more milk, which is just as wrong; in fact, drinking too much water can actually *reduce* milk production rather than increase it.[56] The body's reaction to excessive water intake (well beyond thirst) is to dump the excess fluid through the urine to maintain the proper electrolyte balance.[57] Water is diverted away from the breast, and lower milk volume can result. Pediatrician Tina Smillie explains the misconception this way: milk production doesn't increase because of drinking more fluid; it's actually the other way around. Women who make lots of milk will become thirsty in order to replace the fluid they use to produce milk. When a nursing parent is making less milk, they don't need to drink as much. Until an increased demand stimulates higher supply, the excess forced fluids will be wasted, and you'll just pee more. Jon Gillan, owner of PumpingPal®, also believes that drinking excessive amounts of water can cause the nipple and areolar tissue to swell to the point of compressing milk ducts in the nipple and impeding milk flow. The best advice is to *drink to thirst*. Keep your urine a pale yellow, and you'll be drinking just the right amount to make milk.

## What About Eating Your Placenta?

Ingesting one's own placenta has risen in popularity since the 1970s in some circles. It has a reputation for helping with postpartum depression as well as milk production.[58] Many midwives and doulas offer services for dehydrating raw or cooked placenta and encapsulating it for you after birth, though some nursing parents simply eat it raw (such as in smoothies) or cooked like organ meat. But does it really help? That's a good question. We've heard from some lactation consultants that they've seen mothers ingesting placenta and producing bountiful milk. We've heard from others that they have seen the bottom fall out of mothers' milk supplies when they started ingesting their placenta. What's the truth?

Many mammals do eat their own placentas after birth, for reasons not fully understood. Among humans, however, there is little historical precedent, and it's hard to find a culture where this was practiced,[59] though Traditional Chinese Medicine (TCM) does have a general placental remedy. There are some studies from the early 1900s of low scientific standards showing positive increases in milk production, and a 2013 survey of nursing parents ingesting placenta reported some positive effects as well.[60] On the other hand, blogs by lactation consultants report multiple cases of low supply they believe is tied to placental ingestion that improves when it is discontinued. Again, what's the truth?

It's known that the dried placenta used in capsules contains estradiol, progesterone, and iron. The first two in large amounts can suppress your milk production. Other factors that could account for the positive versus negative effects reported include what preparation of placenta is ingested, the amount and frequency of eating or dosage, and the amount of time since birth. Was it taken just once, for several days, or for some weeks? We clearly need more research to answer these questions, and until then, the jury is out; *proceed at your own risk* and know that if you try it and feel a decrease in milk production, you should stop right away.[61]

## Your Nutritional Profile

Did you identify any nutrition items to work on? The next step is to find foods that you like that that contain the nutrients you need; the table that follows is a good starting place. Some foods may be suitable for snacking, but others may require more preparation. If you're not sure how to work them into your diet, check Pinterest or another favorite online source. If a supplement is the best form, choose a high-quality product.

While this chapter has focused on your nutritional needs during breastfeeding, there are also foods that seem to have milk-boosting properties above their nutritional contribution to your health. You'll read more about lactogenic foods in Chapter 14. Don't skip there now, though; it's important to identify all possible problems first, and the next few chapters will help you do that.

TABLE Good Food Sources of Lactation-Critical Nutrients

| Vitamin B[1] | Calcium[2] (nondairy sources) | Protein[3] | Iron[4] (best absorbed when paired with vitamin C foods) | Zinc[5] | Iodine[6,7] | Fiber and Grains[8] | Omega-3s[9,10] | Healthy Fats[11] | Antioxidants[12,13] |
|---|---|---|---|---|---|---|---|---|---|
| Shellfish (clams, mussels, oysters) | White beans | Poultry | Lean beef | Oysters | Seaweed and sea vegetables such as kelp | Oats | Salmon | Olives and olive oil | Suman bran |
| Crab | Canned salmon or sardines (with bones) | Lean beef | Oysters | Lean beef | Fish, especially cod and tuna | Barley | Mackerel | Ground flaxseed and oil | Berries |
| Tuna | Dried figs | Fish | Chicken | Lobster | Shellfish | Quinoa | Oysters | Avocados | Prunes |
| Beef | Black strap molasses | Pork | Turkey | Pork | Cranberries | Millet | Sardines | Nuts, especially walnuts | Apples |
| Liver | Kale | Milk | Dried beans | Baked beans | Yogurt | Brown rice | Herring | Salmon | Grapes |
| Milk | Black-eyed peas | Greek yogurt | Lentils | Kidney beans | Navy beans | Beans | Anchovies | Fatty fish | Artichokes |
| Yogurt | Sesame seeds | Eggs | Tofu | Chickpeas | Strawberries | | Ground flaxseeds and oil | Peanut butter | Kale |
| Eggs | Almonds | Beans | Nuts | Almonds | Cheese | | Wild rice | Coconut oil | Broccoli |
| Nutritional | Chicken soup (made with bones) | Lentils | Seeds | Seeds | Potatoes | | Chia seeds | Limited amounts of butter | Sweet potatoes |
| Brewers' Yeast | Almonds | Chickpeas | Red beet juice | Poultry | Dried prunes | | Walnuts | | Walnuts |
| | Bok choy | Peanuts and peanut butter | Black strap molasses | Seafood | Himalayan crystal salt | | Fish oil | | Red beans |
| | Turnip or collard greens | Oats | Green leafy vegetables | Eggs | Iodized salt | | Krill oil | | |
| | Broccoli | Quinoa | | Oats | | | Eggs (some brands) | | |
| | Seaweed | Hummus | | Pumpkin seeds | | | Soybeans | | |
| | Oranges | Almonds | | Sesame seeds | | | Canola Oil | | |
| | | Seeds | | Spinach | | | | | |
| | | Soy | | Toasted wheat germ | | | | | |

[1] ods.od.nih.gov/factsheets/VitaminB12-HealthProfessional/
[2] ods.od.nih.gov/factsheets/Calcium-HealthProfessional/
[3] healthline.com/nutrition/20-delicious-high-protein-foods
[4] eatright.org/resource/health/wellness/preventing-illness/iron-deficiency
[5] ods.od.nih.gov/factsheets/Zinc-HealthProfessional/
[6] ods.od.nih.gov/factsheets/Iodine-HealthProfessional/
[7] bda.uk.com/foodfacts/Iodine.pdf
[8] health.gov/dietaryguidelines/2015/guidelines/appendix-13/
[9] ods.od.nih.gov/factsheets/Omega3FattyAcids-Consumer/
[10] ods.od.nih.gov/factsheets/Omega3FattyAcids-HealthProfessional/
[11] eatright.org/resource/food/nutrition/dietary-guidelines-and-myplate/choose-healthy-fats
[12] wikipedia.org/wiki/List_of_antioxidants_in_food
[13] ncbi.nlm.nih.gov/pmc/articles/PMC2841576/pdf/1475-2891-9-3.pdf

## CHAPTER 8

# Is it Something About My Pregnancy or Birth?

You worked hard to have the best pregnancy and birth possible, but it didn't all go as planned. Or maybe the birth went well and everything seemed fine at first, until it wasn't. There is nothing more frustrating than thinking that you've got everything under control . . . *but where's the milk?* There are two issues at stake here: temporary delays in the start-up of the milk factory versus only a partial start-up with reduced output. We will mostly explore some of the first issues here and touch on a few of the second as well. Pregnancy and birth issues fall under the category of *no other lactation inhibitors* in the *Milk Supply Equation* because they can impact multiple things. That's what makes them tricky but also important.

**The Milk Supply Equation**

| | | |
|---|---|---|
| Primary | $\Big\{$ | Sufficient glandular tissue |
| | + | Intact nerve pathways *and* ducts |
| | + | Adequate hormones *and* hormone receptors |
| Secondary | $\Big\{$ + | Adequate lactation-critical nutrients |
| | + | Frequent, effective milk removal and breast stimulation |
| | | AND *no other lactation inhibitors* |
| | = | GOOD MILK PRODUCTION |

## Pregnancy Issues That Can Affect Lactation

### Drugs and Supplements During Pregnancy

#### Anti-contraction Medications

Premature contractions are treated with medications that suppress labor. Keeping your baby inside as long as possible is best for both of you! But we do have information from a small study that those who received such medications during pregnancy had a higher rate of low supply and shorter breastfeeding than those who didn't receive these meds.[1,2] Their usage ranged from 1 week to 7 months, but unfortunately the authors didn't say if there was a relationship between time on the medication and breastfeeding outcome.

#### Betamethasone

When premature birth is imminent, betamethasone is administered to help the baby's lungs mature. In a study that followed women who delivered before 34 weeks, those who received the drug and then gave birth during the window of 3-9 days later experienced a delay in the onset of milk and lower production overall during the first 10 days they were followed. If birth occurred less than 3 days or beyond 10 days after receiving the drug, milk production was not affected.

#### Selective Serotonin Reuptake Inhibitor Antidepressants

Serotonin, the "feel-good" hormone, also plays a role in the breast during involution, the deconstruction of the milk factory.[3] Some mothers who took a selective serotonin reuptake inhibitor (SSRI) antidepressant during pregnancy had a slower onset of milk production. Your mental health is a priority—just know that you need to make sure you are nursing or expressing frequently to counteract any effects.[4]

#### Insulin Treatment

Mothers with gestational or type 2 diabetes who were treated with insulin during pregnancy may have more difficulty establishing milk production than those who didn't receive insulin.[2] This is discussed more fully in Chapter 11.

#### Excessive Vomiting Treatment

Mild nausea and vomiting, also known as morning sickness, is common in pregnancy. When it becomes severe to the point that you can't keep much down, become dehydrated, and even lose weight, it is called *hyperemesis gravidarum*. While conditions like hyperthyroidism can cause severe vomiting, many times there is no explanation. It can last part or all of pregnancy and sends parents in frantic search of a remedy to relieve their misery.

Kelli was one such parent. Following her health care provider's advice, she took pyridoxine (vitamin $B_6$) at a very low dosage (6mg per day) during her first trimester. After birth, she experienced a delay in the onset of milk production but was able to build up slowly to full supply after "constant nursing and pumping." During her second pregnancy the vomiting was worse, and to cope she took 50-100mg of $B_6$ along with 50-63mg of doxylamine daily for 7-8 months all the way until birth. Because iron made her nauseous, she avoided iron supplements this time and developed an iron deficiency as well. After the birth of her second baby, she did not see mature milk until after the first week and then only 30-40ml per day for the next 5 weeks despite frequent nursing and pumping. After receiving an infusion of iron for the anemia, her milk production increased to 200ml per day but then plateaued.

There are no similar cases in the literature, but Kelli's experience is intriguing, and we've heard a few more similar stories. High doses of pyridoxine (150-600mg per day) were once used to suppress lactation in parents who chose not to breastfeed,[5] and it's been tested for the same purpose, though many years ago, with mixed results.[6] Doxylamine is an antihistamine that in high dosages might also suppress prolactin.[7] Kelli's situation was unique in that she took higher doses of $B_6$ along with doxylamine *over an extended period of time* during her second pregnancy. Prolactin normally rises during pregnancy, playing a role in building the milk factory and then kicking off milk production after birth. It makes sense that chronic suppression of prolactin during pregnancy could have reduced normal breast growth and inhibited lactogenesis II for Kelli. The differences in the amount and duration of the medications she took with each pregnancy and the differences in her lactation experiences certainly seem to suggest that there could be a correlation.

Diclectin and Diclegis are both antinausea medications that contain 10mg each of doxylamine and pyridoxine, typically taken at a dosage range of 2-4 tablets daily,[8] though sometimes up to 8 tablets per day. It's hard to say at what dosage this combination might interfere with prolactin action during pregnancy.

If you received any of these medications or supplements during pregnancy and believe that it played a role in a slow start to breastfeeding, it's important to look forward and not backward. Lots of nursing or expressing is on the top of the "what next" list.

## Hypertension

*Hypertension* is diagnosed when blood pressure is higher than normal. Hypertension before pregnancy is called *chronic hypertension*. High blood pressure that starts after 20 weeks of gestation is called *gestational hypertension*. *Pregnancy-induced hypertension* (PIH), also known as *toxemia* or *preeclampsia*, is a form of gestational hypertension accompanied by protein in the urine and sudden swelling of the hands, feet, or face. *HELLP syndrome* (named for its main symptoms: *hemolytic anemia, elevated liver enzymes,* and *low platelet count*) is a severe variation of PIH.

Whatever the origin, hypertension brings a higher risk of delayed and poor milk production.[9-11] We aren't sure exactly why this is because not all nursing parents with high blood pressure have difficulty making milk. We do know that chronic hypertension can affect the placenta[12,13] and thus breast development. This happened in hypertensive rats, who had poor mammary development and less milk.[14] On the positive side, 75% of women with severe preeclampsia who wanted to breastfeed in one study were able to do so.[15]

Questions also have been raised about drugs such as *magnesium sulfate* used to treat hypertension during pregnancy. Women who took it for 4 weeks or longer before delivery were less likely to leave the hospital fully breastfeeding.[2] There is also some evidence that magnesium sulfate treatment started after birth might delay the onset of milk production beyond the risks of hypertension.[16] One possible explanation is that magnesium is a smooth muscle relaxant and may interfere with the letdown reflex by making the myoepithelial cells that squeeze your milk out less responsive. Lactation consultants in one hospital noticed delayed start-up of milk production, higher infant weight loss, and babies who weren't nursing as strongly along with an increased need for supplementing. They now make a point to explain what is likely happening and encourage early and frequent breast stimulation. They also offer donor human milk as a temporary bridge until milk production increases. This proactive approach has reduced discouragement and increased breastfeeding successes for their pre-eclamptic patients.

If you're reading this during pregnancy and have hypertension, expressing colostrum the last 4-6 weeks could help you get a head start in collecting a little bit for after delivery, just in case supplementation is suggested. Even if you don't get much out, you'll learn the process and be ready to provide colostrum if needed after birth, when it's easier to express.[11] Chapter 13 describes this in detail.

For a hypertensive parent at risk of not making enough milk, starting a galactogogue in late pregnancy or right after birth seems like a reasonable secondary strategy. A Filipino study decided to test the effects of malunggay, a local favorite lactogenic vegetable, on the start-up of milk production and infant weight gain in hypertensive mothers. Half started taking malunggay at delivery and continued it for 4 months; their milk came in a day earlier than the control group, and their babies gained more weight, presumably due to more milk.[17] Using galactogogues in this way should be paired with plenty of skin-to-skin contact and lots of breastfeeding. And be sure to talk to your health care provider first. (See Chapter 14 for more about malunggay and other galactogogue herbs with antihypertensive properties.)

## Placental Insufficiency

Jaelynn breastfed 2 other children without incident, but her third baby, born prematurely due to a separating placenta, was not thriving. She reported that her breasts didn't grow or change much this pregnancy, nor did her milk increase much despite excellent management.

Anything that compromises placental function can also affect breast development during pregnancy. The placenta takes over the job of making progesterone after the first trimester, stimulating breast growth and keeping the breast in colostrum mode until delivery. If it doesn't function well, progesterone levels may drop, and breast development might slow down. In Jaelynn's case, her milk factory wasn't in good shape when her baby came early, so her milk volume was less than normal at the start.

When researchers purposely caused placental insufficiency in rats, they saw not only the drop in progesterone but also the premature triggering of milk production *before* birth. Without rat pups to suckle and remove milk, involution set in. The milk factory literally began to tear down before it even opened for business![18,19] A few cases have been reported of women who had preterm labor that stopped, followed by engorgement and milk leakage. Later when the baby was born, their milk didn't come in at all. Although it hasn't been tested in humans, supplemental progesterone therapy at the first sign of a drop in progesterone associated with preterm labor might possibly rescue some of these situations (as it did in rats) by allowing continued breast development and stopping the premature initiation of full milk production.[20]

Chronic placenta problems also affect the growing baby by slowing down the flow of nutrients. Lower birth weight—often referred to as *small for gestational age* or *intrauterine growth restriction*—is common and should be considered a tip-off for possible placental insufficiency (see Chapter 9).

If baby is here and you're reaching the conclusion that a placenta problem may have affected one or both of you, all is not lost. The rat mothers started off poorly, but their mammary glands actually grew more as their pups suckled. Poor glandular development caused by a poorly functioning placenta is a challenge, but *you can still build breast tissue after birth* with frequent stimulation by nursing or pumping. The addition of a breast-stimulating galactogogue might possibly help as well.

## Gestational Ovarian Theca Lutein Cysts

Maya gave birth to twins, her fourth and fifth babies. When her milk didn't increase right away, she didn't panic because she had no problems breastfeeding her other children. Instead, she just started pumping, and in the 3rd week her milk volume finally started to climb until it eventually was enough for both babies. During a consult for latch problems, she mentioned that during her c-section, the doctors had commented on how her ovaries were the size of softballs, though nothing else was mentioned.

Your ovaries produce some testosterone, and a small amount is normally present during pregnancy. Rarely, an ovarian cyst called a gestational ovarian theca lutein cyst (GOTLC) may develop during pregnancy and secrete up to 10-15 times the normal amount. The risk is higher with polycystic ovary syndrome (PCOS), diabetes, ovulation induction, or a multiples pregnancy. Some women experience a dramatic increase in body hair or deepening of the voice,[21] but if symptoms are mild or absent, the condition may not be noticed unless your ovaries are inspected during an ultrasound or surgery. The "cure" for GOTLC is birth, after which testosterone levels gradually drop without treatment.

We've known that high levels of testosterone can suppress milk production by interfering with prolactin, but the fact that GOTLC can interfere with the start-up of milk production was only recognized for the first time in 2002, which is fairly recent in terms of lactation science.[22,23] If no one is aware of the possibility, you might give up too early, assuming that you're "one of those people who just can't make enough milk" (which isn't actually a thing). This is a good reason to have your testosterone checked when there aren't any other explanations. Milk production will eventually pick up so long as breast stimulation by a baby or pump is continued until your testosterone level has dropped low enough. In 4 reported cases, testosterone had dropped to around 300ng/dL before milk production started up, about 2-4 weeks after birth.

## Birth Issues

### Labor Drugs

Labor drugs are used in more births than not these days. Can they affect milk production? In one study, mothers who received labor pain medications reported delayed onset of milk production more often than those who didn't.[24] A review of several studies on epidurals found 50/50 results for negative effects on breastfeeding,[25] while others observed lower breastfeeding rates associated with oxytocin and prostaglandins used to induce or speed up labor.[26-28]

The research on intravenous (IV) oxytocin (Pitocin) during labor is troubling. Bombarding the body with a constant influx of synthetic oxytocin can cause oxytocin receptors in the uterus to tire and become less responsive[29] and even decrease in number.[30] Famed obstetrician Michel Odent expressed concern that receptors in the breast may be affected as well, weakening the letdown reflex.[31] In addition, mothers who received the highest amounts of oxytocin released the lowest amount of their own oxytocin during breastfeeding on the day after birth.[32] This could certainly affect how much colostrum a baby is able to get out, reducing milk removal and dampening start-up of milk production. It would also account for babies who seem frustrated at the breast, unable to get colostrum out. The effects should be short term, but the impact on a mother and baby may last much longer.[31]

If the question on the physical impact of labor drugs on milk production seems murky, the impact on a baby's sucking ability is not. Babies born to parents who received significant amounts of fentanyl (via epidural) or synthetic oxytocin during labor had poorer sucking reflexes the first hour after birth,[33] and some studies also found a trend for decreased sucking in babies when IV magnesium sulfate was given during labor.[2] Weak suck and poor milk removal during the "Golden Hour" certainly doesn't help get breastfeeding off to the best start. We don't know how long these effects on the baby last, but we *do* know that lots of skin-to-skin contact with your baby as well as frequent hand expression of colostrum (feed it back to her by spoon or syringe) is your best counter attack.

## Stressful Birth

There's plenty of research showing that painful, long, exhausting, stressful labors are associated with a slower onset of milk production.[34,35] *The most important thing is to take care of yourself and be patient with the process.* First and foremost, keep nursing (or pumping). Anything that reduces stress, like a massage, acupuncture, reflexology, or other similar therapies, might also help. Chamomile tea is taken by many mothers worldwide to promote relaxation and may even indirectly help with your milk production.[36]

## Cesarean Births

It's been known for a while that it can take longer for full milk production to start-up after a cesarean birth.[10,37] Emergency c-sections bring more stress and separation after birth. Planned c-sections often occur before due dates, with less mature babies, and are associated with delays in the milk coming in.[38,39] Mothers and parents who are in pain also may not nurse their babies or pump as often.[40]

Another piece of the cesarean picture is whether you labored first. Oxytocin is high during and after labor, pushing colostrum forward for easy removal by the baby in the first hour. Oxytocin also stimulates prolactin. When there is no labor, these natural rises are missing.[32]

A third piece of the puzzle may be found in a study that monitored both the sucking strength and the time to noticeable fullness of the breast after delivery, comparing babies born vaginally versus surgically. They discovered a connection between sucking strength and how long it took for the onset of full milk production and further found that babies born by cesarean section often had a weaker suck.[41]

For those who've given birth by cesarean or expect to do so, this can be alarming to read. But it's not the doom of breastfeeding; it just means that early and frequent feedings, lots of skin-to-skin time, and if suction feels weak, pumping at *moderate to higher suction levels* after feedings are needed to compensate. If you didn't get to start this right away, it's water under the bridge now. Just know that you may be working a little harder to catch up.

## Edema

Water retention in the body, called *edema*, is common toward the end of pregnancy. Most individuals laboring in hospitals receive IV fluids, and when fluids go in faster than you can pee them out, they get pushed out into your tissues temporarily. Pitocin (artificial oxytocin), which is chemically similar to antidiuretic hormone (ADH), may bind to or increase the number of ADH receptors and contribute as well, further exacerbating any already-existing edema.[38]

Nurses and lactation consultants report that a number of their patients experience water retention and swelling that seems to develop or worsen during and after delivery. Ankles swell, and breasts may feel hard and swollen to the point that the nipple and areola flatten out as if engorged with milk, causing latch problems.[42] This same edema seems to slow the start-up of milk production,[43] with the milk not coming in fully until the swelling subsides. It's almost as if the milk ducts are being squeezed by all the trapped water so that there's no room to store or transport milk.

Diuretic drugs are rarely prescribed because edema is usually a self-correcting condition. But it may not recede before breastfeeding problems begin. To speed the process of eliminating the excess water to help your milk production increase sooner, there are foods with diuretic properties, such as dandelion greens, dandelion tea, watermelon, cucumbers, asparagus, cabbage, and celery, that you can try, though you'll need to eat a lot of them!

## Retained Placenta

Once the baby is born and the placenta is delivered, progesterone levels drop rapidly, and the milk comes in. On rare occasions, a piece of tissue may break off from the placenta and remain attached to the uterine wall. This will often cause heavy bleeding or even hemorrhaging, so it is usually discovered and treated quickly. But if symptoms are subtler and the piece stays inside, progesterone can continue to interfere with the start-up of milk production. Sometimes lack of milk may be the first clue that a piece of placenta remains. This is more likely to happen in deliveries when the placenta was slow to expel or tension was applied to the cord to help it come out. And while rare, it's happened with cesarean deliveries as well.

Giana had already breastfed 4 other children, but her new baby was not getting enough milk to grow well. A plan was developed to continue nursing, pumping, and supplementing. Two weeks later, the baby was suddenly happily gulping milk at the breast. When asked if there were any significant changes that week, Giana responded, "Well, I did have this really weird thing happen a couple of days ago. I had a lot of cramping and then I passed these big clots...." The improvement in milk production occurred soon after this event. Giana remembered that her obstetrician had kept traction on the umbilical cord until the placenta came out, which could have caused a piece of placenta to break off and remain inside. Case solved.

When postpartum bleeding is in the normal range but milk production is sluggish to start, obstetrician Pamela Berens suggests ruling out retained placental tissue with a blood test for beta human chorionic gonadotropin (β-hCG), a placental hormone that normally disappears rapidly after birth. A transvaginal ultrasound is another possible screening test; a negative result is usually correct, though a positive result could wrongly interpret postbirth debris as placental tissue. As in Giana's case, retained tissue can clear out on its own, but when identified earlier, it's usually removed surgically to avoid the risk of hemorrhage. Increased milk production usually occurs within 48 hours.

In rare cases, a more severe version of retained placental tissue can occur. Rather than merely attaching to the uterine wall, the placenta may grow into the wall and sometimes through the wall and even to other organs. This often causes hemorrhaging because the pieces can't let go and come out easily after birth. Manual removal of the placenta may be attempted, and medications such as methergine or methotrexate may be used to help complete the job and control bleeding. These drugs carry some risk of suppressing or reducing milk production, though short-term use is considered less risky.

Your physicians, working in tandem with a lactation consultant, are the best resources to help sort through this difficult problem. However, not all are aware of the connection between the placenta and the start of milk production, or they may not be open to the possibility because they think that it implies error on their part. This can make it difficult to receive a serious, thorough evaluation if the symptoms are subtle. You may need a second opinion if your caregiver does not fully explore this possibility with you.

## Postpartum Hemorrhage and Sheehan's Syndrome

Severe bleeding after delivery can pose two risks to milk production. Most obvious is the large loss of iron-rich red blood cells and possible anemia. Losing up to 1 pint (500ml) of blood with vaginal births and up to 2 pints (1000ml) with cesarean surgery is considered within normal limits. Higher amounts of blood loss (greater than 1500ml in the first 24 hours after birth or a fall in hemoglobin by 4g/dl or to less than 7g/dl) have been associated with poor milk production.[44,45] In one study, 70% of women who lost less than 2000ml were fully breastfeeding in the first week compared with 50% of those who lost more than 3000ml of blood. Some of this may be the result of a poor start to breastfeeding, which understandably goes by the wayside when someone's health has been threatened. The medically necessary drugs used to treat postpartum hemorrhage (PPH) might contribute as well.[26]

The second risk from hemorrhage involves the pituitary gland, which enlarges during pregnancy. If there is a sudden loss of a large amount of blood, the pituitary gland may collapse and function poorly. Mild to moderate damage is referred to as a *pituitary insult* and causes reduced functioning. Severe damage can cause *Sheehan's syndrome*—lactation failure is typically the first clue (see Chapter 11).

Mona Gabbay, a breastfeeding medicine physician practicing in New York City, finds that baseline prolactin levels are often below 30ng/ml in nursing parents who've experienced PPH and low milk supply. Milk production is unlikely to respond to galactogogues because they can only be as effective as the pituitary's ability to respond.

Despite the seriousness of Sheehan's syndrome, miracles have happened. One mother who developed Sheehan's syndrome and lactation failure went on to have another baby and then to breastfeed.[46] While some degree of reduced pituitary function occurs in nearly one-third of patients with severe PPH,[47] there are also plenty who have experienced serious hemorrhages and blood loss yet breastfed without problems. If you have a suspicious history and aren't sure, ask your health care provider to check your prolactin as described in Chapter 11.

## Essential Self-Care

Did you find some answers in this chapter? This can bring a sense of relief to some and ideas to increase their supplies, while for others, it may dredge up angry or sad feelings. It's almost easier to deal with the practical issues of what you need to do next for breastfeeding than to face the emotions that may be simmering underneath, but do yourself a favor and take some time to work through any negative feelings along the way (see Chapter 18). Just know that you are not alone and that many parents have overcome these obstacles.

## CHAPTER 9

# Is it Something My Baby is Doing?

We've looked at how birth and breastfeeding management can affect milk production, but your baby plays an important role that is easy to overlook. This chapter explores some of the reasons babies may not breastfeed effectively and in the process can sabotage your milk supply if we don't intervene.

### The Milk Supply Equation

| | | |
|---|---|---|
| Primary | $\left\{\begin{array}{l} \\ + \\ + \end{array}\right.$ | Sufficient glandular tissue<br>Intact nerve pathways *and* ducts<br>Adequate hormones *and* hormone receptors |
| Secondary | $\left\{\begin{array}{l} + \\ + \\ \end{array}\right.$ | Adequate lactation-critical nutrients<br>**Frequent, effective milk removal and breast stimulation**<br>AND *no other lactation inhibitors* |
| | = | GOOD MILK PRODUCTION |

## Lisa's Story

When my fourth baby had just latched for the first time, my first thought was that something wasn't right. His latched looked good and he seemed to be getting fed, but Eric "clicked" while he nursed. With my other babies, if I had to get up while nursing, they would hang on like little leeches, but Eric slipped off with the smallest movement. He gained adequately the first couple of months, though not as much as his siblings did on my usually generous supply. Sometimes milk would spurt out through his nose. Over the next few months, I felt my letdowns less and less but figured it was still normal. My periods returned early at

4 months. By 6 months Eric's weight had slowed down, and after that he stopped gaining and even lost weight, and my breasts began to shrink. Neither the pediatrician nor I realized what was happening as we chased other possibilities and pushed solid foods. It wasn't until Eric was 3 years old that I figured out that he really did have a suck problem and realized that it had caused my production to drop off so much that his weight faltered.

## Suck Problems

It's all about suck. Suck draws the milk from the breast and triggers the release of prolactin and oxytocin. A strong, healthy suck stimulates a strong prolactin surge, while a weak suck results in weak prolactin surges.[1] Anything that negatively affects a baby's suck can become a problem for milk production. Effective sucking depends on the baby's ability to coordinate the use of his tongue, cheeks, palate, jaw, facial muscles, and lips to form a seal and create the necessary vacuum to draw out milk. Significant variations in facial or oral anatomy or any type of neurologic issue may affect his ability to remove milk and stimulate the breasts well.

As a new parent, you may not pick up on a suck problem if you don't have any experience with normal yet. But even experienced parents and doctors may not realize when "different" is a problem. One obvious symptom of a sucking problem is nipple pain when the latch otherwise "looks good." Having your nipple come out of your baby's mouth flattened, wedged, or otherwise misshapen is another. There may be bruising, cracking, bleeding, or burning vasospasms, and getting a good latch may seem impossibly difficult (see bit.ly/MMM-NipplePain for a great visual). On the other hand, a baby with a weak suck isn't able to draw the nipple out well or may not hang on to the breast for very long, and when he comes off, the nipple hasn't pulled out much. Clicking sounds during nursing or bottle feeding are a big red flag because they mean that the baby keeps losing his grip, resulting in suction breaks that stop milk flow and shorten suction-induced prolactin surges.

Newborns can develop disorganized sucking habits as a reaction to lack of success at the breast: they were born sucking well, but if they can't draw milk out effectively, then their suck may deteriorate as they desperately try alternate ways to get milk from the breast. Babies are smart, and when one thing doesn't work, they'll try another. Once they experience a little success at the breast and discover the movements that draw milk out most effectively, suck often improves spontaneously without any other intervention.

Accurately identifying and addressing suck problems can be challenging even for lactation consultants. There are three important steps: (1) make sure your baby is latching as deeply as possible, (2) get enough milk into him in a way that supports breastfeeding while you work on the problem, and (3) pump as needed to keep up your milk production. When these bases are covered, there may be suck training exercises or special feeding methods that encourage your baby to move his tongue more effectively. Nursing supplementers or special bottle nipples may also be used. If these techniques don't work, your baby should be evaluated by someone who specializes in infant feeding problems, such as an occupational or speech therapist.

## The Large, Small, Early, or Meds-Affected Baby

Gestational age and overall maturity at birth can affect a newborn's ability to thrive at the breast and help build your milk production. Premature babies have less stamina and can tire quickly; they may also have lower muscle tone that makes sucking more work. Early term babies (37 weeks and no days to 38 weeks and six days weeks' gestation), on the other hand, can look deceptively normal yet not be mature enough to nurse well. Infants who are small or large for gestational age have been affected by something in the uterine environment (placental problems, diabetes) that may also affect their ability to breastfeed.

As discussed in Chapter 8, the greater the dose of pain medication during labor, the greater the chance of suck problems until the meds are cleared from his system. Babies born by cesarean section, or to parents with type 2 or gestational diabetes who received insulin during pregnancy, may also have a weaker suck. In all of these situations, pumping after feedings—"insurance pumping"—is wise until your baby is breastfeeding well enough to maintain a good milk supply.

## Torticollis

Babies with torticollis have tighter muscles on one side of their neck than the other, causing them to favor turning one direction. They feed comfortably when facing that way but do poorly when forced the other direction, such as when changing breasts. Torticollis can also create an imbalance of forces affecting tongue movements and suck that may mimic tongue-tie. Between the two, a baby with torticollis may not remove milk or stimulate the breasts well, leaving you to think that there is something wrong with your breasts as milk production slows.

Understanding what's wrong is half the battle; getting help is the other half. Physical therapists, osteopathic physicians, and chiropractors with pediatric expertise all have skills to help and may also teach you exercises to do at home. *Tummy time* is also important "home therapy" to help babies regain balance in their muscles.

Meanwhile, positioning adjustments can make breastfeeding easier for your baby. Try keeping him facing his preferred direction while sliding his body straight over to the second breast. Or straddle him in your lap, providing support while allowing him to turn his head as needed.[2] You can find links to more good information at lowmilksupply. org/infant/torticollis.

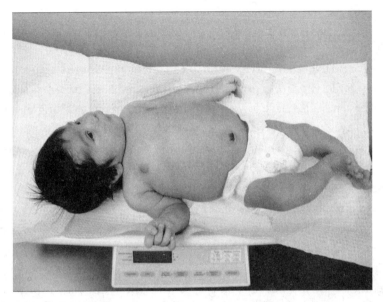

*Torticollis in an infant*

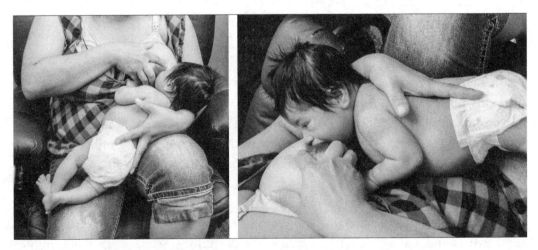

*Positioning to accommodate torticollis*

## Tummy Time Therapy

Since the back-to-sleep campaign began, young babies spend very little time on their tummies. Not only is this a risk for flattening of the head, but it also limits the use and development of their head and neck muscles, some of which are involved in feeding skills. Babies need the opportunity to work on lifting their heads and stretching neck muscles for greater flexibility, especially if they have torticollis, problems tilting their heads back or problems opening wide for breastfeeding. Tummy Time!™ expert Michelle Emmanuel recommends 5 short sessions a day from newborn on up. Some babies may protest at first but soon enjoy their sessions. Every baby needs tummy time, especially when there are feeding issues.

## Tongue Mobility Restriction

A baby's ability to draw milk from the breast depends on his ability to move his tongue freely. Just because he can stick his tongue out doesn't rule out a problem; he needs to be able to *keep* it extended while feeding. He also must be able to cup and elevate (lift) it throughout a whole feeding while maintaining a good seal to breastfeed effectively. The ability to move the tongue from side to side (lateralize) and create wave-like peristaltic movements is also important.[3]

The *lingual frenulum* connects the base of the tongue to the floor of the mouth A normal frenulum is usually flexible to the touch and doesn't interfere with tongue movements. But when the tissue forming the frenulum doesn't recede normally during fetal development, *ankyloglossia* occurs, commonly called *tongue-tie*. The remaining extra tissue can restrict normal tongue movements, interfering with suck and sometimes swallowing as well.[4] Because fighting the restrictions is extra work, a baby may tire before his tummy is full (fatiguing), leading to inadequate intake, slow weight gain, and ultimately low milk production.[5]

A restrictive frenulum may be short or tight and can vary in appearance. It may look and feel like a thin, stretchy web or seem thick and fibrous near the base of the tongue. Most important, it prevents one or more tongue movements that affect the ability to breastfeed effectively. Visual signs that indicate the need for further assessment include but aren't limited to notching at the tongue tip, inability to lift the tongue higher than midmouth (from the base, not just curling the front half of the tongue upward), bunching of the tongue (it looks short and fat) with movements when mouth open wider, inability to maintain extension, and the tongue being pulled down in the center.[6] Other clues that a baby's tongue may be restricted include latch trouble, difficulty opening his mouth widely, persistent chapped lips or sucking blisters, "clicking" or "popping" sounds during feeding, frequent choking on milk flow, flattened nipples, nipple damage, and chronic sore nipples. Suck and swallowing problems can also make reflux worse.

While tongue-tie is the most well-known type of frenulum restriction, a tight lip or *labial frenum* occasionally adds to feeding problems. When this membrane is tight, it may prevent your baby from flanging his lips widely and comfortably and he may purse

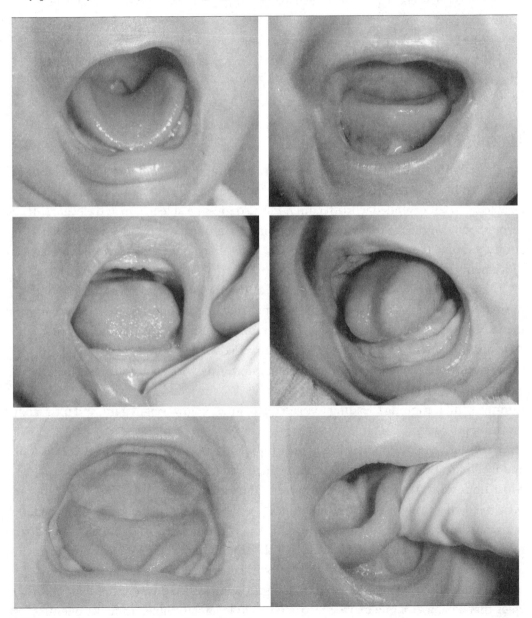

*Visible signs of possible tongue mobility restriction*

them instead, resulting in a shallower latch. If it extends thickly and deeply to the gum ridge or wraps around into the hard palate, it can cause a gap between the front teeth later on. It has also been associated with excess air swallowing during breastfeeding.[7] Restrictive lip frenums occur more often together with tongue-tie than alone. Because both are usually treated at the same time, it's difficult to prove that releasing the lip

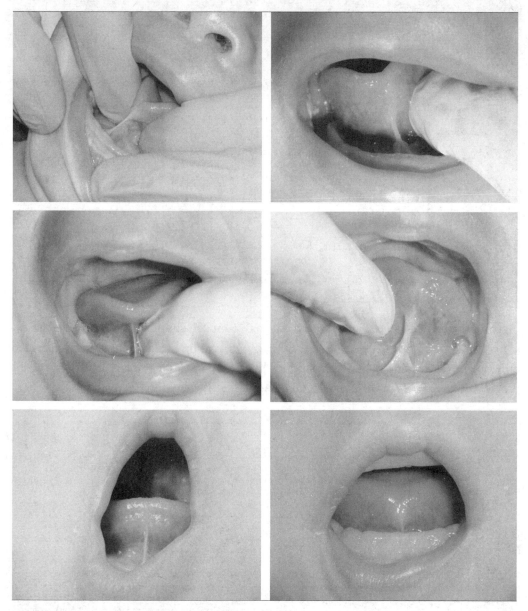

*Variations of restrictive frenulums*

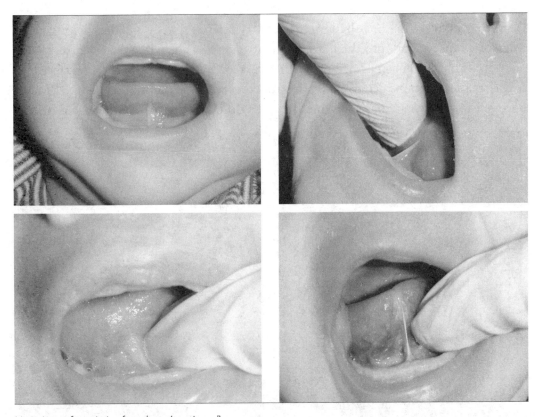

*Variations of restrictive frenulums (continued)*

makes a difference so justifying treatment may be more challenging.[8] However, in one study the combination of releasing both the tongue and lip had a higher success rate than only one or the other.[6] When assessing for lip-tie, visual appearance can flag a possible problem, but *how well it actually functions* should be the deciding factor.

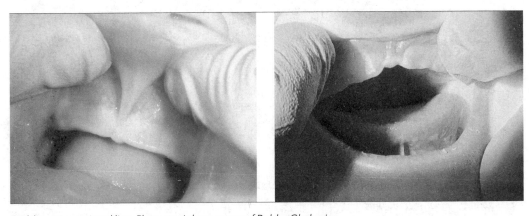

*Problematic restricted lips. Photo on right courtesy of Bobby Ghaheri*

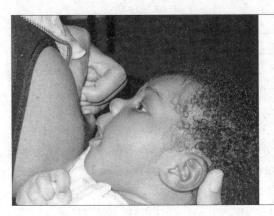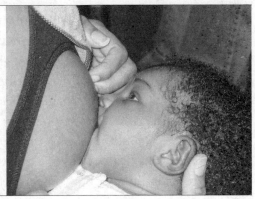

*The nipple flip. Use a finger to pull the nipple just above the baby's upper lip. As you bring him to the breast, let go and allow the nipple to flip on top of the tongue.*

Latching can be tricky when babies have tongue-tie. Special positioning tricks such as breast–nipple sandwiching (see Chapter 10) or the "nipple flip" can help these babies latch or latch more deeply. Bodywork (see end of chapter) may help affected babies who can't open wide or have tight mouths and poor sucks associated with restrictive frenulums. If these are not enough, the most common treatment for tongue or lip mobility restriction is *frenotomy*, a quick in-office surgical procedure using either surgical scissors or laser technology. Baby is wrapped or held to prevent movement, the tongue or lip is lifted, the frenum may be numbed topically, and then the restrictive tissue is released. After completion, the baby can immediately breast or bottle feed and snuggle with you. Frenotomy by a skilled practitioner is safe, and complications are rare.[9] Many babies only experience minimal discomfort, though some may be rather sore and eat less for a few hours to several days, depending on the extent of the procedure. Frenotomy can be performed by a variety of providers (pediatricians; ear, nose, and throat [ENT] doctors; dentists; and others qualified to do minor surgery), but skill and experience can vary a lot. Infant frenotomy is not routinely taught in medical and dental schools, so look for someone who understands what a good release is (not just the visible web) and who does them on a regular basis. Your lactation consultant should be able to direct you to skilled providers in your community if restrictions are suspected.

After the procedure, special exercises can help optimize your baby's tongue mobility and functionality because frenotomy alone often may not fix all feeding issues right away.[10,11] Close follow-up with a skilled lactation consultant will help you develop a sustainable feeding care plan that makes sure your baby gets enough milk and that your milk supply is protected as you work through tongue-tie-related challenges. Less experienced health care providers may suggest waiting to see if the frenulum will stretch or break on its own, but this is rarely the case.[12] Waiting for baby to grow without doing anything to help can jeopardize your milk supply and your chances for a normal breastfeeding experience.[13] In addition, having a restrictive frenulum is not just a breastfeeding issue; it may impact other aspects of health through life such as difficulties with bottle feeding, speech, digestion, reflux, orofacial development (dental or orthodontic issues), airway development (may increase snoring or sleep apnea), neck and shoulder tension, and normal tasks such as swallowing pills or licking an ice cream cone.[14-18]

If you suspect your baby's suck is impaired by tongue or lip restrictions, it's important to find a professional with extensive experience for the best results possible. If your baby's doctor is reluctant to refer but you believe that treatment would benefit you both, ask your lactation consultant for a referral to someone who is familiar with their diagnosis and treatment for a second opinion.

## Palatal Variations

Variations in the shape of the palate may affect a baby's ability to maintain the suction that helps keep the breast in his mouth and creates the vacuum to remove milk. A normal hard palate slopes gradually up and then down from front to back as it reaches the soft palate in the back. The sides are wide, and the pad of a finger should rest comfortably in it, touching the top.

### High Palate

A high palate is shaped like a dome with steep sides, and the top is not as easily touched when a baby sucks on your pad-side-up finger. Smaller fingerprint indentations are known as "bubble" palates. Babies who have high or bubble palates may not feel comfortable pulling the breast in deeply and tend to gag easily. After initially latching well, they often pull back to a shallower position, which causes "clicking" suction breaks more easily.

While some unusual variations in palate shape can be genetic or are caused by breathing or feeding tubes, most high palates are caused by problems with tongue mobility.[3] The tongue normally shapes and spreads the palate during fetal development, but if tongue movement is restricted, so is palate spreading. Bubble palates and tongue-tie are often found together.

Try different positions to help your baby take in more breast tissue. Lying on your back with him on top of you, tummy to tummy, naturally encourages head extension and draws the hyoid bone forward to increase your baby's tongue reach and grasp. Whatever position works best, encourage him to open his mouth widely and keep him tucked close to the breast.

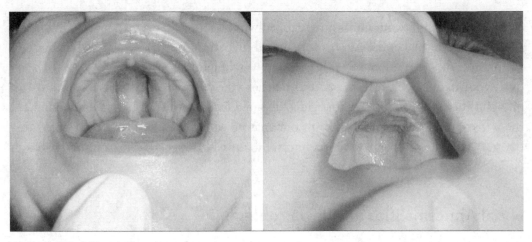

*Examples of bubble palates*

## Cleft Lip and Palate

When there's an opening in the hard palate, it's almost impossible for a baby to create the vacuum necessary to hold the breast in place, let alone draw out milk. Babies with only a cleft lip may be able to form a good seal if they are positioned in a way that allows soft breast tissue to fill in the cleft. Those with a *hard palate cleft*, however, are rarely able to form an effective seal, even with an obturator (a customized device that temporarily covers the cleft).

Babies with a *cleft of the soft palate* have similar problems and challenges. Because the hole is less visible, it may be missed in early newborn exams and picked up only when feeding problems become obvious.

A subtle, lesser-known variation is a *submucosal cleft of the soft palate*, often accompanied by a bifid (split) uvula. The surface of the soft palate is intact, but an opening in the muscle underneath causes an inadequate closing of the soft palate muscle, resulting in a condition called *velopharyngeal insufficiency*. This makes it difficult for the baby to maintain adequate suction. He may have difficulty staying attached to the breast and slip off easily when you move. Clicking sounds from suction breaks may be heard while nursing, and milk can be regurgitated through the nose as he feeds or spits up. Most tellingly, he may not gain weight well. Because they are tricky to identify, milk production can suffer before you realize what's happening. Interventions for submucosal clefts of the soft palate are rare in infants, so compensations such as pumping to keep up production and possibly supplementing may be necessary.

Remember baby Eric? He was the only one of Lisa's children to share her bifid uvula, which runs in the family. It wasn't until later that she learned about the frequent

119

connection to submucous clefts and realized what happened: even though Eric took in enough milk in the beginning, his soft suck didn't stimulate her breasts well enough to maintain good production, so his intake and weight gain fell over time.

If your baby's suck feels weak and neither you nor your lactation consultant can pinpoint the problem, take a short video clip of a feeding to your baby's doctor and ask them to examine baby's mouth to rule out anatomical problems. If they can't determine the source of the problem, ask for a referral to an ENT specialist for a more thorough evaluation.

## Facial Abnormalities and Jaw Problems

Babies can have asymmetric (unequal) facial features, which become more noticeable with growth, or small jaws, called *micrognathia*. When the chin and jaw are set back from the rest of the face, the tongue is also farther back, making it harder to reach the breast and feed effectively. A related issue can be a tight mandible (jaw) that does not open well, sometimes occurring in conjunction with tongue-tie or torticollis. The tongue and jaw work together to drop to create vacuum that draws milk from the breast.[19] If the mouth can't open well, it's harder to feed.

In severe cases, some struggling babies throw in the towel and go on nursing strikes, or they refuse to eat solids later on because it hurts to move the jaw. There may be hidden facial nerve damage affecting suck. Special positioning and latch techniques may be required to help your baby breastfeed, and cranial sacral, osteopathic, or chiropractic treatments may also help. But sometimes he just needs time to grow in order to breastfeed well. In the meantime, pumping will help to maintain good milk production.

## Airway Problems

A baby who has trouble breathing will have difficulty coordinating suck, swallow, and breathing, which makes it challenging to get enough milk out to keep milk production up. Sometimes the problem is simply dried mucus blocking nasal passageways. A drop of milk or sterile saline water can soften it for gentle suctioning before a feed. Chronic stuffy noses may be caused by allergies, and removing the offending substances from the environment or your diet may help. Narrow nasal passages or other structural blockages of the nose are more challenging. With time and growth, the passages usually enlarge. In rare cases, surgery may be required.

*Laryngomalacia* and *tracheomalacia* occur when parts of the larynx, pharynx, or trachea (windpipe) are "floppy" due to poor development, causing a high, squeaky, wheezy sound known as stridor when a baby cries or feeds. Sucking bursts may be very short (3-5 five sucks) with long breaks to recover. Or he may hold his breath for several swallows or let go of the breast entirely, gasping and panting to catch his breath. Feedings often end before the baby is full simply because he is too tired to finish. Unless feeding frequently, he may not take in enough milk to gain weight well, and milk production may suffer over time. Severe cases are usually caught early but only rarely corrected with surgery. The more common mild to moderate cases are often overlooked or not mentioned unless a problem is reported. These conditions usually resolve on their own by the end of baby's second year.

Keeping the airway as open as possible is crucial with breathing issues. Nursing parents often like to hold their baby's head, but this can trap him and block head extension. Cradle holds that create a tucked chin are bad for breathing, too. Try upright positions or an angled cradle hold with your baby's head resting in extension over your arm. Most important, expect and allow short, frequent feedings. In the meantime, post-feed pumping to support your supply may be necessary until feedings become easier.

## Cardiac Problems

Babies with heart problems breathe faster to get enough oxygen into their bodies. Like babies with breathing problems, they tire easily and may stop eating before they've tanked up all the way. Heart problems call for a streamlined approach that maximizes milk intake with the least amount of work to conserve calories. Breastfeeding with a good supply keeps oxygen levels more stable than with bottle-feeding.[20,21] Massaging the breast before feeding and breast compression during the feed can help get more milk into your baby with less effort on his part. It may be necessary to pump after feedings to maintain your production. Many babies with cardiac difficulties do well with nursing supplementation, but others may require topping off with bottles. Short, frequent feedings are often necessary until the heart defect is corrected surgically.

## Nervous System Issues

Nerves relay information about sensations such as pressure, taste, and temperature to the brain, which in turn directs the actions of muscles, including those used for sucking, swallowing, and breathing. Nerve problems from inherited conditions, prenatal drug exposure (recreational or prescription), trauma, cerebral palsy, Bell's palsy, or other medical conditions can affect feeding skills. Some sucking problems are simply caused by immaturity, such as with premies, but other times there just isn't a clear explanation. Whatever the reason, it may take time for your baby's sucking to improve, and in the meantime he may need supplementary feeds. This means you will need to pump after feedings to keep up your supply.

## Low Muscle Tone

Low muscle tone, or *hypotonia*, is common in babies with Down syndrome but can occur with other neurologic issues as well. Babies with low muscle tone have more trouble with the details of latch and suck—getting a good seal on the breast, maintaining suction, and effective tongue movements to remove milk. The suck may feel weak or "light." Dimpling of the cheeks while feeding is a red flag, and when suction is poor, he may slip off the breast easily. To compensate, a baby may tense muscles around the lips while trying to hold on. The feeding may start well, but as the muscles tire, it becomes increasingly harder to get milk out. Low-tone babies tend to nurse better later in the day and into the night when they've gathered more tension into their bodies.

The *dancer hold* is a special way of holding the breast while supporting your baby's jaw and cheeks so that he can put all his energy into sucking. In the cradle hold, slide your

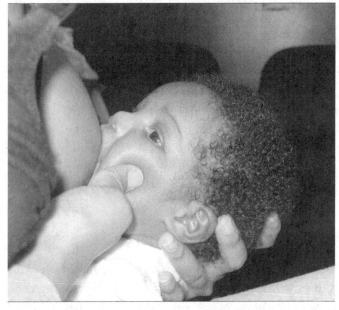

*The dancer hold*

opposite hand under your breast, palm up, and put your thumb on one side of your baby's lower jaw and your index finger on the opposite side. Curl your third finger and place it lightly under baby's chin (you'll have 2 fingers left under the breast). This can also be done in the football hold. Alternatively, some occupational and physical therapists are using kinesio tape on baby's face to duplicate the effects of the dancer hold, much easier on your hand!

Babies with hypotonia may also organize their sucking better if they are positioned to curl around your body, bent at the hip but with the ear, shoulder, and hip kept in line.

## High Muscle Tone

Infants with *hypertonia* have very tight, tense muscles. Their bodies feel stiff, and they don't flex, cuddle, or relax easily into your arms. They tend to breastfeed poorly, popping on and off the breast. They may also clench their jaws while nursing or even clamp down on the breast with their gums. Needless to say, your nipples may be sore, yet your breasts may not get enough of the right stimulation to drive your supply.

True high muscle tone is a physical trait that is present much of the time, regardless of the activity. In other cases, babies stiffen or arch to express frustration or pain but feel relaxed and cuddly when not under stress. Or they may have sensory processing issues. When it happens only at feeding time, the baby is likely reacting to a negative experience. It could be related to aggressive suctioning at birth, frustration with ongoing problems getting milk out of the breast, or painful reflux that starts up during or after feeding. Babies with true hypertonia feel stiff or tense at times unrelated to feedings.

Infants with high muscle tone tend to nurse best in the late night and early morning hours, before the day's tensions stimulate their muscle tone still more. Before nursing, try laying your baby down on a blanket; grab all four corners and gently swing him in a head-to-toe direction to help his body relax. Rocking or walking around with him snuggled closely, even skin-to-skin, may help. Swaddling him into a moderately flexed position may also calm baby and help him to focus. Nursing in the football (side) hold with his hips bent and feet pointing up is a great way to create this flexion if he isn't too big and reflux isn't a problem. On the other hand, some high-tone babies nurse better when allowed to stretch out on a pillow rather than being tucked up close as is usually best. Experiment to find what works best for your baby.

## Sensory Processing Disorders

Sensory processing disorders, also known as *sensory integration dysfunction*, are hard to diagnose in an infant. Sensations that are usually interesting or pleasant, such as the brush of a hand or a soft touch, can be aggravating and even intolerable to these babies.

They are often irritable, don't adapt well to changes around them, and may even seem terrified of certain movements. Sensory defensive babies are easily bothered by noise and baths and diaper changes, or they may seem to crave movement, needing to be carried a lot. These sensitive infants may not nurse well because they are overwhelmed by sensory input and will arch away from the breast, cry, latch poorly, and let go of the breast often,[22] which some parents misinterpret as a sign of high or low supply.[23] Poor breastfeeds can lead to poor milk production over time. Sensory defensive infants often respond better to firm touch with deep pressure; smooth, soft fabrics without irritating zippers, tags, or rough seams; swaddling; swinging head to toe before breastfeeding; breastfeeding in a sling; and low light and noise levels during feeding.

Some sensory defensive babies are calmer with direct skin-to-skin contact rather than being clothed or swaddled. Others nurse better with minimal touching, perhaps preferring a pillow on your lap to being cradled in arms. If they're having difficulty sensing the breast during latch, try aiming the nipple downward toward their tongue rather than toward the palate. The firm feel of a nipple shield may also make latching easier.

If you suspect your baby might have sensory issues, your pediatrician can make a referral to an occupational therapist or early intervention program for a formal assessment. These experts have special training in sensory problems to help both you and your baby. A skilled lactation consultant may also have ideas to help baby nurse better and can work with the therapist. In the meantime, you may need to pump until he is able to handle the job himself.

## Infections

In some cases of poor infant growth, an underlying problem such as a urinary tract infection may be the culprit. Energy requirements may be higher and growth can slow down when the body is fighting an infection. If your baby is suddenly not feeding well or his weight gain has slowed down, see your pediatrician for a thorough evaluation.

## Reflux

All babies spit up some, and some babies spit up a lot. Most of the time, it is largely just a laundry problem. But there are babies who have so much trouble with milk coming back up (reflux) that eating becomes unpleasant and even painful. It may be obvious because they're spitting up large amounts after and in between feedings, or they may have a "silent" version of reflux in which partially digested milk shoots just far enough up the esophagus to cause burning sensations and sometimes disrupt breathing, waking the baby and making him cry and choke. This is usually diagnosed as *gastroesophageal reflux disease* (GERD). Infants with GERD may begin to associate feeding with pain—"I eat then I hurt"—and then put off feedings, eating only when they absolutely have to, resulting in slow weight gain. Or they may stiffen and arch and feed poorly. Either way, milk production can suffer.

GERD is often simply a problem of immaturity, but it can also be triggered by sensitivity to a protein in your diet that passes into the milk; dairy is a common culprit. Mechanical issues such as misalignment of the spine or cranial plates[24] or swallowing problems related to laryngomalacia[25] or tongue- or lip-tie can also contribute to reflux.[7] Regardless of the origin, all babies with GERD benefit from smaller, more frequent meals; having their heads higher than their bottoms during feedings; and being kept upright for 20 minutes after eating. Osteopathic or chiropractic treatment may help if there is a mechanical issue. Medication may be prescribed if nothing else is helping and the baby is miserable. If this all sounds familiar, ask your pediatrician to screen for reflux but be prepared to do some of your own detective work to find the source. In the meantime, you know what to do keep your supply strong if needed—pump! That will buy you time until breastfeeding improves.

## The Self-Limiting Feeder

Babies who are having miserable feeding experiences may self-limit their feeds to minimize discomfort. GERD is often behind this behavior, but other problems can trigger it as well. If your baby needs more calories but you can't get him to take more or feed more often, take a step back and look at the big feeding picture because there is likely something there that needs to be addressed.

## When Nothing Seems to Fit

When anatomical problems have been thoroughly assessed and ruled out and nothing else fits, *bodywork* therapies that treat nerve impingements or other subtle interferences are worth exploring. Some babies respond positively to infant oral motor function therapy by a speech or occupational therapist. Chiropractic treatment also can be effective in improving some suck problems.[26] A third option is *craniosacral therapy* (CST) or *cranial osteopathy*, a very gentle manipulation of the plates of the skull to release subtle pressures on nerves affecting muscles and reflexes. This can be done by CST specialists, osteopathic physicians, and some chiropractors. Cranial therapy has been effective in improving some suck problems.[27] All of these options are generally low-risk, and if one helps, you'll be glad you tried it.

## CHAPTER 10

# Is it Something About My Breasts?

Breast and nipple anatomy form the assembly lines, warehouse, and delivery system of the factory, supported by nerves that receive and send orders in response to the consumer: your baby. When the factory isn't running right, the idea that one of these primary components might be damaged or broken can be perplexing and frustrating. We've already looked at more short-term problems that can be resolved as long as breastfeeding continues to be managed well. But primary issues resulting from either breast structure problems or physiological disruptions related to health conditions or hormonal dysfunctions may require a longer-term strategy. This chapter delves into the known anatomical factors that can affect milk supply, and the next chapter discusses physiological factors. If nothing you've read so far seems to fit, these chapters may shed more light on your situation.

## The Milk Supply Equation

| | | |
|---|---|---|
| Primary | { | **Sufficient glandular tissue** |
| | + | **Intact nerve pathways *and* ducts** |
| | + | Adequate hormones *and* hormone receptors |
| Secondary | + | Adequate lactation-critical nutrients |
| | + | Frequent, effective milk removal and breast stimulation |
| | | AND *no other lactation inhibitors* |
| | = | GOOD MILK PRODUCTION |

# Do You Have Any of the Following Risk Factors for Anatomical Problems?

☐ Breast or chest surgery or medical procedures, even as an infant

☐ Injury to your chest during childhood or adolescence

☐ Damage to any nerves or a spinal cord injury

☐ Unusual breast or nipple features, such as one breast being much smaller than the other or a nipple that's divided into 2 sections

☐ Little or no breast tenderness or changes during pregnancy or after birth

☐ A chronic illness or condition

## Anatomical Variations

Nature isn't perfect. Anatomical variations can start in the womb or be caused by accident, disease, illness, or surgery. Whatever the cause, structural problems with your milk factory and its communications systems can affect milk production.[1]

### Flat and Inverted Nipples

When your baby can't latch well because the nipple doesn't protrude with stimulation, milk supply suffers. Nature programmed your baby via the *rooting reflex* to search for the "top of the hill" using his face. A nipple that doesn't stick out much is confusing and harder to sense. Babies use their hands to knead the breast to make the nipple pop out more (an important reason not to put mittens over their hands), but this doesn't always work when they're flat or inverted.

Your nipples may have always been flat, never protruding even when you are cold. Or they may be normal, but labor fluids caused your breasts to swell, temporarily flattening out the nipples in the process. For this second problem, *Reverse Pressure Softening* (RPS) can help push away the swelling and soften the areola so that the nipples are more manageable (see Chapter 5). If your breasts are really swollen and tender, try the *Therapeutic Breast Massage* described in Chapter 5 to move the fluids out of the breast first.

You can help flat nipples by placing your fingers on one side of the breast and your thumb on the other about 2 inches back from the nipple and compressing lightly to form a "sandwich" that *lines up with your baby's mouth*. She just needs a "here's the top of the hill" landmark to know where to latch, and then she should be able to pull in enough tissue to get the job done. Continue to lightly hold the sandwich until the breast softens; after this, most babies can stay on by themselves. Otherwise, maintain the hold lightly throughout the feeding.

*Making a "breast sandwich" can help some babies latch and stay attached to get more milk.*

Around 3% of women are born with inverted nipples that are turned inward into the breast or that retract inward when you compress with a finger on either side. This is caused by short milk ducts or tight fibers that draw the nipple inward.

**Grade 1** inverted nipples come out easily with stimulation, and babies with a good suck are able to manage them.

**Grade 2** inverted nipples can be pulled out with some difficulty and frequently pull back in soon after letting go. This can make latch challenging and frustrate a baby if the nipple pulls back. Nipple shields can work well in these situations.

**Grade 3** inverted nipples are "tethered" and can be difficult to get your fingers around and behind the ball of tissue, let alone pull the nipple out.[2] Latch is almost impossible, and they also tend to pump poorly, with many drizzling like a kinked hose rather than spraying freely. Baby or pump, milk production can be compromised if milk cannot be removed easily.

Inverted nipples can be surgically released, though not during pregnancy or lactation, of course. The ability to breastfeed later on depends on whether nerves or ducts had to be cut and if scar tissue formed during the healing process.[2]

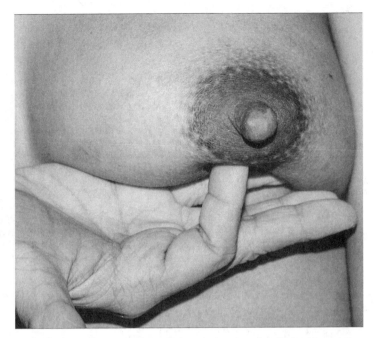

*The "nipple nudge" can help push the nipple out and make latching easier.*

If you are pregnant or between pregnancies, there are low-tech nonsurgical treatment options. The Avent Niplette™ creates sustained suction in a small, hard cup worn inside the bra for several hours at a time. This has been reported to correct all types of inverted nipples (varying degrees of success) but requires at least 1-3 months.[3] Supple Cups™ are similar but made with soft flexible silicone and come in 4 sizes: 11mm (size 1), 12.5mm (size 2), 14.5mm (size 3) and 16.5mm (size 4) diameters; a larger size 5 was discontinued by the manufacturer. The best time to wear either product is between pregnancies, but they can also be worn during pregnancy (except for high-risk pregnancy) or before feedings.[4] If you're interested in other innovative treatments that have been tested, check our website lowmilksupply.org.

Once your baby is here, your two goals are to help her latch and to keep the milk moving. See if you can gently pull your nipple out by pushing your fingers deep into your breast and finding the sides or "back" of the nipple shank. Alternatively, try the *nipple nudge*: press your index finger up into the breast and then outward to push the inverted nipple out farther, then try latching as you hold this. You may need to keep your finger there while the baby nurses.

Another option is the Lansinoh Latch Assist™ or Maternal Concepts' Evert-It Nipple Enhancer™ for drawing nipples out, or you can create your own by cutting the tip end off of a periodontal syringe and then inserting the plunger through the rough side so that the smooth side faces you; apply and pull.[5] Using a pump for a minute or two may also draw out the nipple, but this may cause the areola to swell and form a bulb of tissue that may be too large for your baby to latch to. Whichever you try, the nipple usually retracts quickly once you let go, so you'll have to move fast to latch your baby.

When all else fails, a *properly sized* silicone nipple shield creates an artificial nipple over your own so that the baby can latch, helpful so long as your actual nipple tissue can be pulled inside at least a little. Nipple shields work better for type 1 and 2 inversions but often poorly for type 3. Choose one that is wide enough to pull in the ball of inverted nipple tissue as too small of a shield can obstruct milk flow.[6,7] Turn the dome of the shield halfway inside out, then press the inverted edge on the areola and smooth out from the

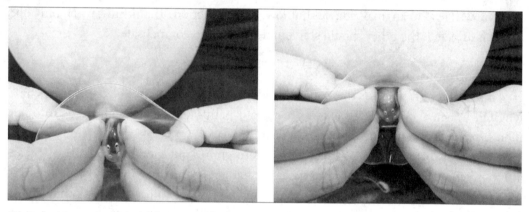

*When applying a nipple shield, first turn the dome halfway inside out, center on the nipple and then smooth out.*

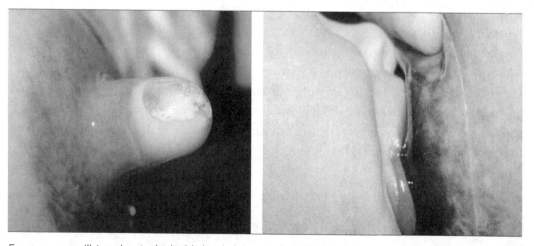

*Express some milk into the nipple shield, then help your baby latch deeply, beyond the cone. Lower photos from Wilson-Clay B, Hoover K. The Breastfeeding Atlas, 6th edition. Lactnews Press, Manchaca, TX. 2017*

center outward. The dome should pop back up, drawing in some nipple with it. Before your baby latches, hold the shield in place with one hand and compress from farther back to express some milk into the dome to encourage sucking. (You can also inject milk through a hole with a periodontal syringe.) Make sure your baby latches as deeply as possible! Finally, you'll want to pump after feedings to ensure good breast drainage. A shield is usually temporary until your baby learns how to make your breast work.

## Unusually Shaped Nipples

Nipples are generally round but can also come in unusual shapes such as bumpy, elongated, or even separated into two distinct parts. Many function normally, but a few may have blind ducts with no exit through the nipple. If milk can't get through, lack of milk removal will lead to an unavoidable shutdown in production. Thankfully, when only one breast is affected, the other should step up production to compensate.

## Large Nipples

If you have large nipples or they've enlarged after years of nursing, latch can be challenging. When the mismatch is too great, your baby can't get enough tissue into her mouth to milk the breast. Lactation consultant Jan Barger jokingly refers to this as "oro-nippular disproportion." The solution is to pump and then feed your baby by an alternative method—you'll need extra-large flanges—until her mouth grows bigger. Try latching every so often until she can get on and remove milk well; this can take 1-3 months. Some babies may become opinionated after all the struggle; if so, see "Breast Refusal" in Chapter 4 or contact a lactation consultant.

## Nipple Piercings

Nipple piercings aren't usually a problem for milk production; if anything, they may add additional outlets in the nipples. (Do remove any nipple rings or bars during feedings.) However, unusual or extensive scarring from infections or poor piercing technique could obstruct milk flow, and a few cases have been reported.[8] If this happens, there isn't much you can do about it; the lobes that can't drain will eventually dry up. One parent who had problems with just one side was able to nurse exclusively on the other "good" side.

# Breast Structure

Two basic breast structure issues can affect milk production. *Tissue density* is the relative elasticity and compressibility of the breast, areola, and nipple, ranging from very firm to jello-soft. *Glandular development* refers to the overall amount of milk-making tissue.

## Soft Breast Tissue

Soft, flaccid breast tissue can be difficult for babies to grasp. In some instances, the skin is so loosely attached to the underlying gland that your baby has mostly skin in her mouth and can't extract milk efficiently. Firmly shaping the breast and pulling back toward your chest wall to tighten the skin against the gland can help baby get her mouth around the milking area. Or try the "nipple nudge" described earlier in this chapter to make the nipple and areola stick out farther. Holding your baby against your side with her feet pointing behind you may align her to latch more easily. Breast compressions are usually necessary to remove all of the available milk to keep up your supply.

## Insufficient Glandular Tissue

Parents with small breasts often worry about having enough milk-making tissue, while those with large breasts may assume they have plenty. However, it isn't the outer size of the breasts that matters but the amount of glandular tissue *inside* them. Most of the time, differences in breast size are related to the amount of fat in the breast, not the gland.

Having "enough" for a good milk factory starts with a healthy basic tree in place before pregnancy and then having that tree respond to pregnancy hormones with new growth. If you have a normal amount of breast tissue but it doesn't blossom during pregnancy like a fruit tree in spring, you won't have enough milk-making tissue, but not because there wasn't enough to start. Placental problems or insufficient prolactin are two possibilities for this kind of "pseudo" hypoplasia.

True *insufficient glandular tissue* (IGT), or *mammary hypoplasia*, refers to *what you started with* before pregnancy and typically involves a lack of fullness in part or all of the breast. Small IGT breasts may look as if they never finished puberty and are often less than an A cup, with little palpable tissue. Larger IGT breasts may look "deflated" or have an unusually long tubular or bowed shape, with the nipples pointing down or away from the body. This is caused by the missing tissue that would normally provide support (see type I to IV drawings). They may be asymmetric in size, with one side much larger than the other. Stretch marks that aren't related to pregnancy or pubertal growth may be present, and there may be little or no visible veining.[9]

Less tissue on the chest means more flat space between the breasts[10]—greater than 1.5 inches (4cm) signals a higher risk for IGT and milk supply problems[9]. The areolas may also be disproportionately large and "bulbous," almost as if they're a separate structure attached to the breast.[11] Breasts that are classified as "tubular or tuberous" seem to have abnormal glandular tissue.[12]

Affected individuals usually experience few, if any, breast changes during pregnancy and have difficulty identifying when the breasts start making milk after birth.[13]

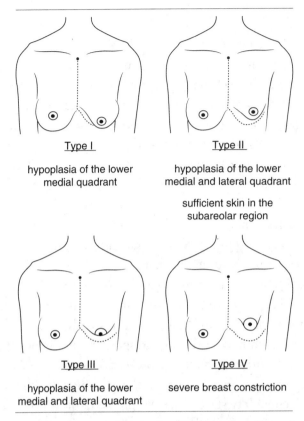

Type I

hypoplasia of the lower
medial quadrant

Type II

hypoplasia of the lower
medial and lateral quadrant

sufficient skin in the
subareolar region

Type III

hypoplasia of the lower
medial and lateral quadrant

Type IV

severe breast constriction

*Plastic surgeon's grading of severity of tubular hypoplasia.
From von Heimburg, Exner, Kruft and Lemperle, 1996.*[14]

However, more mammary growth may occur after birth with frequent milk removal and stimulation.

There are two types of hypoplasia: *congenital* (the defect is present at birth) and *acquired* (the result of a later event). Congenital hypoplasia is considered rare and is usually the result of a syndrome such as Jeune or Poland.[10] However, back in the 1980s, someone noticed that women with the heart condition mitral valve prolapse were also more likely to have breast hypoplasia. The theory was that both the breast gland and the mitral valve develop from the same layer of tissue during fetal development, so when something goes astray, both can be affected.[15] Breast hypoplasia also seems to occur more with scoliosis—the more severe the condition, the worst the hypoplasia.[16]

Fetal breast development could also be altered by a high androgen (male hormones) environment or exposure to hormone-disrupting chemicals during pregnancy. Abnormal breast development was discovered in a group of young teens who were conceived and born in an agricultural region with high pesticide exposure. *The breasts looked normal*

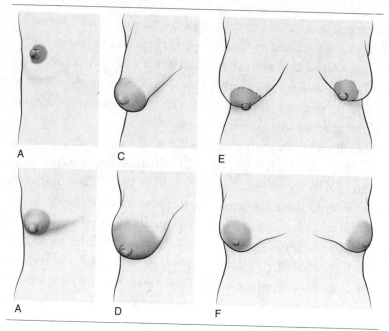

*Real-life hypoplasia variations: **A**, Incomplete development before puberty with prominent nipple. **B**, Poorly developed upper portion with scant lower tissue. **C**, Tubular breast with bulbous areola. **D**, Long, mildly tubular, bowed to outside, with extra-large areola. **E**, Classic wide-spaced and uneven. **F**, Wide-spaced with scant tissue.*

*on the outside,* but on the inside there was less glandular tissue than usual,[17] leading to the prediction that they might have difficulty breastfeeding—making enough milk—later on.[18] Unfortunately, no one has followed up to find out what happened. Such breasts represent a "hybrid" of congenital and acquired hypoplasia because fetal development was altered by environmental contaminants and are trickier to identify because the outer breast may appear normal.

Acquired hypoplasia is often considered "idiopathic," which simply means that no one knows what went wrong.[10] But we are starting to identify more causes now, which will at least bring some peace in knowing the "why." Here's some of what's been identified so far:

- Chest surgeries before puberty if they cut through budding glandular tissue[19]
- Chest traumas such as caused by a burn or seat belt during an accident[20]
- Hypoplasia after radiation to an infant breast[21]
- One-sided breast atrophy (shrinkage) attributed to mononucleosis[22]
- One-sided hypoplasia occurring in the breast with an infantile hemangioma[23,24]

- One-sided hypoplasia caused by scarring after treatment for a breast infection at age 1; the breast was unable to form properly through the scar tissue[25]
- One-sided hypoplasia in the breast with a Becker's nevus has been reported. These brown patches often develop in early puberty and seem to make androgen receptors hypersensitive. In one case, treatment with spironolactone, an anti-androgen drug, resulted in the affected side growing bigger.[26,27]
- History of hormonal or ovarian problems[28-30]
- Exposure to hormone-disrupting chemicals during puberty. Organochlorines such as TCDD and DDE and substances such as BPA and PCBs stunted mammary development in rats. There also are human reports of poor glandular development and early weaning among women living in heavily exposed areas, the latter presumably due to poor milk production.[31] The less glandular tissue there is, the less milk can be produced.[32] Prolonged exposure to low doses of triclosan, present in antibacterial soaps and products, and methylparaben, found in many personal care products, can result in more fat and less actual mammary gland tissue. Puberty is a time of extra vulnerability to chemical influences.[33]

In addition to what's been documented, two other red flags for a higher risk of IGT have been suggested as well:

- An eating disorder during puberty resulting in a scant fat pad, which is needed for pubertal breast growth
- Obesity and insulin resistance during puberty, which may alter glandular development.[34,35] Diana Cassar-Uhl, author of *Finding Sufficiency: Breastfeeding with Insufficient Glandular Tissue*, believes that this may be a major cause.[35,36]

Bianca had underdeveloped breast tissue that she believes was caused by a childhood infection: "I had a freak but pretty severe case of mastitis on both sides when I was 11. It didn't get treated for quite some time because I was embarrassed and my mother thought I was just talking about normal growing pains when I said I was hurting. I don't think my breasts ever developed much more beyond that 11-year-old point, except a little at the sides during pregnancy." Interestingly, the one thing that seemed to help Bianca was goat's rue, which has mammary-stimulating properties.

Author and lactation consultant Nancy Mohrbacher has a deformity of her chest that prevented one breast from growing during puberty. At age 21, she had a breast implant inserted to even them out and went on to have three babies and breastfeed using both breasts. Years later, during a mammogram, it was discovered that her implant had migrated into the hole of her deformity, yet she still had a full breast! Having nursed for a total of 12 years, she credits the nursing activity with stimulating growth to fill in that tissue. You can read her full story at bit.ly/MMM-Magical.

With hard work, many parents are able to boost their production, but others seem to hit a ceiling quickly.[9] *One of the biggest hurdles is getting enough stimulation* because not all babies will continue to suck vigorously when milk flow is low. Supplementing at the breast preserves the breastfeeding relationship and is a great way to keep your baby sucking while simultaneously getting her fed. Adding breast compression also helps drain the breast more thoroughly. Additional hands-on pumping (see Chapter 13) afterward helps complete breast drainage and provides the extra stimulation that is often needed to continue stimulating hormones and receptors. If your baby sucks strongly for at least 15 minutes per side and drains you well and the pump gets only drops out, extra pumping may not always be necessary.

Galactogogues can make a difference but are often disappointing in these situations, perhaps because expectations tend to be high! The best herbal choices are those that have a dual reputation of also stimulating mammary growth, such as goat's rue (see Chapter 14). It's uncertain whether you'll grow more tissue, but if they can at least help what you have work harder, great. Prescription galactogogues also stimulate the existing tissue to work harder. Good results for either depend in part on how much functional breast tissue there is to work on.

Lactation with hypoplasia can be challenging, but some parents who persistently continue to stimulate their breasts by nursing or pumping long-term—well past a year— have reported glandular tissue growth and more milk the next time around. You never know what might happen!

## The Great Pretenders: Breasts That Look Normal But Aren't

There are two possibilities here. The first are breasts filled largely with fatty tissue and only a small amount of glandular tissue.[11] The problem isn't obvious by their shape; one clue may be little or no visible veining during pregnancy and lactation. The second breasts appear to have plenty of glandular tissue, but it doesn't function well. Such problems may be the result of hormonal issues as discussed in the next chapter but can have external causes as well.

We mentioned earlier that chest irradiation before puberty can prevent the breast from developing normally. When irradiation occurs *after* pubertal development, the breast can appear normal but respond poorly to pregnancy hormones due to damaged cells. A review of multiple studies on radiation found that while lactation after radiotherapy was possible in 50% of treated women, milk production was reduced. A number of them also had problems with nipple protrusion that caused latch difficulties.[37]

We've seen how hormone-disrupting chemicals can cause permanent damage to fetal breast tissue or alter pubertal development. A third possibility is to have normally developed breast tissue that is affected *later on* by hormone-disrupting chemicals. The contaminants may be stored in fat tissue before pregnancy, or first-time exposure could happen during pregnancy. A lack of normal pregnancy breast changes and growth may lead some parents to conclude that they must have insufficient glandular tissue when the problem really is *unresponsive* glandular tissue. While the end result of poor milk production may be the same, the breast was not deficient in the amount of glandular tissue prior to pregnancy.

There are blood tests for chemicals, but they aren't done routinely, so it's hard to know if you're being affected. Living in an area with contaminated water or soil or having occupational exposures to chemicals or pesticides can up the risk. But even low-dose exposure over a long period of time can disrupt hormone functions,[38] as seen with the study on chemicals in personal care products mentioned earlier.[33] How many of us might be affected and not have a clue? Of all the possible explanations for why women's breasts are not functioning properly, hormone-disrupting chemicals might be the sleeping giant responsible for many mysterious cases. On the positive side, some of the negative effects might be reversible if the chemicals can be cleansed from the body, as happened for a man who wasn't able to lose weight and help his diabetes without getting sick from chemical contaminants until olestra, a fat substitute, was added to his diet to help pull out and excrete chemicals as they were released during weight loss.[39,40] If this is a real possibility that you'd like to rule out, talk to your doctor about testing for these chemicals.

## Breast Surgeries

With few exceptions, most parents who've had breast surgery (either for cosmetic or medical reasons) are able to produce some amount of milk, so the question is not *if* you'll produce milk but rather *how much* you'll be able to make. This is determined by the amount of damage to the ducts and nerves, the functionality of the milk glands before surgery, the healing process, the amount of time since the surgery, and any other lactation experiences between the surgery and your current baby. Scarring or the complication of an infection may have an additional effect on lactation, depending on the extent.

Ducts can regenerate over time in response to the stimulation of pregnancy and lactation.[41] If you had a partial milk supply with your first baby, you may find that you get progressively more milk with each subsequent baby, sometimes even a full supply. The subtle stimulation from each menstrual cycle also plays a role in this regeneration process, so the more time between babies, the better.

The number of ductal openings in the nipple makes a difference. The average number is 9 but can be as few as 4.[42] A mother with lots of openings can afford to lose a couple when ducts are severed during surgery, and the milk will still be able to get out, but someone with only 4 can't afford to lose any because some areas of the breast may no longer have an outlet. There isn't an easy way to know how many openings you have because they're very small and don't all drain at the same time. Milk that builds up behind the severed ducts triggers production shutdown and involution of the milk-making cells in the immediate area. Meanwhile, the unaffected areas of the breast will continue to function and work even harder as long as milk continues to be removed from them.

Like ducts, nerve fibers can also regenerate. The most critical nerve to lactation is the *fourth intercostal nerve*, which is generally located around the 4 o'clock position facing the left breast and the 8 o'clock position facing the right. It is the primary carrier of messages to the brain for the release of prolactin and oxytocin, and when injured, letdown doesn't happen as easily.[43] Unlike ducts, nerve regeneration is *not* influenced by lactation, past or current, but grows at a consistent rate of 0.04 inches (1mm) per month after an initial period of repair.[41] Normal response to touch and temperature indicates that the nerve network is improving, although the healing process can vary, and it's possible that your nipples may become very tender as they heal or never regain all of their previous sensitivity and functionality. The longer it's been since the surgery, the greater the chances that the critical nerves have regenerated to their ultimate potential. Chapter 12 discusses ways to stimulate or enhance the letdown reflex.

Maximizing milk removal is the best starting strategy for making the most milk possible after breast surgery. Pumping, galactogogues, and techniques to stimulate letdowns may also be necessary. Thoroughly massaging your breasts both before and during feedings and using breast compressions may move milk through obstructed areas. Massaging and compressing while pumping can also be effective; try leaning over periodically to let gravity help draw the milk out. If you have implants above the muscle, you can avoid the risk of rupture by placing your hand on top of the breast, with your fingers on one side and your thumb on the other. If your baby has difficulty latching deeply because the tissue under your areola isn't as full, try the "nipple nudge" illustrated earlier in this chapter as your baby latches.

## Diagnostic and Surgical Procedures

Biopsies that remove samples of breast tissue, aspirations to remove infectious or suspicious fluids from the breast, and removal of tissue such as lumps may potentially interfere with lactation, although the impact is usually mild. Ducts or nerves may be severed, depending on where and what direction the surgeon cut.[44] Incisions that are oriented toward the nipple like the spoke of a wheel are less likely to damage nerves and ducts.

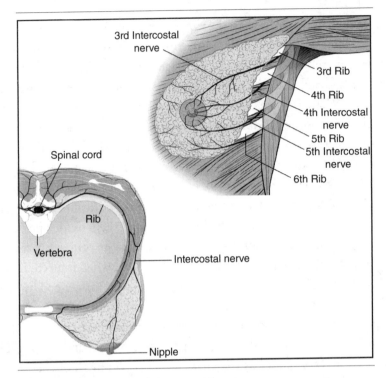

*Nerves that directly affect the breast and lactation.*

One of the most vulnerable periods for significant damage from any surgery is before puberty when the immature mammary gland is very small. Invasive cuts during that time can interfere with a greater number of ducts and nerves simply because they are closer together, eventually affecting the internal structure of the breast as it matures.

## Breast Lift

Breast lift surgery, known as *mastopexy*, repositions the breasts to reduce sagging without removing breast tissue, resulting in fuller, rounder, and higher breasts. Breast implant surgery is often performed at the same time to further increase breast fullness. Breast lift surgery alone doesn't usually affect milk production because no glandular tissue is removed and the incisions are not usually deep enough to sever critical nerves.[41]

## Breast Augmentation

*Breast augmentation* is a common cosmetic procedure undertaken for many reasons: to enhance appearance, to correct abnormal breasts, to even out breasts when one side is significantly larger than the other, or for reconstruction after other breast surgery. It is most commonly done with silicone or saline implants, but sometimes liposuctioned fat

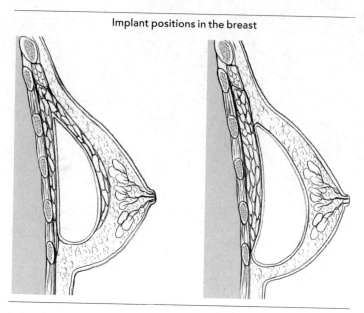

Implant positions in the breast

*Left: submuscular implant placed under the chest muscle.*
*Right: subglandular implant placed above the muscle.*

or polyacrylamide hydrogel (PAAG) may be used. Individuals who've had this procedure have a higher risk of problems establishing lactation than those who don't.[45,46] The impact on lactation depends on the entry location and the placement of the implants. An incision around the areola, particularly in the lower, outer portion, can reduce nerve response to the nipple and areola. A large implant can also reduce nipple and areolar sensitivity.[47] An implant positioned directly above the chest muscle is more likely to put pressure on the glandular tissue and obstruct milk flow, resulting in reduced milk production over time, compared with an implant positioned under the chest muscle away from the tissue.[48] But above or below, any significant pressure on the glandular tissue could cause a false sense of fullness and trigger a "cut back production" message to your milk factory, especially when the skin is tight and inelastic. Feed or express frequently to minimize fullness or engorgement and maintain the "keep making milk" message.

Another important factor to consider is the reason for your surgery. If your breasts were unusual in shape, perhaps lacking the normal amount of glandular tissue, the cause of a low milk supply later on could have more to do with a smaller amount of milk-making tissue than the surgery you had to even them out.[49]

## Breast Reduction

Breast reduction surgery, known as *reduction mammoplasty*, can reduce your ability to make milk because it removes mammary tissue and can damage nerves. In an analysis of

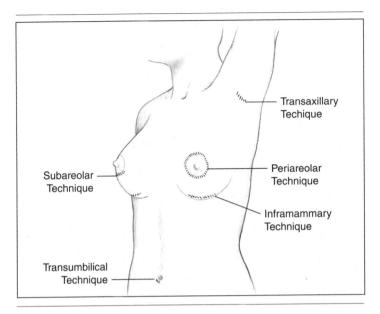

*Breast implants can be inserted from several different locations. Some are riskier for lactation than others.*

51 studies, the amount of breast tissue and the time since the surgery were less important than the surgical method itself.[50] It was discovered that:

- When the nipple and areola were completely severed from the breast during surgery (free nipple graft), breastfeeding "success," usually defined as *any* breastfeeding, was lower.
- When pedicle techniques that preserve the connection to the nipple and areola during surgery were used, individuals who had the "inferior" or "central" pedicle technique had the best breastfeeding outcomes compared with other pedicle locations.
- Breastfeeding success was highest when the attachment of the column of tissue to the chest wall was fully preserved compared with partial preservation.

It is rare not to produce some amount of milk after breast reduction surgery—it's more a matter of *how much* you can make. Remember how some of the branches in the breast tree actually connect? It's possible that if a duct was severed, the affected area of the breast might be able to drain through another branch. If that is not the case, the blocked area will eventually shut down, and the rest of the breast will have to step up to compensate. Nerve damage is trickier; nerves sometimes reconnect over time, but if there is significant damage, it's harder for the brain to get the message to release prolactin and oxytocin.

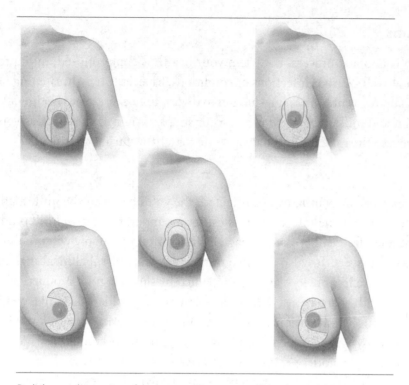

*Pedicles are the portion of the breast with nerves and blood vessels that is left attached to the nipple and areola during reduction surgery. They may connect completely down to the chest wall or be partially severed. Top left: inferior pedicle; top right: superior pedicle; middle: central pedicle (no skin attachment); bottom left: medial pedicle; bottom right: lateral pedicle.*

Expressing colostrum the last few weeks of pregnancy as described in Chapters 5 and 19 may give you a head start. After that, the most important thing you can do from your baby's birth is to remove milk often. Frequent breastfeeding, with the possible addition of hand expression in the first 3 days, helps to launch your milk supply. Breast massage and compressions also aid in draining the breast more thoroughly while breastfeeding.[41]

Some parents choose to pump after breastfeeding for additional stimulation. How much that extra work pays off depends on the individual. If you want to give your body its best chance, set a goal for how many weeks you're going to pump before you decide if it's beneficial or not. Galactogogues may also be helpful in superstimulating your active mammary tissue to make the most milk possible if breastfeeding and good breast drainage are not enough.

For more information and support, check out the Breastfeeding After Reduction (BFAR) groups on Facebook (Facebook.com/groups/179939525406788 and 458224110894529).

## Infections

Lactation is a robust process, but when your health is compromised, milk production can suffer as well. Serious infections or conditions, especially life-threatening ones, may cause your body to cut back on production to divert more energy into healing. As long as stimulation and milk removal continue, your supply usually comes back as your condition improves. The milk is almost always safe for a baby during treatment.

### Mastitis

If your breast becomes inflamed or infected, the gates between the milk-making cells open up to clear out the infection. This causes a temporary drop in milk production.[51] With continued frequent breast drainage by baby or pump, supply will usually rebound as the breast recovers. It's also possible to have subacute or subclinical mastitis, when the symptoms are less obvious and accompanied by sluggish milk production. If you've been dealing with sharp pains, dull achiness, or clumpy milk for a while, consider getting checked out by a lactation consultant. While antibiotics are often used to knock down chronic low-grade infections, many organisms are becoming resistant to medications. Certain probiotics—*Lactobacillus fermentum* CECT5716, *gasseri* CECT5714, and *salivarius* CECT5713 in particular[52]—have shown good results in reducing symptoms and preventing recurrence. Topical curcumin (turmeric) is also good for reducing inflammation and may be effective.[51]

On rare occasions, breast tissue damage from abscess, extreme prolonged engorgement, or severe mastitis may account for some otherwise inexplicable cases of unresponsive low milk production.

## Injuries

Various injuries have the potential to interfere with milk production by damaging glandular tissue or critical nerve connections. The types of injuries that are described next are the most likely to cause problems with milk production.

### Breast and Other Cancer Treatments

Cancer evolves from cells that start to grow out of control and harm the body. Nonsurgical treatments are designed to stop this growth in its tracks, if not kill the cancer cells completely. Since milk-making cells are designed by nature to grow and regress through multiple pregnancy cycles, therapies to stop cancer cells from growing have a high likelihood of damaging healthy mammary cells as well.

A comprehensive review of articles and case studies on breastfeeding after irradiation reported that approximately 50% of nursing parents produced milk on the affected side, but it took longer to increase and the volume was lower than from the non-treated side. Radiated breasts did not grow or change much during pregnancy, and not surprisingly, tissue samples showed damage to mammary cells. What was *not* expected were the changes in nipple function after radiation—*they no longer extended well*—making latch difficult as well. Overall, tumor location, the type of surgery, and the radiotherapy dose determined breastfeeding outcome. On the positive side, the remaining well-functioning breast is usually able to compensate.[37]

In women who were diagnosed with cancer during pregnancy, those who received chemotherapy until 3 weeks before delivery were most likely to report little or no milk production compared with those who didn't have it. The chances of reduced milk production were 75% if therapy was started at 17 weeks of pregnancy and 50% if started at 24 weeks, with only 34% of chemotherapy patients able to exclusively breastfeed versus 91% of untreated patients. Some types of chemotherapy regimens affected lactation more than others.[53]

## Spinal Cord Injuries

The nerves that supply the breast enter the spinal cord in the middle of the back at the T3, T4, T5, and T6 vertebrae.[54] Spinal injuries below this should not affect milk production directly, but injuries above T6 carry the potential to cause problems. A complete injury results in the loss of all motor and sensory function at the level of the injury and below, while an incomplete injury may allow for some sensory or motor function at the level of the injury or below.[55] Spinal cord injuries are a concern for breastfeeding because they interfere with the normal messages sent by the suckling baby to your brain that stimulate the release of prolactin and oxytocin. They can also affect one side of the body more than the other.[56] It has generally been accepted that injuries above T6 usually result in a decrease in milk production between 6 weeks and 3 months after birth. In a survey of breastfeeding parents with various degrees of spinal cord injuries, those with injuries above T6 breastfed for a shorter time than parents with lower level injuries.[57]

An interesting report may shed light on why the decreases occur and what compensations are possible. Three women had neck injuries resulting in paralysis of both the lower and upper body. Two were first-time mothers, while the third had successfully breastfed a baby before her injury. In each case, their milk came in normally, but the letdown reflex wasn't consistent. To compensate, they learned to bypass the physical and tap into their secondary emotional pathway of mental imaging and relaxation to trigger letdown, often multiple times during feedings. Oxytocin nasal spray was also used for the same purpose. Both of these strategies helped the babies to get more milk and the mothers to sustain higher milk production for a longer time.[58]

## Blunt Force Trauma

Blunt force trauma occurs when the body is suddenly impacted by an object with great force. Breast tissue can be damaged, such as during a bad car accident when a seat belt across the chest crushes the breast and causes bruising. Damage from blunt force trauma may be intensified in young girls and teens whose breasts haven't started or completed development. Imagine dropping a rock on a flower and then dropping the same rock on a flower bud. The fully bloomed flower may be bruised, but not all of it will be harmed. The bud, however, is smaller and more completely crushed, and it may never bloom normally. The potential damage to breast tissue before and after puberty is similar, but each case is individual. If the side you were hurt on has lower milk production, your injury is a likely cause of the problem. This may be a permanent condition, but most nursing parents should be able to make enough milk with the undamaged breast to compensate. You may find that the higher-producing breast becomes larger because it is doing most of the work. It's a temporary inconvenience that will gradually diminish throughout lactation and weaning.

## Burn Trauma

Damage to the breast tissue from burns on your chest varies depending on when it happened, how deep the burn went, and the extent of scarring. If the burn wounds were superficial, scarring is probably the biggest problem, with possible blockage of the nipple pores and poor elasticity of the skin that can make latching more difficult. Deeper wounds may destroy milk-making tissue. Burn injuries to a young girl's chest can damage the undeveloped gland and prevent normal growth later on. A lactation consultant can help you strategize and work around the damage as much as possible.

## Muscular-Skeletal Problems

A variety of situations ranging from accidents to repetitive motions can result in subtle muscular-skeletal problems that can affect nerves and obstruct lymphatic and blood flow, resulting in areas of numbness, tingling, or other unusual symptoms. This may reduce the sensations that trigger hormones, or a kink elsewhere in the nerve pathway might prevent messages from getting to the brain. If you've had such symptoms and your milk supply problem doesn't seem to have another cause, it may be worth exploring the possibility of a mechanical interference with an osteopath, a chiropractor, a doctor of Chinese medicine, or another holistic practitioner.

## CHAPTER 11

# Is it My Hormones?

In the female body, sex hormones cycle up and down on a monthly basis, climbing higher and higher during pregnancy, then dropping and flattening out during lactation. With all these fluctuations, is it any wonder that we might be more prone to hormone problems in general?

This piece of the equation—the role of hormones in the milk-making process—is often overlooked by health care providers yet is one of the most important links. The body follows a "recipe" for making milk, and your hormones and their complex interactions are what bring everything together and direct milk production. If you haven't found your answer yet, you may find some clues here that will help you solve your personal mystery.

**The Milk Supply Equation**

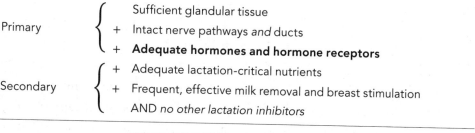

Primary
{
+ Sufficient glandular tissue
+ Intact nerve pathways *and* ducts
+ **Adequate hormones and hormone receptors**

Secondary
{
+ Adequate lactation-critical nutrients
+ Frequent, effective milk removal and breast stimulation
AND *no other lactation inhibitors*

= GOOD MILK PRODUCTION

## Hormonal Issues: The Big Spider Web

Probably the most confusing and confounding aspect of trying to understand hormonal issues is the many complex interrelationships among conditions. Sometimes the question becomes, "Which came first, the chicken or the egg?" Is the hormone problem causing my low milk supply, or is it a symptom of another issue?

Hormones are complicated, interrelating like the many threads of a giant spider web. They can affect their own receptors, other hormones, and other hormone receptors. The timing of an imbalance can determine whether lactation is affected or not. For instance, problems with key hormones during the critical window of puberty could alter breast development.

Certain conditions that affect various mammary gland and lactation hormones will be discussed individually in this chapter, but it also helps to look at the big picture as you try to understand what may be askew in your body when milk production doesn't seem to be working right. A problem with any of the three major milk-making hormones—prolactin, insulin, and cortisol—could certainly throw a monkey wrench into your milk production machinery. However, thyroid hormones have direct influence over breast development and milk production, and androgens (male hormones) can have a negative effect if they are out of balance. If there's a problem with oxytocin, it could cause a decrease in your ability to release milk, which can then lead to decreased milk production.

The receptor side of hormone function has also been a neglected element in the *Milk Supply Equation*, yet having a receptor problem is the same as not having enough hormone because the hormone can't get where it needs to go. Insulin resistance, the underlying cause of gestational diabetes and type 2 diabetes, is an example of a concerning receptor problem that you'll be learning more about later. As you read through this chapter, keep an open mind to all the possibilities of what may be affecting your own supply.

## Prolactin

Prolactin is the queen of lactation hormones; without it, you can't make milk. Any problems with prolactin or its receptors has the potential to muck things up. Two logical questions that follow are, "How much prolactin do I need to make milk?" "What is the right amount?" These are great questions that aren't easy to answer. When researchers tried to pin down a normal range of prolactin for lactation, they discovered that the numbers were all over the map.[1] It is believed that the more prolactin receptors a person has for prolactin to bind to, the less will be left in the blood to measure. This is likely why mothers on their second or more baby have less measurable prolactin in their blood: they've had more time to develop receptors with earlier babies than first-time mothers.[2] Nevertheless, parents with higher prolactin levels during pregnancy and lactation *in general* seem to breastfeed longer than those with lower levels.[3,4] If your prolactin is low despite feeding often *and* you have low supply, prolactin becomes a key concern.

Beyond being a first-time or "repeat" mother, another important factor is how well and how often milk is taken out of the breast. A baby who sucks well stimulates a stronger prolactin surge than a baby with a weak suck.[5] A baby who suckles often provides lots of surges. The more frequent and strong the surges, the more prolactin will be in your system, available to make milk. Think about medications—some you take once a day, or twice a day, or more. Prolactin clears your system in about 3 hours; a baby who nurses well every 3 hours or less (more than 8 times per day) is going to keep your baseline prolactin higher. The same applies to pumping and milk expression: you need frequent, good-quality suction to maintain a sufficient amount of prolactin. Doctors urge us to be sure and take our medications regularly and not to skip doses so that we get well faster; feeding/pumping regularly and not skipping sessions keeps prolactin higher and helps us make the most milk possible.

## Low Prolactin (Hypoprolactinemia)

A true deficiency in prolactin is considered rare, largely because there are only a handful of documented cases.[6,7] However, it may not be rare so much as under-identified, simply because it hasn't been on many people's radar.[8] Low prolactin isn't life-threatening, so few health care providers take the time to rule it out.

Despite this, in a couple of intriguing cases, a lack of milk production was pinpointed to extremely low prolactin levels due to prolactin-specific autoimmune antibodies. Who would've guessed? This is a good example of how the more we look, the more we're going to learn.

It's been suggested that women with a history of pituitary problems who want to breastfeed should have their prolactin measured in the 3rd trimester of pregnancy or around the time of birth to know what to expect and so they can strategize in advance if a problem is anticipated (more on this in Chapter 19).[6]

Some other risk factors for prolactin-related breastfeeding problems:

- Cranial radiotherapy (CRT) treatment for childhood cancer.[9,10]
- Mothers with a *family* history of alcoholism had smaller prolactin surges during breastfeeding and may need to nurse more frequently to compensate.[11]

- Women with a body mass index (BMI) greater than 26 before pregnancy had smaller prolactin surges the first week.[12]
- *Sheehan's syndrome* (rare; see Chapter 8). Prolactin and milk production can be moderately to completely suppressed.[13]

Addressing low prolactin caused by breastfeeding or pumping problems should help milk production. But when there isn't a clear explanation, prolactin-stimulating drugs or herbs may be beneficial (see Chapter 14). If the pituitary is unable to respond to these treatments, replacement prolactin—*recombinant human prolactin*—would be the logical next step and worked well in early research.[14,15] Sadly, the development of this promising therapy was shut down due to lack of research funding and because the manufacturer discontinued it in the belief that there was little need for it. We fervently hope that this changes in the future because replacement prolactin is the *only* possible solution for some parents. Until then, galactogogues such as domperidone or moringa that stimulate prolactin secretion may help to a limited degree (see Chapter 14).

## High Prolactin (Hyperprolactinemia)

It's normal for prolactin to be high when you're breastfeeding, but not in the absence of a pregnancy or baby. *Hyperprolactinemia* (greater than 25ng/ml) can be caused by a number of things, including prolactin-stimulating medications, pituitary tumors (prolactinomas), hypothyroidism, head injuries, radiation of the pituitary, empty sella syndrome, Cushing's disease, and Addison's disease, but sometimes the source is never pinpointed. Those affected often experience suppressed ovulation, irregular menstrual cycles, and infertility.[16] Some also produce milk (*galactorrhea*), leading to the false assumption that breastfeeding will be easy for them.

So how can having too much prolactin cause problems with lactation? High prolactin suppresses ovulation. Becoming pregnant often involves treatment with prolactin-suppressing drugs such as bromocriptine or cabergoline. Stopping the medication once pregnancy is confirmed provides the best chance of a normal milk supply since prolactin *needs* to rise during pregnancy. If radiation or surgical removal of a tumor is necessary, this may affect the ability of the pituitary to respond to pregnancy and lactation. Some experts suggest checking prolactin every trimester during pregnancy and every 3 months afterward to ensure that all continues normally.[17]

Beyond the impact of treatment, there's another way that hyperprolactinemia may throw a monkey wrench into the milk factory machinery. Prolactin comes in three sizes: "regular" monomeric prolactin, which is the most common (80-90%) and active form,

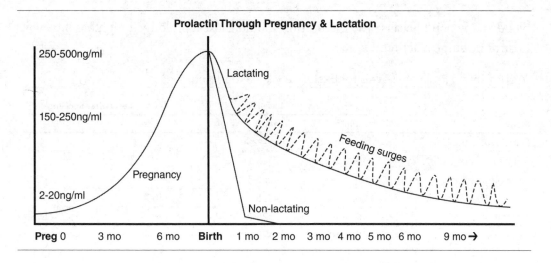

**Prolactin Through Pregnancy & Lactation**

and the less active "big" dimer and "big-big" macroprolactin. Women with high prolactin may have less of the regular and more of the low-active macroprolactin. Standard lab tests only measure total prolactin and don't distinguish these types, so you aren't likely to get this information. Research is currently underway to determine if this can affect milk production.

## Measuring Prolactin

Prolactin is tricky to measure and interpret because it varies depending on the age of your baby and the frequency of nursing. It's highest around birth and then declines over the next few months to a lower plateau. For *baseline measurements*, blood is drawn when there's been no nipple stimulation for 90-120 minutes. For *reactive prolactin*, the surge response to sucking stimulation is measured by drawing blood about 10-15 minutes after the end of a 20- to 30-minute breastfeeding or 15-minute double-pumping session. If you can only have one blood draw, the surge may be the better choice because you can see how much prolactin is actually released before the body starts to process it.

Standard lab reports typically list the ranges for nonpregnant, nonlactating female bodies. Some breastfeeding parents have been told that their baseline prolactin level was "normal" when in fact it was quite low for lactation because not all health care providers are familiar with changes during lactation. Baseline or surge, the following chart gives you an *approximate* idea of what to expect either way for lactation. Note: If testing is done while you are taking a prolactin-stimulating drug such as domperidone, you can draw blood at any point because the medication should cause a prolonged high baseline with little or no surge reaction.[18]

Approximate Prolactin Levels for Exclusively Breastfeeding

| Stage | Baseline | | Level after Suckling | |
|---|---|---|---|---|
| | ng/ml | mIU/L | ng/ml | mIU/L |
| Female menstrual life | 2-20 | 42-425 | | |
| 3rd trimester of pregnancy | 100-550 | 2128-11700 | | |
| Term pregnancy | 200-600 | 4255-12766 | | |
| First 10 days postpartum | 200 | 4255 | 400 | 8510 |
| 1 month | 100-140 | 2128-2978 | 260-310 | 5532-6596 |
| 2 months | 100-140 | 2128-2978 | 195-240 | 4149-5106 |
| 4 months | 60-80 | 1277-1702 | 120-155 | 2553-3298 |
| 6 months | 50-65 | 1063-1383 | 80-100 | 1702-2128 |
| 7 months to 1 year | 30–40 | 638-851 | 45–80 | 957-1702 |

**Collated from:**
Cox D, Owens R, Hartmann P. Blood and milk prolactin and the rate of milk synthesis in women. *Exp Physol*. 1996;81(6):1007-1020.
Lawrence RA, Lawrence RM. *Breastfeeding: A Guide for the Medical Profession*. 8th ed. Philadelphia: Elsevier; 2016:65.
López MÁC, Rodríguez JLR, García MR. Physiological and pathological hyperprolactinemia: can we minimize errors in the clinical practice? In Prolactin: InTech; 2013. https://www.intechopen.com/books/prolactin/physiological-and-pathological-hyperprolactinemia-can-we-minimize-errors-in-the-clinical-practice-. doi: 10.5772/54758

## Your Metabolic Profile

Metabolic health is evaluated by looking for high blood pressure, high blood sugar, higher waist circumference, low "good" high-density lipoprotein (HDL) cholesterol, and high triglycerides. Having *fewer* than two risk factors is considered healthy. In a small study of nursing parents trying to increase their milk, all those with poor metabolic health versus a quarter of those considered healthy experienced persistently low milk output (less than 10oz [300ml] per 24 hours) throughout the study.[19] Our metabolic health matters! Next we will examine some of these factors in more detail.

### Overweight and Obesity

It's no secret that overweight and obesity are now epidemic. Diet and lack of exercise are common underlying reasons, but there are metabolic disorders such as hypothyroidism and polycystic ovary syndrome (PCOS) that also cause weight gain. Whatever the reason, it is now recognized that nursing parents with high BMIs may struggle more to sustain lactation. What's new is that we're finally gaining an understanding of the mechanisms behind the problem, both physically and psychosocially.[20]

### Physical Impact

On a physical level, the earlier excess weight is put on, the more potential for problems.[21] Obese mice developed large mammary fat pads (think breasts) during puberty, but the milk ducts were abnormal, and there were fewer of the milk-squeezing myoepithelial cells for letdown,[22] something that was also seen in breast tissue samples from obese women. (On the good side, some of these effects were reversed with weight loss in the mice.[23]) Excess fatty tissue in the breast can also camouflage hypoplasia.

Both certainly would help explain how someone can have large-appearing breasts and yet not make lots of milk; they simply may not have enough well-functioning glandular tissue inside. We've also seen that high BMI parents with poor milk production report less breast size *changes* during pregnancy than those who made enough milk,[24] which means their glandular tissue likely did not respond to pregnancy as much as expected. Meanwhile, having fewer muscle cells to squeeze the milk to the nipple might explain in part why some of those large breasts seem to have a slower milk flow.

### Hormonal Impact

Excess body fat changes our hormones, too. When prolactin was tested in both high and normal BMI parents after birth, their levels were the same right after delivery. However, the prolactin *surge* during breastfeeding in the first week was lower in those with a higher BMI, causing concern for their ability to maintain sufficient milk production over time.[12] In obese rats, prolactin *resistance* impaired lactation performance by preventing prolactin from doing its job.[25]

Being overweight also raises the risk of insulin resistance and diabetes, which can directly impact milk production.[26] Some overweight parents may have high androgen (male hormone) levels, which potentially could affect breast development and milk production as well,[27] and the estrogen dominance that may occur with more body fat might also have an inhibitory effect (see bit.ly/MMM-Estrogen).

If you believe that your breasts did not develop properly during puberty because of early weight gain, this is a tougher situation. But if the weight gain came after that or even during pregnancy, anything that you can do to lower your weight has a good chance of improving your metabolic health and, with it, your milk production. In the short-term, if your breasts drain slowly, compressions during breastfeeding and breast massage and expressing leftover milk with your hands will be your first line of defense. After this, galactogogues may help also, but it depends on your individual weight and health issues.

### Psychosocial Impact

Beyond the physical factors are the more intangible but equally important psychosocial issues of low self-esteem, shaming, and discrimination. Parents with a high BMI are not always comfortable with exposing their bodies and may not want to nurse in front of others, even at home. They are more likely to be harassed and therefore less likely to breastfeed in public, reducing nursing and milk removal opportunities that can contribute to less milk over time.

Professional discrimination can be another serious barrier if your health care provider is more focused on fat than on what you need help with—namely, making more milk.[28] Sad but true, some parents' concerns are overlooked entirely when their provider chooses to address fat only rather than the breastfeeding problem, which may or may not be related! The delay in obtaining help, whether from reluctance due to shaming or simply having your requests put off, can lead to more damage to your supply before having the opportunity to turn things around.

If this has been your experience, don't give up; keep looking for someone who is interested in supporting and helping you with breastfeeding.

## Insulin and Diabetes

The breast is a major consumer of insulin, a key hormone that plays a role in mammary development and milk production. Insulin receptors in the breast are somewhat resistant during pregnancy, but become very sensitive to insulin when it's time to start up the milk factory. Diabetes is a disease in which the body either does not produce enough insulin or has difficulty using it. There are three types of diabetes mellitus: type 1, type 2, and gestational (pregnancy) diabetes.

### Insufficient Insulin: Type 1 Diabetes

*Insulin-dependent diabetes mellitus* (IDDM), also known as type 1 diabetes, occurs when the pancreas is unable to manufacture enough insulin to meet the body's needs. As a result, additional insulin is required to make up the deficit. During pregnancy, both prolactin and human placental lactogen can be lower in type 1 diabetic individuals, possibly affecting breast tissue development and lactation. As milk production increases after birth, the body's metabolic needs change dramatically, and insulin requirements may also change. Depending on how quickly medication adjustments are made, this can slow the increase of milk production for up to 24 hours.[29] Any significant fluctuations in insulin can cause a decrease in milk production at any time during lactation, so tight control of blood sugar will help to maintain consistent milk production. Insulin therapy is safe for lactation because the molecule is too large to pass into the milk. People with type 1 diabetes also have a higher risk of developing hypothyroidism, another issue described in this chapter.

Much of this information comes from studies conducted before more recent advancements in treatment. In a more current Danish study, type 1 diabetic mothers breastfed for a shorter amount of time than non-diabetic mothers. But the most predictive factors for problems were delivering before 37 weeks, c-section, mother's age, and whether breastfeeding was established by the time of discharge from the hospital, *not* diabetes status![32] The most likely reason is that early deliveries and c-sections are more common in diabetic pregnancies, and these things impact the early days of breastfeeding. Lots of support, including minimal separation after birth and early, frequent nursing, can give you the edge when you have type 1 diabetes.

### *Insulin Resistance: Type 2 and Gestational Diabetes*

With type 2 or *non–insulin-dependent diabetes mellitus* (NIDDM), the body can make insulin but is not able to use it well due to a problem with receptor binding. The resulting *insulin resistance* creates a "rusty lock" effect that makes getting enough insulin and glucose into the cells more difficult. The body's response is to compensate by increasing insulin production further, resulting in *hyperinsulinemia*. Brown, velvety patches of skin located around the neck, armpits, inside the elbows, or even under the breasts—called acanthosis nigricans—are symptoms of insulin resistance, while the growth of multiple skin tags can be a sign of hyperinsulinemia.

Although genetics and chemical exposures can play a role in the development of insulin resistance and type 2 diabetes,[31] diet and weight are common underlying causes. This is the reason diet changes and/or weight loss are frequently used to control the condition. When this is not enough, oral medications such as metformin may be used. If the effort of overproducing insulin burns out the pancreas, insulin treatment eventually may be required.

You don't have to be overweight to be insulin resistant, however; some families simply have a higher genetic risk. It's also possible to have a normal BMI, but the way the fat is distributed (belly versus all over, sometimes referred to as TOFI—thin outside, fat inside[32]) is a clue to possible insulin resistance. More exercise and changing the foods you eat—less of the bad carbs and sugars and more whole foods and fiber-rich carbs along with good sleep—are typical starting recommendations for treatment.

Insulin receptors in the body naturally become a little more resistant than usual during pregnancy, but when they become *too* resistant, a temporary form of type 2 diabetes called *gestational diabetes mellitus* (GDM) can occur. If you were overweight before conception, gained a lot of weight during pregnancy, have PCOS, or have a family history of type 2 diabetes, you're at higher risk of GDM. The condition usually improves in the weeks after delivery, but mothers who've had GDM are also at higher risk of developing type 2 diabetes later in life.

We've suspected for a while that insulin resistance could slow lactation and it has now been confirmed. Ground-breaking research discovered that the main difference between those whose milk production started to increase around 34 hours after delivery versus those whose milk didn't increase until 74 hours was good versus sluggish insulin activity.[33] When they investigated parents struggling with milk production, those who were more insulin resistant were also making the lowest amounts of milk.[34]

We've also learned that in parents with GDM, higher fasting glucose, hemoglobin A1C, and BMI (over 34) all increased the risks of breastfeeding ending sooner than desired.[37] *Even mild glucose intolerance during pregnancy below the threshold for diagnosing gestational diabetes* increased the risk of premature weaning.[36] Higher BMI and insulin resistance have also been linked to less breast growth during pregnancy and "shorter lactation."[24] This is alarming news, but it explains the struggles that some parents face.

How diabetes is treated during pregnancy may affect lactation as well. A Danish study compared breastfeeding outcomes for parents with type 1 and 2 diabetes. In that country, it is standard to treat type 2 and GDM with insulin during pregnancy rather than diet or medication, regardless of the severity of the condition. Contrary to what everyone expected, those with pre-existing type 2 diabetes breastfed only half as long as those with type 1 diabetes.[37] This raises the question of whether giving insulin for type 2 and gestational diabetes fails to correct the underlying problem that affects milk production.

*For low milk production related to insulin resistance*, the first priority is to address the underlying cause. In the long-term, this may involve lifestyle changes concerning diet, weight, and overall physical health. In the short-term, certain medications, supplements, or herbs may be beneficial. Talk to your health care provider about your suspicions and the best options for your situation.

Research is underway to see what effect metformin, a common medication for type 2 diabetes, may have on lactation. Over the years, we've heard varying stories of modest to large improvements in milk production. In a small study of mothers with low milk production, those treated with metformin did not experience much increase but were able to sustain their current level of milk production, while those who were not treated experienced a decline.[38,39]

You might be wondering whether taking metformin during pregnancy, rather than waiting for a problem to become apparent after birth, might help the milk factory get off to a better start. This question was explored in the same study that looked at breast size changes; mothers with PCOS were either given metformin or no treatment during pregnancy. No differences in how long they breastfed were observed between the groups.[26] *However*, the researchers also didn't report whether these mothers had insulin resistance or not, and they excluded mothers who were diabetic or had high glucose at the start of the study, the very group who would likely benefit the most from treatment. Metformin is frequently used to help women conceive and then to control blood sugar and reduce complications during pregnancy. Infertility specialist Randall Craig, MD, reports that mothers in his practice who needed metformin for conception and stayed on it throughout pregnancy and into lactation seem to have better overall glandular development and milk production. It just makes sense that helping the body to function better during pregnancy might help the milk factory run better after birth, though at this time it has yet to be proven.[39]

But here's a wrinkle: the American College of Obstetricians and Gynecologists (ACOG) issued a practice bulletin in 2018 supporting insulin therapy over oral antidiabetic medications for gestational diabetes, though they acknowledge that metformin is acceptable.[40] ACOG's recommendation doesn't take into account the possible negative effects of insulin therapy on lactation discussed earlier, so parents may not be given a choice depending on their health care provider's treatment preference.

During lactation, very little metformin passes into your milk, so it is considered safe for breastfeeding.[41] But it is not for everyone. Metformin can cause stomach pain, nausea, or diarrhea in some people who just cannot tolerate it, and because it can deplete vitamin $B_{12}$, supplemental $B_{12}$ with annual monitoring of levels is usually recommended. Metformin may not be metabolized as easily by those with *MTHFR* gene mutations.

A more natural alternative to metformin currently being explored is inositol, a family of naturally occuring sugars found widely in nature, especially in fruits and beans. Myo-inositol and d-chiro-inositol play specific roles in the use of insulin in our body, and an imbalance between them is associated with insulin resistance.[42] Correcting this imbalance has become the focus of new therapies for diabetes and PCOS, either with myo-inositol supplementation alone or a special 40:1 combination of myo- and d-chiro-inositol.[43] Best of all is that side effects of inositol are rare and mild. No one has yet reported trying this to improve their milk production, but the potential is promising, and research is starting to look at inositol for use during pregnancy as well.

Anything that helps insulin resistance should boost the efficiency of your milk factory over time, all other things being equal. Cinnamon improved insulin resistance in women with PCOS who took 1.5g (about ½ teaspoon) per day for 12 weeks,[44] though other research seems to go both ways. It's tasty and easy to throw into a smoothie or your oatmeal. Resveratrol, magnesium and chromium also seem to help insulin resistance.[45-47] While they can be found as supplements, look for them in their natural food sources as well. (Note: Due to anecdotal reports of mothers who started taking magnesium alone as a supplement and then experienced a drop in their pumping output that rebounded only after they stopped, it is suggested that magnesium be taken in a combination such as with calcium to counter or neutralize potential effects on lactation.)

Some of the most popular herbal galactogogues also have "antidiabetic" properties. Fenugreek has been used in many cultures for this purpose, while metformin was originally developed from galegine, which is found in goat's rue. (See Chapter 14 for other antidiabetic galactogogue herbs.)

If you believe that insulin resistance may be affecting your milk production and are feeling a little overwhelmed by all of this, you are not alone. A need to make more milk may have brought you to this book, but there's more at stake: your health. Addressing blood sugar and insulin resistance issues could help milk production and definitely should help your long-term health. Beyond this, research suggests that breastfeeding may contribute to a healthier metabolism.[50] Dr. Alison Stuebe explains that pregnancy changes our metabolism to store more fat temporarily and that lactation switches us back to burning that fat. Breastfeeding may help to "reset" our metabolism[49] as well as reduce your risk of developing type 2 diabetes later in life.[50]

## Infertility

A long-standing assumption has been that if someone can become pregnant, they should be able to breastfeed. We now understand that this is not always the case; those requiring assisted reproductive technology are at risk for "early termination of breastfeeding."[51,52] Causes of infertility vary, of course. When it's related to an underlying hormonal issue on your side, there is potential for interference with breast development before or during pregnancy or with the milk-making process after delivery. Quite often infertility treatments don't directly correct a problem but "leapfrog" over it to achieve pregnancy. The breasts are ignored, yet they may be missing some of the materials needed to build your milk factory. If you had difficulty getting pregnant and haven't found any other reasons for your low milk production, try to learn as much about the cause of your infertility as possible. Any clues you collect could give you a starting point for what might be wrong and then what you might be able to do about it, as you'll read next.

## Polycystic Ovary Syndrome

PCOS affects 5-15% of all women and is considered a leading cause of infertility.[55] Many parents with PCOS have plenty of milk and some even complain of overproduction, but at the same time, it seems that those with PCOS struggle with low milk supply more often than unaffected parents. There are a number of reasons why this may be so.

PCOS often causes higher levels of androgens, estrogen, cholesterol, and insulin, the last because of insulin resistance. It also causes lower progesterone when ovulation is infrequent and disrupts other reproductive hormones as well. Hypothyroidism may be present, especially with obesity or insulin resistance.[54,55]

These hormonal problems can cause a number of symptoms. Too many androgens can result in excess body hair growth, male-pattern balding, and persistent acne. Insulin resistance is common, and individuals with PCOS often develop type 2 diabetes in their 30s and 40s. Half are obese, which may be related to problems with carbohydrate metabolism. Infrequent ovulation is also common, in turn causing ovarian cysts, irregular menstrual cycles, endometriosis, infertility, and/or miscarriage.[56] Pregnancy complications such as hypertension, gestational diabetes, preeclampsia, and preterm birth occur more often in women with PCOS, who also seem more vulnerable to depression as a result of their hormonal imbalances.[57] Because PCOS is a syndrome rather than a disease, every case is unique and any combination of problems can be found, making diagnosis tricky.[58] For this reason, some health care providers skip the formality of a diagnosis and simply treat the patient's individual problems and symptoms.

A connection between PCOS and milk supply problems was first proposed in a case study of 3 mothers with low milk production and common symptoms of PCOS.[29] Most researchers have overlooked the breast in lactating parents with PCOS, but over the years a few have written about underdevelopment of the glandular tissue within the breast, underdevelopment of the outward appearance of the breast, or both. They also mention women who had very large breasts that "simulated excessive growth" yet were mostly filled with fat rather than glandular tissue.[60] *These findings don't apply to everyone with PCOS*, but they're significant for PCOS parents with lactation problems.

If PCOS symptoms start very early, before or around the time of the first menstrual period, the breast development that normally happens during puberty may be affected, resulting in hypoplasia. But even if the breasts developed normally, hormonal problems could still interfere with normal pregnancy breast changes, resulting in insufficient glandular growth for breastfeeding. It's also possible that sufficient glandular tissue may be present, but hormonal problems are interfering with the milk-making process.[61-63]

When researchers first looked at PCOS and breastfeeding, they were unable to confirm a connection to low milk production.[64,65] But they did observe some relationship between higher levels of androgens at mid-pregnancy (testosterone, androstenedione, the free testosterone index, and DHEAS [dehydroepiandrosterone sulphate]) and duration of breastfeeding, though that evidence has been contradictory.[27] What we *have* learned is that within PCOS, the risk of lactation problems seems to be higher when someone is overweight, obese, has high blood pressure, and/or is insulin resistant.[66] Poor pregnancy breast growth is also more common in this subgroup and linked to a shorter duration of breastfeeding.[26] While obesity and insulin resistance seem to be the main factors,[26,67] not everyone with PCOS who has trouble making enough milk fits this description.[68]

If you have PCOS and you're struggling to produce enough milk, first make sure that you haven't overlooked the most common causes of low supply. Then, identifying and addressing your own underlying hormonal problems such as insulin resistance, high androgens, or thyroid problems is your best shot at improving your milk production capability. Patience is important. For some, working on weight loss may be part of a longer-term strategy to improve hormone imbalances that are causing problems. Pumping and galactogogues may help but aren't always enough. Metoclopramide is not a good idea for depression-prone individuals with PCOS because of its risk of inducing depression (see Chapter 14), but domperidone may help get more from your breasts.

Hannah's doctor was willing to try metformin for her low milk supply while they ran some lab tests. Within a few days, she noticed an increase, and the amount of supplementation her baby needed started dropping. One night she found herself waking her baby to feed out of discomfort, for the first time ever! When the lab results came back, her doctor reported that her A1C was normal but that continuing the metformin was reasonable because of her overall PCOS profile that included abdominal fat.

Metformin, which improves PCOS symptoms for many women even when they aren't clearly insulin resistant, has reportedly boosted milk production for some women modestly, some a lot, and some not at all, though research has not validated this yet. Dosages vary, typically starting at 500mg and working up to 1000-2500mg daily. If you've taken metformin previously, ask your doctor about trying the dosage that was initially needed to improve your symptoms. Metformin during pregnancy reduces the incidence of miscarriage, gestational diabetes, pregnancy-induced hypertension, and premature delivery[69,70] and may set the stage for better lactation.

As discussed earlier, inositol appears to work similarly to metformin and is being promoted as a more natural, lower risk remedy for PCOS and insulin resistance.[71,72] Berberine is another natural treatment being explored for PCOS that might be useful, though it is not a good choice in the early weeks after delivery.[73]

Goat's rue is one lactogenic herb that seems especially appropriate for PCOS-related low milk production. It contains galegin and is the herb from which metformin was originally developed. Saw palmetto is another herb reputed to reduce excessive body hair, a symptom of high testosterone, as well as stimulate breast growth and lactation. One PCOS parent who tried saw palmetto reported a tripling of their previously low milk production. Chasteberry has long been used for PCOS and for milk production, and a few PCOS mothers feel it has helped them, but it must be dosed carefully as too much may decrease prolactin. You can read more about these in Chapter 14.

## Thyroid Dysfunction

Thyroid hormones come from the butterfly-shaped thyroid gland in your neck and are vital to the proper regulation of lactation hormones. Thyroid function involves a complex interaction between the hypothalamus, pituitary, and thyroid glands. The hypothalamus uses thyroid-releasing hormone (TRH) to tell the pituitary when to release thyroid-stimulating hormone (TSH). This hormone directs the thyroid gland in the production of thyroxine ($T_4$) and triiodothyronine ($T_3$), which in turn control your metabolism. Any dysfunctions in this complex process can affect milk production.[74] Problems with your thyroid can be hard to detect and diagnose if the symptoms or lab results are not obvious and straightforward. They can also occur together with other conditions such as PCOS and even cause PCOS-type symptoms.

Thyroid dysfunctions generally fall into two main categories. *Hyper*thyroidism involves overproduction of thyroid hormones that is usually caused by overactivity of the thyroid gland. In *hypo*thyroidism, the problem is inadequate production of thyroid hormones caused by underactivity of the thyroid gland. *Postpartum thyroiditis*, or *postpartum thyroid dysfunction*, often doesn't show up until sometime after the baby is born. Only a little research exists on the effects of hypothyroidism and hyperthyroidism on human lactation, but animal research is providing us with some great insights.

### Hypothyroidism

Hypothyroidism is diagnosed when there are high levels of TSH and low levels of $T_3$ and $T_4$ (thyroid hormones), typically slowing metabolism and causing fatigue, constipation, weight gain, and even depression. Hashimoto's disease is the most common form, caused by the immune system attacking the thyroid gland. Deficiencies in iodine, selenium, iron, magnesium, coenzyme Q10, and possibly vitamin D can also reduce thyroid function.[75,77]

Hypothyroidism may exist beforehand but can also occur for the first time during pregnancy in a small percentage of people. Slightly lower levels of thyroid hormones are normal during pregnancy because some go to the developing baby. This isn't usually a problem, but if you're already hypothyroid, the additional burden can make your condition worse. Untreated or poorly controlled hypothyroidism can cause pregnancy-induced hypertension, preeclampsia, placental abruption, anemia, postpartum hemorrhage, and low birth weight. It may also reduce the amount of good fats normally manufactured during pregnancy for making milk after the baby comes.[78,79] For these reasons, hypothyroid nursing parents should be monitored carefully, and their medication may need to be increased during pregnancy. Until recently, it was believed that hypothyroidism affected only milk production, but rat research shows that it reduces oxytocin as well, impairing the letdown reflex. Without treatment, hypothyroid rats experienced premature involution of the mammary gland—the factory started to shut down early despite continued demand.[80,81]

Not all thyroid problems show up with the usual tests. Parents with low milk production and "low normal" thyroid levels may not be treated because their levels aren't considered low enough. Some whose TSH and $T_3/T_4$ are considered normal, even though they don't feel well, are eventually diagnosed with *subclinical hypothyroidism* after more thorough testing.[82] It can be difficult to find a provider who will pursue borderline cases, so you may need to be persistent. If you've been treated during pregnancy and now are having problems making milk, ask to have your thyroid checked right away—don't wait for your 6-week check-up. Thyroid hormone needs often decrease after birth, and if medications are not quickly adjusted, this can lead to fluctuations in your thyroid function and milk supply.

Treatment is the #1 strategy for addressing low-thyroid-related breastfeeding problems. If your health care provider is unaware that thyroid dysfunction can affect breastfeeding or is not sure if lactation is a reason to treat, the 2017 *Guidelines of the American Thyroid Association for the Diagnosis and Management of Thyroid Disease During Pregnancy and Postpartum* (bit.ly/MMM-Thyroid) is a good resource to share. Recommendation 74 states that thyroid function should be assessed when lactation is poor with no other obvious causes, while Recommendation 75 further suggests that because of the adverse impact of hypothyroidism on milk production and letdown, both subclinical and obvious low thyroid should be treated.[83]

Replacement of thyroid hormone ($T_4$) is the usual treatment, but we've learned from mothers that just because the medication returned them to the "normal population range" didn't mean that all was well. For some, their normal turned out to be different, and they did not produce enough milk until further adjustments were made.[84] For others, they still didn't feel right, and milk production did not improve until they switched to natural desiccated thyroid (from pigs), an alternate prescription treatment that contains $T_3$ as well as $T_4$.

Metformin is used to treat insulin resistance but surprisingly also seems to improve low thyroid without affecting individuals with normal thyroid function.[85] Myo-inositol coupled with selenium seems to have a similar effect.[86] Naturopathic physicians take a holistic approach and incorporate natural remedies such as inositol in their treatments.

Parents with low milk supply and low thyroid function should know that large amounts of both fenugreek and moringa reduced thyroid hormones in rats.[87-79] While eating moringa as a vegetable or fenugreek as a spice is not a concern, it would be wise to avoid larger amounts of either; choose a thyroid-supportive or thyroid-neutral galactogogue instead.

## Hyperthyroidism

An overactive thyroid is diagnosed when TSH is low and $T_3$ and $T_4$ are high, and it can cause accelerated metabolism, weight loss, jitteriness, and insomnia. The most common cause of hyperthyroidism is Graves' disease, an autoimmune disorder. Hyperthyroidism occurs less commonly in pregnancy (2 in 1000) than hypothyroidism.[90] If you were already hyperthyroid, you will usually experience improvement of your symptoms because baby takes some of your hormone, pulling you closer to normal. As a result, you may need less suppressing medication during pregnancy, though symptoms usually rebound shortly after birth. Poorly controlled hyperthyroidism in pregnancy can cause premature delivery, preeclampsia, and fetal growth restriction.

Studies of rats made severely hyperthyroid during pregnancy show multiple problems. First, while they had rapid mammary gland growth, they also burned up mammary fat stores before birth, affecting the amount left to make milk. Second, they had an early surge of prolactin before delivery but lower prolactin and oxytocin surges during lactation.[90] The milk came in quickly, but because of significant problems with letdown, little or no milk came out, depending on the severity of the hyperthyroidism.[91,92]

A case was reported in which a mother had a history of very little milk while developing Graves' disease in the weeks after birth.[93] Beyond this, there are no published human case reports, but we've informally documented some experiences. One mother became severely hyperthyroid (TSH 0.001mIU/L) during the pregnancy and experienced breast growth of multiple bra sizes. Her milk increased rapidly in the first 24 hours after birth. She became severely engorged, and neither baby nor breast pump could get milk out. Without answers, she ultimately had to stop breastfeeding.

Another mother came for a prenatal consultation to discuss whether she "could breastfeed this time around." With her first two babies, the milk came in quickly, and she also developed unrelieved engorgement, leading her to stop breastfeeding efforts after the first week. She had the same history of uncontrolled hyperthyroidism with each pregnancy. Based on the rat research, she was strongly encouraged to pursue control of her condition as soon as possible. A secondary plan was hatched to have oxytocin nasal spray on hand after delivery to see if this might help her letdown reflex. Unfortunately, both her obstetrician and the hospital IBCLC who were part of this support team were on vacation when she delivered, and without knowledgeable help, history repeated itself.

It must be mentioned that a few isolated cases of hyperlactation in hyperthyroid mothers have been informally reported as well. If occurring as postpartum thyroiditis, it's possible that increased metabolism may drive high production because the breast was not affected during pregnancy, but until we have more detailed information, we can't fully explain the paradox. Anyone experiencing problematic over-production should have their thyroid checked.[94]

If you suspect hyperthyroidism is affecting breastfeeding, your first strategy is identification and treatment. The *2017 Guidelines of the American Thyroid Association for the Diagnosis and Management of Thyroid Disease During Pregnancy and Postpartum* discusses the research above but stops short of recommending treatment because there is less information.[83] Don't let that deter you, though; the problem was formally acknowledged, and you can still make your case for testing and subsequent treatment. If letdown seems to be a problem, oxytocin nasal spray (Chapter 12) theoretically might help.

## Postpartum Thyroiditis

*Postpartum thyroid dysfunction* (PPTD) is an autoimmune disease that occurs in 3-8% of all pregnancies.[95] Type 1 diabetes or smoking triples this risk. Diagnosis of PPTD often takes time because it can take different patterns. It may start with hyperthyroidism that lasts for a few to several weeks and then switch to hypothyroidism that continues for a few to several months; this is often overlooked because symptoms like fatigue may be mistaken for normal postpartum adjustments.[96] In some cases, the hyperthyroid stage starts just days after birth, accompanied by severe hypertension. But PPTD can also start with hypothyroidism and change to hyperthyroidism, or it can stay just one or the

## Testing for Thyroid Problems

What's a normal thyroid level for breastfeeding? We don't know yet, and in fact, the question of what should be normal for reproduction is still under debate. Some experts lean toward tightening the range for thyroid-stimulating hormone (TSH) to 0.5-2.5mIU/L, noting that the miscarriage rate starts to increase when TSH rises above 2.5mIU/L,[1] but others would allow for 0.3-3.5mIU/L.[2] Either way, each individual has their own unique hormone profile that doesn't always fit the standards, so explain your concerns to your doctor and ask for an in-depth assessment.

other. When hyperthyroidism occurs first, PPTD is often not caught until the swing to the hypothyroid phase, which has more obvious symptoms. Even when postpartum hyperthyroidism is detected, many doctors will treat only the hypothyroid phase if it occurs.[83]

Galactogogues may be helpful but probably won't make much difference if the thyroid dysfunction isn't corrected at the same time. For herbal galactogogues, consider those that are reputed to support thyroid function or help with letdown (see Chapter 14).

## Autoimmune Issues

One of the emerging themes of illnesses in general is autoimmunity, a condition in which the body's immune system mistakenly identifies some of its own cells as foreign invaders and attacks them. We've discussed how certain autoantibodies can destroy the cells that make prolactin or cause hypo- and hyperthyroidism, all of which can affect lactation. Research is also linking low vitamin D with autoimmune thyroid disease associated with PCOS.[98] It may be that autoimmunity underlies some of the perplexing lactation problems we see, but more research needs to be done to determine this.

## Menstruation

Milk production can sometimes decrease before or during periods once cycles have returned, probably due to temporary shifts in hormones. But before jumping to the conclusion that your periods are causing your low milk production, keep in mind that the return of menstruation may actually be a *symptom* and not the main cause. A drop in the number of feedings a day, long periods of time without stimulation (such as your baby sleeping through the night), or weaker suckling reduces prolactin and can trigger the return of fertility and menstruation.[99] Hormonal birth control can also artificially induce periods in a nursing parent before she might otherwise have started. We don't understand all of the hormonal changes during lactation that cause the body to resume ovulation, but *one of the results of low production can be the return of menstruation.* Did your milk supply drop *before* your periods came back or after? If it decreased beforehand, then low production or a drop in prolactin triggered the periods, not the other way around. If it's consistently low, then your period isn't the likely cause.

This hasn't been formally studied, but lactation consultant Patricia Gima reports that a daily dose of a calcium and magnesium supplement (1000mg/500mg) has helped several of her clients, often within 24 hours. Try taking it 3 days beforehand through the first 3 days of bleeding , or just take it daily for good measure.

## The Age Factor

The relationship between age and milk production has often been debated but is much less studied. There are plenty of mothers in their later 30s or 40s (and sometimes beyond) who make lots of milk for their babies. On the other hand, there are also older mothers who have problems with milk production with no apparent explanation. Most perplexing are the cases of parents who previously breastfed other children and then find themselves facing inexplicable low milk production for the first time.

At age 42, 8 years after the birth of her fifth child, Laura gave birth to Chloe. For the first time in her life, Laura struggled with milk production. Her lactation consultant noted that Chloe's suck was weak, though it was unclear whether this was caused by not getting enough milk or because of a true sucking problem. Pumping and herbal galactogogues were begun, and milk production rose slowly but still not enough. Laura decided to try domperidone, and finally her supply reached and then surpassed Chloe's needs. It became clear over time that Laura's breasts weren't functioning as enthusiastically as they had with her other children and needed a boost.

In the past decade, a number of studies have identified older age (defined variously as over 30, 32, 35, or 38 years) as a risk factor for delayed lactation, which if tracked longer could also be persistent subpar milk production. On the positive side, research has shown that the fat content of colostrum in older mothers is higher[100,101]—a bonus for your baby.

A key question to ask first is, "What are the surrounding circumstances of my baby's conception and birth?" Is this your first baby after fertility problems or years of health or hormonal problems, or did you simply wait until now to have a baby for other reasons? If the new baby was conceived in the midst of long-term health or reproductive problems, those factors—not age directly—may be the culprit. However, the problem could also be the reverse: health or reproductive problems could be the natural result of an aging process that is now extending to milk production as well.

Another intriguing possibility is the effects of aging itself. Some researchers believe that hormone receptors become resistant to binding with their own hormones as we age. Could this be an issue when older nursing mothers experience low milk supply?

## Lactation Labs

The question often arises of whether there is a "Lactation Panel" of blood tests to determine problems. This doesn't formally exist (yet), but we've outlined hormonal imbalances that may cause problems in this chapter. That doesn't mean they should *all* be checked,

| | Reason to Check | Possible Tests | Levels |
|---|---|---|---|
| Prolactin | • Low supply with normal breast tissue and despite frequent feedings; no other risk factors<br>• History of hemorrhage, pituitary tumor, head injury | | *See prolactin table in this chapter* |
| Testosterone | • Excess facial or body hair, thinning hair of head, and adult acne indicate excess androgens that may not show up on tests | Free testosterone<br>Bioavailable testosterone | 0.06-1.08ng/dl (varies by age)<br>0.8-10ng/dl (varies by age) |
| Thyroid | • Personal or family history of thyroid problems<br>• Extreme fatigue (hypothyroidism)<br>• Unexplained weight gain (hypothyroidism)<br>• Unexplained weight loss and jitteriness (hyperthyroidism) | TSH<br><br>Free T$_4$<br>TPO-Ab (thyroid antibodies) | 0.5-2.5mIU/L is ideal<br>0.3-3.5mIU/L acceptable<br><br>0.7-1.9ng/dl<br>Negative is normal<br>*Acceptable levels during pregnancy vary* |
| Insulin resistance | • Family history of diabetes<br>• Recent borderline glucose tolerance test or gestational diabetes.<br>• Baby with high birth weight<br>• Persistent acanthosis nigricans indicates IR; testing is optional | Hemoglobin A1C<br><br><br>2-hr oral glucose tolerance test (OGTT) | Normal     4%-5.6%<br>Prediabetes 5.7%-6.4%<br>Diabetes    ≥6.5%<br><br>Normal, <140ng/dl (7.8mmol/L)<br>Impaired, 140-199ng/dl (7.8-11mmol/L)<br>Diabetes likely, >200ng/dL<br>*values different for pregnancy |

IR, insulin resistance; T$_3$, triiodothyronine; T$_4$, thyroxine; TPO, thyroid peroxidase; TSH, thyroid-stimulating hormone.

though. Breastfeeding medicine physicians approach the question by taking an in-depth health and lactation history and then ordering any lab tests based on suspicions that need to be validated or ruled out. The problem arises when your health care provider doesn't have the background to think this through—that's why we've included detailed information in this chapter. If you've identified possible problems, share the applicable information and ask for testing to rule them out. That's a fair and defensible request and more likely to happen than if you drag in a long list of hormones to check. Other than prolactin, please note that these numbers are based on non-pregnant, non-lactating women because we don't have much research to show whether they might be different during lactation.[102]

One last factor that is unlikely to show up in standard tests is the hormone-disrupting chemicals discussed in Chapter 10. It's possible that hormone function could be off due to chemicals that you've absorbed or ingested over time, interfering with your normal hormones and receptors.[103] When nothing else makes sense and especially if you know you've had exposures, it may be worth seeking testing and further help. This article has a good summary of the issues: bit.ly/MMM-Chemicals.

## What do I do Now?

If you identified yourself in one or more of the scenarios in this chapter or had lab tests indicating possible causes, you may be wondering, "What do I need to do next?" First, read the chapters on increasing milk production so that you know all your options; then discuss them with your health care providers. If one isn't interested in exploring them, find someone more sympathetic and knowledgeable who will. Then share this information with a skilled lactation consultant so they can help you sort through your options and decide which plan is best for you and your baby.

## CHAPTER 12

# Is My Letdown Reflex Letting Me Down?

I'VE GOT 25,000 HITS FOR LETDOWN. WHICH ONE
DO YOU WANT?

We tend to assume that having milk is the main issue, not getting it out. But what if you feel milk in your breasts but it doesn't seem to come out easily? There's no point in having a warehouse full of milk if you can't deliver it! And if goods in the warehouse aren't flowing out the door, the assembly lines will eventually slow or shut down, and the customer will complain. We're going to take a closer look at the components of milk delivery—things that can affect it both physically and psychologically and ideas to counteract interferences.

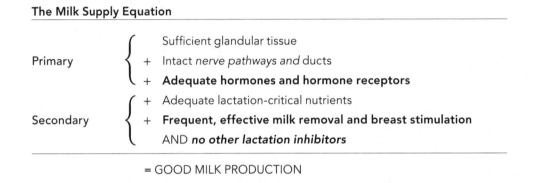

**The Milk Supply Equation**

| Primary | { | + | Sufficient glandular tissue |
| | | + | Intact *nerve pathways and* ducts |
| | | + | **Adequate hormones and hormone receptors** |
| Secondary | { | + | Adequate lactation-critical nutrients |
| | | + | **Frequent, effective milk removal and breast stimulation** |
| | | | AND *no other lactation inhibitors* |

= GOOD MILK PRODUCTION

## Letdown Reflex Under the Looking Glass

As described in Chapter 1, the letdown reflex starts with messages to the brain to release oxytocin, which is then carried through the blood to the breast. When oxytocin connects to receptors on the cells surrounding the milk sacs, it triggers a message for the cell to contract and squeeze milk down the ducts. Anything that interferes with oxytocin release, binding to its receptor, or the message pathway could affect milk delivery.

When there's a lot of milk, the letdown reflex is more apparent than when supply is low. Think of a water balloon: if you fill it up really full and then let go, the water will shoot out in a fast stream. But if there is a small amount of water in the balloon, it tends to dribble out more slowly because there isn't as much force. The more water stretches the balloon, the stronger the water shoots out when released. If you take a large balloon and a small balloon and fill each with a cup of water, which will squirt it out faster when you let go? The smaller one, because it's stretched out more. There are more nuances to letdown than this, but it's a fair starting explanation for why parents with low milk production may not feel their letdown reflex even though it is working.

This is an important point: *just because you don't feel it doesn't mean it isn't happening.* On the other hand, if the breast feels full yet the milk takes a long time to start flowing or it drains slowly, this raises a legitimate question about how well the reflex is working. If you feel or notice it more strongly on one breast or the other, chances are that breast is fuller. In fact, milk release does not occur uniformly across both breasts or even inside a single breast; rather, the fullest alveoli may be squeezed first, and others later on in the feeding.[1] Think of your warehouse as having multiple compartments; when one fills up, it will be the next to ship milk to your baby. Just because the milk stops flowing doesn't mean there isn't anything left; the alveoli just may not be ready to empty yet. One other frequently overlooked influence on letdown is the role of the baby. Strong sucking tends to trigger strong letdowns, while the breast does not respond as enthusiastically to soft or weak sucking. It's not always you![2]

## Physical Techniques to Help Trigger Letdown

### Nipple Stimulation

One of the first things to try is *nipple stimulation*. Gentle tickling, rolling, or pulling of the nipple can wake up the breast and get things moving. Oaxacan mothers from Mexico place the palm of their hand over the nipple and areola and then push in lightly while rotating several times before putting their baby to the breast. This makes perfect sense if you want to get the milk flowing for your baby.

### Warmth

*Warmth* is another great trigger and hot showers are famous for getting the milk to flow, though they may not always be convenient. Next to that, you can wrap your breasts in warm, wet towels. Alternatively, you can make a warm compress by filling a sock with uncooked rice and tying the end closed. Lightly dampen it and microwave for about 30 seconds until it is warm but not hot. Or you can buy a commercial breastfeeding compress. For some nursing parents, just drinking a glass of water or a cup of tea can stimulate letdown as well—both have been recommended for decades, if not much longer.[3]

### Reverse Pressure Softening

This technique, as described in Chapter 5, is another option that can be very effective, especially when the breasts are engorged or very full.

### Massage

Breast massage may also be helpful; research suggests that it most likely works on letdown,[4] though in a worldwide survey of breast massage techniques, it is used for both

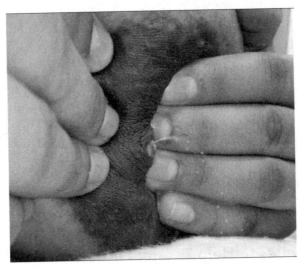

*Spraying milk as letdown is triggered by Reverse Pressure Softening.*

letdown and stimulation of milk production.[5] Lactation consultant Maya Bolman often taps the breast several times as part of her massage, which for some individuals seems to help with letdown more than massage alone.

There are also other points on the body that, when stimulated, seem to trigger the letdown reflex. As a kid, did you ever play a joke on a friend, running your fingernail quickly up their spine to give them the shivers? That can trigger the letdown reflex. Similarly, one mother discovered that when she leaned her back up against a cold wall, she would get the shivers, and her milk would letdown. An innovative study from India compared back and spine massage (neck down to buttocks) on mothers 4 times daily for 3 days starting 2 hours after delivery against regular postpartum care. Babies from the massage group transferred more colostrum or milk than babies from the other group.[6] Another Indian study tested back massage versus an herbal treatment in new mothers struggling to establish breastfeeding on the day after delivery and found greater improvements in the back massage group.[7] Who doesn't like a nice back massage? Sounds like a great excuse for a "spa day" for you and your baby with a professional masseuse. Or have someone massage your shoulders and walk their knuckles up and down your spine to help with letdown. Whichever you do, be prepared to feed or pump!

## Traditional Chinese Medicine

Traditional Chinese Medicine (TCM) is a non-Western therapy that can also be helpful. *Acupuncture/acupressure* points Shanzhong REN-17 and Jianjing GB-21, among others, stimulate the letdown reflex.[8] Reflexology, auricular and tuina therapy are variations of acupressure applied to hands, feet, ear, or by body massage and also have trigger points that coincide with stimulating oxytocin release. Some of these methods can be continued at home as well. Check out bit.ly/MMM-Letdown for a demo of acupressure points for letdown.

## Mechanical Adjustments

If you've had neck, back, or shoulder strain or pain from any cause, including a difficult birth, something as simple as a nerve impingement could be interfering with the letdown reflex. This problem is easily addressed by a good chiropractor or osteopathic physician. Janae first sought help for engorgement and breast lumps after her milk came in. Her baby would latch but wasn't getting much out. Therapeutic breast massage helped to soften the breasts, but milk still wasn't flowing well. When this failed to improve over the next 2 weeks despite good management, the lactation consultant became suspicious and suggested a chiropractic evaluation. The doctor found and treated significant nerve impingements in Janae's body. Within 24 hours, she started to "feel more milk coming down" and the need for formula supplementation dropped thereafter (see also Chapter 17).

## Mind vs Matter

Throughout history, our emotional state has been considered very influential on milk production. This is reflected in the popular proverb of many cultures that says, "Don't upset a nursing mother or her milk will dry up." Similarly, some have been told they won't make enough milk because they're too "high-strung." Then there's the favorite, "It's all in your head." While making milk is not *all* in your head, your thoughts and feelings *do* play a role in the bigger picture and fall under the *Milk Supply Equation* category of "no other lactation inhibitors."

The brain is wired in such a way that the nerve pathways for letdown run through the emotion-processing area of the brain. As a result, the responsiveness of your letdown reflex can sometimes be influenced by your emotional state or thought processes.[9] A positive example of this is how your breasts may start leaking when you hear your baby's cry. Your maternal instinct responds to this basic cue, ready to feed the baby in need. On the other side of the coin is the self-conscious new parent nursing in public for the first time. Worried about drawing unwanted attention, they may experience a delayed letdown, which may cause baby to protest and draw the very attention they feared.

Research on oxytocin, the hormone of letdown as well as love and bonding, is still in its infancy, but we're learning that not only is oxytocin released in response to both physical and emotional stimuli, it also influences other hormones and is in turn influenced by them. Oxytocin stimulates prolactin, and prolactin may also play a role in the release of oxytocin.[10] We don't know how important this interrelationship is, but it's possible that problems with oxytocin could affect production in subtle ways beyond milk removal.

As we explore the role of the mind, remember that your body is wired with overlapping "fail-safes" to help you succeed. In fact, frequent surges of oxytocin from breastfeeding actually have a calming effect, making us less reactive to stress. If lactation was as fragile as some people seem to believe, the human race would never have survived. *Nature wants you to succeed!*

## Potential Inhibitors of Your Letdown Reflex

Amy was a high school teacher who had planned ahead for her return to work. On her first day back, however, she called her lactation consultant in a panic when little milk came out during her first pumping session. Further conversation revealed that the curtains had been removed from her office during her maternity leave, and she felt like a fish in a bowl on display for all the students walking by. Uh, duh—no wonder she couldn't pump milk! Once they discussed how to create more privacy, the milk started flowing, and pumping was fine after that.

In this situation, Amy was worried that she was losing her milk, when in fact she was experiencing a temporary inhibition of her letdown reflex. Such short-term episodes aren't going to impact milk production. However, chronic long-term inhibition could reduce production over time because when less milk is taken out on a regular basis, less milk is made in the long run. Had Amy not fixed her uncomfortable environment, her milk supply might have been affected.

Unlike the more tangible physical or management-related causes of low milk production, the impact of psychological inhibition often lessens once the issues are identified. In most cases, it's possible to work through them by identifying or facing your stressors to understand them better and then making any necessary changes, such as Amy creating a more private environment. Even if the issues remain, understanding them will help you feel more in control, which may itself reduce your stress and allow the milk to flow more easily.[11]

### Chronic Stress

Stress is a normal part of life. While it may not be fun to experience, it heightens our senses through the release of cortisol and adrenaline to ensure our survival. Long-term stress, however, can take a toll on our body over time, which is why there is so much emphasis on stress-reducing activities in health promotion.

The amazing thing about breastfeeding is that oxytocin actually dampens the stress response and helps you cope.[12,13] When you're breastfeeding, you actually have a *lower* response to stressors than other people, nature's way of keeping you on top of your parenting game at a vulnerable time. Once again, nature wants you to succeed! At the same time, sudden periods of high stress can have a variable impact on breastfeeding; for some, milk production might actually surge temporarily because stress can stimulate prolactin,[14] while for others, the letdown reflex may be temporarily impaired,[15] making it feel like you have less milk. Most of these will resolve on their own as things settle back down.

For a few people, long-term stress can make breastfeeding more challenging.[16] It's so easy today to buy into the idea that you're one of many who "just can't make enough milk" when in fact life's circumstances—poverty, unstable relationships, depression—may affect oxytocin and play a role in some struggles.[17] Mindful awareness of your feelings and reactions can help you identify any issues that might be affecting your letdown.

### Pain and Negative Conditioning

Breastfeeding shouldn't hurt! Chronic or severe pain while nursing is an understandable reason for wanting to put off nursing. One parent told her lactation consultant, "I actually put my finger in to check her mouth—I was sure she had some sharp metal razor blades in there." No wonder she dreaded feedings even though she really wanted to breastfeed. The anticipation of pain can slow letdown temporarily, and inhibition can become chronic (negative conditioning) if breastfeeding is not fixed. When pain is an element of a low supply situation, it's time to get help.

### Birth Trauma and Posttraumatic Stress Disorder

Childbirth is good work, but it's hard work as well. At times, a difficult birth may become traumatizing due to any number of disturbing personal violations and even violence. *Any* severe psychological trauma that is related to the baby has the rare but possible potential to spark fear-related inhibition. Cynthia Good, a lactation consultant and clinical counselor who specializes in the emotional needs and experiences of breastfeeding parents, explains that someone may be traumatized if they felt intense helplessness, terror, or horror during birth because they feared for their own or their baby's life or if they experienced or witnessed serious injury during delivery. Birth may also bring back memories of abuse or assault in childhood or adulthood. Or labor and delivery may have been challenging and joyous—yet circumstances surrounding birth, such as a family tragedy, may still have left you feeling traumatized.

Posttraumatic stress disorder (PTSD) due to childbirth is estimated to occur in just a little more than 1% of Swedish and Dutch births,[18,19] while 3-6% and 9% of mothers in two US studies developed full-blown PTSD after delivery.[20,21] A striking difference between the two groups is that birth is treated as a normal event with few interventions in Sweden and the Netherlands, while in the US it is viewed more as a risky event to be managed, with a significant increase in interventions (and sometimes mistreatment). PTSD can occur alone or simultaneously with depression. It may also be confused with mood disorders such as generalized anxiety disorder. Because experiencing trauma is subjective and screening is not done routinely during pregnancy, labor, or after birth, caretakers may not realize that a parent has been traumatized, let alone understand how much time may be required for recovery.

Parents with PTSD related to childbirth may experience nightmares or flashbacks, reliving the traumatic experience again and again. Two frequent themes are the perception of extreme pain and a sense of loss of control. It's also common to feel emotionally detached from the event or family members and to be anxious and irritable, with outbursts of anger. Places and things that never bothered you before may suddenly trigger fear, putting you constantly on guard. Concentration and memory may be affected, and you may feel as if you are in a daze and life is not real. Emotions may be numb with little or no conscious love felt for your baby or other family members and friends. This may even extend to a vague discomfort when simply holding or nursing your baby. You may find yourself going through the motions of parenting but feel secretly relieved when others take over care of the baby. Or you may feel intense guilt for your detachment. Fearful of reliving the memories, you may avoid the place where the birth occurred and switch doctors. The normal lack of sleep that comes with parenting a newborn may be compounded by insomnia. Such symptoms may begin immediately or months or even years after the traumatic event.

Trauma of any kind, especially in the year before birth, increases the risk of early weaning.[16] Coping with the experience of a premature or very sick baby can also cause PTSD, and the stress is compounded for low-income minority parents, who may have lower oxytocin levels as a result.[17] Recognizing what is happening to you is the first step. Fortunately, treatments such as psychotherapy for childbirth-related PTSD have progressed tremendously. Look for someone who is knowledgeable about both trauma recovery and the importance of the breastfeeding relationship, and who will be committed to treating you and your baby as an inseparable unit. Certain complementary therapies may also be helpful, including acupuncture, mindfulness, and expressive writing.[22,23] *LactMed* or *Medications and Mothers' Milk* by Thomas Hale, PhD, are excellent resources for evaluating any medications that may be suggested. For a list of great resources on healing from birth trauma, see lowmilksupply.org.

### Grief and Loss

Shakara contacted a La Leche League Leader because her baby wasn't feeding well at the breast. She would latch easily and suck well but then fuss and didn't seem to get much, even though she was clearly full of milk. Shakara was encouraged to pump while continuing to work on breastfeeding and found that she was able to express plenty of milk, leaving the Leader to wonder why the baby was having such a hard time. Following a hunch during a follow-up call, she gently asked her how she felt about being a mother. Shakara burst into tears and poured out a story of feeling guilty and unworthy of her new baby because of an abortion she had when she was younger. They talked about her pent-up feelings, and a referral was made for more in-depth help. Several days later, Shakara called excitedly to say that her son had started feeding at the breast. To her delight, the milk had begun to flow easily, and she was now finally feeding happily at the breast.

The loss of a baby, whether by miscarriage, abortion, stillbirth, disease, SIDS, or accident, is a profound loss in anyone's life. In Shakara's case, she had suppressed remorse for a decision in her youth that was brought to the surface by the birth of her new baby, and that burden was subconsciously inhibiting her letdown reflex as a consequence. Once she acknowledged her hidden feelings and shared them openly, she was able to shed her burden and move more fully into her role as a nurturing mother.

Loss, especially that which occurs suddenly and without warning, can be a great shock. We all deal with traumatic experiences differently, and at times nursing parents have reported "drying up" that was more likely the inhibition of the letdown reflex. Such a reaction is usually temporary and doesn't have to mean the end of breastfeeding. The best thing is to keep your baby close as you grieve and process your loss. Well-meaning people may offer to take her in the mistaken belief that this will reduce your stress. What they don't understand is that babies can bring comfort and healing, and milk will soon flow again if nursing is maintained rather than put off.

### History of Sexual Abuse

This topic is often glossed over because it's not something we want to think about, but it has potential to affect breastfeeding. The following story illustrates the complexity of the human mind in coping with conflicting emotions.

Jenna contacted a lactation consultant while pregnant with her fourth child. With her other children, Jenna's milk came in, and her breasts felt very full, but the milk did not come out, either for the babies or a pump. So she fed them formula but wanted to give nursing one more try. While asking Jenna about her experiences with her other babies, the lactation consultant learned that she had not experienced spontaneous labor with any of them, requiring synthetic oxytocin induction each time. A previous consultant had raised the possibility that Jenna had an oxytocin deficit, but because laboratory tests for oxytocin are uncommon, this could not be confirmed. Further questions revealed that Jenna had experienced severe sexual abuse as a child that continued into adulthood with an emotionally abusive marriage. Jenna consciously worked very hard as a parent to overcome the effects of her nightmare childhood, yet it seemed clear that somewhere deep down, her mind and body were reacting to a past that she had not yet resolved. Once her baby arrived, the same scenario repeated itself. Jenna later sought counseling, and it was the opinion of her therapist, who had dual expertise in lactation and psychology, that the sexual abuse issues most likely did negatively influence her oxytocin release and letdown reflex and possibly affected her birthing as well. Hormone-releasing inhibitions as deep-seated as Jenna's are rare but do occur. Help for Jenna came after she had completed her family, but she wished she could have worked on these issues beforehand.

Unlike Jenna, who was very comfortable with the concept of breastfeeding on a conscious level, some parents are deeply uncomfortable with the intimacy of breastfeeding and may not realize that a disturbing past physical experience underlies the anxiety they now feel. If you've been sexually abused, your desire to give your baby your very best may be overshadowed by feelings of revulsion when she suckles at your breasts. You may also believe that your baby is rejecting you if she has difficulty latching or fusses when your milk flow is slow.

The experience of abuse may only be vaguely remembered. It may not even have been an actual sexual encounter so much as a physically threatening intimacy. In rare cases, a long-suppressed memory may stir up old feelings of threat or panic even though you cannot recall anything specific. Counseling may eventually reveal the underlying roots. A healthy breastfeeding relationship can help you become comfortable with intimacy and human touch again, providing the opportunity to work through feelings and experience a greater degree of healing.

### Abusive Partner

Anyone who is being battered or emotionally abused by a partner is also a trauma victim. During crisis, adrenaline begins to flow as the body goes into self-protective "fight-or-flight" mode. From nature's standpoint, your survival ranks higher than survival of a baby, and the body will inhibit other processes, including the delivery of milk, under such circumstances. When the danger has passed, milk will flow more easily again, but frequent battering could lead to chronic, extreme stress that in turn could affect milk production over time. Even more concerning, violence can escalate quickly, making escape difficult. If you are experiencing any kind of physical or emotional abuse, you *must* get help for your and your baby's safety sooner rather than later.

## Overcoming Inhibitions
### Create a Peaceful Space
Traditional cultures understand that breastfeeding works best in a calm, peaceful space. When you sit down to nurse or pump, try to minimize negative elements in your immediate surroundings. This may mean moving to a quiet room away from the rest of the family, especially anyone who is not entirely supportive of breastfeeding. Before you begin, take a few slow, deep breaths to clear your mind and body of any remaining tension. The influence of your environment on milk release is a factor that can change over time. Confidence is built with experience, and soon your mind will work effortlessly and efficiently in the busyness of day-to-day life.

### Relaxation
Relaxation techniques that helped you cope through childbirth can also help your milk to flow. There are two basic methods: physical relaxation and psychological relaxation. With the first, you concentrate on progressively relaxing all the muscles in your body from your toes to your scalp while breathing deeply. The resulting deep muscular relaxation calms and clears the mind of concern, worry, aggravation, and stress. The second technique starts with the mind, allowing the physical relaxation to follow naturally. Envision anything that gives you a feeling of peace and well-being, such as hanging out at the pool or beach.

### Guided Imagery, Meditation, and Hypnotherapy
When stress or fear is affecting letdown, relaxation therapy may help the milk to flow.[24] Listening to a guided relaxation audio recording created specifically for breastfeeding was associated with an increase in milk output in one study; the more sessions a parent listened to it per day, the more they pumped.[25,26] There are several audio recordings available that have been developed for this purpose: *Hypnosis for Making More Milk* by Robin Frees; *Letting Down* by James Wierzbicki and Betsy Feldman (Willow Music); *A Bond Like No Other* by Anji, Inc.; and *Breastfeeding Meditations* by Sheri Menelli. Or

search YouTube using the terms "guided imagery," "hypnotherapy," or "relaxation" with "breastfeeding," "pumping," or "making milk" for additional options. See Harnessing the Mind" in Chapter 17 for more information.

## Music

Listening to music can also help the milk to flow. In a small study of mothers of premature infants, milk output increased more over 4 days when they listened to music before and during pumping sessions than for those who did not.[27] In another study, mothers who listened to music right after delivery expressed more drops than those who didn't.[28] But when researchers studying mothers of premature infants compared standard breastfeeding support (group A), a verbal script for progressive muscle relaxation followed by guided imagery only (group D), the script + pre-chosen music (group B), and the script + music + pictures of their baby (group C) over a 2-week period, the results were surprising. Group C had the greatest increase in milk output followed by D, B, then A.[29] Group C also had more fat in the milk. Relaxation scripts and music were better than standard breastfeeding support, but pictures of their baby pushed the combo to the top. If the mothers had been able to choose their own music, this might have altered the results. This is one of those can-only-be-good-for-you things; use whatever combinations *you* find most relaxing. Read more about this at bit.ly/MMM-Music.

## Biofeedback

This technique trains users to relax and alter their reactions to stressors. One study developed a breastfeeding-specific protocol to see if it could help pumping mothers get more milk out. Out of 7 mothers, 5 expressed more milk during biofeedback, though it was not considered statistically significant.[30]

## *Distraction*

Talking to or texting supportive friends, reading books and magazines, and watching television while nursing or pumping can be wonderfully effective in facilitating letdown. When your mind is occupied by other activities, you aren't thinking about how much milk you are producing or how long the nursing or pumping session has lasted. They also help ease stress and relax your tension.

## *Visualization*

You can also learn to provoke letdowns by noticing what triggers them and then mentally picturing the trigger happening. For instance, if your baby's cry is a trigger for you, then imagine that you hear your baby crying to be fed. Some nursing parents find that a more abstract image, such as a waterfall, helps to trigger a rush of milk. The more vividly you use your imagination to re-create the physical or emotional sensation of the trigger, the easier it will become to stimulate letdown.

Visualization has been used to trigger letdowns even when primary nerves have been damaged. The mothers with spinal cord damage in that fascinating case described in Chapter 10 used mental imagery to induce letdown, resulting in significantly increased milk flow:

> One of them always breastfed in a quiet location that had no distractions. She began by counting to relax and then by mentally cycling through a series of images and thoughts that most commonly involved thoughts of loving and nurturing her infant. She reported recycling these image patterns several times in the months that she breastfed, because they became less effective if used for several days in a row. She also reported finding it useful to intersperse the periods of inducing [letdown] with a distracting task, such as reading or watching television. Finally, she reported becoming better at inducing letdown . . . such that she could tolerate some distractions.[31]

Notice that it took some experimentation, but she figured it out.

### Self-Talk

While learning to relax is an important part of helping letdown to happen, there are other ways to use your mind to get the same results. "Self-talk" is based on the principle that we all have an ongoing internal dialogue. For example, when waking up in the morning, we think, "I really don't want to get out of bed. I'm tired and I don't want to change one more diaper." Or at the end of an enjoyable evening at the movies, "That was fun! I should get out more often."

Self-talk can be positive or negative and is influenced by what we hear around us and choose to internalize. Negative self-statements are usually in the form of phrases that begin like these: "I just can't do it," "If only I could or didn't," or "I just don't have the energy." This type of self-talk represents the doubts and fears we have about ourselves in general and about our abilities to deal with discomfort in particular. In fact, negative self-talk can worsen symptoms like pain, depression, and fatigue.

What we say to ourselves plays a role in determining our success or failure in becoming good self-managers. Women whose mothers and grandmothers did not breastfeed may be less confident and more vulnerable to believing that they are doomed to fail at the first sign of difficulty.[32] Learning to make self-talk work for you instead of against you can help improve your mental frame of mind and ability to relax. Like all changes, this requires practice and includes the following steps:

- **Listen carefully to what you say to or about yourself, both out loud and silently.** Pay special attention to the things you say during times that are particularly difficult.
- **Work on changing each negative statement to a positive one** that reflects your potential, strengths, and capabilities. For example, negative statements such as "I'll never make enough milk" or "I can't pump all the time, so why bother?" become positive messages such as "My breasts were designed to make milk" or "I can pump 5 times a day, and that is really good."
- **Rehearse these positive statements**, mentally or with another person, as a replacement of those old, habitual negative statements.
- **Practice these new statements in real situations.** This practice, along with time and patience, will help the new patterns of thinking become automatic.

### Condition Your Letdown Reflex

Remember Pavlov's dogs? Because he fed them every day, they began to associate his entry into the room with food and would start to salivate in anticipation of a meal when they saw him. The letdown reflex can also be conditioned to respond to a stimulus that you create through a routine. After you experiment with the techniques above and find what works for you, keep doing it! Over time and with repetition, your body will begin to letdown in response to the trigger that works best for you.

## Matter Over Mind: Organic Problems with Letdown

Kristin's first breastfeeding experience was no picnic. Her baby had low muscle tone and suck problems, forcing her to rely on pumping to keep her production up and provide milk for her daughter. Despite her efforts, Kristin was never able to meet all of her daughter's needs. When her son was born and similar problems began to repeat, she started pumping again. But that first experience taught her something about her body—that her letdown reflex was slow to happen and sluggish when it did. If she depended on it alone, she could not pump enough milk, but if she used her hands to "wring out her breasts" for 30 minutes, she could extract more milk. Doing this, she eventually was able to express up to 40oz (1200ml) per day. Kristin had unusually long, elastic breasts that pulled deeply into the flange of the breast pump. No matter what she tried, her letdown reflex remained sluggish, and her hands were her most important tool.

## Thyroid Imbalance

Both *hypo-* and *hyperthyroidism* can disrupt oxytocin release and affect the letdown reflex (see Chapter 11). Childbearing-related thyroid dysfunction can pop up during pregnancy or anytime in the first year after birth. If you're also experiencing unexplained weight gain, weight loss, depression, or anxiety, and especially if there's a family history of thyroid problems, you might want to ask your health care provider to screen you for this.

## High Body Mass Index

One discovery from animal research is that high-fat diet-induced obese mice had fewer myoepithelial cells. The authors were concerned that this could lead to poorer letdown and lactation problems.[33] On the positive side, another related study discovered that weight loss could reverse some of these effects on the mammary gland, so all is not lost.[34] Whether there are fewer myoepithelial cells or simply longer, pendulous breasts, hand compressions while nursing will help you and your baby get the most milk out.

## Artificial Oxytocin

As mentioned in Chapter 8, prolonged use of oxytocin in labor may cause the body to temporarily stop releasing its own oxytocin, or it may cause overstimulated receptors to tire out and become unresponsive, or even to reduce in number. No one has looked at whether this could affect the letdown reflex, but if it does, the effect should be short term.[35,36] Use hand compressions in the meantime.

## Lactogenic Substances for Letdown

If the hormone system is having a problem, what about bringing some oxytocin in from the outside? Oxytocin nasal spray or drops have been used in the past, largely to help with overcoming stress-induced letdown problems. Most of the research has been done on mothers of premature infants on the assumption that stress inhibition of letdown is the reason for their lower milk yield. A Cochrane Review of studies before 2000 concluded that oxytocin nasal spray may be helpful at times.[37] If you feel strongly that your letdown reflex is impaired, oxytocin nasal spray is worth a try. It's not intended as a long-term treatment but rather a short-term jump start. Talk to your health care provider

## Oxytocin Nasal Spray for Letdown

When normal methods fail, oxytocin nasal spray may stimulate the letdown reflex. In the US, a compounding pharmacist can make it for you if you have a doctor's prescription. Pharmacist Frank Nice gives the following ingredients and directions:[38]

Nasal spray bottle = 2 or 5ml

Each milliliter contains:

**Oxytocin:** 40 USP units

**Preservatives:** chlorobutanol (0.05%), methylparaben, propylparaben

**Buffers:** citric acid, sodium phosphate, sodium chloride

**Vehicles:** glycerin, sorbitol, purified water

Use 1 spray in one or both nostrils 2-3 minutes before nursing or pumping. If results are not seen within 48 hours, it's time to re-evaluate.

about a prescription, then find a compounding pharmacy, either locally or online. Some parents are purchasing oxytocin spray online, but be aware that these products are not regulated. The actual content of the active ingredient can vary widely, and improper storage conditions can affect potency, with unpredictable results.

On the herbal side, *chamomile* is often recommended to stressed, anxious nursing parents because of its calming effects; drinking a cup of the tea may help with letdown, which in turn could lead to more milk. An article described the experience of a Portuguese mother who had been drinking 4 liters of water daily (recommended by her health care provider) but substituted 2 liters with weak chamomile tea when she grew tired of plain water. She would experience a boost in supply, pumping 90ml instead of 60ml, for the rest of the day.

Bach's five-flower homeopathic *Rescue Remedy®* has been recommended for a number of years to help with stress-related letdown problems. Retired lactation consultant Pat Gima recommends four or five drops under the tongue before nursing, or even better, putting a few drops in your water bottle to sip on throughout the day, plus drops under the tongue before a feeding. If you're tempted to use more than directed, don't; homeopathy works on the premise that a teeny bit is best for stimulating your body to do its job. More can be counterproductive.

Mechell Turner, herbalist, lactation consultant, and owner of Simply Herbal Organics, created Let-Down Formula, her own special blend tincture with black cohosh, shizandra berries, and motherwort. In the herbal galactogogue world, anything that is "contraindicated" in pregnancy due to concerns of stimulating contraction activity would be great for letdown.

Chapter 14 lists more herbs that are reputed to help with letdown.

## Moving Ahead

You can't make more milk if you can't get milk out. If there have been letdown problems, hopefully you now have a better grasp of why and what to do about it. This is important as you move to the next section on ways to make more milk, especially when expressing and pumping are involved.

# PART IV

# Increasing Milk Production

## Janelle's Story

I always had strangely shaped, tubular breasts, and during my first pregnancy they never enlarged. At 1 week of age, my daughter Hannah was well under her birth weight, and we made an urgent call to a lactation consultant. We discovered that I didn't have a lot of milk-making breast tissue, even though my breasts were long. I did make milk, but only a little—just ¼oz (8ml) per feeding. I started pumping immediately, along with taking goat's rue and More Milk Plus™ tincture every feeding. Every 2 hours, I nursed Hannah on each side, pumped for 10 minutes, fed her what I'd pumped, and then finished with formula. My milk production gradually increased, and I soon had enough milk to make it through night feedings with just me! At 2 months, because I breastfed very often and Hannah nursed willingly, we decided to stop pumping but maintain the herbs. By 3 months, I was down to two evening bottles, and at age 4 months, Hannah decided not to take a supplemental bottle at all. She continued to gain weight at the same pace and was a healthy baby. The work was hard, but the rewards were great!

With my second baby, I had high hopes that things would kick in right away, but again my breasts didn't grow, and my milk did not come in. I was so crushed, but I knew there was light at the end of the tunnel. I started pumping and taking the herbs, eventually replacing the More MIlk Plus™ with domperidone while continuing the goat's rue. It wasn't long before my milk supply was over the top and able to fill her little belly. Would I do it the same way all over again? You bet! I feel so fulfilled as a mother of two breastfed babies.

## CHAPTER 15

# *Move That Milk!* Pump It Up!

**Milk removal** is *the* most important principle of making milk. Remember demand and supply? We'll be talking about other milk-boosting options later on, *but if milk isn't being removed often and effectively, they're unlikely to help*. Your baby is the number one choice to do the job. If he isn't up to the task yet, you'll have to help out.

**The Milk Supply Equation**

| | | |
|---|---|---|
| **Primary** | { | **Sufficient glandular tissue** |
| | + | Intact *nerve pathways and* ducts |
| | + | Adequate hormones *and* hormone receptors |
| **Secondary** | + | Adequate lactation-critical nutrients |
| | + | Adequately frequent, **effective milk removal** and stimulation |
| | | AND no lactation inhibitors |

= GOOD MILK PRODUCTION

## Breastfeed More Frequently

Not breastfeeding enough is the number one cause of low milk production and the easiest to reverse. How often has your baby been nursing in a 24-hour day? Especially in the first few weeks, parents with vulnerable supplies shouldn't allow longer than 2-3 hours between daytime feedings or longer than one 4- to 5-hour sleep stretch each 24 hours. It's normal for a newborn to nurse *at least* 8 times in 24 hours. When milk production is low, feeding *more often* than this is nature's way of telling the breast that your baby needs

# Basic Strategy for Boosting your Milk Supply[1]

To stimulate higher production, increase the frequency and thoroughness of breast emptying:

- Watch infant feeding cues and offer the breast at the earliest signs of interest.
- Keep baby awake at the breast and encourage him to take both sides. Compress and massage to increase flow when he starts to slow down, or switch back and forth between sides to keep him active.
- Make sure that he breastfeeds *at least* every 2-3 hours during the day and 3-4 hours at night (*at least* 8-12 times in 24 hours; the more often the better). Keep any supplement to a minimum to encourage more breastfeeding.
- If your baby doesn't feed well at the breast and leaves milk he needs behind, express immediately after using hands-on techniques.

more milk. If you don't change anything, the breast won't change what it's doing, either. Would your baby nurse more often if you offered? The simple solution is to offer the breast more often and find out.

## Express to Plug the Gap

When your baby just doesn't want to nurse more often or as long as you need him to, or his suck just isn't strong enough to drive your supply, expressing milk can help fill that gap. *Your ultimate goal is to mimic normal breastfeeding*—frequent, thorough breast drainage. If this isn't happening sufficiently, expressing makes up the difference so that your breasts receive the messages that stimulate production. Milk can be removed by hand or mechanically with the aid of a breast pump.

## Hand Expression

Our hands are the original "manual pump" and can be very effective, especially in getting more cream out.[2,3] Hand expression is an art that comes naturally to some people but takes more practice for others. We strongly recommend learning this skill because it is the best way to extract colostrum and can also remove milk that a pump leaves behind.

There are some general do's and don'ts for how to do it, but techniques must be adapted for your particular anatomy. Do use a "C" hold and place your fingers a couple of inches back from the nipple base so that they are positioned over the milk ducts. Don't put your fingers on or near the actual nipple or pinch it, which would be like pinching a straw. Don't allow your hands to slide down the breast, where friction could cause a bright red "rug burn." Don't squeeze to the point of pain. Be patient as you prime the pump. Don't end up like Kim, who ruefully shared, "When I was beginning to express and hadn't learned how to do it properly, I wrung those boobs out like they were wet washcloths! I probably damaged some ducts."

You'll find a few different techniques being taught. The Marmet technique has been in use for many years; position your thumb above the nipple on top and your fingers below it, forming a C with your hand; push back into the chest wall and then roll your fingers together and forward. Pediatrician Jane Morton also recommends forming the C with fingers lined up with the nipple, pulling back toward the chest wall and compressing your fingers together and then relaxing: press-compress-relax. Lactation consultant Maya Bolman suggests positioning your fingers in a straight line with the nipple and then bringing the fingertips together while gently compressing or rolling the fingers behind the nipple. She sometimes also adds a finger from the opposite hand during compression to assist drainage from other areas of the breast. For links to explanations and video demonstrations, see lowmilksupply.org/hand-expression.

Whatever technique you go with, *massage the breast* for a minute or two first to trigger your letdown reflex. Maya adds kneading and rolling the breast between your hands along with fingertip tapping. Once you start expressions, it can take several compression cycles before the milk starts to flow so be patient; it's coming! Rotate your hand to

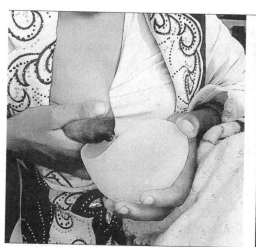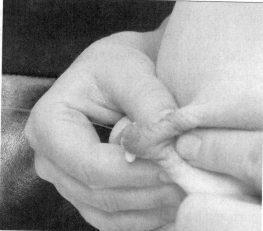

*Hand Expression: Place your thumb on one side and fingers on the other, lining up with the nipple; compress. Photo by Annie Aloysius. **Third Finger Technique:** As you compress, you can add a finger from your other hand to reach more of the milk glands at the same time. Photo by Maya Bolman.*

find the most effective placement, then express 10-15 minutes per side until the breast is drained and soft. When the milk flow subsides, stop and massage again to stimulate another letdown. Expressing into a soft plastic cup or bowl lets you aim into a large container that can be squeezed for pouring.

## Pumps

Pumping is often the first strategy recommended to increase milk production. It can be an excellent tool but isn't *always* necessary. If your baby is nursing often *and effectively* and is willing to do some comfort nursing, extra pumping may not be needed. Instead, supplementing at the breast or supplementing first and finishing at the breast may be adequate. But if your baby isn't nursing effectively or if he sucks only the short time that milk is flowing easily, pumping becomes the primary way to stimulate the breasts and send that "make more milk" message. Successful pumping starts with a quality pump, properly fitting flanges, and a good strategy for when and how long to pump.

### Choosing a Breast Pump

There is no one best breast pump, though certain models seem to perform well for more parents than others. The best pump for you is the one that fits you best and is both effective and comfortable.

#### Manual Pumps

The earliest pumps were single-side manual pumps, and there are many out there of varying quality. Virtually all are one-hand models, which makes pumping one breast while nursing on the other side an option. This also allows you to use a free hand to compress and get the most milk out. Most nursing parents will express more milk with a good electric pump, but there are always a few who prefer and seem to respond best to a manual pump.

One intriguing newcomer to the market is the Haakaa® silicone suction pump (preferably the smaller second generation model with a suction cup base). Rather than rhythmically cycling, you simply squeeze it and apply so that it virtually hangs on by itself. If you tend to drip milk from one side as you nurse on the other, this little gem can collect all that milk. *But be aware*— if your baby hasn't nursed that side yet, it may take out too much and leave him less, so you'd want to monitor that. It would be great for "clean-up," conveniently removing leftover milk from the first side while baby feeds on the second. (Note: If used for "clean-up," you might want to try hand expressing or pumping afterward to test how well it did before relying on a silicone suction pump alone.)

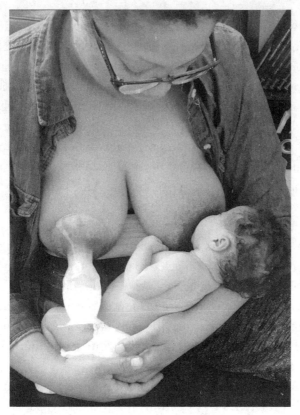

*Nursing on one breast while collecting milk from the second side with a silicone suction pump. Photo courtesy of N. Killings.*

### Electric Pumps

There are many brands of electric breast pumps available, some as rental and many for purchase. One thing to check out is whether they are open or closed systems because tubing is more vulnerable to moisture and mold contamination in open systems.

*Multi-user* "hospital-grade" electric pumps are built for both performance and endurance.[4] The top models are typically rented rather than purchased because they are expensive (US $700-2000), and rental rates are more affordable (US $40-90 per month, plus the cost of the kit). All models are auto-cycling and have adjustable vacuum suction and cycling speeds. Ameda's Platinum™ allows independent adjustment of suction and speed, while Medela's Symphony™ uses one knob, continuously linking lower suction to faster speeds and higher suction to lower speeds. Both are commonly found in hospitals and rental depots, though Ardo's Carum and Limerick's PJ Comfort® are challenging the place of the pioneer pumps and get good reviews. Occasionally, you may run across some of the older workhorse rental pumps—Ameda's SMB™ and Lact-E™ and the Medela Classic™ or their working-parent rental models, Ameda Elite™ and Medela Lactina™. They don't have all the bells and whistles and are larger and bulkier than the new generation of pumps, but they can do the job; in fact, some lactation consultants feel that the old workhorses are still the best for low supply even though they're being phased out. Gabrielle, mother of six, agrees: "My youngest daughter was born at 28 weeks, and I ended up pumping exclusively for months. At about a month postpartum, my supply dropped, and I couldn't keep up with her needs. I tried herbs, power pumping, sleeping more, but then a colleague suggested trying her old Ameda Lact-E™ and that made all the difference. Newer is not always better!"

*Consumer-grade* electric pumps are usually single-user and range from highly effective pumps that can last 1 or more years under heavy use to light-duty pumps intended for use a few times a week. Most must be connected to an outlet, though some have car-adaptor, internal rechargeable battery, or replaceable battery options. (Note: The pump may not be as powerful when running on batteries.) A few of the newest models now come with Bluetooth tracking technology that records your use, some claiming even to measure your milk output. Being able to track all of this is intriguing, but you'll have to decide whether the added cost is worth it.

As of this writing, the most popular better-performing consumer pumps include Ameda's Finesse™, Limerick's PJ's Comfort®, Ardo's Calypso, Lansinoh's Signature Pro™ and Smart Pump™, Medela's Pump in Style™ and Sonata™, and the Spectra® models S1Plus and S2Plus; costs range from US $150 to 400. Hygeia's Enjoye is used by many WIC offices and is also sold to consumers. Once upon a time, cost predicted quality, but among this group of pumps, that is not the case anymore.

While many parents have used a consumer pump successfully, there are some who really do need the smoother cycling curves of a top rental pump to maintain or build their milk production. They cost more for a reason, and it may be worth trying or returning to.

Additionally, there are a few pumps on the market designed to allow you to move around while pumping. Medela's Freestyle® requires the use of some type of hands-free bra, with the tubing attaching to a small motor at your waistband or pocket. It seems to work better for some parents than others and may not sustain milk production in long-term use. Freemie® collects milk inside the hollow flange, which you can wear under your clothes, and is similarly attached to an external motor. Reviews suggest that Freemie's motor isn't very effective, but the collection kit can be adapted for use with other pumps (see bit.ly/MMM-Freemie) and is popular for pumping discreetly in the car and elsewhere. (Note that manufacturers of some of those other pumps may void the warranty if parts other than their own are used.) The Willow® pump is a fully contained

# Insurance Pumps

The 2010 Affordable Care Act in the US mandated insurance companies to provide breast pumps to nursing parents at no cost. This has been a boon to families, but caution is called for because the insurance companies have found clever ways to minimize their costs. The quality of the pump is not dictated, so the quality of your options may be good or poor. Some insurers offer basic models but allow you to upgrade to a better model for an additional fee. Check your model options carefully to make sure they have what you need. Pump options for Medicaid participants are all over the map, so it's important to check multiple durable medical equipment providers for the best options. Some manufacturers will even process a Medicaid pump for you directly!

motor-flange-milk collection unit that uses bags that must be repurchased. It's a great concept, but customer reviews suggest that it's a little trickier to place on the breast, depending on your shape, and may take longer to extract milk. If it becomes dislodged by movement, the suction must build up again. There are drawbacks to each of these portable pumps, but it may mean the difference between being able to pump at all for some people (surgeons have used them during long operations) and anything is better than nothing!

## Qualities of a Good Pump

Effective pumps balance both suction strength and cycling speed to mimic the sucking of a baby. If they reach their pressure too quickly or take too much time to build up appropriate pressure, they can cause tissue damage. Some automatically adjust the speed according to the suction level—low suction, fast cycle; strong suction, slow cycle. Another feature on many pumps is 2-phase expression technology. Phase 1 starts you at a set low-suction, fast cycle for 1-2 minutes to stimulate letdown. Once the milk starts to flow, you hit a button to jump to the 2nd phase with adjustable strong, slow cycling for maximum milk expression. Other pumps allow you to adjust suction and speed separately for a more customized experience. For specific details, see our pump summary on lowmilksupply.org/pumps.

Breast flanges, also known as "breast shields," are the funnel-shaped parts that fit against the breast. Ameda, Ardo, Hygeia, Medela, and Spectra offer two to four flange sizes that may or may not all be included in your basic kit to improve the comfort and effectiveness of a pump. Limerick has a soft flexible silicone breast shield they claim accommodates all sizes of nipples. Whichever you have, proper fit is critical for effective milk removal. A flange that is too small can cause soreness and can even pinch milk

## What About a Secondhand Pump?

It's common to see pumps at yard sales and online resale sites such as eBay and Craigslist. They may also be handed down from a friend or family member. Used consumer-grade models abound but can be contaminated with bacteria, mold, and viruses, or the motors may simply be worn down from use so that they no longer draw milk out well as they once did. Your supply is vulnerable; why take a chance and waste your hard work by using a pump that may not perform optimally?

ducts and affect milk flow. A flange that is too large may pull in too much tissue, causing swelling and redness, and compromise the milk flow. The average flange tunnel is 24-26mm, but many nursing parents seem to do better with the next size up, which is 27-30mm. To know if the flange you're using fits well, watch the way your nipple draws into the flange tunnel as you pump. It's normal to touch the sides of the tunnel, but your nipple should move easily and your areola should move slightly as well. A small amount of olive or coconut oil can lubricate the tunnel and alleviate friction, but a properly sized flange shouldn't need it. Any marks or redness on the areola or at the nipple base after pumping that do not go away before the next pumping session are signs of poor flange fit. Try the next larger size. If larger doesn't feel better, try smaller. Softer silicone flanges are available, though they may come in fewer sizes.

If your nipples require larger or smaller flanges than what came with your pump, or if you have problems with how the angle of the flange works with your breast, PumpinPals® offers multiple sizes with graduated openings and angled tunnels to accommodate breast tissue comfortably and allow milk to flow into the bottle more easily without leaning over. A favorite of many lactation consultants, they are available in both standard hard plastic for most nipple structures and a softer silicone model for more flexible areola tissue, and can be used with many of the popular pumps (check pumpinpal.com for more information).

One last point to keep in mind: the flange size you need can change over time. If you had really sore nipples, for instance, you may have needed a larger size that didn't touch the sore area. But when your nipples are feeling better, a different size might actually work better. Your nipple size may also change over time. Keep this in mind if you're questioning your pump's comfort or performance.

## Clean Parts, Clean Milk

When you regularly wash your parts thoroughly with soap and water in a clean basin or a dishwasher and then air-dry them, your milk should be fine. Sadly, the death of a fragile hospitalized infant that was traced back to contaminated breast pump parts caused both the US Food and Drug Administration (FDA) and the US Centers for Disease Control and Prevention (CDC) to roll out rigorous cleaning guidelines in 2017 for *everyone* that seemed overreaching and unnecessarily scary, especially for those with limited time and restricted environments (see lowmilksupply.org/pumps). We agree with Robyn Roche-Paul of *Breastfeeding in Combat Boots*, who wrote in her handout: "From a high ranking officer working at the Pentagon with access to a sink and a microwave in a dedicated lactation room, to a Private First Class pumping in the field during a 2-week long training exercise with no water or electricity, personnel pumping breast milk in the military may or may not always have access to a place to pump let alone a dedicated sink or any way to sanitize breast pump parts." We share Robyn's concern that these guidelines are not realistic for every family and can be safely modified for parents with low-risk babies. Many experts agree as well, as Heather Marcoux from *Motherly* explored in an excellent web article.[5] Of greatest relief is the acknowledgment in this article by a CDC public affairs specialist that the practice of refrigerating used pump parts between sessions is likely fine *so long as the pump kit has been well-maintained.*

The take-home message is simple: clean your parts well, *taking apart all pieces* (we've seen some nasty valves when the membrane was not removed for cleaning), and consider periodic sterilization for extra precautions. Tubing isn't usually washed because milk does not run through it, but should moisture collect, trying running the pump without the flange for a while to dry it. If mold develops, replace it immediately. Your pumped milk lasts longer when your parts are clean!

## Maintain Your Pump

Hastily washed pump parts can affect performance as well. For instance, caked milk can stick a valve and membrane together and reduce suction if they aren't routinely separated for washing. Valves can also stretch or tear, and sometimes cracks occur in tubing or flange sets. If your pump doesn't seem to be working as well as before, first check that everything is clean and intact, and replace any questionable pieces. Another reminder: An older consumer pump motor can wear out so gradually that you don't realize it's not working at full capacity anymore, and there are also occasional new pump "lemons." If your pump seems sluggish or not very strong, have a lactation consultant check it out with you—and be sure to bring all the parts!

## Optimizing Your Pumping Technique

Simultaneously pumping both breasts is usually the fastest and most effective way to remove milk and seems to stimulate a higher prolactin surge.[1] While you can hold one

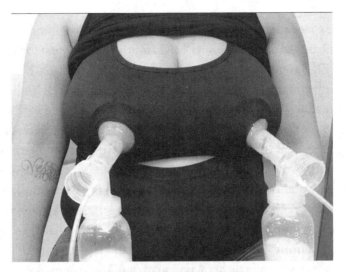

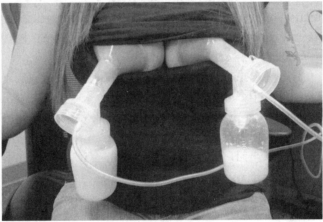

*Hands-free pumping with a commercial bra and a homemade setup.*

bottle with each hand the old-fashioned way, going "hands-free" allows you to eat, drink, surf the net, or massage your breasts. You can buy specialized hands-free pumping bras and bustiers, or better yet, create your own by cutting small slits or circles in a snug sports bra. One ingenious mother figured out how to use her bra to trap the flanges on the bottom side while using her shirt to trap the top portion (see bottom photo above).

Single pumping may be more comfortable if you make a lot more on one side than the other. This also allows you to alternate breasts while pumping, which for some parents yields more milk. It definitely makes it easier to do breast compressions on the breast that is being pumped.

### Find a Comfortable Position

As with nursing, it's important to be comfortable while pumping. Many people jam the flanges deep into their breasts, elbows sticking out, and their backs hunched over so they can watch the milk come out or because they've been told they have to lean over to pump, ending up with kinks in their necks and sore shoulders. No wonder some say it's a miserable experience! Instead, find a comfortable spot with supportive cushions or pillows so you can lean back. The amount of milk pumped doesn't increase with leaning forward, so you may as well be comfortable. One caveat: The milk may stay in the flange tunnel because of the angle and can leak back onto the breast if you don't rock forward periodically to empty it into the bottle. Those PumpinPals® tilted flanges might be a good fix since they're angled to help the milk flow forward when you are leaning back, eliminating leakage.

### Get Your Letdown Going

The best pump in the world won't drain you well if your letdown reflex doesn't trigger. The sight, sound, and smell of your baby can be powerful triggers, so keep your cell phone nearby with pictures and videos of him to view. Smelling a piece of clothing he recently wore can help, too (Note: Thoughts of your baby are usually helpful, but for some parents they can be painful reminders of separation or struggles. Try this technique only if the feelings are positive). When you first start pumping, letdown may not happen as quickly, but over time, your reflex should become conditioned. There are even downloadable hypnosis scripts for pumping parents. Alternatively, playing electronic games can distract and relax you, helping letdown. Follow the suggestions below and in Chapter 12.

### Massage and Heat

You'll get more milk out and with a higher cream content if you massage your breasts first. One study looked at the effect of simultaneous massage with pumping and found that 40-50% more milk was removed when pumping with massage than without it.[6] Use a circular motion, kneading, rolling . . . just be gentle and work gradually from the back of the breast forward toward the nipple, giving special attention to any lumpy areas. Spend a minute or two doing this first. Applying a warm compress to the breasts for a couple of minutes[7] or using a prewarmed breast shield while pumping[8] can increase the amount of milk pumped, too. (This works for breastfeeding as well!)

### Mimic the Baby

Start your pump with Phase 1 "low-suction, fast-speed" cycling. When your milk starts to flow, switch to Phase 2 or gradually increase suction while slowing down the speed—healthy full-term babies tend to suck about 50-60 times per minute during letdowns and at suction levels of approximately -150 to -200mmHg. In a study of post-caesarean mothers, a level of -150mmHg helped bring in the milk more quickly than a lower setting (-100mmHg).[9] In another study, the most milk was extracted when the vacuum reached 190mmHg for 0.7 second and cycled at a speed of one suck per second.[10] You don't need to know these numbers, though; your goal is the highest *comfortable* suction level combined with a moderate speed, which equates to how long the suction is held (aka how long the milk is allowed to spray per cycle!). Parents sometimes make the mistake of thinking that fast and strong is advantageous, but in another study, the best milk producers settled with slightly lower suction and speed levels.[11] Experiment to find what's best for you. Ultimately, the amount of milk you'll get each letdown is determined by the vacuum pressure of the pump and how full your breast is and will decrease with each letdown.[4]

### Hands-On Pumping

One of the biggest lessons we've learned since the first edition of this book is that relying on a pump alone to drive supply is often not enough. Massaging before you start and then using your hands to compress when the milk flow stops can make a big difference. In fact, compressing during letdowns can also increase milk yield.[12] When pediatrician Jane Morton compared pumping alone with hands-on pumping or frequent hand-expression the first 3 days plus hands-on pumping in mothers of premature non-nursing babies, the difference was striking![13]

We've seen this to be true even later on: Renee's baby was unable to latch and feed effectively due to an undiagnosed tongue-tie. She had generously sized breasts and remembered feeling fullness early on, but she was never able to extract more than 1oz (30ml) of milk at a time and became discouraged. After 2 months, her partner convinced her to seek help. During their visit, the lactation consultant observed Renee's pumping and then showed her how to use her hands, adding compressions while pumping. Renee extracted 3oz (90ml) in that session, and she felt hope for the first time ever. Using these new techniques, Renee was able to rebuild her supply to meet 100% of her baby's needs! It was clear that her large breasts needed more than just the pump to fully drain. In our experience, this technique is useful for everyone but may be especially critical for parents with larger breasts and lower milk supplies. Morton recommends finishing up with hand expression to remove milk left by the pump. For some nursing parents, this can be quite a lot! Watch this video clip for the full story at bit.ly/MMM-HandsOn.

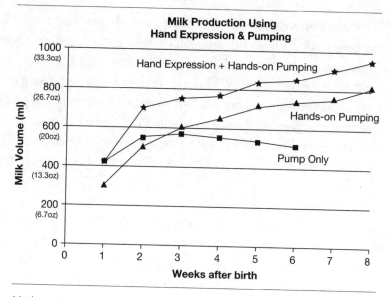

**Milk Production Using Hand Expression & Pumping**

Mothers who relied on the pump alone to remove milk made the least milk. Adding hands to compress and massage while pumping boosted production higher. Those who hand expressed the first 3 days in addition to hands-on pumping stimulated the highest supply of all. Used with permission of Jane Morton.

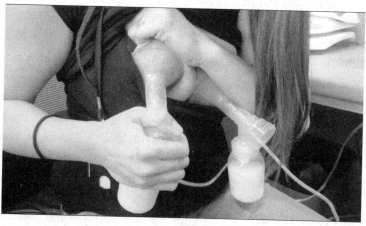

*Hands-on pumping, whether one side at a time or both at the same time, helps extract milk that the pump may have left behind.*

## Reboot your Letdown Reflex

One thing about pumps is that they are very consistent. Babies will speed up, slow down, and take breaks, but the pump just drones on. It's a blessing that pumps never give up, but on the flip side, this absolute consistency is less likely to signal the need for another letdown. The compressions described earlier help, but you can also trigger another let-down by going back to that Phase 1 expression cycle of faster speed and lighter suction. You can even vary suction and speed a few times. Or turn off the pump completely for 1-2 minutes and start pumping again. Make your pump act more like a baby wanting another letdown, and your breasts are likely to respond sooner than if you just sit and wait. Switch back to a strong and slower cycle when milk flows again.

We've presented several techniques, but there is no one set that works for every person. Experimentation is the best way to discover what works best for your breasts.

## Expression Strategies

Pumping requires patience, persistence, and a workable plan, but there is no one right way to go about it. The best way to express is the way that works for you—flexibility is the key. If you struggle with pumping every feeding, then maybe a goal of pumping every other feeding is more realistic and attainable. Occasionally, you might even breast-feed one feeding and pump the next. Figure out what you *can* do and start with that so that you can feel good about it rather than guilty about what didn't happen.

### Express After Feeds

The most common approach to increasing supply by pumping is to nurse as long as your baby will *actively* suck and then pump. This is especially appropriate when a baby is leaving a lot of milk in the breast but also for a baby who sucks well only the short time that milk is flowing strongly and not long enough to stimulate more. Whatever residual milk the pump removes then becomes his next supplement before any formula. Pump until the milk stops, but at least 5-20 minutes (the shorter the feed, the longer the pumping time), even if there is no milk flowing during some of this time. If you don't get much out, it's likely because baby did a good job. *Your goal is extra stimulation to tell your body to either keep up the current supply or make more milk than it is making right now.* If your baby tends to nurse actively for a short while but then quickly closes his eyes and hangs out with just occasional sucks, you may need to limit his time on the breast to active suckling—even if that's only 5 minutes per side—so that you have enough time to supplement him, pump, and keep your sanity.

### Express Between Feeds

If seeing only a little milk is discouraging, pumping between feedings or halfway through a nap rather than right after can provide encouraging visible feedback you want. It also may become more of an extra session rather than the continuation of your feeding session as far as your body is concerned. At the least, having more milk to remove means more for your body to replace. The downside is that there may be less milk in the breast for your baby if he wakes up soon after you pump, and having less milk there may affect his opinion of the breast, not to mention require feeding the milk back to him (more work for you in the end!).

### Express During the Night

If you can handle it, pumping at night takes advantage of higher prolactin levels in addition to removing more milk. However, getting adequate sleep is also important to your overall health and well-being and can affect your milk production. The trick is to be flexible in balancing the two. Try to plan for at least one pumping session in the middle of the night if you can. Or don't set an alarm, but if you happen to awaken, use that opportunity. The sedating effects of oxytocin being released while pumping may help you get back to sleep when you're done. Taking a couple of short naps in the daytime can help you stay rested.

### Expressing in Lieu of Nursing

If you can't nurse directly or need to take a break, it's really important to pump at least as often as your baby feeds. This can easily be done by simply feeding baby with your alternate method first and then pumping when he's done. The caveat here is that your baby is feeding 8 or more times per day. Some babies may start taking larger amounts and going longer between feeds—this can seem like a great thing to a weary parent but may result in a reduced pumping frequency that ultimately isn't helping your progress. Use paced-feeding techniques to help your baby take less each time and hopefully feed more often. Otherwise, you may need to uncouple pumpings from feedings and just set an alarm for 8-10 times per 24 hours.

### Frequency Pumping

In nature, if a baby wants more than you're making, he will nurse frequently until production rises. When your baby isn't available, you can replicate this by extra frequent pumping. Lactation consultant Cathy Genna coined the term *power-pumping* for a short-term strategy for nursing parents of healthy, full-term babies who are having a difficult time fitting pumping into their busy daytime routines. Place the breast pump in a convenient location that you will pass often and where you'll be comfortable sitting or standing. Every time you pass the pump, use it for 5-10 minutes or so, as often as every 45-60 minutes. Stop when you begin to feel "antsy," restless, or annoyed. Aim for pumping at least 10 times every day. Continue for 2-3 days and then resume your normal pumping routine. In an alternate version dubbed "pump like crazy day" by lactation consultant Barbara Robertson, you pump once an hour for 5-10 minutes at a time from 8 am until 9 pm (or whatever you choose). Either way, you'll want to refrigerate the milk and re-wash the kit every 4-5 hours.

Author Stephanie Casemore sometimes suggests *cluster pumping*, a very short-term variation: pump 5-10 minutes on, 5-10 minutes off (or your own chosen times) for an hour or two to mimic a baby's cluster-feeding. This can be done every 1-3 days as desired.

## Managing Triple-Feed Fatigue

The *nurse–supplement–express* routine, aptly nicknamed "triple feeding" by parents, sometimes feels like a never-ending hamster wheel that can become overwhelming, especially if you have other children who also need attention. How long you should continue depends on your goals. If you're trying to increase production, you'll want to keep going until there's no further change for several days (assuming you're working with good equipment),then try backing down on pumping. If production seems stable, maintain the routine for a few days before trying another decrease in pumping. But if production dips when you pump less, you may need a revised long-term strategy.

Streamlining the work when you've hit your plateau can make it more manageable. Instead of pumping after every feeding, pump after every other feeding. Or pump after all feedings in the daytime but skip the night. Rather than seeing it as all or nothing, what *can* you handle? Can someone else supplement the baby while you pump so that you're only doing two things instead of three?

Another idea to drop from triple to "double-time" is to pump one breast while nursing your baby on the other—*parallel pumping*.[14] You'll only pump one breast each feeding, but if you're on the mental edge, this drops you from triple- to double-time and has been a lifesaver for some families. It also adds the advantage of the baby and pump helping each other with letdowns.

A similar trick is to find a way to pump and bottle-feed (if you're using a bottle) at the same time. Some people have even managed to coordinate feeding at the breast with the supplementer on one side while pumping on the other! You don't have to aim for perfect—just aim for what you can handle, especially if it's going to last for a while.

If you need a break, *that's okay,* as long as you keep your baby fed and the milk flowing. Lactation consultant Jan Ellen Brown suggests simplifying the routine temporarily by just pumping for 2-3 days (be sure to do it at least 8-10 times a day!) and feeding your baby that milk by an alternate method. A few days off allows you to catch your breath and might even result in increased milk from thorough, consistent milk

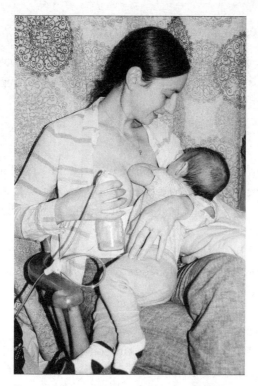

*Pumping the starting breast when your baby has moved to the second side.*

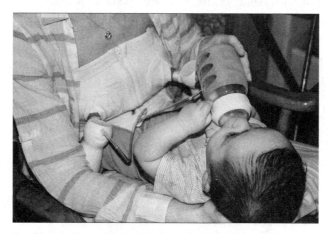

*Double pumping while completing a feed by bottle*

removal. When you're feeling better, add breastfeeding back in. Most babies don't have difficulty coming back to the breast after such a short time when using the alternative feeding techniques described in Chapter 4, especially bottle-feeding methods that support breastfeeding.

205

# What If Baby Cries When You're Pumping?

Your baby's needs come first. Is it possible that he's still hungry and needs a little bit more? If he's fed but still fussing, try snuggling him while at least single pumping. If this doesn't work, you made have to skip until the next time. Pumping should never cause you or your baby emotional stress.

Some parents sustain triple-feeds for quite a while, but it's not for everyone. It may help to set a time limit—lactation consultant Ellen Rubin calls it a "Breastfeeding Campaign" because campaigns have an ending point. Give it your all during the campaign, then at the end decide how you want to proceed from there.

Finally, don't forget the option of supplementing at the breast. This drops you down to doing two things, and if your baby sucks strongly for a good amount of time, you may even be able to discontinue pumping.

## More Tips and Tricks

- If you can afford it, buy multiple pump kits so that you always have a clean one on hand.
- Use the smallest bottle with your pump that is still large enough to ensure it won't overfill, such as the 30 or 60ml sizes. It's psychologically

*Put a sock on it! Courtesy of Johanna Sargeant*

more satisfying, and it's easier to get all the milk out later when amounts are smaller.

- Put a sock on it! When pumping became a stressful and demoralizing experience, Johanna Sargeant put a baby sock over the bottle, hoping the scent of her baby would help with letdown; she also couldn't see how much or little milk was flowing into it. Later she shared this idea with other families, and to her amazement started hearing stories of increased pumping yields. Johanna now routinely makes this suggestion and says that some parents report pumping 2-3 times more in a session than before. (See bit.ly/MMM-PumpHack and bit.ly/MMM-MilkMotherhood)

- Feed the baby, not the freezer. Some parents become so focused on maintaining a milk stash that they don't realize when they've reached the point where the baby can get enough milk out of the breast and not need to be supplemented—*if they just leave the milk in the breast.* One example is when a baby with a weak suck in the beginning grows and strengthens over time but is not given a chance to see what he can do with a full breast. It can be a mental hurdle, but a trial of backing off pumping may be in order.

- If young siblings vie for your attention every time you sit down to pump, consider how you can turn that time into a positive. Keep a basket nearby with snacks, drinks, and books. Make pumping or nursing time also book-reading time so that they are getting some attention, too. Or let them watch a favorite movie or play a favorite game only when you're pumping.

- If you're upstairs at night and the kitchen is downstairs, keep a small cooler with ice packs by your bedside to throw your pump parts and any milk you won't use right away into so that you don't have to get out of bed. Or you may be able to find an inexpensive used dorm-style refrigerator to keep in your room. Just be sure to wash those parts thoroughly in the morning!

## Milk Storage and Leftover Milk

For low milk supply parents, you are likely using any collected milk for supplementation within a few hours; in average room temperatures, you don't even need to refrigerate it. But when there is more milk than you can use right now, the Academy of Breastfeeding Medicine has provided milk storage guidelines based on the most recent evidence. Frozen milk is like frozen food: the better wrapped it is and the colder the freezer, the longer the milk will last. Deep freezers are ideal when available; otherwise, put bags or bottles of milk inside a freezer storage bag and store them in the back of the freezer, which typically stays the coldest.

## Milk Storage Guidelines

| Location of Storage | Temperature | Maximum Recommended Storage Duration |
|---|---|---|
| Room temperature | 16-29°C (60-85°F) | 4 hr optimal |
| | | 6-8 hr acceptable under very clean conditions |
| Refrigerator | ~4°C (39.2°F) | 4 days optimal |
| | | 5-8 days under very clean conditions |
| Freezer | 0°F (-18°C) | 6 mo optimal |
| | | 12 mo acceptable |

From Eglash A, Simon L. ABM Clinical Protocol #8: Human Milk Storage Information for Home Use for Full-Term Infants, Revised 2017. *Breastfeed Med.*2017;12(7), 390-395.

## How Long Do I Keep This Up?

Once you've reached your goal, your baby can often keep your supply going, and you can stop pumping. Awesome—you're done! But what if you need the pump to keep supply up? Or maybe you've hit a ceiling and find you aren't getting any more milk no matter what you do. If you've been pumping very often, try *reducing* the frequency by 1-2 sessions and see if your body maintains your production level. If so, great! If production drops just a little, decide if it's worth the extra effort to maintain the higher level. A small number of people find that they actually get *more* milk when they back off. Ultimately, your goal is to use the pump as little as you can get away with. Experimentation will help you find the balance where you get the most milk for your work.

## CHAPTER 14

# What the Galactogogue? Milk-Boosting Medications, Foods, and Herbs

Imagine a rocket headed to orbit around the earth, only it failed to reach the outer atmosphere where it needed to be. What's next? Mission Control might choose to ignite the boosters and give that rocket a little extra power to push it higher into the proper orbit. If your milk production is like that rocket, you'll first do your best to gun the motors with extra stimulation—frequent feeds or pumping. If there's a problem with the motor, you might have to address some physical or hormonal problems. And if you want to get things going faster, a milk-boosting galactogogue is another option.

In every country and culture, nursing mothers have taken special foods or herbs to bring in a strong supply or boost a lagging one. These traditional practices are supported by centuries of experience and continue to be passed on from one generation to the next. Scientific support for traditional knowledge has lagged, and skeptical professionals have

## Reading This First??

If you bypassed earlier chapters and skipped to this one hoping for a shortcut, be forewarned that *galactogogues can't take the place of frequent milk removal*. Take the time to identify and address whatever is tanking your supply first. *Then* galactogogues may help speed up the process. Putting the cart before the horse rarely gets you very far.

argued "there is no research" or "there is no evidence that galactogogues work," but that simply isn't true. There are many supportive animal studies, and veterinary galactogogue products are available precisely because they help![1] And an increasing number of human studies have been published over the past several decades on various galactogogues as well, even though they aren't all of high-quality. A Cochrane review of galactogogue studies involving healthy nursing mothers and infants is currently in the analysis phase as of the writing of this book.[2] Over 200 studies were screened, with the majority favoring the galactogogue. Due to weaknesses in how the research was conducted or reported—along with the fact that there were many different galactogogues grouped together—the quality of the overall evidence is considered to be very low. This doesn't sound very impressive, but the quality of new research continues to improve, so stay tuned for updates on "Where's the evidence?"

The decision of *when* to use galactogogues depends on your circumstances, personal comfort level, and any health issues or medications. It typically takes at least 2-5 days to start feeling a difference; if nothing has happened by the end of a week, it likely isn't working for you. Simple situations where either your baby or infrequent milk removal caused a drop in supply usually require only short-term use, approximately 1-4 weeks, along with necessary changes. Once full milk production is reestablished, the galactogogue is gradually reduced over 1-2 weeks' time. In more difficult cases, a galactogogue may be required indefinitely to sustain a higher level of milk production, though many nursing parents find that they can reduce their dosages after the first 6 months.

## Targeting: Choosing the Best Galactogogue for Your Needs

Galactogogues work in different ways for different situations. The best galactogogue choice usually depends on what's affecting your supply.

In the Western world, the most common strategy is to boost milk production with prolactin-stimulating medications.[3] As we learned earlier, prolactin is high at birth to get milk production started but then normally decreases to moderately elevated levels as milk removal takes over driving milk production. However, extra prolactin can boost milk production further in many nursing parents, especially when their prolactin is low. And it can slow down or even reverse the process of breast involution—the tearing down of your milk factory—that might otherwise happen when production has slowed.[4] This helps keep your milk-making cells alive, which is especially important if there are fewer due to problems such as insufficient glandular tissue or breast reduction surgery. Extra prolactin may also compensate for mild deficiencies of some hormones.[5]

## Baby's Here: When's the Best Time to Start a Galactogogue?

Research on nursing parents of premature babies suggest that the earlier it is started, the better the chance that it may help, with best results in the first 3 weeks after delivery.[6] One hospital's pharmaceutical galactogogue protocol triggers when milk output is less than 10oz (300mL) a day at 1 week or about 17oz (500ml) a day at 2 weeks after birth.[7] In other situations, it's certainly reasonable to start a medication or herb when you've made course corrections but results are lagging.[8] Lactogenic foods can be started at any time, however, and can be a great starting strategy.

Although boosting prolactin can be effective, it doesn't bring the best results for everyone. Just as there is no one best antibiotic to treat every infection, there is no one best substance for milk production in all situations. And sometimes they don't work at all.

When selecting a drug, herb, or food to help with your milk production, consider which have other properties that are helpful for your situation, such as an anti-androgen herbal galactogogue if you have excessive testosterone or a high-iron herb if you are anemic. Some herbs may actually assist indirectly by helping your letdown reflex so that milk is extracted more easily; look at these if stress has been a part of your picture. *Targeting your choice to your situation may improve your chances of boosting milk production.*

If available, the guidance of a trained practitioner is invaluable. *Herbalists* have training from lore passed down from one generation to the next, formal or self-education, research, or apprenticeship. *Doctors of Traditional Chinese Medicine* (TCM) are formally trained to use herbs based on a 1000-year-old tradition, while *naturopaths*, doctors whose specialty includes the use of botanical (plant) medicine, are familiar with both modern and traditional herbal medicine and represent a blending of Eastern and Western thought.

## Pharmaceutical Galactogogues

There are no pharmaceutical medications that have been specifically designated as galactogogues. However, several drugs that are marketed for other disorders do have the side effect of stimulating milk production—such "off-label" use is a legitimate practice. Some people believe that pharmaceutical galactogogues are more effective than herbal ones, but others report better results from herbs. The differences in opinion may be due to how appropriately each one addressed the underlying problem, or to varying dosages or potencies.

For medications that boost prolactin, pharmacist TM McGuire believes they have the best chance of helping when started within the first 3 weeks after birth and may take at least 2 weeks of treatment "for the breast changes required to sustain milk production."[6] But don't worry if your baby is older—they've helped many nursing parents well past this time.

## Domperidone (Motilium™)

Domperidone is a prescription anti-nausea and stomach-emptying drug that is used for gastrointestinal disorders in adults and children. It also stimulates prolactin, which in turn can boost milk production.

### Effectiveness

Formal research into this "off-label" use reports modest to moderate increases. Most of the evidence is in parents of preterm infants,[7,9-11] but there also are many individual stories describing moderate to dramatic increases. Overall, domperidone has an excellent track record and is considered the drug of choice for increasing milk production where it is available.[7] Dr. Thomas Hale rates it L1 (compatible) in *Medications and Mothers' Milk*.[12]

Domperidone is tolerated well by most nursing parents, though a few may experience headaches, abdominal pain, or dry mouth. Most people respond to domperidone quickly, usually within 48 hours but no longer than 7 days. The maximal effect is typically reached in 2-4 weeks.[13] It seems to work best when started in the first 4-6 weeks after birth, though it can still be helpful later. Not everyone responds to this medication, likely due to prolactin already being high or other underlying issues. If possible, consider having your baseline prolactin checked (see Chapter 11) before starting and also 2 weeks into therapy. If your milk output doesn't change much, seeing whether your prolactin has risen as expected will help you understand what is and is not working in your body. Weaning from domperidone should be done gradually to avoid a sudden drop in supply or withdrawal side effects. If you've taken it long-term (months), taper off at 10mg per week.[14]

### Safety

Domperidone is considered to be relatively safe and effective by the regulatory agencies of European countries and is available without prescription in some places. Domperidone is not manufactured in the US, and the FDA has taken a stubborn stance against it despite the pleas of nursing parents and breastfeeding medicine practitioners. In the US, domperidone now has "orphan status" with the FDA, which will allow for compassionate use and lactation research. However, despite the long positive history of the drug in other countries, the FDA's opposition continues to make it difficult for US families to obtain domperidone. As a result, breastfeeding parents are turning to international online pharmacies and self-prescribing without medical oversight, which is a concerning trend. We strongly recommend conferring with your medical provider first.

We are sometimes asked if it's safe to take domperidone with another drug or galactogogue. Some people take it together with metformin, and some take it with a botanical galactogogue such as moringa or goat's rue, reporting their combinations to be more effective together. No problems have been reported to our knowledge.

### Dosage

In Australia, where domperidone is commonly used for lactation, the typical galactogogue dosage is 30-60mg per day.[15] Two small studies investigated both infant safety and the dosage response of 30 and 60mg, one with six Australian mothers conducted over 1-2 weeks[16] and the other with 15 Canadian mothers over 6 weeks.[17] In both studies more milk was made at the higher dosage, but it wasn't considered statistically significant.[16,17] No infant side effects were reported.

In North America, 20-30mg taken 3-4 times daily (80-90mg total) has been commonly used.[18] No research has tested the effectiveness of this range nor the higher dosages of 120-160mg used by some desperate nursing parents.[14] The relative safety of higher dosages—especially more than 90mg per day—is a concern to many healthcare providers.[19] Weight gain or difficulty losing weight at higher doses has been reported in online groups.

## Metoclopramide (Reglan™, Maxeran™)

Metoclopramide is commonly used to treat gastroesophageal reflux in both adults and children.

### Effectiveness

Since it increases prolactin and can stimulate milk production, metoclopramide has also been prescribed off-label to increase milk production effectively for nearly 4 decades.[6]

### Safety

Unlike domperidone, metoclopramide crosses the blood-brain barrier and can cause side effects such as restlessness, drowsiness, fatigue, irritability, depression, and involuntary body movements,[20] especially when used longer than 2-4 weeks. These problems are considered uncommon when taken for gastrointestinal problems, but postpartum parents seem to be more vulnerable, and complaints of fatigue and blueness are common. On

## Domperidone vs Metoclopramide: What's the Scoop?

Hale, Kendall-Tackett, and Cong surveyed 1990 mothers in 25 different countries to find out what kinds of side effects they experienced when taking one or both drugs. When mothers were given the same amount of either domperidone or metoclopramide (10mg taken 3 times daily for 10 days), they experienced similar increases in milk production; however, more side effects were reported with metoclopramide.[20] Women taking metoclopramide were almost 4 times more likely to report a side effect than those taking domperidone. Cardiac symptoms were reassuringly very low in both groups—less than 1%—though those taking metoclopramide were 7 times more likely to report a racing heart. Central nervous system problems also occurred more often in the metoclopramide group, with the risk of developing depression 7 times higher and the occurrence of tardive dyskinesia (tremors, involuntary grimaces, jerking) 4-19 times higher among others.[22]

occasion, side effects have persisted even after stopping the medication, especially with use longer than 12 weeks, the reason for an FDA 'black box' warning (see bit.ly/MMM-Reglan for more information). Metoclopramide also may not be compatible with selective serotonin reuptake inhibitor (SSRI) antidepressants.[21] If you have a personal or family history of depression, it's probably wise to avoid using metoclopramide. Hale rates it L2 (probably compatible).[22]

### Dosage

The most common effective dose is 10-15mg taken 3 times daily, with a stronger response at the higher dosage. The research has been mixed when testing the 10mg dose dosage, but clinical experience has seen significant increases of up to 100% at times.[6,23] The bottom line is that like domperidone, some nursing parents respond well and others do not—50-85% of those with low supply experience an increase.

## Metformin (Glucophage™)

Metformin is an insulin receptor sensitizing agent used for type 2 diabetes and often for PCOS as well. Its earliest version, phenformin, was originally created from galegin, found in herb goat's rue.

### Effectiveness

Metformin is not a galactogogue per se. It may help milk production for some insulin-resistant nursing parents, though research hasn't yet confirmed this yet. In a case of a mother with PCOS, insulin resistance, and hypoplasia, it was metformin and not domperidone that boosted milk production, though the overall amount of milk was still low.[24,25]

Another study followed fifteen nursing parents (1-8 weeks postpartum) with low milk production and signs of insulin resistance for a month. Those who received metformin had a small improvement in milk output, while those taking the placebo experienced decreasing production. This small study suggests that those who are insulin resistant may be at risk for decreasing milk production—a premature drop in their lactation curve—and that metformin may at least help maintain milk production and possibly help increase it.[25,26]

If you have a history of insulin resistance or you've taken this drug before, metformin might be worth trying. Talk to your health care provider first.

### Safety

Because very little of the drug passes into human milk, metformin is considered compatible with breastfeeding.[27]

### Dosage

Typical dosages range from 500-2500mg per day, but informal reports of success for lactation seem to occur in the 1500- to 2500mg range. Canadian breastfeeding medicine physician Shawna Lamond uses it together with domperidone and sometimes moringa, combinations she finds effective for patients with signs of insulin resistance. See Chapter 11 for more about metformin and also inositol, a possible natural alternative.

## Lactogenic Foods: Can You Really Eat Your Way to Making More Milk?

It's hard to find a person these days who hasn't heard about some food reputed to stimulate more milk. While we've heard some wild ones, there really are foods that seem to boost milk production. In fact, traditional societies figured this out centuries ago and developed strategies to "stack the deck" in the mother's favor by loading her up with these special foods in the early weeks and months—commonly referred to as "recovery" foods. What's great is that there's virtually no risk of harm, and at worst, you're eating better for your own health.

A hospital in Thailand actually tried a novel experiment: For one month, all newly delivered mothers were fed a menu loaded with the local favorite reputed galactogogue foods (hot basil, lemon basil, sweet basil, banana blossom, garlic, garlic chives, ginger, and pepper). The next month, the menu excluded lactogenic foods. More women in the galactogogue group reported feeling "breast heaviness" after 48 hours than the plain menu group (72% vs 57%), and their babies were less likely to lose more than 7% of their weight at 48 hours (15% vs 24%).[28]

We want to emphasize *functional foods*—those that offer additional health or therapeutic benefits beyond their nutritive value. A number of foods are considered lactogenic, some stronger than others. After reading Chapter 7 about the role of nutrition in making milk, you now have a better appreciation for critical nutrients that are in many lactogenic foods. Look through those discussed in this chapter to find the ones you might want to incorporate into your diet. Two other good resources we recommend are Hilary Jacobson's book *Motherfood* and Pharmacist Frank Nice's article *Selection and Use of Galactogogues* that lists suggested dosages of a number of lactogenic foods and herbs (bit.ly/MMM-Galactogogues).

## Whole Grains, Beans, and Yeast

Whole grains and beans are high in fiber and vitamins, among other things. Breastfeeding parents who ate a lot of fiber and protein had "longer lactations."[29,30] Remember the Metamucil® mom in Chapter 7? Fiber was her magic ingredient. Some whole grains that are considered to support or stimulate milk production include *brown rice, millet, amaranth, and maize*. Among legumes, *kidney beans, black or white beans, lentil beans* and *chickpeas*, all high in fiber, protein, and iron, are promoted for milk production in several traditional cultures.[31-33]

### Quinoa (Chenopodium quinoa)

One of the hot lactogenic whole grains of the day is *quinoa* (pronounced keen-wah). A YouTube video (bit.ly/MMM-Quinoa) chronicles a nursing mother's accidental discovery when she cooked quinoa for the first time and woke up to "rock hard boobs" in the middle of the night. When it happened again after she ate leftovers, she put two and two together and decided to share her experience for the benefit of low-supply parents everywhere. Quinoa is high in protein and frequently used by Peruvian mothers to boost milk supply, most often in soup.[34] Try 2 regular servings or 1 large serving a day. Tip: Make a pot of quinoa and store in the fridge to add to soup, toss with salad, mix with rice or oatmeal, or however you like it.

### Oats and Oat Pods (Avena sativa)

*Oats* are high in iron, fiber, and minerals. They're good for exhaustion, anxiety, and pituitary support, and have a strong reputation for boosting milk production.[35] In the

Hispanic tradition, oats are often used in *atole con avena*, a hot milk drink for new mothers. US parents eat oatmeal cereal, and oatmeal is a common ingredient in "lactation cookies" and bars. Oats are very nutritious and easy to work into the diet—think oatmeal cereal, oatmeal cookies, and oatmeal in breads, muffins, or meatloaf. Steel-cut or rolled oats are more nutritious and likely to be more effective than instant oats. (Anyone with celiac disease should take care to read labels carefully and look for gluten-free oats.) Naturopathic physician Sheila Kingsbury prefers an infusion of dried oat pods, the dried milky top of the oats (1 cup whole oat pods soaked in 1 quart of water overnight and then strained and sipped during the day),[36] or her Milky Oats Tea (see Customize Your Own Blend). A few herb companies offer milky oats tinctures as well.

### Barley (Hordeum vulgare)

If you've ever heard "Drink a beer to make more milk," it was more than just an old wives' tale. We now know that a polysaccharide in *barley* is responsible for boosting prolactin and milk production.[37,38] Alcohol isn't recommended for nursing parents, but a dark, non-alcoholic beer such as O'Douls or St. Pauli's Girl is acceptable; keep in mind that brand recipes vary. Better yet, just try barley in soup or any number of your recipes that have grains, or find some new ideas online.

Another option is "barley water," an Old World remedy made with ½ cup of flaked or pearled barley simmered in 1 quart/1 liter of water for 20 minutes, with powdered fennel or fenugreek seed added. There are also roasted barley and barley malt beverages available commercially such as Roma, Pero, Cafix, Karamalz and Dandy Blend, enjoyed by European women to boost supply. If you're missing your coffee these days, a roasted barley drink is a perfect double-duty substitute!

### Hops (Humulus lupulus)

*Hops* are another ingredient in beer and also considered lactogenic. Research on hops and prolactin are inconclusive, but they may promote milk production by aiding digestion, relaxation, and sleep. Due to sedating effects, hops should not be taken if you're depressed.[36] Naturopath Sheila Kingsbury uses hops in herbal combinations, 50-100mg taken 2-3 times per day.

### Brewer's Yeast (Saccharomyces cerevisiae)

*Brewer's yeast* is also used in beer-making and has been a popular galactogogue in the past. It is high in B vitamins, and there is supporting animal research though no studies with humans, only historical mention.[39] Many parents over the years have reported this to be helpful, and it's a common ingredient in lactation cookies. Do not take it if you are prone to yeast (*Candida*) infections. Be aware that it can make you gassy and occasionally cause diarrhea or abdominal upset. Brewer's yeast can be found at the health food store as a powder or a tablet; try 1-2 tablespoons per day or 2-3 tablets taken 1-3 times per day.

## Nuts and Seeds

Certain nuts and seeds are considered to be milk-boosters. Two of the most well-known are *almonds* and *sesame seeds*, both high in calcium.[40] To increase their supplies, Turkish mothers eat sesame halva, a treat made with tahini.[33] In the East Indian Ayurvedic tradition, almonds, coconut, and sesame seeds are considered to promote "rich" milk; Indian women eat roasted and pounded sesame seeds twice a day.[41] Rice pudding with milk and sugar, *pumpkin*, and *sunflower seeds* is also often recommended to support or increase production.

Bekki had a history of hypoplasia, weight struggles, hormone problems, and very low milk production. She had tried many different strategies to boost her production, with little success. One day she bought some packaged carrot muffins at the grocery store; a little while after eating one, she pumped significantly more than usual. Every time she ate a muffin, she experienced a bump in milk volume—magic muffins! Bekki checked the ingredients and tried to replicate the recipe at home, but her own version initially didn't work, not until she added one overlooked ingredient: almond meal. Then it worked!

## Dark Green Leaves

*Dark green leafy vegetables* are high in fiber, iron, magnesium, and calcium and are eaten for milk production by Turkish women.[33] *Lettuce* (*Lactuca sativa*) is believed to help with letdown.

### *Dandelion Leaves* (Taraxacum officinale)

*Dandelion leaves*—yes, those yard weeds—are good for your production. Though there are no studies of it specifically for milk supply, dandelion is mentioned in many cultural records.[8,33,42] It has diuretic properties (good for that ankle swelling after birth), is a mild laxative and anti-inflammatory, and helps regulate blood sugar.[43] Dandelion is also a good source of vitamins A and C and potassium and is rich in antioxidants; in fact, it is considered more nutritious than kale or spinach! Dandelion greens are best picked young as they become bitter as they go to seed.[44] Take care not to harvest from areas treated with weed killers. Health food stores also often sell fresh dandelion greens, which are typically sweeter than those in yards. Use fresh in salads, sautéed in a little garlic, or make a tea. Alternatively, you can purchase dandelion tincture or tea.

### Moringa (Moringa oleifera)

The leaves of *Moringa oleifera*, known as *malunggay* (rhymes with "balloon guy") in the Philippines, and *drumstick tree, horseradish tree,* or simply *moringa* elsewhere, are eaten as a vegetable in salads, soups, stews and casseroles, similar to how Westerners use spinach. Moringa can be found in most countries of the dry tropics, where its super-food status is well known; it's often called the "miracle vegetable." Moringa is high in vitamins A, C, and E, as well as antioxidants, protein, calcium, potassium, and iron.[45] It's also known in the Philippines for boosting milk, and multiple studies using capsulized dried leaf powder have been conducted to prove its lactogenic effects. All found increases in prolactin, milk yield, or infant weights.[46,47] One unpublished study wanted to find out if giving malunggay capsules during the last month of pregnancy would help the milk to increase faster and stronger after delivery, and it did appear to do just that.[48] This seems a reasonable approach because moringa leaves are also promoted in Africa for healthy pregnancies.[49,50] Malunggay is eaten commonly in the Philippines, where they have no restrictions on its use, and it is a common vegetable in their diet. (For more information, see bit.ly/MMM-Moringa.)

If you're lucky enough to have access to fresh moringa leaves, they are traditionally used in soup, but you can eat them in stirfries or however you wish. Frozen moringa is available in many Asian food stores. Otherwise, powdered moringa leaf (start at ½-1 teaspoon) can be added to smoothies, baked goods, vegetables, casseroles, and even spaghetti sauce. If you're not fond of powdered moringa, you can also purchase it in capsules or try moringa tea.

## Other Fruits, Roots, and Vegetables

A study from Thailand found positive associations between *banana flower, lemon basil, Thai basil,* and *bottle gourd* and milk volume.[51] *Ginger* is also considered lactogenic in multiple cultures. Thai mothers started on powdered ginger capsules after birth had higher milk output on the 3rd but not the 7th day,[52] while in another Thai study a combination product started at 1 month that included equal amounts of ginger, fenugreek and turmeric boosted milk production by almost 50% after 2 weeks and 100% after 4 weeks.[53] *Palm dates* (10 dates, taken 3 times daily), popular in Middle Eastern countries, performed about the same as fenugreek (2g in tea, 3 times daily) in Egyptian mothers.[54]

### Green Papaya (Carica papaya)

Cooked green (unripe) *papaya* is used throughout tropical regions for milk production, often in soups.[33,41,55] Two Chinese studies, one that fed rats an octopus and papaya soup and one that fed human mothers pig's feet and papaya soup, observed increases in milk output.[56,57] If you enjoy Asian cuisine, papaya salad or dishes with added green papaya are a delicious way to sneak this one into your diet.

## Blue Drinks??

Have you heard that Gatorade or similar sports drinks—blue is often specified—are lactogenic? Personal testimonies abound, though there is nothing special about the ingredients that stand out except maybe potassium, which is important for dehydration. Myth or fact, there are healthier drinks (mentioned in this chapter) that both contribute to your health and your milk supply.

### *Traditional Soups*

Many cultures feed new mothers special lactogenic soups. In the Philippines, *Tinola* is made with a chicken broth (high in calcium if made with the bones), moringa leaves, green papaya, and other vegetables—truly a super galactogogue soup! *Torbangun* or *Bangun-Bangun* ("wake-up") soup, a Bataknese post-birth recovery food made from the leaves of the *Coleus amboinicus Lour* and either chicken or fish, boosted milk production by 65% in normal breastfeeding mothers.[58] Other Asian countries favor seaweed soups (high in iodine and calcium), fish soups, pork leg/knuckle/feet soups, and there are several Chinese studies of various combinations.

## Lactogenic Treats and Recipes

There's been an explosion of commercial lactation cookies, bars, and now chews on the market, which seem to help some people more than others. They are a great convenience for busy parents but are also pricey, and some have lots of added sugar, which is not good for any of us and especially counter-productive for those with insulin resistance. If you or a family member or friend enjoys cooking, consider creating your own lactogenic dishes and menus. Pharmacist Frank Nice's *The Galactogogue Recipe Book* has recipes that are designed to include therapeutic amounts of the lactogenic foods. *Boost Your Breast Milk* by dietician and lactation consultant Alicia Simpson also contains 75 recipes. You'll find even more ideas on how to incorporate lactogenic foods into your daily menus in Hilary Jacobson's *MotherFood* and at bit.ly/MMM-Lactogenic.

## Navigating the World of Herbal Galactogogues

Despite centuries of herbal galactogogue use in traditional cultures, and despite a growing body of research validating their effectiveness and safety, their use in the Western world is still often viewed with distrust and suspicion. Nevertheless, they are more popular than ever for a simple reason: Western medicine has largely ignored the dilemma of low milk supply and offers little help beyond "pump, breastfeed, and just keep trying." This is especially true in the US, where domperidone is difficult to obtain, and it's what spurred lactation professionals like us to dig a little deeper on behalf of our clients. Navigating herbal galactogogues can be overwhelming because of frequently conflicting information—especially online!—but we hope that this next section will break it down so you can make informed decisions about what's right for you.

## Effectiveness of Herbal Galactogogues

We're happy to report that quite a bit has been written or researched about a number of herbal galactogogues since our first edition and that the quality of research is improving, though few studies are "gold-standard" quality yet. Herbal galactogogues likely help by doing one of three things: stimulating lactation directly, stimulating lactation indirectly by aiding the letdown reflex for more milk removal, or helping hormonal imbalances or nutritional deficiencies that may be interfering with good production.[2,59] Many herbs have multiple beneficial properties and may help at more than one level. Interestingly, a number of herbal galactogogues are known for aiding digestion just as domperidone and metoclopramide do or for "bringing on the flow of menses" (think contractions and letdown). Some, including those reputed to increase breast size, contain phytoestrogens that may stimulate prolactin naturally to increase milk production.[60]

## Herbal Galactogogues Safety

Toxicology studies have shown the more widely available herbs to be relatively safe, although much of the formal research is on animals.[62] Be aware of the safety of your herb source; some imported from Asia can be contaminated with heavy metals.[63]

A question frequently asked is whether an herb will get into the milk and if that's a problem. There isn't much research, but it's reasonable to apply the same principles as for medications used while nursing, which have an average transfer rate of about 3% of the

## Are Phytoestrogens Safe?

Plant-based phytoestrogens are weak compared with pharmaceutical or our own natural estrogen. Many foods contain some phytoestrogens, and chances are you've been eating them and didn't even realize it.[61] They've come into the news because of cancer risk concerns, but in foods and herbs taken in moderation they are unlikely to increase cancer risk. Many galactogogues have phytoestrogens that underlie how they stimulate breast growth and prolactin—Nature's way of supporting lactation.

dose.[64] As with medications, transference into the milk is rarely an issue for your baby. We've provided some basic safety information in our herb monographs and the tables at the end of the chapter. Another good resource is Sheila Humphrey's book *The Nursing Mother's Herbal*, which rates a long list of commonly used herbs according to their relative safety for nursing. *Be sure to tell your baby's health care providers whenever you take herbs to increase milk production.* If you or baby have allergies, you may want to research herbs of interest before trying them. Also keep in mind that larger amounts of some herbs can interact negatively with some drugs or cause side effects, such as diarrhea or a maple syrup-scented urine, that might be misinterpreted if the doctor doesn't know about them.

## Herbs Come in Many Forms

If you stroll down the aisle of your local drug or health food store, you'll quickly notice a variety of options. There are whole-herb preparations that grind up all the usable plant parts and package them as powders, tablets, or capsules, and there are "standardized extracts" that guarantee a certain amount of active ingredients from the herb for a standard dose. Tinctures may be created by extracting certain plant properties by soaking the herb in alcohol or another medium at various concentrations, while teas steep dried leaves, flowers, seeds, or roots in hot water to extract their water-soluble properties.

Which form is best? Not even the experts agree, as they each have their own philosophy, and the method of preparation also plays a strong role in the herbs' effectiveness. Tea is a good example—if not brewed long enough, the therapeutic properties won't be as strong. Some herbs in tablet form have a small proportion of active ingredients, while others are quite potent. The right form, in most cases, is probably the one you like best, but if we're aware that one works better than another, we'll let you know.

## Quality Matters

Not all products are created equal. Quality may vary by manufacturer and can also deteriorate over time if exposed to heat and light. It may be tempting to buy the cheapest version on the shelf, but for best results, choose a reputable brand that is well within its expiration date. We list some recommended brands for various herbs on our website, lowmilksupply.org/herbs.

## How to Take Herbal Galactogogues

Some herbs and medications should not be taken together. For instance, those that contain a lot of fiber—typically dried herbs or seeds, loose or in capsules—can slow the absorption of some medications. It's important to research your other prescription medications for any known interactions with herbs, keeping in mind that many sources simply list every possible theoretical risk without considering how much you're taking or if anything has ever been researched or problems actually reported. (See bit.ly/MMM-HerbsDrugs and bit.ly/MMM-Herbs.)

Some herbs taste very bitter. Sweeteners can be added to teas, and tinctures can be mixed with a *small* amount of strong juice or tea to mask the flavors (larger amounts might diminish effectiveness). However, some herbalists believe that it is necessary to experience the bitter flavor in order to stimulate gastric juices enough for full absorption into the bloodstream. Foods taken at the same time as herbs may aid or interfere with absorption, depending on the individual qualities of the herb. For this reason, it's important to pay attention to any instructions regarding when and how to take each herb. Consider taking herbs and medications at different times as well.

Some experts recommend rotating your galactogogue herbs every few weeks because they believe that your body can become used to a substance and respond less and less over time.[65]

## Herb Dosages: How Much Should I Take?

One of the challenges in using herbs as galactogogues is the lack of research-based information on effective dosages. With the exception of a few like blessed thistle and fenugreek, most recommended dosages are standard amounts for general purposes. There is little or no research on whether these amounts are enough (or more than enough!) to boost milk production or if the amounts needed might vary according to the underlying problem.

Some herbs are completely benign and can be experimented with freely, while others may be potentially toxic in large amounts and must be used much more carefully. Start with the basic recommended dosages and give it a few days before playing with the amount. Primary low milk supply may take much longer to respond than simple management or baby-related problems. The concept of "if a little is good, more is better" is *not* true for all herbal galactogogues. When you find something effective, use no more than is necessary, and when you want to cut back, do so gradually to help the body begin "taking back" its own duties. Allow at least a week between changes as long as you aren't experiencing any negative side effects.

## Targeting Herbs to the Cause of the Problem

You may be wondering where to start in choosing herbs. Alfalfa, fenugreek, blessed thistle, goat's rue, moringa, nettle, and shatavari are good all-purpose galactogogues that usually work well for low milk supply due to secondary causes. If you prefer familiar culinary herbs, try cooking with or making a tea from crushed anise, caraway, coriander, dill, fennel, or fenugreek seed. But if you have specific issues related to your low supply, look more closely for herbs with additional properties that may address them.

The Galatogogue Tables at the end of this chapter provide a summary of form, dosage, herb properties, and other information.

## Overview of Lactogenic Herbs

### Alfalfa (Medicago sativa)

A popular and commonly used galactogogue,[31,55] *alfalfa leaf* is often taken in combination with blessed thistle, marshmallow, and fenugreek. It's a good source of vitamins A, C, E, and K, along with calcium, potassium, phosphorus and iron.[35] Alfalfa is phytoestrogenic and said to contain thyroid-releasing hormone (TRH)-type material, either of which might stimulate prolactin and milk production.[38] Some people believe that it can worsen lupus symptoms and should be avoided with a history of autoimmune disorders, but this has not been proven.[66] There is no evidence for or against taking alfalfa in pregnancy.[62] Many parents have done so and credit it with getting milk production off to a faster start after delivery.

### Aniseed or Anise Seed (Pimpinella anisum)

One of the "aromatic" culinary herbs and a traditional medicine in France, *anise seed* is known for helping colic and gassiness along with increasing milk production. It hasn't been studied much on its own but is included in several galactogogue teas.[67] Both water and alcohol extracts boosted production in rats.[68] Anise contains anethole, considered to be estrogenic, and some believe it may help with letdown. Anise is *not* the same as *star of anise* and should not be used interchangeably.

### Ashwagandha (Withania somnifera)

Known for being an adaptogen (hormone balancer), supporting the adrenal glands, and helping with stress, *ashwagandha* is often paired with shatavari in Ayurvedic galactogogue combinations.[1,69] It also helps normalize thyroid function when thyroid hormone is a bit low.[70] Though not considered a direct galactogogue, it seems to work synergistically.

### Black Cohosh (Actaea racemosa or Cimicifuga racemosa)

Native American women historically have used *black cohosh* for a variety of female health issues, including as a galactogogue.[1,71] Black cohosh is believed to be anti-androgenic[72] and has phytoestrogens that may stimulate mammary growth.[69,73] It's also reputedly oxytocic and used by midwives to start labor,[43] which may explain its reputation for helping with letdown.

### Black seed (Nigella sativa)

*Black seed*, also called black cumin, is a cooking herb found in eastern Mediterranean countries, Pakistan, India, and Iran. Its use as a galactogogue is well known[55,60,74] and even promoted in Islam.[75] Indian women may take powdered black seeds first thing in the morning to support milk supply.[76] There are no human studies, only those in animals; of the most recent, rats fed water or alcoholic extracts of blackseed produced more milk than control rats.[77]

### Blessed Thistle (Cnicus benedictus)

The use of *blessed thistle*, a member of the ragweed family, has been recorded as far back as the early 16th century for treating many ailments as well as for loss of appetite and milk production. It is a popular galactogogue that is most often taken in conjunction with fenugreek, but it has not been formally studied. Most parents prefer to take blessed thistle in capsule form as the teas and tinctures are quite bitter.[35,78] Naturopath Sheila Kingsbury notes that she has sometimes seen this work when fenugreek did not; she uses 1000mg taken 2-3 times per day.[36]

### Borage Seed Oil (Borago officinalis)

A lesser-known lactogenic herb, *borage* also has a reputation for helping with anxiety, premenstrual syndrome, endometriosis, and fibrocystic breasts and has some laxative effects. Its leaves contain small amounts of toxic alkaloids, making them controversial for use by breastfeeding parents despite the ability to increase milk production.[42,79] *Borage oil* is made from borage seeds and contains very little of these alkaloids, so it can be safely consumed when used appropriately.[62] High in the beneficial fat gamma-linolenic acid (GLA), it boosts these in human milk,[80] which may be why it also has the reputation of increasing the creaminess of the milk.

### Caraway Seed (Carum carvi)

Another of the aromatic culinary galactogogue herbs, *caraway* is also known for appetite stimulation, anticolic, antianxiety, and antiflatulence properties and increasing libido.[42,81] In Spain, mothers may drink an infusion of ½ teaspoon per cup of water, 3-4 times a day to stimulate milk production,[38] but caraway is more often combined with other galactogogue herbs.[42]

### Chasteberry, Chaste Tree Berry, and Vitex (Vitex agnus-castus)

Mia had difficulty getting pregnant. Her doctor thought that maybe she had PCOS and had her try metformin and clomid. Six months later with no success, she stopped the clomid and decided to try Vitex instead, and became pregnant in the third month. But when the baby came, milk production became the next hurdle. Her milk was slow to increase, just 6oz (180ml) per day at 1 week and 13.5oz (400ml) a day at 2 weeks despite frequent pumping and normal prolactin and thyroid labs. A lactation consultant suggested trying the Vitex again at the same dosage used when she became pregnant (400mg daily). Mia's milk started to increase rapidly, reaching 22.3oz (670ml) at 3 weeks, 24.3oz (730ml) at 4 weeks . . . eventually peaking at 36.7oz (1100ml) per day by 6 weeks!

Chasteberry, also known as chaste tree berry and Vitex, is known for its normalizing effects on the pituitary gland and especially on progesterone (probably by helping ovulation) and is believed to regulate prolactin. Some women take it for premenstrual syndrome (PMS), irregular periods, infertility, and even acne, as it seems to have anti-androgen properties as well.[72] Chasteberry has also been used for increasing milk production as far back as 50 CE, when Dioscorides recommended an extract of crushed fruits in wine "to increase the flow of milk."[82]

Some research has documented decreases in prolactin, calling into question chasteberry's use as a galactogogue. A study in men showed that low doses of a chasteberry extract (120mg per day) stimulated prolactin, while high doses of another product (480mg per day) lowered it.[83] Rats injected with large amounts had decreases in milk production. This has caused many people to shelve chasteberry as a galactogogue, though the issue of dosage may hold the key.[35] While Mia's effective dosage was on the higher side, herb expert Sheila Humphrey suggests starting low, around 30-40mg per day.[84] We aren't sure about its use as a general galactogogue, but chasteberry may be appropriate if hormonal imbalances are part of your milk production problem.

### Coriander (Coriandrum sativum)

The seed of cilantro, *coriander* has a light, lemony flavor and is helpful for gassiness, has diuretic properties, and is also mildly antidiabetic.[42,85] Indian mothers drink an infusion of the dried fruits twice a day to boost milk supply.[41] Palestinian parents take it after childbirth to "strengthen the body, increase the production of milk and increase sexual desire,"[74] and it's used to boost milk supply in Africa as well.[33] Brew 1 tablespoon of crushed seed in a mug of boiling water and drink a few times daily.

### Cotton Seed (Gossypium herbaceum)

*Cotton seed* has been used since antiquity in the Unani tradition for boosting milk production and is also considered an aphrodisiac to boost libido. It stimulates prolactin in both female sheep and rats[38] and enhances milk production in buffaloes.[86] In the first known study in human parents with milk supply problems using 10g of powdered kernels per day for 1 month, those taking cotton seed had higher rates of reducing or eliminating supplements than those taking a placebo.[87] Caution is advised if there is a bleeding disorder or medications that increase the risk of bleeding.

### Cumin (Cuminum cyminum)

Another of the aromatic herbs, *cumin* is used in multiple cultures as a galactogogue. An old rat study observed growth of mammary tissue though not stimulation of milk production.[88] Indian parents boil a handful of seeds in 2 cups of water, strain, add 1 spoonful of honey, and drink it every morning for their milk supply.[41] Cumin may also have antidiabetic properties.[85]

### Dill Seed (Anethum graveolens)

Widely used since ancient times for digestive issues, *dill seed* is part of the recipe for "gripe water," traditionally used to soothe infant colic. It has antidiabetic, antispasmodic, and diuretic properties but is also high in sodium. Dill seed is included in many popular commercial galactogogue products because it seems to work well when combined with others (synergistic). It's supposed to "increase the flow of milk in nursing mothers," which suggests that dill may assist the letdown reflex.[89] Sprinkle dill on food or drink it as a tea.

### Fennel (Foeniculum vulgare)

A popular European galactogogue, *fennel* is also known for its ability to reduce intestinal gas and improve digestion. Nursing parents of colicky babies may take fennel tea to simultaneously help their milk production and possibly calm a baby's digestive upsets. Fennel is also reputed to be diuretic and anti-androgenic,[89] and may promote letdown. It has been studied for its ability to reduce hirsutism (male-pattern hair growth) in women.[90] Its phytoestrogens likely play a role in its breast-enhancing reputation. Additionally, fennel may have appetite-suppressing properties—one parent reported that it helped mitigate their hunger while taking domperidone. Fennel is the second main ingredient of the traditional lactogenic barley water drink.

### Fenugreek Seed (Trigonella foenum-graecum)

*Fenugreek* is probably the most recommended galactogogue in North America and is popular in many other countries as well. It is known as methi in India and enjoyed in all parts of the world as a culinary herb. Fenugreek leaf and seeds lend a distinctive flavor to a wide variety of baked goods and foods, including curry dishes and imitation maple syrup. It contains protein, iron, vitamin C, niacin, and potassium; the whole seed provides fiber. Mothers from India traditionally chew the seeds, soak them overnight and heat up the liquid to make a tea the next day, or soak the seeds then eat them mixed in milk and honey. One mother tells of simply swallowing ½ tablespoon of seeds with water directly, finding that this was more effective for her than capsules and commercial teas. The seed powder can also be mixed into other foods.

Several studies of fenugreek as a milk booster have been done in the past decade, testing it either in tea form or as a powdered seed capsule at various dosages.[91,92] In all but one study, those taking fenugreek pumped more milk or their babies gained more weight than those who didn't, though the differences were generally modest.

The most frequently recommended dosage today is 3-6g of powdered seed per day.[35] If you have a sensitive stomach, start with a low dose and work up gradually; a few people experience cramping or diarrhea, and on occasion a baby may have digestive upset as well. These go away quickly when the herb is stopped. Your sweat and urine may smell like maple syrup when taking it.[93] Allergic reactions to fenugreek are uncommon, but if you're prone to asthma or allergies, try a tincture rather than capsules.

Fenugreek is known for its antidiabetic properties, but it doesn't seem to lower blood sugar therapeutically (for diabetes) when taking less than 25g per day.[79] Nevertheless, it is best to stay in normal lactation ranges not exceeding 10g per day. A few people have reported mild hypoglycemic effects; this is unlikely when fenugreek is taken as a food, or mixed in hot cereal or taken with other foods. Type 1 diabetics should not use fenugreek without medical supervision. Fenugreek may not be a good choice if you have low thyroid because it lowered thyroid hormone ($T_3$) in rats, though at high doses.[94] Due to its uterine-stimulating properties, fenugreek is not recommended for pregnancy.

There have been a few isolated reports of milk production actually decreasing with fenugreek rather than increasing. One low-supply parent who had been pumping 4oz (120ml) *total* a day reported her output plummeting to just drops in a short amount of time on fenugreek; it took a week after she stopped it to recover her previous 4oz (120ml) production. In an online group for adoptive parents inducing lactation, several members reported a drop in milk output when they added fenugreek to their domperidone regimen. The common denominator among them was hypothyroidism, and we're suspicious that these rare cases may be occurring in parents with low thyroid. If you have a similar experience, ask your health care provider to check your thyroid function.

### Goat's Rue (Galega officinalis)

*Goat's rue* is a popular galactogogue for French and other European parents and is increasing in popularity in North America, where it's sometimes even taken during the last month or two of pregnancy to support breast growth and milk production. Its use originated in southern Europe and western Asia and was first mentioned in 1873 by dairy farmer Gillet-Damitte, who reported that his cows produced 35-50% more milk when they grazed on the plant. It comes from the same family as fenugreek and has similar antidiabetic properties. Goat's rue contains galegin, from which the insulin-sensitizing drug metformin was eventually developed. Goat's rue is also considered a diuretic and is reputed to stimulate breast tissue growth.

Despite the positive reports on cattle, toxic effects in sheep have made goat's rue somewhat controversial. The most plausible explanation for this is simply the fact that different animals can have different responses, and sheep typically pull up and eat entire plants, roots and all, including parts not typically used for galatogenic purposes. We haven't found any reports of human problems either anecdotally or in the literature. Herbalists who have clinical experience with goat's rue remain comfortable with its use,[36] and LactMed notes that it is generally well-tolerated.[95]

Goat's rue is a good general galactogogue and especially appropriate if you have insulin resistance, hypoplasia, PCOS, or had gestational diabetes during pregnancy. If taken at the same time as metformin, pharmacist Frank Nice suggests self-monitoring for any signs of hypoglycemia. Goat's rue is an ingredient in many lactation teas, combination tinctures, and some new products that combine it with silymarin, a milk thistle extract. It's definitely one of our favorites!

### Ixbut or Hierba Lechera (Euphorbia lancifolia)

In the Mayan language, "Ix" means "woman," and "but" means "an increase in flow," thus Ixbut means to increase the flow of milk in women. Used largely in southern Mexico and Central America, the leaves of ixbut are made into a tea for new parents who are having trouble making milk. It's also used to induce milk production. They tell stories about old women with "withered breasts" who were able to relactate after eating it and how a great-grandfather used it to induce lactation when his granddaughter died in childbirth.[38,96]

Ixbut is very high in calcium. The dosage often mentioned is 3 cups per day for 3-5 days, though a study in 1949 used 6 cups (5 leaves or sections of stem, about 5g total, brewed to make 1 cup of tea).[96] Ixbut tea for breastfeeding parents is available commercially in Guatemala and now in the US (Tea-Tas® by Legendairy Milk®).

### Jivanti (Leptadenia reticulate)

The root of *jivanti* is not only considered a galactogogue but is also reputed to have anti-oxidant, antifungal, and antidiabetic properties. Jivanti is high in quercetin, which may be how it boosts milk production,[97] and is a major ingredient of Leptaden,™ a popular galactogogue product from India backed by animal and human studies dating from the 1960s to the 1980s.[98] Lactancia™ is a newer Indian product combining jivanti and shatavari with additional vitamins and minerals and reportedly increased milk production in parents with insufficient milk.[99]

### Lemon Balm (Melissa officinalis)

*Lemon balm* has calming nervine properties and is typically found in galactogogue combinations. Tustanofskyj mentions an old story in which Russian mothers who drank an infusion of the leaves and stems experienced an increase in milk volume.[60] One study showed that large amounts had anti-thyroid effects in mice,[100] but moderate use, especially in blends, should not be a concern due to its adaptogenic hormone-balancing properties.

### Marshmallow Root (Althaea officinalis)

Nutritious *marshmallow root* has a long reputation for boosting the lactogenic effectiveness of fenugreek, blessed thistle, and alfalfa,[1] along with "enriching the milk." It contains high levels of vitamin A, calcium, and zinc, as well as smaller amounts of iron, sodium, iodine, and B-complex vitamins, and has diuretic properties.[42] While the root is usually used, some cultures use the flowers and leaves.[55] Combine marshmallow with other galactogogue herbs for maximum benefit. Naturopath Sheila Kingsbury believes that the mucilage content also helps keep the milk emulsified and flowing better, reducing clogged milk ducts.[36] She prefers a cold water extraction: Add ¼ cup of cut root per quart of water (not hot) and allow it to sit overnight; strain and drink throughout the day. It can be sweetened with a little honey. Her second choice is powdered root capsules.

### Milk Thistle (Silybum marianum)

*Milk thistle*, sometimes called Mary's thistle, blessed milk thistle, or Lady's thistle, has been used medicinally for a wide range of liver and gallbladder problems since the first century in Europe. It has a long-standing reputation as a galactogogue[101] and is considered to be supportive of thyroid function. Like mulunggay, the fresh leaves and peeled shoots can be eaten in salads or cooked as a spinach substitute.[74] Milk thistle tea is a favorite galactogogue of physician and herb expert Tieraona Lowdog. Capsules of the seed typically come in standardized form to guarantee the content of the active ingredient, silymarin. New galactogogue products using micronized silymarin or a combination of micronized silymarin and goat's rue to enhance absorption have been developed and tested, with mixed but promising results.[102,103]

### Nettle or Stinging Nettle (Urtica urens or Urtica dioica)

*Nettle* has also enjoyed a long tradition of medicinal use, dating back to ancient Greece. Rich in iron, calcium, vitamins A, C, D, and K, potassium, and phosphorus,[78] it is considered antidiabetic, diuretic, hypotensive, and supportive of thyroid function. Nettle has a consistent history of being a powerful galactogogue and is a significant ingredient of many commercial galactogogue products, though usually not used alone. The freeze-dried version of the herb, which is used in capsules and tinctures, is considered the most potent form. It's also the safest because leaves that have been dried in the usual fashion can contain mold spores, which could cause an allergic reaction in those sensitive to mold.

### Red Clover Blossoms (Trifolium pratense)

As a galactogogue, *red clover blossoms* are usually combined with other herbs. They have multiple phytoestrogens to promote mammary development and also help to reduce edema. Sheep fed 3.5 kg of fermented red clover feed daily for 2 weeks had significantly increased total and free $T_3$ thyroid hormone.[104] There is no information on whether normal doses of unfermented red clover affect thyroid hormone in humans, but the herb might be beneficial for nursing parents with low thyroid.

### Red Raspberry (Rubus idaeus)

*Red raspberry* leaf is found in many galactogogue combination teas and tinctures, though it also is not considered a direct galactogogue. Its beneficial effects may come from the nutritive value of the herb, and it may also aid letdown. Due to the astringent (drying) qualities of red raspberry, some herbalists believe that it may be useful in the short-term but could cause a decrease in milk production if used long term.[84] Interestingly, one study noticed that mothers drinking the tea during the last couple months of pregnancy seemed to have their milk volume increase sooner after delivery.[105] Red raspberry is usually combined with other galactogogues and may have a counteractive effect with those that cause loose stools.

### Saw Palmetto (Serenoa repens)

Most known for its usefulness in treating male prostate conditions, *saw palmetto* is reported to have anti-androgenic and hormone-balancing properties when used by women.[72] Those who struggle with excessive body hair, male-pattern hair loss, or adult acne have turned to saw palmetto as a natural treatment for their problem.[106]

Saw palmetto is often found in "natural" bust-enhancing products because of historic reports of breast enlargement with long-term use.[73,107] Seminole Indian women used it to treat "underdeveloped breasts" and to increase their milk: "It increases the size and secreting power of the mammary glands where they are abnormally small and inactive."[108,109] The berries have also been used as galactogogues in animals, with reports of increased and richer milk in cows.[110] The use of saw palmetto in nursing parents in general has not been studied, but we know of several cases when other herbs didn't help but saw palmetto did. This herb is a good choice for anyone with PCOS, hyperandrogenism, or insufficient glandular tissue.

### *Shatavari* (Asparagus racemosus)

From the Sanskrit, "she who has a hundred husbands," *shatavari* (or shatavri or shatawari) is known for its beneficial effects on women's reproductive function and is very popular as an all-around female tonic in India and China. It has traditionally been used for infertility problems and increasing milk production and is an ingredient in Lactare, an Indian commercial galactogogue product.

Shatavari increased the size of the mammary gland in rats and increased milk production in both rats and buffaloes.[111] One human study claimed that it was ineffective for increasing milk production and had little effect on prolactin. However, the researchers used only a very small dose, did not measure prolactin reliably, and combined shatavari with other herbs, so their conclusions are questionable.[112] In a better study of 60 nursing parents using 60mg of root powder per kilogram of parental weight per day, prolactin rose 33%, and the babies gained 16% in weight versus 6% in the placebo group.[113] And here's an interesting fact: when a water-decoction was compared with a milk-decoction of the root in mice, production was higher in the milk-decoction group.[114] In India, *shatavari kalpa* is traditionally taken as a hot milk drink with the powdered root, a little ghee, and honey. Clearly, it's wise to check how it's traditionally taken if you try a different form and it doesn't seem to help!

Shatavari is also reputed to block oxytocin receptors in the uterus, which may be why the Ayurvedic tradition considers it useful for preventing miscarriage or premature labor.[115] (Note: High doses of shatavari extract—100mg per kilogram of weight daily—were associated with fetal development problems in rats.[62,116]) It may seem that this could interfere with letdown, but such complaints have not been found. In an informal survey conducted on our website, 75% of nursing parents with a variety of situations reported an increase in milk production, and some even weaned from domperidone to shatavari, maintaining most of their milk supply. Few side effects were reported, although several mentioned breast tenderness, breast enlargement, and increases in vaginal fluid and libido.

### *Vervain* (Verbena officinalis)

Another lactogenic herb with diuretic and calming properties, *vervain* has a historical reputation for increasing milk production by Europeans and Native Americans[82] and is most often used in combinations. Vervain may also stimulate uterine contractions, so it shouldn't be used during pregnancy but would be good for letdown after the baby is born.[42]

## Using Herbs to Increase Milk Supply During Pregnancy

If you want to continue breastfeeding during a new pregnancy and have experienced a drop in production due to hormone changes, a galactogogue may help maintain some of your milk production. However, you're working against nature—your body's first priority is to prepare for the new baby. A decrease in volume and return to more colostrum-type milk is normal.

Not all herbal galactogogues are appropriate for pregnancy, especially those that are reputed to have oxytocic or uterine-stimulating effects. Herbs generally considered safe for pregnancy include *alfalfa, dandelion leaf, fennel, milk thistle, nettle, oat straw,* and *red raspberry.*

If you had milk supply problems in the past and are now pregnant again, you may be wondering if taking a galactogogue during pregnancy might improve your odds for making more milk the next time around. A study mentioned earlier had mothers take *moringa* from 35 weeks until delivery to see if it made a difference and it did, though they didn't have a history of low supply. Using low-risk herbs in moderate amounts is certainly a reasonable strategy. Depending on the root problem of previous low supply, some galactogogues such as alfalfa might help build milk-making tissue when the milk glands didn't seem to respond with normal growth during a prior pregnancy. Many women have taken *goat's rue* for this purpose during the last couple of months as well, and we are not aware of any problems.

## Commercial Herbal Products

There has been an explosion of commercial galactogogue products on the market in North America, and they can work well in a number of circumstances. Although not reviewed by the FDA for effectiveness nor regulated in the same way as drugs, herbs used as dietary supplements do fall under the FDA's "food and spice" category. They must meet the same basic standards for sterilization and handling, and their packaging can't contain unproven health claims. However, quality is not guaranteed and can vary by manufacturer (see lowmilksupply.org/herbs).

### Nursing Tinctures

Several combination galactogogue tinctures on the market can be very effective. A few large companies offer them commercially, while there are also small businesses that offer their own combinations for sale. Some are tinctures of just one herb, and others are blends of herbs specifically combined for their lactogenic properties. Most are alcohol based (the small amount ingested is not a problem for breastfeeding), though some are available in glycerin form. Tinctures may be made from fresh or dried herbs, and this can affect the potency as well as the price. Remember that suggested dosages are not set in stone. You may need more or less, depending on your situation.

### Commercial Galactogogue Capsules

For anyone who doesn't want to taste anything strong or unpleasant, capsules can be a great option. Most contain dried herbs singly or in combinations, though one company capsulizes concentrated tinctures. One big difference between the two is that dried herbs contain fiber and fats, which for some herbs may be important components of their lactogenic effects.

### Nursing Tea Combinations

Historically, most herbs were brewed into teas, and remedies for increasing milk production were no exception. Teas are preferred by many herbalists for the comforting ritual of their preparation. Many lactation consultants consider lactation teas to be milder in effect than tinctures or capsules, but that may depend on using the right amount and preparing it properly. Experience has shown that it may take several cups of some lactation teas to get a good effect rather than the 2-3 cups a day that's recommended. Try brewing several cups at a time and then sip on the tea all day long.

Various commercial brands offer slightly different herb combinations. Steeping time is very important for the proper diffusion of the herbs into the tea—too short will make a less effective product. Covering the tea with a plate during steeping helps to prevent evaporation of the water-soluble components into the air. While some products call for only 5 minutes of steeping time, a minimum of 10 minutes may give a better result.

## Customize Your Own Galactogogue Blend

Creating your own combination is another alternative and provides the opportunity to tailor the herbs to your situation. Some low-supply parents have simply bought bulk herbs and created their own tinctures, custom teas, and decoction blends. Although we often correctly assume that multiple herbs will add to a stronger overall effect or at least help each other, keep in mind that *there is also the possibility that they may cancel out some of each other's properties, negating the advantage.* You may want to try herbs one at a time and then try combining them to see if the effect is better or simply overlapping. Why use (or spend) more than you need?

After struggling and never making quite enough milk for her first baby, Cindy researched and created her own special blend of herbs. For pregnancy, she devised a bulk tea mix to enhance her breast growth made from a generous handful each of red raspberry leaf and nettle and slightly smaller amounts of alfalfa and red clover. She added a handful of this mix to 1 quart (946ml) of almost boiling water and allowed it to steep overnight. Cindy drank 1 cup each day during the first trimester and worked up to 1 quart a day by the end of pregnancy. After the baby was born, she added other herbs that would enhance milk supply to her mix: handfuls of hops flower, blessed thistle, and marshmallow root. When she made a batch, she added a heaping teaspoon (about 5g) each of fenugreek powder and goat's rue powder to the pot. Cindy continued to drink 4 cups daily, usually iced to mask the bitterness of some of the herbs (sweeteners can be used, too). She credits her "lactation brew" for her full supply with her next baby. For Cindy and a few other parents, this selection of herbs seemed to be helpful. It's important to remember, however, that *there is no one magic combination that is perfect for everyone.*

A good source of lactation tea recipes is *A Fountain of Gardens* by Jennifer Maiden. And here's a recipe from herbalist Sheila Kingsbury:

# Milky Oat Tea

¼ cup hops flowers (fresh or dried)

½ cup goat's rue leaves

¼ cup anise *or* fennel seed

½ cup oat pods

Mix all in a bag. Put ½ cup of the mixture into 1 quart of hot water and let steep for 30 minutes. Strain and then drink throughout the day.

## Other Traditional Tea Combinations[60]

- Mix 20g anise seed, 20g dill seed, 30g fenugreek seeds, and 30g fennel seed. Brew 1 tsp of tea blend in 1 cup of boiling water and drink 3 cups per day.
- Mix 10g anise seeds, 20g melissa leaves, 20g galega, 30g dill seeds, and 40g fennel seeds. Brew 1 tsp of this tea blend in 1 cup of boiling water; drink 2-3 cups per day.
- Mix 30g galega, 10g anise seeds, and 10g fennel seeds. Brew 1 tsp of this tea blend in 1 cup of boiling water; drink 2-3 cups per day.

## Herbs for Letdown

There are several herbs with varying reputations for helping with letdown. When stress is a factor, *chamomile* tea is well known for its calming effects and is sometimes taken before nursing to help with relaxation and milk release. Naturopath Sheila Kingsbury likes to use *lemon balm, hops,* and *oats* for calming effects as well. Herbs that have a reputation for increasing milk flow include *anise, black cohosh, black seed, chasteberry, dill, fennel, red raspberry leaf,* and *vervain.* Lactation consultant Margie Deutsch-Lash prefers red raspberry leaf tincture, 1ml held under the tongue for 30 seconds before swallowing, 10 minutes before a feeding, but says that if a parent likes tea better, it is best taken 20 minutes before feeding as it is absorbed more slowly in the stomach.

## Homeopathic Galactogogues

Homeopathy is a healing philosophy that is counterintuitive to Western medicine. The prescription of homeopathic remedies and medicines is based on the ancient Law of Similars, or "like treats like," rather than the Western approach of treating a problem with something designed to counteract it. Homeopathy interprets physical and emotional signs and symptoms as the means by which the body is trying to restore order when it is out of balance and so facilitates the choice of a medicine capable of actually causing that same particular set of signs and symptoms as a way to assist the body in its attempts to heal.

Some homeopathic remedies can be used generally for particular problems, but ideally they are chosen by an experienced practitioner after a detailed screening of your history and situation. The homeopathic approach is complex and not easily reduced to a list because there are dozens of possible remedies depending on what the practitioner determines the root problems to be.

Because homeopathy doesn't easily fit into the Western paradigm of medicine, it is difficult to list homeopathic galactogogues in an absolute sense. There are some that are appropriate for general application to low milk production, but the vast majority require specific tailoring to a nursing parent's unique situation. Remedies and medicines usually come in X (1:10), C (1:100), or LM (1:50,000) potencies and may be liquid or pills. For use without the advice of a practitioner, 6C or 12C dilutions are usually most appropriate.

## Lactogenic Homeopathic Remedies and Their Clinical Indications

| Homeopathic Remedy | Low Milk Supply Cause |
| --- | --- |
| Agnus castus | Depression |
| Calcarea carbonica | General use; hemorrhage or anemia |
| Causticum | Short-term exhaustion; works best with personality that resists rather than "rolls with the punches" |
| Dulcamara | Sudden loss of milk after exposure to cold and damp; engorgement |
| Galega | Anemia or poor nutrition |
| Helonias | Extreme maternal exhaustion ("super mom syndrome") |
| Ignatia | Sudden loss of milk related to shock and grief |
| Lactuca virosa | Strong; general use |
| Ricinus communis | Hemorrhage or anemia |
| Urtica urens | General use; hemorrhage or anemia |

Source: Hatherly P. *The Homeopathic Physician's Guide to Lactation.* Chapel Hill, Australia: Luminoz Pty Ltd; 2004.

To save cost on medicine and effect the smoothest possible healing response, homeo-pathic practitioner Patricia Hatherly suggests placing either 3 pills or 3 drops of the rem-edy into a small bottle 10-17oz (300-500ml) of spring water and taking a teaspoon (5ml) 3 times daily, shaking the bottle in between.

The table above lists several homeopathic remedies more commonly used for low milk production. For best results, consult an experienced practitioner as skilled at choosing the most appropriate prescription for your unique situation.

## When Can I Stop Taking a Galactogogue?

When to stop depends on your circumstances. In uncomplicated low milk supply, you can start to cut back as soon as you've reached full production and your baby is able to keep it going. Reduce your galactogogues gradually to avoid a drop in milk produc-tion. If your body seems to be struggling, such as with an iron deficiency, a hormonal problem, or a lack of sufficient breast tissue, you might need to keep taking it for weeks or months or possibly even the entire time you're breastfeeding. Sometimes the body seems to "kick in" after a time of additional support, but other times the breast needs long-term support. But even then, some parents find that they are able to cut back some, if not completely, around 6 months or so when their baby starts to eat solids. You can always try reducing your dosage or frequency (or both), no more than 25% every week, and if you begin to experience a drop in milk production, just start back up again.

# Galactogogue Tables

*Note: Do not use the information in these tables without first consulting the explanations about appropriate use of galactogogues in Chapter 14. Internal use of essential oils is not recommended.*

## Ratings

**US Federal Drug Administration**

GRAS = Generally Regarded As Safe

**Humphrey, *The Nursing Mother's Herbal*[84]**

A = No contraindications, side effects, drug interactions, or pregnancy-related safety issues have been identified. Generally considered safe when used appropriately.

B = May not be appropriate for self-use by some individuals or dyads. May cause adverse effects if misused. Seek reliable safety and dose information.

C = Moderate potential for toxicity, mainly dose related. Seek an expert herbalist as well as a lactation consultation before using. Consider using safer herbs.

**American Herbal Products Association's *Botanical Safety Handbook* (BSH) based on normal, not excessive, consumption[62]**

Safety Class 1 = Can be safely consumed when used appropriately

Safety Class 2 = Some restrictions apply

Safety Class 2a= For external use only, due to toxicity concerns

Safety Class 2b = Not to be used during pregnancy

Safety Class 2c = Not be used while nursing

Interaction Class A = No clinically relevant interactions with drugs expected

Interaction Class B = Clinically relevant interactions with some drugs theoretically possible

Interaction Class C = Clinically relevant interactions with some drugs are known to occur

**TABLE 1** Galactogogues Quick Reference Table

| Herb | Therapeutic Dose | | | Other Reputed Beneficial Qualities | Potential Side Effects | Cautions or Notes | Rating |
|---|---|---|---|---|---|---|---|
| | Tea | Tincture | Capsule | | | | |
| Alfalfa leaf (*Medicago sativa*) | 1-2 tbsp leaves steeped in 2/3 cup (150ml) water; drink 2-4 times per day | 0.5-4ml 3-4 times per day; less effective | 1-2 capsules 4 times per day | Diuretic, mammary stimulation, pituitary support, phytoestrogen, nutritive: vitamins A, C, E, K; calcium; iron | Loose stools; allergenic for some people; seeds may increase risk of sunburn | Related to peanut and legume families; avoid if taking warfarin; safe for pregnancy | GRAS (spice) Humphrey: leaf: A Seed: C BSH: 1, A |
| Anise seed (*Pimpinella anisum*) | 1-2 tsp crushed seeds steeped in 1 cup (240ml) water 10-20 min; drink 3-6 times a day | 3ml 2-3 times per day | | Antiflatulent, anticolic, aromatic, phytoestrogen, letdown aid; relaxing | Can be allergenic for some people | Not the same as star of anise and should not be used interchangeably; avoid if allergic to anethole; tea safe for pregnancy but not alcohol extract | GRAS (spice) Humphrey: B BSH: 1, A |
| Ashwagandha root (*Withania somnifera*) | | | One 500mg capsule concentrated extract twice a day | Hypotensive, relaxing, thyroxine-stimulating properties[2] | None known | | Humphrey: C BSH: 2b, A |
| Black cohosh (*Actaea racemosa*) | | 1ml 3 times per day | | Hypotensive, letdown aid, mammary stimulation, anti-androgen | Possibly allergenic, occasional gastric discomfort | Not for use in pregnancy; better for short-term; avoid large amounts | Humphrey: B BSH: 2b, A |
| Black seed or black cumin (*Nigella sativa*) | 1 tsp crushed seeds steeped in 1 cup (240ml) water for 15 min; drink 4-6 times per day | 1 tbsp seed oil daily | | Antidiabetic, antihistamine, hypotensive, mammary gland stimulation; nutritive | Possible contact allergy with oil | Not recommended during pregnancy; contraindicated with bleeding disorder; avoid large amounts of essential oil | GRAS (spice) Humphrey: B BSH: 1, A |

*continued*

Dosages are suggested starting points; you may need more or less depending on your situation. Teas should be made with boiling water and loose herb or tea bag unless otherwise noted.

**TABLE 1** Galactogogues Quick Reference Table   *continued*

| Herb | Therapeutic Dose | | | Other Reputed Beneficial Qualities | Potential Side Effects | Cautions or Notes | Rating |
| --- | --- | --- | --- | --- | --- | --- | --- |
| | Tea | Tincture | Capsule | | | | |
| Blessed thistle aerial parts (*Cnicus benedictus*) | 1-2 tsp dried herb steeped in 2/3 cup (150ml) water; drink 5-6 times per day (bitter) | 1-3ml 2-4 times per day (bitter) | One to three 250-300mg capsules 3 times per day when combined with fenugreek; up to 6g if used alone | Digestive aid, diuretic | Occasionally allergenic member of the ragweed family; high doses (more than 1 tsp per cup of tea) may cause gastric irritation | Typically discouraged for pregnancy | GRAS Humphrey: B BSH: 1, A |
| Borage seed (*Borago officinalis*) | N/A | N/A | 1-2g oil capsules per day | Diuretic, enriches milk, high gamma-linolenic acid (GLA); relaxing | Loose stools, minor stomach upset | Leaves contain small amounts of toxic alkaloids not found in seed oil | Humphrey: seed oil: A leaf: C BSH: seed oil: 1, A Leaf: 2a, A |
| Caraway seed (*Carum carvi*) | 1-2 tsp freshly crushed seeds steeped in 1 cup (240ml) water; steep 10-15 min; drink 5-6 times per day | 3ml 3 times per day | ¼-½ tsp powder 3 times per day | Antianxiety, antiflatulent, antidiabetic, antihypertensive, letdown aid; relaxing | None known | Avoid large amounts of essential oil | GRAS Humphrey: A BSH: 1, A |
| Chaste tree berry (*Vitex agnus-castus*) | 1 tsp ripe berries infused in 1 cup (240ml) water for 10-15 min; drink 3 times per day (bitter) | 0.5-1ml (1:5 tincture) 3 times per day or up to 5ml total daily | 250-500mg per day | Hormone balancer, mammary gland stimulation, letdown aid, pituitary regulation, anti-androgen | Itching, rash | Higher dosages decrease prolactin in men and may counteract effects of metoclopramide and domperidone, hormonal contraceptives; best used with professional advice | Humphrey: B BSH: 1, A |
| Coriander seed (*Coriandrum sativum*) | 1 heaping tbsp (5g) crushed seeds steeped in 1 cup (240ml) water for 10-15 min; drink 3-5 times per day | | | Antidiabetic, antiflatulent, diuretic, letdown aid; nutritive | Related to celery; increased photosensitivity (rare) | Avoid large amounts of the essential oil; occasional contact allergic reactions reported | GRAS Humphrey: A BSH: 1, A |

| Herb | Tea/infusion | Tincture | Capsule | Actions | Side effects | Cautions | Safety |
|---|---|---|---|---|---|---|---|
| Dandelion leaves (*Taraxacum officinale*) | 1-2 tsp (5-10g) finely chopped or coarsely powdered leaf steeped in 1 cup (240ml) of water; drink 3 times daily | 3ml 3 times per day | Two 500mg capsules 3 times per day | Antidiabetic, diuretic, good iron source, thyroid support; nutritive (iron) | Contact dermatitis (rare) | Avoid harvesting from lawns or areas treated with chemicals or pesticides | GRAS for oil extract; Humphrey: A BSH: 1, A |
| Dill seed (*Anethum graveolens*) | 2 tsp crushed seeds steeped in 1 cup water (or 3g in 300ml) for 10-15 min; drink 2-3 times per day | ½-1 tsp (2.5-5ml), 1-3 times per day | | Antidiabetic, antiflatulent, diuretic, letdown aid; relaxing | None known | None known | Humphrey: A BSH: 1, A |
| Fennel seed (*Foeniculum volgare*) | 1-3 tsp (5-15g) crushed seeds steeped in 1 cup (240mL) water for 10-15 min; drink 2-6 times per day | 3ml 3 times per day | 1000mg 2-3 times per day | Anti-androgen, antiflatulent, aromatic, diuretic, phytoestrogen, hypotensive, mammary gland stimulation, letdown aid; relaxing | Contact dermatitis, possible allergic response in gastrointestinal or respiratory tract | Essential oil may be toxic in very large amounts; fennel tea OK for pregnancy; avoid essential oil during pregnancy and lactation | GRAS (spice) Humphrey: A BSH: 1, A |
| Fenugreek seed (*Trigonella foenum-graecum*) | 1 tsp (5g) whole or ¼ tsp (1g) powdered seeds steeped in 1 cup (240ml) water for 15 min; drink 2-3 times per day | 1-2ml 3 times per day | One to four 580- to 610mg capsules, 3-4 times per day, or equivalent | Antidiabetic, appetite stimulation, iron rich, mammary gland stimulation | Can cause maple syrup smell in mother or baby; stomach upset; loose stools or diarrhea, hypoglycemia; powdered seed form may cause allergic reactions, especially in people with asthma | Consult health care provider first if history of hypoglycemia or diabetes; take with food to minimize any hypoglycemic effects; reduces thyroid hormone (T$_3$) in mice and rats; not for use during pregnancy; caution if taking warfarin; high mucilage content in powdered seed- avoid taking medications at same time. | GRAS (spice) Humphrey: B BSH: 2b, A |

continued

**TABLE 1** Galactogogues Quick Reference Table  *continued*

| Herb | Tea | Therapeutic Dose Tincture | Capsule | Other Reputed Beneficial Qualities | Potential Side Effects | Cautions or Notes | Rating |
|---|---|---|---|---|---|---|---|
| Goat's rue aerial parts (*Galega officinalis*) | 1 tsp (5g) leaves steeped in 1 cup (240ml) of water for 10-15 min; drink 2-5 times per day (bitter) | WiseWoman Herbal: 2.5ml 1-4 times per day; Simply Herbal Organics: 3-4ml 4 times per day  Motherlove: 1-2ml 4 times per day  Dr. Low Dog: 1 tsp in 8oz water 3 times per day | Motherlove: 1 capsule 4 times per day or 2 capsules 3 times per day for over 175 lb; 0.5-1 tsp 3 times per day | Antidiabetic; diuretic; mammary gland stimulation, | Hypoglycemic; may have blood-thinning properties | Consult with health care provider if taking any other diabetes-related medications; take with food to reduce any hypoglycemic effects; observe for hypoglycemia if taken together with antidiabetic medications such as metformin; no research or reported problems with use during pregnancy | Humphrey: B BSH: N/A |
| Hops flower (*Humulus lupulus*) | 1 tsp (5g) leaves steeped in 1 cup (240ml) water for 10 min; drink 1-2 times per day | | | Mammary gland stimulation; relaxing; letdown aid | Contact allergy | Use with history of depression controversial | GRAS (oil, extract) Humphrey: B BSH: 1, A |
| Lemon balm leaf (*Melissa officinalis*) | 1.5-4.5g cut leaf several times daily; fresh leaf tea is ideal | 0.5-1ml glycerite form 2-3 times daily | Follow manufacturer's instructions for dried herb capsules | Calming; antiflatulent; antidiabetic; gastrointestinal spasms; adaptogen | Large amounts had antithyroid effect in rats; moderate amounts not a concern for hypothyroidism | Caution advised if already taking sedatives | GRAS Humphrey: A BSH: 1, A |
| Moringa leaf (*Moringa oleifera*) | 3-5 cups per day | Motherlove concentrated tincture capsules 4-6 per day | 1-3 350mg capsules leaf powder 3 times per day | Nutritive, antidiabetic, antioxidant | Large amounts had antithyroid effect in rats; root and bark have abortifacient properties | Caution if taking warfarin | Humphrey: leaf A, fruit B BSH: n/a |

| Herb | Tea/infusion | Tincture | Capsule | Properties/uses | Side effects | Notes | Safety |
|---|---|---|---|---|---|---|---|
| Marshmallow root (*Althaea officinalis*) | 1 tbsp (15g) root powder to 5-8 oz (150-140ml) in *cold* water; let stand 30 min and drink immediately | Ineffective form | 2-4 capsules 3 times per day | Diuretic; enriches milk; nutritive: vitamin A, calcium, zinc, iron, sodium, iodine, and B-complex vitamins | Allergic reactions possible but extremely rare | High mucilage content-avoid taking medications at same time | Humphrey: A BSH: 1, A |
| Milk thistle seed (*Silybum marianum*) | 1 heaping tsp (5ml) freshly crushed or chopped seeds steeped in 5oz (150ml) water for 20-30 min; drink up to 5-6 times per day | Less effective form | Two 500mg standardized capsules 3 times per day | Antidiabetic; liver and gallbladder protective | Possible allergen; possible mild laxative effect in first few days | Take with food if any hypoglycemic effects; may increase clearance of metronidazole; best used with other herbs, not alone | Humphrey: A BSH: 1, A |
| Nettle or stinging nettle leaf (*Urtica urens* or *Urtica dioica*) | 1 tbsp cut herb steeped in 1 cup (240ml) water for 10-15 min; drink 2-3 times per day | Less effective form | One to two 300mg capsules 3 times per day | Antidiabetic; antiinflammatory; diuretic; hypotensive; nutritive: iron, calcium, vitamin K, potassium | Mild diuretic, mild gastrointestinal upset | None known | Humphrey: A BSH: 1, A |
| Red clover aerial parts (*Trifolium pratense*) | 1-3 tsp (5-15g) herb steeped in 1 cup water for 10-15 min; drink 3 times per day | 2-6ml 3 times per day | 2-3 capsules 3 times per day | Diuretic; mammary gland stimulation; nutritive; phytoestrogen; increases thyroid hormone in ewes | Rarely may cause loose stools or nausea | Use during pregnancy somewhat controversial though moderate amounts probably fine; usually taken with other herbs | GRAS (spice, oil) Humphrey: B BSH: 1, A |
| Red raspberry leaf (*Rubus idaeus*) | 1 tsp (5g) steeped in 2/3 cup (150ml) water for 5 min; drink 2-4 times per day | 3-4ml 3 times per day | Three 300mg capsules 3 times per day | letdown aid; nutritive: iron, calcium; antidiabetic | None known | Short-term use only; may cause lowering of milk production with long-term use (more than 2 weeks) | Humphrey: A BSH: 1, A |

continued

**TABLE 1** Galactogogues Quick Reference Table *continued*

| Herb | Therapeutic Dose | | | Other Reputed Beneficial Qualities | Potential Side Effects | Cautions or Notes | Rating |
|------|-----|---------|---------|------|------|------|------|
| | Tea | Tincture | Capsule | | | | |
| Saw palmetto berries (Serenoa repens) | ½-1 tsp (2.5-5g) berries in 1 cup (240ml) water; bring to a boil and simmer gently for 5 min; drink 3 times per day | 1-2ml 3 times per day | 1-2 capsules berries 2-3 times per day | Anti-androgen, diuretic, hormone balancer, mammary gland stimulation | Occasional stomach upset, diarrhea, headache; take with food to avoid | Avoid with bleeding disorder; not for pregnancy use | Humphrey: A BSH: 1, A |
| Shatavari root (Asparagus racemosus) | Beverage: 2 tsp (10g) root powder stirred into warm milk once or twice a day | | One or two 500mg capsules twice a day | Diuretic; mammary gland stimulation; nutritive | May have laxative effect; may increase libido | Traditional use of beverage form during pregnancy in Ayurveda; see text for details | Humphrey: B BSH:1, A |
| Vervain aerial parts (Verbena officinalis) | 1 tsp (5g) steeped in 2/3 cup (150ml) water for 10 min, drink 3 times per day or ¼-½ cup (30-60g) herb in 1 qt (1L) water 10-15 min drink ½ cup 3 times per day | 2-4ml 3 times per day | | Antianxiety; hypotensive, thyroid support | None known | Usually combined with other herbs rather than taken alone; bitter flavor; not recommended during pregnancy | GRAS (flavoring) Humphrey: B BSH: 2b, A |

Source: See Chapter 14 citations.

**TABLE 2** Symptoms and Lactogenic Herbs that May be Beneficial to Them

| Symptom | Herbal Properties | Herbs |
|---|---|---|
| Heavy bleeding, hemorrhage, anemia | High iron content or pituitary support | Alfalfa, dandelion, fenugreek, moringa, nettle, red raspberry |
| Hypertension (high blood pressure) | Hypotensive | Ashwagandha, black cohosh, black seed, caraway, nettle, vervain |
| Postpartum edema (water retention) | Diuretic | Alfalfa, dandelion, nettle, shatavari |
| High blood sugar or insulin resistance | Antidiabetic (check with your physician also) | Black seed; caraway, coriander, dandelion, fenugreek, goat's rue, milk thistle, moringa, nettle |
| Hormonal imbalances | Hormone balancer | Ashwagandha, blessed thistle, chasteberry, saw palmetto |
| Hyperandrogenism | Anti-androgen (male hormone) | Saw palmetto, fennel, chasteberry, black cohosh |
| Hypothyroid (low) | Thyroid-supporting qualities | Ashwagandha, dandelion, nettle, vervain, red clover |
| Hyperthyroid (high) | Antithyroid | Fenugreek, moringa, lemon balm |
| Mammary hypoplasia or poor pregnancy breast development | Mammary gland stimulation (often estrogenic) | Goat's rue, chasteberry, fennel, fenugreek, red clover, saw palmetto, shatavari, alfalfa, black seed, black cohosh, hops, milk thistle |
| Maternal or infant gassiness | Antiflatulent (gas) carminatives | Anise, caraway, coriander, dill, fennel, hops, lemon balm |
| Nutrient deficiencies | High in vitamins and minerals | Alfalfa, dandelion, moringa, nettle, red raspberry leaf |
| Slow milk letdown | Increase flow of milk or relaxing to help milk flow | Anise, black cohosh (short-term), blessed thistle, caraway, chasteberry, coriander, dill, fennel, hops, red raspberry (short-term only), wild lettuce (lactuca virosa) |
| Stress | Relaxing aromatic herbs | Anise, caraway, dill, fennel, hops, lemon balm, oat pods, vervain |

Sources: See Chapter 14 citations.

## CHAPTER 15

# Making More Milk When You Return to Work or School

Mothers always worked while breastfeeding, though what this looks like has evolved throughout time. In previous centuries, they farmed, sewed, cooked, and more at home, but today's parents can continue breastfeeding while attending work and school both inside and outside their home. What's changed most is the demands placed on us—the sometimes-fractured support systems, the shortcomings of available tools and pumps, and entirely new parenting challenges. Whether you're reading this with a supply that's already low or you need ideas because it dropped after returning to work or school, this chapter will help you pinpoint issues and strategize ways to make the most milk possible for your baby.

## Develop Your Game Plan

Before you return, you'll need a plan for how to manage expressing and feeding while you're away from your baby. There is no single right approach because work, school, and childcare situations vary. The main factors that affect your plan are the baby's age when you start work, how long you'll be separated each time, how close your caregiver is, and what baby will be fed during the workday. If you want him to have only your milk, or at least as much of it as possible, you'll need to express for when you aren't together. Just like the first few weeks after birth, returning to work or school may be a little bit awkward as you find your way and settle into a routine. The following suggestions will help minimize the impact on your milk production. Most important, *be flexible so you can adapt to the unexpected.*

## "Stack the Deck" in Your Favor

Your best chance for maintaining the supply your baby needs starts with investing the time to establish maximum milk production *before* you start working. As discussed in Chapter 5, the higher you can calibrate your initial milk production, the more resilient it will be if you have difficulties later on.[1]

Some parents opt to express one or more times a day after nursing to deliberately overstimulate production and build up a stash for the inevitable bumps down the road. But unless you're returning to work very quickly after birth, consider focusing on breastfeeding the first couple of weeks before adding pumping to the mix. Enjoy the moment and establish your nursing relationship first. Babies eat a lot in the early weeks and you need to make sure there's milk left in the breast for a baby who is just learning and wants to top off the tank. You'll produce more milk and make the transition back to work more easily if you put your baby first and fit preparations in as you go. Once you do start expressing, if you find yourself feeding the milk back to your baby because he wanted more after you pumped, one way to balance this is to express the leftover milk from the *starting breast* only. The yield will be less but this allows for extra stimulation, collection of some milk, *and* still leaves milk for a baby who may want to come back for a little more.

If you don't express very much at the start, don't panic; this doesn't mean you'll have problems when you return to work. The point of expressing is to tell your breasts to make *more* than they're currently making. If necessary, you can always add another session or two but keep in mind that it can take a few days to see a difference. Just remember that once you're back at work you'll be collecting at least what your baby normally takes.

## Get a Good Pump

Even if you're very skilled at hand expressing, you'll probably find it more efficient and time-effective to express with a high-quality double pump when away from your baby. If you start with a good supply, a high-end consumer pump is usually sufficient; but if you struggle with milk production, a high-end multi-user rental pump may be a wiser choice, at least temporarily. Your equipment can make or break your experience, so invest in the best that you can afford. For helpful information on choosing a pump, see Chapter 13.

## Get That Letdown Going

After weeks or months of nursing before you return to work, your letdown reflex should be conditioned to the sight, sounds, and feel of your hungry baby. If you haven't done much pumping before now, you may need a little time to make the mental adjustment and get the milk flowing quickly for the pump. Lactation consultant Barbara Robertson talks about how nursing parents need to "feel the love" for their pump and bond with it, but this can take time.[2] Anything that reminds you of your baby can help elicit your letdown reflex. Photos can be very powerful, as can smelling clothing or blankets with baby's scent or listening to a recording of his sounds. One mother was able to condition her letdown reflex to the pump by practicing with the pump on one side while nursing her baby on the other breast. This helped her associate the pump with the baby, and soon she was able to letdown for the pump by itself. Another person used guided imagery and hands-on pumping techniques as their "magic bullets." Chapter 12 has more ideas for triggering or conditioning your letdown reflex that can be adapted for pumping as well.

If privacy is the issue, see if you can find either a more secluded place to pump (not the bathroom!) or a way to make your pumping location more private. Can you put up a sign to discourage visitors? Can you install a lock on the door? Can you hang curtains? Can you pump in your car? Ask your employer for help if you can't come up with a solution on your own, though bringing an idea to them usually gets faster results. For families in the US, the Affordable Care Act spells out how employers should be accommodating nursing parents, including privacy and breaktime issues (see bit.ly/MMM-Laws).

## Work Out Your Feeding and Expressing Routine

How many times does your baby normally feed during the time period you'll be away? Aim for fitting in that many pumping sessions, adding extra opportunities for feeding and expressing while at home into your schedule to help keep your supply up.

Here's an example for an 8-hour day: If you normally get up at 6 am for your workday, wake your baby at 5:30 am for an early feeding, preferably in bed, where you can rest for a few more minutes. Once he's content, you should be able to get ready. Give him a "top off" feeding right before you leave home or at the caregiver's. If you have time, express as soon as you get to work or school to drain the remaining milk. Then express again during your morning, lunch, and afternoon breaks. Ask the caregiver not to feed the baby close to the time you're due to arrive so that he'll be ready to nurse when you pick him up or get home. If you're late, baby can be given an ounce or so to keep him happy until you get there. Nurse once or twice more in the evening, right before he goes to sleep, and at least once during the night.

By now you've fit more than 8 sessions of pumping or nursing into your day! Even though you've been away for 8-10 hours, you're still nursing or pumping as many times as parents who are with their babies full time. That's going to go a long way toward keeping your milk production high.

*Hands-free pumping allows you to multitask. Photo courtesy of Syreeta Elie*

For some busy parents, there just doesn't seem to be enough free space in the day to get all those sessions in, at least not at home or work. But what about during your commute? Clever parents have used hands-free pumps or pumping set-ups while commuting, and for some, it's the longest stretch of expressing that they get and the key to their long-term success.

## Find Your Magic Number

We've outlined a standard workday example, but schedules vary, and so do our bodies. Lactation consultant Nancy Mohrbacher talks about the *Magic Number*—the minimum number of times an individual needs to remove milk by either breastfeeding or expressing in 24 hours to keep up their supply. Your *starting point* is the average number of feedings per 24 hours when you are home together, given that your baby is older than 6 weeks, you are nursing on cue, and the baby has been gaining well with exclusive breastfeeding. Moms with smaller breast storage capacities typically feed more often and will have higher numbers, while those with larger storage capacity may have longer feeding intervals and thus lower numbers. Nancy estimates them to be *around* 8-9 times per day for small-capacity, 7-8 times for medium-capacity, and 5-6 times for large-capacity breasts.[3] As long as your pumping and feeding sessions add up to your personal magic number or more, you should be able to sustain your milk production. For more details, see bit.ly/MMM-Number.

Make breastfeeding a high priority when you're not working. Consider setting a rule that your baby gets bottles only when you're at work, and breastfeed the rest of the time as much as possible. Try to resist the temptation to let someone else feed a bottle of pumped milk just because it's already prepared and handy and you have something else to do. These situations usually mean skipping pumping as well, which can lead to slower milk production. Frequent bottle use can also lead to breast refusal if your baby spends more time with the bottle than the breast. On evenings and weekends, consider taking him with you wherever you go so you can nurse when he wants to, even at the movies or out to dinner. If—when—the going gets tough, keep in mind that it's a short period of your life that will be over before you know it.

## Be Creative

Don't overlook creative scheduling possibilities. Can you minimize the time you and your baby are separated? How about working or going to school part time at first? Or taking online classes or working from home? Can baby come with you for some or all of the time, at least in the early weeks or months? Can your baby be brought to you, or can you go to your baby, for at least one nursing each day? Could you take part or all of Wednesday off so that you have to rely on pumping to maintain your milk supply for only 2 days at a time? Would fewer longer days or more short workdays work better in your situation? How important is privacy compared with convenience to you? Don't hesitate to express your needs to those who can help, especially your employer or professors.

Jennie struggled with pumping. Instead of isolating herself with a machine, she opted to use her hand pump because she felt more comfortable using it in front of her co-workers. "It made me hate pumping a lot less, and it was light years faster to do it one-handed and massage one breast at a time, plus I got to chat with friends while doing it. Pumping when around others always made the task more bearable." While most people prefer privacy, Jennie recognized her need for socializing time and modified her pumping regimen to allow her to comfortably stay among her co-workers.

## Common Pitfalls

It's so common to hear about working parents having problems with their milk supplies that it seems inevitable. Milk production may start off very well at the beginning of the week but lag by the end. An expression routine that works well on Monday may not yield the same amount of milk on Thursday or Friday. Other times, mothers find that milk production seems to decrease around 2-3 months after they've started back. These experiences aren't inevitable, but there are many reasons they can happen.

## Inadequate Milk Removal

The most likely suspect when a working parent's milk supply drops is a decrease in pumping. If your job or class schedule keeps you running most of the day, it can be challenging to fit in enough pumping sessions, especially if you're limited to just the time of your break. Or you may start off expressing 3-4 times each day but eventually find that you're pumping only a couple of times at most on busy days, and there seem to be more busy days than not. One solution may be to use a hands-free kit or set-up so you can multitask while pumping. Another idea is to set an alarm on your cell phone. If you don't have enough time for a full pumping session, *it's better to pump for even a few minutes than not at all.* Anything is better than nothing.

Feeding less at night is another common reason for production dropping. Has your baby started sleeping longer at night? Or have you started sleep training? It might seem great at first because you're getting more rest. But your baby has to make up those feedings in some way, and it's probably going to be during the day with the caregiver, demanding larger bottles. To keep up with his need for more milk then, you'll need to add in another 1 or 2 pumping sessions at other times, wake your baby for an additional feed right before you go to bed, or reconsider the value of uninterrupted sleep.

If you can get your baby to nurse at least once during the night, you can minimize the disruption of night feeding by having him sleep with you or near you for the next few months. This worked for Charlotte: "Sleeping with my baby made getting enough sleep while nighttime parenting and nursing on demand so much easier! My husband compared notes with his friends and swears we got more sleep because of this." Remember: The more baby eats at home, the less he'll need while you're away and the less milk you'll have to provide. (For info on bedsharing safety, review the *Safe Sleep Seven* in Chapter 5.)

Having a freezer stash can actually be the downfall of milk supply for some mothers. While it's great to have a back-up, dipping into it often because of a shortfall in what you're pumping is a red flag. It's easy to lose that sense of urgency about taking action if production falters when you've got a freezer full of milk, but if you wait until it's gone to make changes, it will be harder to recoup your production.

Another possibility when frequency is an issue is how you determine when it's time to pump. Do you wait until your breasts feel full? That can lead to longer and longer pumping intervals because production slows down when milk builds up in the breast for a while.

Some parents choose not to express at all while they are away from their baby, nursing only at night and on weekends and opting for the caregiver to give formula instead. This creates a challenge for keeping milk production up, especially if the time away is long, yet some have done this successfully. *The key is making sure to nurse as much as possible when you and your baby are together.*

## Pump Effectiveness

The second most likely suspect when milk production decreases while working or attending school is the equipment. How good is your pump? A high-end unit may be necessary to remove milk effectively. Make sure your flanges fit well and all the parts are cleaned and connected properly. If valves and membranes haven't been washed separately, residual milk can cause them to stick together and reduce suction. If those aren't the issue, try adjusting the cycling speed either up or down to better match the way your baby nurses. If you're using a consumer-grade pump, how old is it? As discussed earlier, they're not designed to work at top efficiency for much longer than a year and can deteriorate so slowly that you may not notice. If you used it with your last baby or you borrowed it from someone else, try renting a pump for a week to see if you get more milk. If so, you may want to invest in a new pump. It may also help to read back through Chapter 13 for tips to increase your pumping output.

## Travel

For some families, it's traveling out of town that throws off the pumping schedule. That's usually followed by the dilemma of where and how to store pumped milk. You may need to think creatively to work around any travel-related obstacles, such as expressing in a car or plane lavatory or bringing your baby and a helper with you. Some airports and public places now have designated breastfeeding areas and even specially designed private pods that can make everything easier.

Many of today's electric pumps are quite compact, but if you're worried about the hassle of hauling something around, a manual pump is easily tucked away and can be used almost anywhere. Insulated cold storage products allow you to conveniently store and transport your milk as well. On long trips, determined parents have even shipped milk home. But another option is to "pump and dump" (or "pump and sacrifice" as some moms call it!). It seems a shame to waste milk, but it keeps your supply up. Whichever you choose, just keep the milk flowing.

## Caregiver's Feeding Management

You may think there's a problem with your milk supply because your caregiver said your baby needs more milk during the day than you're bringing. If what he gets at home decreases for any reason, he may indeed "demand" more with the caregiver. But if all is the same at home and the amount you're expressing hasn't changed, the problem is more likely how your caregiver is feeding your baby.[1,2]

Is the bottle being offered as a first resort when your baby fusses? Some babies will take a bottle to soothe themselves regardless of hunger, when what they really need is the cuddling that comes with the feeding. Encourage your caregiver to try other ways to soothe the baby than just reaching for a bottle. If he takes a pacifier, offering it after the bottle until his brain gets the message that he's had enough may help.

Is your baby being fed on a schedule rather than on cue? Caregivers may encourage larger intakes to keep him on the daycare center schedule; you may need to speak to them about flexible, responsive feeding.[4]

Is your baby taking more and more milk? This may happen if he drinks faster than his stomach can register satiety. Is the bottle being held above him, creating a steady fast flow? Have you upgraded to a nipple size larger than "newborn" or "slow flow"? Or has the caregiver cut the opening to make it flow faster? These can all contribute to over-feeding. If your caregiver is unaware that breastfed babies don't usually need the larger amounts that fully bottle-fed babies take because they typically feed more frequently and have better appetite regulation, they may believe more is necessary without checking things out first.[4] Demonstrate how to pace the feeding by keeping the bottle more horizontal or periodically leaning baby forward or tipping the bottle downward for a break; this will help both them and your baby learn to regulate the feeding naturally (see Chapter 4). The Milk Mob has a good demo video at bit.ly/MMM-Paced.

Is the feeding being ended when your baby seems satisfied, or is he being encouraged to finish the bottle so none is wasted? Find out if any milk is being thrown away at the end, and if so, how much. Leftover human milk keeps longer than formula and can safely be reused for *at least* a couple of hours after a feeding,[5] with research suggesting this number may eventually be lengthened.[6] If milk is being thrown away frequently, send smaller packets and ask the caregiver to offer extra only as needed.

For all these situations of caregiver mismanagement, Nancy Mohrbacher offers a great handout that you can share with them at bit.ly/MMM-Caregivers.

## Growth Spurts

Even when the caregiver feeds your baby in all the right ways, there will be days when he goes through all the milk you pumped yesterday by noon and nurses nonstop when you get home. He's probably going through one of those infamous "growth spurts" and will want more milk than usual until it passes. During this time, you may need to add an extra pumping or two to keep up. If that isn't possible, it's a good time to dip into your frozen stockpile if you have one. This usually only lasts for 2-3 days, and then he'll be back to his usual amount.

## It Isn't Always About Work

What if you're pumping often enough with a quality pump and your caregiver isn't overfeeding, but there's still not enough milk? If milk production was great until you returned to work, the first question to ask yourself is, "What's changed since then?" and consider the possibilities listed in Chapters 6 and 7. Are you feeding less at home now? Could you be pregnant? Have you taken any decongestants or new medications or eaten a lot of mint candy or sage? Are you skipping meals a lot? Have you started taking hormonal birth control? Has your baby started sleeping through the night? If nothing fits, it's possible that a hormonal problem such as postpartum thyroiditis has developed, but it's usually one of the previous issues.

# Increasing Your Supply While Working

The faster you take action to correct a drop in milk output, the easier it will be to bring it back up. Don't hesitate, hoping that it will get better on its own. Addressing the cause now will help you get back to normal sooner. If the problem is caused by a faulty pump or scheduling problems, the following ideas may help.

## Increase Frequency At Home

One of the most effective ways to compensate for a decrease in pumping output is to offer the breast more often on your days off. Extra feedings help to rebuild your supply for the new week. If your baby doesn't want to nurse more often or other things interfere, "power pumping" as described in Chapter 13 can accomplish the same result.

## Breast Compressions

Breast compressions increase the amount of milk removed while pumping by adding pressure inside the breast so that milk flows more forcibly through the ducts, almost like creating another letdown. It often speeds up the time it takes to drain the breasts, too.

## Reverse Cycling

Seeking to avoid the pressure of pumping enough milk for daytime feedings while working the demanding schedule of a resident, Dr. Marilyn Grams developed her own unique strategy that she calls "reverse cycling"—deliberately feeding more at night than during the day. She discovered that when she encouraged lots of nighttime nursings, her baby needed less pumped milk during the day. She also found that she was able to maintain a strong supply under challenging work circumstances. The quality of her rest didn't suffer because she learned to nurse comfortably while lying down and to sleep through the feedings. It's a counterintuitive strategy that has worked well for some working parents and is worth trying. Babies have also been known to initiate this themselves, taking little at the caregiver's and waiting until mom returns, after which they start feeding in earnest.

If you're worried about sleep, go to bed an hour or two earlier than usual (after feeding) and let your partner care for the baby so you can sleep alone for a while. On weekend mornings, have someone else get up with him (after feeding) so you can go back to sleep. Nap with your baby whenever possible.

## Galactogogues

If you've done your best to maximize milk removal but are still falling short, galactogogues may help fill the gap. For a modest boost, one great idea is to brew and ice a pitcher of commercial or homemade lactation tea, pour it into a water bottle, and sip on it throughout the day. You may also want to include lactogenic foods as a snack or part of your lunch (see Chapter 14 for ideas). If that isn't enough, a galactogogue herb or herbal combination may provide enough boost to keep you going.

## Solids Take the Pressure Off

Once your baby begins taking solids, they can be used as part of his meal at the caregiver's. This can take some pressure off how much milk you need to provide each day. Of course, solids should be offered only in small amounts at first, so this transition will be gradual. When given at home, be sure to breastfeed first so he fills up on your milk. However, when your caregiver gives your baby solids, they should be given *before* the bottle to reduce his need for milk while you are away.

## CHAPTER 16

# Making More Milk in Special Situations

Coping with low milk production is difficult even in the best of circumstances. Additional challenges such as exclusive pumping, premies, multiples, co-nursing families, relactation, or induced lactation for a surrogate-born or adopted baby require specialized strategies to increase milk production.

## Exclusive Pumping

Long-term pumping and bottle-feeding happen for a variety of reasons. You may have had problems that made feeding at the breast difficult or impossible. Or you may want to provide your milk but don't feel emotionally comfortable with nursing. Whatever the reason, exclusive pumping can challenge milk production because the infant has been taken out of the equation. Even when given human milk, babies fed by bottle tend to develop feeding patterns that are different from how they would have breastfed, *so a baby's eating pattern is not always the best guide for developing an appropriate pumping routine for your body.* Nor does the same schedule work equally well for every exclusively pumping parent. After the first couple of months, some are able to sustain pumping large amounts of milk in just a few sessions a day, but most of us need to pump more often to maintain adequate production.

The most successful parents pump very frequently in the early weeks and months and aim for a slight oversupply, with extra milk stored in the freezer as insurance against any future hiccups. For the first several weeks, aim for pumping *at least* 8 times per 24 hours, for a total of 120-140 minutes. Just be sure not to "wait" for your breasts to get really full before pumping—otherwise, production may start to slow down—and try not to go longer than one 4-6 hour stretch.[1] When most of the available milk has been removed, your breasts will feel lighter and softer. Erratic milk removal is the enemy of a good long-term milk supply; consistency helps you maintain it.

Most parents pump for 15-20 minutes at a time, but there are a *few* who find that 30 minutes or sometimes much longer seems necessary to fully drain the breasts; they may pump 240 minutes or more per day. It may be that their letdown is sluggish or their pump is not working well. Others only pump 4-5 times per day, which is risky. Long pumping periods are rarely necessary, and if this seems to be the case, consider exploring the reasons *why* as this is not typical and takes up more time in your life.

Exclusively pumping parents report that milk supply can continue to build for up to 12 weeks, so it may pay to keep pumping often for a while. After this, you can experiment to determine how often you need to pump to sustain you milk supply. Stephanie Casemore, author of *Exclusively Pumping Breastmilk*, suggests dropping only one session at a time and increasing pumping time for the remaining sessions to keep the total minutes per day the same. Don't make any more changes for at least a couple of weeks.

If you're having difficulty meeting baby's daily needs, *first make sure that your pump is still working well and your flanges fit properly* (see Chapter 13). After this, increasing the number of pumping sessions per day or short-term power pumping may help increase your supply. *Don't panic when you get less milk out each time when you increase frequency*—that's normal and production should start to increase by the third day. Many parents turn quickly to galactogogues, but they're less likely to help without adequate frequent milk removal. Stephanie Casemore's book is a great comprehensive resource for more how-to details.

Exclusive pumping for an extended period of time requires dedication, and sometimes it can be hard to stay motivated, but it *is* possible and many families have met or surpassed their goals. There are several online support groups, including one for exclusively pumping "under suppliers" (facebook.com/groups/375843826087267). Connecting to others who are exclusively pumping may make all the difference.

## Premature Babies

When a baby is born prematurely, lactation rarely begins normally because of the events surrounding the early birth. A small but otherwise healthy baby may be able to breastfeed soon, but chances are good that she may not be strong enough to get all her nourishment from the breast right away or stimulate the breasts well. Quite often, preterm infants aren't ready to breastfeed at all after birth; the earlier they come, the more likely this is true. Mothers of preterm infants have historically struggled to establish a good milk supply and maintain it. But after a decade of research, we now understand what sets the better producers apart from those who struggle when the cause isn't a primary issue.

You may not have much control over the physical factors, but there are other things under your control that can make a big difference because *the rule of demand and supply is still in effect*. In the first week, those who give birth prematurely often start off producing the same amount of milk as mothers who give birth at term, yet may end up with much less milk than full-term parents after 6 weeks. Part of the difference lies in the fact that premie parents may not start pumping right away and typically pump less often than term parents breastfeed.[2,3] For best results, start pumping in the first hour after birth if it's possible.[4] Pump frequently—8 or more times per day—and ignore the temptation to try to get by with less. The tiny premie who at first needs only a few ounces of milk daily will eventually grow and develop a bigger appetite.

Frequency is an obvious difference, but there's more. Remember pediatrician Jane Morton's discovery that mimicking the nursing behaviors of newborns boosted long-term milk production? She observed that hand expression removed colostrum more effectively, so she had nursing parents hand express as frequently as possible in the first 3 days *along with pumping*. The more often they hand expressed, the more milk they made later on (see Hands-On Pumping in Chapter 13 and the graph below).

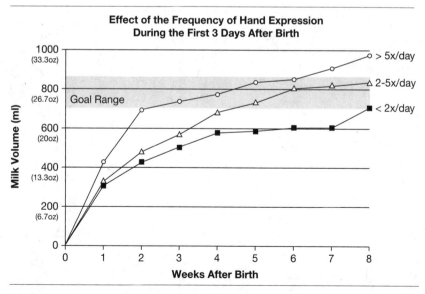

**Effect of the Frequency of Hand Expression During the First 3 Days After Birth**

*Morton's study: All groups pumped the same number of times each day; the only difference was how many times they hand expressed the first 3 days in addition to pumping. Adapted from Morton et al.[5] Used with permission.*

## Maximizing Milk Production for Premature Babies

- Start expressing in the first hour after delivery and continue at least 8 times daily, 15-20 minutes total each time, if at all possible. Try not to go longer than one 4-5 hour stretch without pumping.
- Use a high-quality rental-grade breast pump as much as possible.
- Make sure that your flanges fit properly and that your pump's cycling feels comfortable.
- Once your milk volume increases, use your hands to massage and compress the breast while pumping and hand express any milk left by the pump at the end.
- Express as close to your baby as possible; holding her at the same time, if you can manage it, is even better.[6]

A good pumping goal is at least 17oz (500ml) per day, but preferably 25-33oz (750-1000ml) by 2 weeks postpartum to attain a full supply.[7] If you don't reach this range, just keep working steadily and perhaps consider a galactogogue.[8] When milk production seems to fluctuate significantly at times, take a look at what else is going on in your life. It's common for the amount of milk you pump to drop temporarily if you receive distressing news about your baby. This usually rebounds when things improve and you're

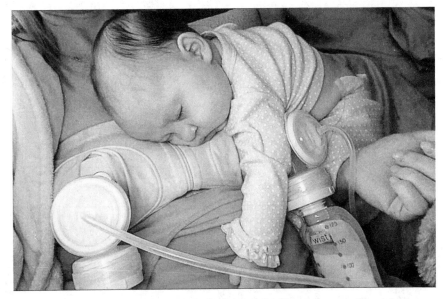

*Pumping while holding baby can increase your milk yield. Photo courtesy of Sarah Lester*

feeling better again. Parents of very ill babies are under a tremendous amount of pressure, and it's understandable that occasionally this may affect your letdown reflex.

## But My Baby's Already Here! Now What?

If you missed this early opportunity, it's water under the bridge now. The good news is that all is not lost. You can pump more often, and if you haven't already added breast compressions and massage during pumping and hand expressing leftover milk at the end, starting this now can still help you get more out of your breasts. Some of the ideas in the next chapter might be helpful, too.

## Other Factors in Play

One question is whether the breast is "fully operational" when you've delivered prematurely. Because the basic glandular structures are complete by the first half of pregnancy, it has been assumed that the milk factory is fully operational by that time. This may not be true in all cases, however, especially when delivering between 22 and 34 weeks of gestation.[9] Milk-making cells enlarge and "mature" during the second half of pregnancy, and research shows that starting milk volume is directly related to a baby's gestational age at birth and rises as gestational age increases.[10]

There is also the question of why the baby was born early, because pre-existing medical or infertility conditions that can result in premature births might also subtly affect the developing breast. If your baby was small for gestational age (SGA), intrauterine growth restricted (IUGR) or a problem with the placenta was suspected, be sure to read about placental problems in Chapter 8 and remember that breast tissue can still be built up after birth.

## A Common Mistake

It's easier to understand the need to pump in the beginning, but now that baby's home and latching, can you stop pumping? You may be longing to just feel like a "normal" breastfeeding parent, but proceed cautiously. We've seen many situations where milk supply was quite good *until* the baby came home and started nursing full-time. It takes time for an early baby's suck to mature, and while she initially may be able to get enough from you, she may *not* be able to provide enough stimulation to sustain your production.[11] Unless your baby's suck is truly vigorous, it's usually wise to continue pumping for top-off feedings or just as insurance for a little while longer. Once she becomes a proficient feeder, you'll need to pump or use galactogogues only if you haven't reached a full supply. Otherwise, you can gradually wean from pumping.

## Multiples

Supporting a single baby can seem challenging enough, but when you have twins or more, milk supply worries can double or triple! Fortunately, most mothers who give birth to multiples are able to produce enough milk for twins and even triplets or more.[12,13] Animal studies show that the more total placental weight, the more mammary gland development occurs during the pregnancy.[14] This appears to be equally true for humans. So the fact that you had two or more babies is itself a bonus—your starting milk factory is likely to be larger than if you had only one baby.[15]

Still, it's common for parents of multiples to have concerns about their milk production. Each baby's weight gain and diaper output should be considered independently. If one is doing well but another is not, it may be that the baby who is not getting enough milk is not being brought to the breast often enough or is not allowed to nurse long enough, perhaps because she is a more leisurely breastfeeder than her sibling. It's also possible that one baby may not be removing milk from the breast efficiently due to immature, disorganized suckling patterns; she may need supplementation until she matures. Or she may have a tongue mobility problem that requires evaluation and treatment. In the meantime, you may want to alternate the side from which each baby is fed to ensure that both breasts receive equal amounts of stimulation and express for the baby who isn't transferring milk efficiently yet. If the suck of one or more of your babies isn't effective yet, which commonly happens because multiples are often born early and with varying degrees of maturity, a visit with a lactation consultant is often helpful. Reviewing Chapter 9 may also be helpful.

When multiples are born prematurely and you must express milk until the babies are able to nurse, there is a greater risk of having problems with low milk production. The expression routine normally used to establish a milk supply for one baby must now create milk for two or more babies. If this doesn't happen, milk production may not calibrate high enough. If one or more babies are at home from the hospital, use the strategies in Chapter 4 for supplementing in a way that is supportive of breastfeeding as you work to increase your milk production.

Begin hand expression along with pumping as soon after birth as possible, preferably within the first hour, with a goal of 8 or more double-pumping sessions per day. Don't forget to add hands-on compressions when milk flow slows and to manually express any residual milk at the end. Trying to fit in that many pumping sessions when you are also visiting your babies in the hospital each day can be difficult. Don't stress about spacing pumping sessions evenly—it's fine to cluster some of them closer together, just as your babies are likely to cluster some of the feedings together when they begin nursing. Keep in mind that when you first start pumping more frequently, you are likely to see less milk in each pumping session, but the total amount will be the same and higher later on.

When it comes to building your milk supply for multiples, equipment quality is especially critical. Lactation consultant and multiples expert Karen Gromada strongly recommends a high-quality multi-user pump if possible for *at least* until adequate milk production is established for all babies or they are all breastfeeding effectively. Such pumps are most often rented, and while the cost may be higher, so is the "payout" in milk production (see Chapter 13).

Once all babies are breastfeeding, you may be able to decrease pumping or discontinue it altogether, depending on how effectively each breastfeeds. If you're uncertain, a little extra "insurance pumping" will guarantee that the breasts are drained well and adequately stimulated. But if the babies aren't removing milk effectively overall, it may be better for both your sanity and milk production to spend more time on pumping and less on breastfeeding until both/all babies can nurse better.

Simultaneous nursing, often referred to as "tandem nursing" by many parents of multiples, can be a real time saver, with the added advantage that the babies can help each other in stimulating letdowns.[16] It doesn't work well for everyone, but it's worth giving a try. There's no rush; wait until at least one baby is able to latch and nurse effectively before you attempt both babies together. It may be easier to start with the baby who has more difficulty and then let the second one latch. If it doesn't go well, try again in a few weeks or another month or two because it often goes better when babies are older and more skilled feeders.

If milk production is a struggle even though you've been "doing everything right," one additional thing to consider is whether the babies were conceived with or without fertility assistance. If there was a hormonal problem that affected your ability to conceive, it may now be affecting your milk production. You're also at higher risk of postpartum hemorrhages, anemia, placental insufficiencies, and thyroid problems, which may affect the milk factory. Addressing these problems, when possible, may improve lactation (Chapters 8 and 11 cover these issues). For more information about nursing multiples, read Karen Gromada's excellent book, *Mothering Multiples*, and visit her website, karengromada.com.

## Relactation

*Relactation* is the process of rebuilding a milk supply weeks, months, or even years after stopping breastfeeding, which can happen for many reasons. Sometimes milk production appeared to be so low that it just didn't seem worth the bother to continue nursing.

In other cases, parents were told they had to wean in order to take certain medications or undergo diagnostic tests, or it was recommended as the solution to breastfeeding problems when the health care provider didn't know how to help. Long separations from baby, breast rejection, or the concern that baby isn't tolerating her parent's milk can also lead to unintended weaning.

Whatever may have happened, relactation is possible. In general, it may take about the same amount of time to resume exclusive breastfeeding as has elapsed since the baby weaned, provided you once had a full supply. This means that if your baby was weaned a month ago, it may take up to 1 month to reestablish full milk production. If you're currently nursing but want to breastfeed a new baby you aren't birthing, you may not be able to increase milk production enough to meet the new baby's needs fully because you're in the autumn season of the lactation cycle. But it's always worth trying because your new baby will benefit from whatever extra you can make.

The actual process of relactation is simple: *very frequent breast and nipple stimulation signals the milk factory to start production back up again.* This is accomplished with either a baby or milk expression via hand or pump.[17] In the Western world, parents tend to rely on breast pumps, often because the baby has become accustomed to the bottle and refuses the breast, but sometimes just for convenience. But frequent pumping can be tiresome and certainly isn't as emotionally rewarding as a baby, and many parents quit before reaching their goal. In contrast, mothers in more traditional cultures simply put the baby to breast very frequently for 10-15 minutes per side, then offer nutrition by cup or spoon. If the baby balks at nursing without reward, milk is dripped on the breast (the "drip-drop" method) or added via a supplementer tube to entice her. Using this method, the first drops of milk often appear around 6 days on average but anywhere from 2 days to a few weeks,[17,18] with maximum production reached between 1 week and 2 months.[19]

The collective experience is that most are able to relactate at least partially, if not completely; total failure is less common. The younger the baby and the shorter the time period since breastfeeding stopped, the faster and easier the process tends to go.[20,21] When the lactation gap was less than 2 weeks, milk production returned the fastest, and in one study, the success rate was 95%.[22] This makes sense because the process of involution, tearing down the milk factory, usually takes longer than this. But even with up to a 2-month lactation gap, milk can often be brought back, though the success rate drops with increasing time to around 50%.[22,23] And miracles happen! In one case of a 14-week gap, the first drops of milk were seen on day 6, and by day 11, supplementation at the breast was no longer necessary.[24] In another with a 2-month lactation gap, milk appeared by day 3 and exclusive breastfeeding was reached on the 8th day.[25] These amazing stories have taught us to never say never.

*So what are their keys to success?* Parents were more likely to succeed if they ditched bottles and pacifiers and offered their baby milk either by tube at the breast or by cup or spoon after nursing.[21] Doing *Kangaroo care*—keeping baby skin-to-skin as much as possible—boosted the success rate further.[26] But one of the most important factors was hope. Those who believed it was possible and had a strong desire were more likely to achieve their goals.[18] When families *didn't* reach their goals, bottles, latching problems, colic, and breast refusal were the most common barriers. Recognizing the difficulty of parents dealing with these issues alone, some savvy clinicians found success with hospitalizing mothers and babies together so that lactation experts could help them through the process.[18,21] What a great idea!

If your baby balks at the breast, try to keep in mind that babies are born to breastfeed, and there are many ways to gently entice them to the breast. For some babies, it may be necessary to get milk production back up before they'll agree to nurse. Nursing supplementers can help because they provide the immediate reward of milk at the breast. A nipple shield, with or without a supplementer, can provide a baby with a familiar form that he may be more willing to try at first. Switching from a bottle to a cup may be met with protests but can make a big difference. If she still won't latch, don't hesitate to enlist the aid of an experienced lactation consultant, who may provide some helpful tips customized for your situation. Once your baby is latching easily, encourage her to nurse at every opportunity. Galactogogues can help the process along, but frequent nipple stimulation and milk removal are the most important things you can do.

In instances when it's difficult or impossible for a baby to nurse, milk expression is mandatory. Pumping or expressing frequently and consistently helps the process happen faster. Use your hands to massage and express a little along with your breast pump and hold your baby as much as possible, especially skin-to-skin.

## Induced Lactation

*Induced lactation* is the process of creating a milk supply when you've never given birth, but the term is also often used when someone who has birthed previously wishes to bring in a milk supply for a baby they have not birthed. With a long historical tradition in native societies, it is now becoming more common as parents and medical professionals learn that it's actually possible.[27] Whether you are adopting, a non-gestational parent, or a parent of a surrogate infant, breastfeeding is about more than the milk—it's a way to connect at a deeper level with your new baby and contribute to her growth beyond the pregnancy. Although it will require time, motivation, perseverance, tenacity, and patience, nursing your baby can be highly rewarding.

As with relactation, the younger the baby, the more likely she is to latch onto the breast easily. A nipple shield can be a good transitional tool if she balks. Babies older than 3 months have begun to overwrite their instincts with learned experiences and may have more difficulty re-learning what to do. Most babies nurse more willingly when there is more milk, so it helps to do all you can to maximize your production or otherwise provide milk flow at the breast. Achieving a full supply may be possible provided there aren't underlying problems such as hormonal dysfunctions or underdeveloped breast tissue. If you struggled with infertility in particular, there may be a hormonal problem that could limit your milk-making capability. However, most parents can make at least some milk, and the total amount of milk need not interfere with a satisfying nursing relationship. While you may or may not produce colostrum, the milk you make will be the same as a birth parent's milk.[28,29]

There are two basic approaches: (1) induction by nipple stimulation via hand, pump, or baby alone, or (2) induction via medications and/or herbals along with nipple stimulation. Whichever method you choose, keep in mind that in the beginning, you have only your standby skeletal crew of milk-making cells to start up milk production. Be patient. Induced lactation really is more like building a milk factory by hand from bricks and mortar instead of having the construction company—pregnancy—do the job with all their specialized parts and equipment. It's a slower process, but sooner or later new workers and assembly lines will slowly start to kick in, and your production should pick up.

## Suckling to Induce Lactation

In traditional cultures, women—and yes, even a few men—have successfully stimulated milk production just by putting the baby to the breast very frequently.[27,30] Western parents tend to rely more often on breast pump technology, but as discussed with relactation, pumping is an imperfect method because it is cold, mechanical, and usually vacuum-centered only. Plus, it takes time to become comfortable and proficient at pumping. Even birthing parents with excellent milk supplies aren't always able to pump effectively, especially in the beginning. A nursing baby adds a positive emotional element; not only does suckling stimulate the letdown reflex, but the psychological effect of baby's smell, sight, and sounds triggers additional oxytocin releases that a pump cannot. If possible, combining pumping with nursing your baby using a supplementer can provide the best of both worlds. Adding hand expression can provide another level of stimulation and may extract milk sooner than a pump. The addition of galactogogue medications and/or herbs can result in significantly higher milk production for some parents.

## Pumping to Induce Lactation

Breast pumps are typically used to develop a milk supply before the baby arrives. Because they don't evoke the same warm feelings as a baby, adding breast massage can help the process along.

### Basic Pumping Protocol for Induced Lactation

1. About 2-4 weeks (or more) before the baby's arrival, begin manual massage of nipples and breasts for 10 minutes 8 to 10 times per day for 2 weeks.

2. After 2 weeks, begin double pumping with a hospital-grade pump for 10-15 minutes 8 to 10 times per day. If you find pumping without a flow of milk to be uncomfortable, try lubricating the funnel with a bit of olive or coconut oil. Sometimes the discomfort is caused by less elastic nipple tissue (pregnancy hormones increase nipple elasticity). In this case, lactation consultant Alyssa Schnell suggests that Dr. Nice Breast Gel™ may be helpful. You might also do some gentle nipple stretching with your fingers or try Supple Cups™ (see Chapter 10) to help with nipple elasticity.

3. When baby arrives, use a nursing supplementer to provide feedings at the breast (see Chapter 4). Pump after feedings or several times per day, as time permits. Keep a close watch on the baby's weight gain to ensure that she's getting enough milk.

4. As your breasts begin to feel full, heavy, and slightly tender, see if baby will nurse at the breast without supplementation for the first few minutes of the feeding if she is willing. Continue to watch diapers or track weight gain.

5. As long as hunger cues aren't frantic and weight gain is sufficient, gradually decrease either the amount of milk in the supplementer or the length of time the milk is allowed to flow from the supplementer during the feeding. Eventually, you may reach a point where you can no longer decrease the amount of supplement you offer without leaving baby hungry. That is the amount that will be needed for now, and possibly for the long-term.

## Hormonal Protocols to Induce Lactation Prior to Birth

The strategy here is using hormones to simulate a pregnancy in order to build a milk factory before the baby arrives. When time allows, a birth control pill containing estrogen and progesterone is taken first to stimulate the growth of more milk-making breast tissue.

Then a prolactin-stimulating medication safe for long-term use is introduced (see Chapter 14). Finally, pumping is begun to kick-start milk production.

In many cases, hormonal protocols result in greater milk production than pumping or sucking alone. The more time you spend in the pregnancy-mimicking phase, the more milk-making tissue will be created. Starting at least 4 months before baby is expected to arrive produces the best results, but if you don't have that much time, any prep can still help.

Milk production doesn't start up until the pumping phase and first appears as drops that may be clear or opaque. As the volume increases, you may begin to see small sprays that eventually become streams of milk. The amount of time it takes to see streams of milk varies from one person to the next and depends on the type of protocol that is followed. It may take days, weeks, or months for milk production to begin. You'll know your body is gearing up to make milk when your breasts increase at least one bra cup size and feel full, heavy, and slightly tender.

Because hormonal protocols entail the use of prescription drugs, *it is essential to work closely with your health care provider.* Share the entire protocol and explain that the birth control pill is being used to develop lactation tissue rather than for contraception. Medication can be started at any point in the menstrual cycle because the purpose is to simulate a pregnancy rather than prevent one. The hormonal protocol *is not* recommended if you have a history of blood clotting problems, a heart condition, or severe blood pressure problems.

The Newman-Goldfarb Protocols for Induced Lactation® were first developed by Dr. Jack Newman for Lenore Goldfarb and her first baby, and then refined as a result of their subsequent work with adoptive and intended families. They haven't been formally tested in clinical trials but are reportedly effective for many parents.[31] Similar protocols using medications to stimulate lactation hormones have been tested and found to be effective as well.[27,32]

There are three versions of the protocols—regular, accelerated, and menopause—to accommodate the varying amounts of time available before the baby arrives, and your hormonal status. Generally speaking, the more time you have to prepare, the greater the amount of milk you are likely to make by baby's arrival. The one caveat is the condition of your breasts; results may be less with hypoplasia. For more information, visit bit.ly/MMM-Protocols.

For additional comprehensive information about induced lactation, we highly recommend Alyssa Schnell's book, *Breastfeeding Without Birthing*, and her website BreastfeedingWithoutBirthing.com. The Adoptive Breastfeeding Resource website at fourfriends.com/abrw is another good resource.

# LGBTQ Lactation and Co-Nursing

One of the biggest changes since our first edition is the surge in the desire to breastfeed/chestfeed among gender-diverse individuals and families. Each situation brings unique challenges, and knowledge on this topic in the lactation field is still in its infancy; we offer the best information available at this time.

## Lesbian Co-nursing

Lesbian co-nursing typically involves inducing lactation using one of the previously described methods for the partner who did not birth the baby.[33] In many families with two nursing mothers, the challenge arises when both partners wish to share the responsibilities of nursing the baby. Biologically, lactation works best when it is launched strongly. Often, the birthing partner will exclusively nurse for the first few weeks to establish a good milk supply while the other partner spends a lot of time skin-to-skin, pumping, and hand expressing. The nonbirthing parent may or may not do some comfort feeding. The way this looks is very individual for each family. If baby spends a lot of sucking time with the second parent, the birthing parent's breasts may not be stimulated sufficiently to maintain adequate long-term milk production. It's important for you both to discuss these issues first. Once a thoughtful plan is developed, many couples have successfully shared duties and provided fully for their babies.

## Transgender Female Nursing

Transgender women, who were assigned as male at birth, may take female hormones to suppress male characteristics and enhance female characteristics, and may or may not have confirmation "bottom surgery" to further a physical transformation. Lactation in transgender women is similar to cisgender (born)-male lactation, which has been documented in history.

In the first published medical case report of transgender lactation, the gestational parent didn't wish to breastfeed, so the transgender parent decided to induce lactation. She had been taking spironolactone, estradiol and progesterone, and already had well-developed breast tissue. Her estradiol and progesterone were increased, and domperidone was added to mimic pregnancy hormones. She also pumped a few times daily. Droplets of milk occurred after the first month and medications were increased along with doubling her pumping time. By 3 months, she was producing 8oz (240ml) per day. Estradiol and progesterone were reduced, and when the baby was born 2 weeks later, she started breastfeeding, nursing exclusively for 6 weeks before supplementation was required. The use of an anti-androgen drug is somewhat controversial; the concern is more for potential effects on a male baby, though only a small amount of spironolactone (2-4%) passes into the milk and is likely insignificant. You can read the full case report at bit.ly/MMM-TransWoman.[34]

If you've been taking estrogen, you're already ahead of the game because the hormones have likely started developing more mammary tissue. The choice then is whether to pursue a full hormonal induction of milk production or simply use demand and supply. In the latter option, frequent sucking stimulates the start-up of milk production. A breast pump may be used, or the baby may simply be put to the breast. It can be difficult to persuade a baby to take a breast that is not producing milk, but with the addition of a nursing supplementer, she's more likely to give it a try. Parents who choose to rely on sucking stimulation only may be less concerned with the volume of milk produced than in simply establishing a nursing relationship.

For those who want more milk, a hormonal-medical protocol as discussed previously and described in detail at bit.ly/MMM-Protocols2 is the next option. This may require switching from estrogen to a birth control pill to simulate pregnancy and then reducing and eventually dropping this while adding a prolactin-stimulating substance such as domperidone. It's important to note that induction protocols are largely still experimental and are best done with medical oversight.

Herbal galactogogues may also be used in addition to demand and supply, in lieu of medications, or with medications. Saw palmetto and fennel have anti-androgen and mammary-stimulating properties that may be especially appropriate. Goat's rue also reputedly stimulates mammary tissue and is a good choice as well.

If your partner is the gestational parent and also wishes to nurse, you'll want to consider that sharing lactation can put the establishment of full milk production at risk in the gestational parent, as discussed earlier. Sarah, whose story is chronicled in a blog (bit.ly/MMM-TransWomen), chose to deal with this by having her wife exclusively breastfeed the first 6 weeks while she exclusively pumped to bring in her milk, having started the milk induction process early in her partner's pregnancy. For the first few months, each would pump when the other nursed, but this was eventually dropped. In this arrangement, the birth parent did not maintain a full supply, but between them both they were able to supply their baby's needs.

## Transgender Male Nursing

Transgender males, who were assigned as females at birth, may or may not choose to take hormones or have confirmation chest-contouring (top surgery) or reproductive organ surgery as part of their transformation process. Lactation can be more or less complex

A trans man feeding his baby human milk with the aid of a
supplementing tube and bottle.

for trans men because you have the option of carrying a pregnancy, which brings the
advantage of lactation hormones. Psychologically, however, the desire to nurse may be
counterbalanced by gender dysphoria and emotions related to the birthing experience
and the growth of breast tissue, which can complicate the milk-making process. Each
individual desiring to nurse must weigh the goals of the nursing relationship and making
milk versus chest image dysphoria. The overall strategy hinges on this decision.[35]

Nursing after a pregnancy is easy from a hormonal perspective. If chest surgery has
taken place, this lactation scenario is more similar to cisgender (born) female nursing
after breast reduction surgery. In the absence of surgery, the potential to produce milk
is high, but even those with surgery still have mammary tissue that can grow during
pregnancy. Layered on top of this is the issue of testosterone use; if taken to suppress
mammary growth during the lactation period, milk production may be affected as testosterone has an inhibitory effect on lactation, though nursing can continue with the use
of a nursing supplementer.

On a practical and emotional level, preserving your masculine identity while nursing
can be trickier. Some parents prefer to chestfeed privately to avoid the risk of being scru-
tinized and judged. Well-thought-out clothing selections such as the use of layers and
buttoned shirts can reduce dysphoria while making nursing easier. Any chest binding

should be considered and undertaken carefully because it limits the space for milk to collect and can both reduce milk production and possibly contribute to plugged ducts.

Some trans men want to induce lactation or relactate for babies they did not birth. Nursing usually happens with the aid of a feeding tube at the chest, and the individual can choose whether to do additional stimulation with pumping, prolactin-stimulating medications, or herbal galactogogues.

For more information, La Leche League's article on transgender and non-binary parent nursing (llli.org/breastfeeding-info/transgender-non-binary-parents) is a great place to start and includes links to articles on specifically related concerns. You can also read more stories in the study we referenced at bit.ly/MMM-TransGender.

## CHAPTER 17

# Thinking Outside the Box: Complementary and Alternative Therapies

When the usual strategies aren't making enough of a difference, or maybe just because you aren't one to be constrained by Western norms, it may be worth looking further. *Alternative therapies* are those used *in place of* standard treatments, whereas *complementary therapies* are non-mainstream treatments that are used *together* with standard treatments. Some are backed by research evidence, while others lack solid backing.

Today many health care providers are starting to recognize that Western medicine doesn't have all the answers. Holistic and integrative medicine broaden treatment options to consider the use of non-traditional therapies that offer something standard treatments don't. We love the integrative approach and the willingness to think outside the box, especially because this is where some parents have found help, supported by research or not.

In the spirit of leaving no stone unturned, we offer the following ideas. Some have long histories from other cultures, some are relatively recent strategies, and a few are more theoretical and "out there" a bit. We've opted to tell you all of what's out there so you can make your own decision.

## Chiropractics

Chiropractics focuses on the neurologic effects of nerve impingements known as *subluxations*. Somewhat accidentally, it was discovered that chiropractic adjustments sometimes can help increase milk production in nursing parents who've experienced physical stresses or trauma. Three cases are recounted in a chiropractic journal article. While all the mothers had low milk supply, only one was actually seeking help for that specifically. It was her second baby, and she had made plenty of milk for her first. The second mother had back pain, while the third thought her baby's suck was the cause and so wanted help for her baby. Problems were identified with the first two women for treatment. In the third case, the doctor found nothing wrong with the baby, so she evaluated the mother instead and found several vertebral problems. Each case was very different in history and problems, but within the first couple of treatments, milk supply improved dramatically for all three.[1]

A lactation consultant worked with a nursing parent who had nursed several children without problems. Supply was sluggish from the start, making the consultant wonder if the parent's age was a factor, but the baby also had a poor suck that could contribute to the problem. When milk production did not improve with expressing and galacto-gogues, they decided to have the baby evaluated by a local chiropractor experienced with babies. During that appointment, the mom was asked how *she* was feeling and she mentioned having some back pain since the pregnancy, so she was treated, too. Shortly thereafter, milk production began to rebound and normalize. This goes to show that sometimes we bark up the wrong tree before we find the right one!

Chiropractic treatment may work by restoring nerve communication in key areas that have been reduced or cut off. This approach may be worth checking out when there aren't any other good explanations, especially if you've experienced physical trauma, nerve pain, numbness, or impingements before pregnancy, during pregnancy, or during childbirth.

## Traditional Chinese Medicine, Acupuncture, and Acupressure

*Acupuncture* is a Traditional Chinese Medicine (TCM) therapeutic practice during which specific areas on the body are pierced with very fine needles. Although not as common in the Western world, acupuncture has been used to treat low milk production for more than 2000 years. Research from multiple countries suggests that it can be effective.[2-4] Acupuncture can stimulate both prolactin and oxytocin, depending on the points chosen by the practitioner, and it's also used to treat a number of hormonal problems, including low thyroid function and fertility issues. Acupuncture and the variations described next are less likely to help when there are anatomical problems such as insufficient glandular tissue. On the other hand, you have little to lose in trying!

*Acupressure*, also called shiatsu, uses thumb or fingertip pressure instead of nee-dles. One study found better sustained milk production after acupressure treatment as opposed to no treatment in women with low milk supply.[5] *Auricular* therapy stimulates similar specific places on the ear, while *reflexology* focuses on trigger points in the foot or hand. Both seemed to increase milk output in studies.[6-9] Check out bit.ly/MMM-Acupressure for a demo of acupressure to boost milk production.

TCM relies on a thorough screening of the patient to select the proper treatment locations. While you can do some self-help techniques found online, it's smart to seek an experienced and qualified practitioner in case you have other underlying issues that need to be addressed at the same time for best results. They often will teach you techniques that can be used at home as well. In addition to these techniques, TCM practitioners may offer their own special blend of Chinese herbs based on their assessment of your situation. Ask around for a reputable doctor of TCM in your area. For more information, see bit.ly/MMM-Acupuncture.

## Breast Massage

*Breast massage* is promoted in some cultures as a way to stimulate milk production. Korean mothers who were given 30-minute massages twice daily in the first 10 days after birth had less sodium in their milk than those who didn't get it, indicating that milk production was ramping up faster.[10] In a Chinese study of cesarean section parents, breast massage was started at 2, 12, or 24 hours after delivery for 3 days. Those who started the earliest had the highest prolactin levels and reached "adequate lactation" the fastest.[11] The *Oketani* method of breast massage is popular in Japan and said to help milk production.[12] A recent worldwide survey found 10 different breast massage methods, only some of which were specific to milk production, and 30 YouTube video demonstrations.[13] A systematic review of the studies on the effectiveness of breast massage for breastfeeding problems, including milk production, is currently underway and should provide more information.[14] In the meantime, if you know of someone skilled in breast massage for lactation, there's nothing to lose in trying. A one-time breast massage session may be helpful to get milk flowing when letdown is an issue; for milk production, multiple sessions may be more helpful.

## Kinesio Tape

Chiropractors, occupational therapists, and physical therapists use kinesio tape for a variety of rehabilitation purposes. It differs from athletic tape in that it assists rather than restricts movement while providing support. The placement and direction it is applied determine the stimulation effect. Kinesio tape is sometimes used on babies with suck problems instead of hand support for facial muscles, and it's also been tried for engorgement because of its ability to lift the skin and allow lymph drainage. A small study of 11 New Mexican nursing parents with low supply reported increases in milk output (and immediate letdown in some cases) when the tape was applied in a fan-like pattern designed to inhibit or relax the pectoralis muscles and help fluids move. The individual situations varied, from pumping drops after returning to work to breast implants and induced lactation. Kinesio tape was placed for 3-5 days at a time and sometimes reapplied several times for maximum improvement.[15] This concept seems to have a lot of potential when applied by a skilled practitioner.

## Yoga

*Yoga* is a system of exercises to promote control of the body and mind. Awtar Kaur Khalsa, a registered yoga teacher and lactation consultant, reports that several breastfeeding yoga students experienced spontaneous increases in milk volume after attending her Kundalini yoga classes. She believes that arm movements increase blood circulation, which in turn causes relaxation and easier milk flow. Other mothers have reported increases after various upper arm activities, supporting the idea that such movements can stimulate milk production. From a practical standpoint, yoga is an effective means of exercise and relaxation that is safe for pregnant and nursing parents. At the very least, the relaxation it affords can help facilitate the letdown reflex.

## How About a Little Romance?

If it's not too soon to bring up this topic, orgasm during sex releases a surge of both oxytocin and prolactin.[16] Sexual activity has actually been suggested as an option for treating low supply without the drawbacks of drugs.[17] We'll leave it up to you whether to tell your partner about this one!

## Harnessing the Mind

Linda Pincus started a postpartum hypnotherapy class to help her clients cope with the stresses of early parenthood. Much to her surprise, several came back reporting more milk after the class, regardless of whether they had supply problems. Realizing the potential, she created a self-hypnosis CD for nursing parents with lactation problems.[18] Hilary Jacobson, who uses hypnotherapy in counseling mothers with childbirth and lactation related traumas, says that PCOS-type chronic low milk supply seems to "even out"—a reduction of highs and lows—with hypnotherapy and that it similarly seems to help parents dealing with tough issues such as tongue-tie related lactation problems to work through their doubts and despair, with improvement in supply.

Back in 1989, a study was conducted with mothers of preterm babies. Starting at 3-5 days after delivery, 1 of 2 groups was asked to listen to a 20-minute relaxation and imagery recording before pumping over a week's time. They averaged only 1 session a day but still pumped 60% more milk than mothers who didn't listen to it. Even more interesting, the more times daily a mother listened to the recording, the more milk she pumped.[19] The results were so impressive that the authors believed the effects might go beyond oxytocin and letdown to actual stimulation of prolactin. This is quite possible because oxytocin can influence the release of prolactin.[20] An Indonesian study that found strong prolactin responses after hypnotherapy treatment appears to support this theory.[21]

Several audio recordings are available online that have been developed for this purpose: *Hypnosis for Making More Milk* by Robin Frees (newbornconcepts.com), *Letting Down* by James Wierzbicki and Betsy Feldman (Willow Music), *A Bond Like No Other* by Anji, Inc. (anjionline.com), and *Breastfeeding Meditations* by Sheri Menelli. Or go to YouTube and search on hypnotherapy, relaxation, or meditation along with breastfeeding, lactation, milk supply, or milk production for more options. This is one of those no-risk, might-help ideas that is definitely worth considering.

## Further Out There

Back in the late 1800s, Dr. Edward Routh wrote about a novel treatment that he and a colleague used to help stimulate milk production. "Another mechanical mode of stimulating the breast to secret milk is electricity . . . experiments are still in their infancy. It has, however, been known for some time that the secretion of glands is increased when an electric current is passed through them." They understood that nerves run on electrical impulses and astutely applied this to lactation problems. Dr. Routh goes on to recount stories where this treatment brought milk back in cases of abrupt cessation of lactation or generally poor output.[22] With this in mind, the following ideas may not be quite so far-fetched.

### Transcutaneous Electrical Nerve Stimulation

*Transcutaneous electrical nerve stimulation* (TENS) is sometimes used to manage pain by sending localized gentle, low electrical impulses that block pain messages and help release feel-good endorphins. In the world of adult lactation, TENS is sometimes applied to the breast to help induce lactation and has also been promoted for adoptive parents trying to induce lactation. There's no research on this, but a midwife shared the story of one of her clients who was using TENS for low back pain and later told the midwife that she thought it was also causing her to make more milk. If this intrigues you, check it out online (bit.ly/MMM-TENS) and talk to your health care provider about any contraindications.

### Laser

Low-level laser therapy is being used for wound healing and an ever-widening number of other issues, so it's not surprising that someone decided to find out if it could help mothers with lactation insufficiency to make more milk. After 12 sessions over 3 weeks, those in the laser group had significant increases in prolactin and lactose and reported increases in their milk production, though the measurement method was too subjective to say with certainty.[23]

### Ultrasound

Along the same lines, low-frequency ultrasound, 5 or 10 minutes per day for 7 days, increased prolactin and milk production in rats, with better results in the 10-minute group.[24]

## Pursuing a Complementary Therapy

Did you find something interesting worth trying? If a therapy seems to address what you think may be an underlying problem, such as meditation for stress or a chiropractic adjustment for back or neck pain, it has a greater chance of helping. But some out-of-the-box methods may stimulate lactation in general and may be worth trying as well. We'd love feedback if you found something that helped; please consider visiting us at lowmilksupply.org to share your story.

# PART V

# Surviving the Present and Planning for the Future

## *"The Real Reason I Breastfeed" by Gina, Mother of Five*

Because I have insufficient mammary tissue and have struggled with low milk production with all 5 of my babies, I have been asked many times, "Why do you bother? Why do you keep trying to breastfeed with all the problems you have?" I usually answer in several ways, such as, "It's better for my baby to have some breast milk than none," or "For bonding and closeness and visual and oral development." My favorite answer is, "Because breastfeeding is so much more than milk," but that answer is rarely understood. Well, the other day my little guy showed me how real that answer is. He had just finished nursing on one side, and I straddled him on my lap while I situated the SNS, an at-breast supplementer. When I lifted my shirt, his eyes lit up, he smiled, and one hand went on each breast. He looked back and forth like a kid in a candy shop, trying to decide which one he wanted. His eyes were wide with excitement, and he was full of giggles. It was so very cute! After several times of looking back and forth, he just plopped his head down and nestled between my breasts. He had one arm around each as if he was hugging them. This tender and sweet moment was the ultimate reward for a battle long fought and the perfect illustration that "breastfeeding is so much more than milk." So why do I persevere despite the problems? The answer is easy . . . because it brings my baby joy and because my breasts offer more than milk. We aren't measured by the ounces in bottles but rather by the grit and determination behind those ounces. By that measure, none of us fail!

## CHAPTER 18

# Coping with Low Milk Supply

## You ARE *Successful*

At the end of the day, it's not about how much milk you are able to produce or how long you are able to nurse *but the commitment you make to give your baby the best start in life and the tremendous effort you put into pursuing that goal.* Breastfeeding may not turn out quite the way you dreamed, but you're climbing mountains that others have never faced. You have every right to be proud of your efforts! Celebrate what you *can* do rather than focusing on what cannot be.

## The Many Emotions of Low Supply

Parents coping with low milk supply describe a wide array of emotions as they navigate their breastfeeding journey. Whatever you're feeling, chances are someone else has felt it, too. There is no right or wrong to emotions—identifying them is an important step in helping you find a plan that you can live with.

### Feeling Grief

Grief is one emotion that is rarely acknowledged. Hilary Jacobson coined the term "breastfeeding grief" in her book *Healing Breastfeeding Grief.* People get that parents grieve if they experience the loss of a baby, but few comprehend that the loss of our breastfeeding dreams can also be deep and painful. Insensitive comments like, "just be glad there's formula," do nothing to assuage your pain and can drive you to hide those feelings. We're here to tell you that breastfeeding grief is real and you have a right to mourn. We hope that in acknowledging this and sharing the journeys of other families, you will also find your own pathway to healing.

## Feeling Guilt or Regret

Some parents feel guilty about decisions they made, such as cosmetic breast surgery or using a poor-quality pump, that affected the amount of milk they could produce. Others feel as though they starved their baby before realizing they weren't getting enough milk. Guilt can also be imposed on you by a health care provider or family member who blames you for one thing or another. But it's important to distinguish guilt from regret. *Guilt* assumes that you made a deliberate decision knowing what the outcome would be. *Regret* happens when we realize that different choices might have altered the outcome. You made the best choices you could with the information available to you at the time. There is no reason to accept guilt for something you didn't know or understand beforehand.

## Feeling Envy, Anger, or Resentment

It's hard to spend time with other nursing parents whose milk seems to flow like a river while you're scraping precious drops out of bottles. Let's be honest—it's just not fair that some of us have to work so much harder than others to breastfeed. Envy, anger, and resentment are understandable emotions when breastfeeding doesn't happen the way you originally envisioned. When the problem is on your side, you may feel betrayed by your own body. Maybe a health care provider or someone else you trust was unsupportive or gave you inaccurate information that contributed to your difficulties. You may even feel anger toward your baby if the problem was on her side and then feel guilty because you know that she doesn't understand and is doing her best.

Defusing anger and resentment starts with acknowledging your feelings—bottling them up doesn't relieve the pressure. Emily shared this about her experience: "It's just like any grieving process; the anger, hurt, and frustration come and go. I've found solace in helping others who are also struggling with breastfeeding. The more I've opened up about my struggles, the more understanding has happened. It's been healing as many people have said things like: 'I wish my aunt, sister, friend, etc., would have known about the tools available.'" When she was feeling particularly sad and angry one day and her husband asked if he could help, she told us, "I was with it enough to say angrily, 'Yes! Remind me that this is all temporary and that he's going to be ok even if I can't give him every drop of food from my breasts!'" What a great answer! Rather than simply lashing out, Emily responded with something she needed, and it gave her husband a way to support her in her pain.

## Feeling Like A Failure

It's common for parents struggling with milk production to confide that they feel like they've let their baby and family down. For Janelle, not only did she feel like a failure, but she sometimes also felt like a fraud when she told people she was breastfeeding. Three years and two babies into the journey, she sought help to process her feelings: "I think that it's very important to explore the depth of that feeling [with] the proper help . . . someone that can dig in deep with you. I'm just now finally getting the help that I need to emotionally deal with the rawness and hurt and anger and sadness around why I can't fully feed my baby at the breast and others can. . . . It's helpful to me when I focus on what I *am* doing rather than what I'm *not* doing."

When the focus is on what you can't provide, failure looms large. But if you've provided any amount of colostrum or milk, that is more than some babies ever get. There are many unpublished stories of how just a few ounces of human milk a day has helped people with conditions like Crohn's disease or cancer—what wonderful things the milk you're able to provide is doing for your little one![1-3] And there's far more to nursing than just nutrition—it's also about attachment and bonding, meeting needs, establishing trust, and building a foundational relationship.[4] These things are every bit as important as food, and some would say more. *Success is about quality, not just quantity,* and doing the best with the cards you've been dealt.

## Feeling Rejected by Baby

In the midst of all your hard work, it can be dismaying if your baby seems more satisfied by the supplement than by your milk. Even worse, if she fusses while feeding at the breast, it can feel like she's rejecting you. This can profoundly affect the way you feel about yourself and undermine your confidence. In these moments, it's important to realize that feelings of rejection are an *interpretation* of your baby's feeding behavior, not the *reality* of how your baby feels about you. Keep in mind that you are your baby's mother/parent, no matter what. You are the person who knows her best. You are the person *she* knows best. You are the person your baby turns to for comfort. That need and love for you are deep and unchanging, even when your baby gets frustrated with the food delivery system. Do yourself a favor and set aside time to just enjoy your baby skin-to-skin to remind yourself of all the good feelings you have for each other.

## Feeling Selfish for Wanting to Breastfeed

It's ironic that in the midst of the struggle, you may feel or be told that you're being selfish for wanting to breastfeed your baby. This usually comes from people who resent or are concerned about the extra time and effort you are putting in or from you feeling you're neglecting other parts of your life. Coping with low milk supply is a balancing act—your baby, your family, your job, your own well-being—all require your attention. Each person balances them differently. Listen to those outside voices and consider them because they're part of your balancing act. But in the end, it's *your* balancing act, not theirs.

## Feeling Judgmental of Others

If you've been struggling to breastfeed, it can be very hard to see other nursing parents overflowing with milk who wean early. The reality is that we can never truly know what they are going through. Their reasons for not breastfeeding or their apparent lack of persistence in the face of problems may be related to personal issues that make breastfeeding as difficult for them as nursing with low milk production is for you. Or maybe they simply didn't have accurate information or the support they needed to overcome other obstacles.

## Feeling Hurt by Insensitive Remarks and Criticism

A new mother's baby was cluster-feeding on the second night when her nurse came by and made the demoralizing comment, "Why are you working so hard? Just give that baby a bottle!" People sometimes say things like this without realizing how much it can hurt to hear it. It's similar to wanting to comfort a bereaved person after a death but not knowing quite what to say and uttering something insensitive instead.

The natural reaction to hurtful comments is defensiveness, usually expressed by an angry reply or stunned silence. However, standing up for yourself doesn't have to mean a full-blown confrontation. An easy way to deflect such remarks is to respond with, "Why do you ask?" or "Why would you think so?" These neutral-sounding questions often stop people in their tracks.

Another approach is to acknowledge the other person's concern without agreeing with it, which tactfully asserts your right to your position. Take a moment to think about what the underlying concern is, then reflect this back and correct it. For instance: "It sounds like you're worried that I'm spending too much time on breastfeeding and not enough time enjoying my baby. It may look that way from the outside but here's what I'm doing and why. . . ." Addressing the underlying concerns may lead to a genuine, respectful discussion that can help you both understand each other better.

It can feel even more hurtful to be criticized by another nursing parent for not breastfeeding exclusively. Many have shared how judged they felt by other parents at breastfeeding support group meetings because they were supplementing with formula. Don't wait for the shoe to drop. Misassumptions can be avoided by explaining up front that you have to supplement because you don't have enough milk yet and that you're there because you need support. They are much more likely to empathize and support your efforts to breastfeed if they hear your story up front. If not, don't be discouraged. Look for a more accepting group even if it is farther away. Consider contacting the group's leader in advance to explain your situation. It's worth the effort to find a group that is open-minded and understanding of the challenges you're facing. For more ways to cope with criticism about breastfeeding, visit llli.net/nb/nbcriticism.html.

## Feeling Lonely

Breastfeeding in the face of low milk supply can be difficult and lonely. Support is as important as good information; it's very hard to do it all alone. Meeting other nursing parents who have felt the same way and faced similar challenges is reassuring and validating. They may even have ideas to help that only someone who has experienced similar issues personally could know. Online support groups such as IGT and Low Milk Supply and Mothers Overcoming Breastfeeding Issues (MOBI) on Facebook provide a safe place to connect with others who are walking your same path. Keep in mind, though, that it's worth the effort to find parents you can meet in person who understand what you're going through (ideally because they've been down the same road themselves) and can provide the kind of in-person support you need and deserve.

## Feeling Depressed

Most mothers experience some moments of depression when they have a new baby, even when their road is smooth. It can be a normal response to the sudden shift in self-image and identity as you undertake the great responsibility of parenting. But there is also exhaustion from adjusting to the nighttime needs of a baby, and postbirth hormonal changes (especially in the first month) can magnify these feelings of depression. Bridget recalled this time:

> *The crushing blow of reality and needing to supplement with formula was so much more intense than I could have imagined. I would go to lactation appointments and my baby would transfer ⅓ - ½ oz (10-15ml). I'd hold it together, only to get home and sob about how hard I had it and how people didn't understand my specific situation. I knew that I was doing my best but I couldn't make my brain keep my emotions in check. I'm not a very emotional person otherwise, so it was very out of character for me. I was head over heels about having my daughter and never had other issues, just related to breastfeeding.*

285

Coping with low milk production can put you at higher risk for depression because you are under additional stress as you do double-duty, taking care of baby and working to build your milk supply. Have people begun hinting that you should wean? Weaning doesn't necessarily solve the problem, and the loss of mood-buffering lactation hormones often leads to increased depression, not less.[5] In fact, depressive symptoms are often less and resolve faster in nursing parents,[6] and breastfeeding also protects babies when their mother is depressed.[4] However, the real question is not what others think you need to do, but what do *you* want? What do *you* feel needs to happen?

If your emotional state is seriously interfering with your ability to function or care for your baby, you may be experiencing postpartum depression (PPD). Let your health care provider know how you are feeling so that they can help you. In some cases medications or herbs are helpful, while in others, therapy works well. Medication and therapy combined can also be very effective. In most cases, the drugs to treat PPD are compatible with breastfeeding.[7] When your baby is getting supplements, his exposure is even lower. Most lactation consultants have a copy of *Medications and Mothers' Milk* or can check LactMed for the latest information on each medication.

## Feeling Overwhelmed

Being a new parent can be overwhelming, and the added burden of coping with low milk supply can push you to the brink. Something needs to give! First-time mother Lani describes her struggle along with her breakthrough moment when friends came to the rescue:

*I felt incredibly overwhelmed at times, beginning when my mom left a week or so after the birth. I had a baby born at 37 weeks weighing in at only 5½ lb, who also had a yet undiagnosed tongue and lip tie. Needless to say, I was dealing with the nipple pain and struggling with the shield. We were doing triple feeds and supplementing with donor milk. We had to move to a new house when she was only 2 weeks old, and I was still sore from delivery. Baby quickly developed colicky/reflux symptoms and wouldn't sleep flat for more than 30 minutes at a time. I was also the sole provider for my family and knew I would have to go back to work in a couple months. Meanwhile we were living on a fraction of my normal salary. So, yes, I felt very overwhelmed. Looking back, I recalled the time that I was able to make the most milk. In fact, all the milk in the freezer when I returned to work was from this time. When my baby was 2 months old, my college girlfriends came for a vacation. We rented a house together and I essentially had a "staycation." The girls cooked, and there was no cleaning to do. I used dispos- able diapers that week instead of cloth. I had my own room downstairs away from everyone and co-slept with the knowledge that a crying baby would not bother anyone. They worked around my 8-times-a-day pumping schedule and celebrated every drop of milk I stored up in the fridge. I was completely surrounded by supportive friends in an uplifting environment, and the feeling of being overwhelmed vanished for 7 glorious days.*

Lani's story of how stress relief positively impacted her milk production is insightful—she was lucky to have friends pamper her for a week. There are many other ways to reduce stress as well, as you'll read in the next section.

## Coping Ideas from Real Parents

When you're feeling overwhelmed, the question is not "*Can* something be changed?" but "*What* can be changed?" It's easier to pull a loaded wagon than to drag the load on the ground. So what wheels can you add to make each day more doable? Below are some survival strategies shared by parents in the trenches:

- First and foremost, remember that *nursing doesn't have to be all or nothing*! There are many in-between options that have worked for numerous families.
- Set short-term goals that are easy to achieve. *Just for today*, maybe you want to pump six times or try a new way to supplement. Aiming for one thing is more doable than a list, and at the end of the day, you'll feel good about accomplishing a goal.
- Make a list of all the things you accomplished today, including getting dressed and growing a baby's brain and bones, and put it on the refrigerator.
- Nap once or twice a day when your baby sleeps. The to-do list can wait, or better yet, be done by others.
- Enlist support—friends, family, church, nanny, neighbor, doula, anyone! Make a list of things that need to be done and post it on the fridge, maybe starting with those dishes and washing pump parts, so that people know how to help.
- Surround yourself with supportive friends and family, whether physically or virtually. This may mean banishing (at least temporarily) those who are critical of your efforts and undermine your confidence. You need people around who help re-energize, not drain, your emotional reserves.
- Ask for help with meals or order takeout if the budget allows.
- Stock your nursing or pumping place with snacks and water and give yourself permission to just sit and binge watch your favorite movie or show while you nurse, pump, and snuggle your baby.

- Have a friend bring coffee over instead of hauling yourself, your baby, and your equipment somewhere else.
- Take your baby for a walk, even if it's just a short walk around the block or in a local mall. The change of pace and scenery can be good for both of you, and exercise and bright light are mood lifting.
- If you don't have time for a walk at least step outside. Look up at the sky, see the bigger world, and take a few deep breaths—it's amazing how re-energizing even a quick breath of fresh air and view of the world outside can feel.
- Stay with a good friend or family member for a few days (or even just for a day) where you won't be tempted by laundry, cooking, or cleaning. If you have other children, ask someone to take them so that you can focus on your baby and milk-making activities.
- Add omega-3 fatty acids (especially eicosapentaenoic acid [EPA] and docosahexaenoic acid [DHA]) to your diet. It can help improve feelings of depression,[8,9] as may aromatherapy.[10]
- Vent your feelings with a trusted friend, family member, or partner. There's a reason they call it "unloading"—a shared burden is much lighter than one carried alone. Sometimes just saying, "I'm really frustrated today" can reduce that frustration.
- Keep your baby in your room at night—the American Academy of Pediatrics recommends for *at least* 6 months.[11] This will reduce the risk of sudden infant death syndrome (SIDS), make breastfeeding easier by reducing the number of nighttime steps you take, and thus increase your sleep.
- Stash all the supplement you may need in a cooler by your bedside so you don't have to get out of bed.
- If you still find yourself at the brink of serious exhaustion, sometimes one good long sleep is necessary to reboot. Feed or pump until your breasts feel drained; then have someone take charge of your baby while you sleep until you wake up on your own. You'll be amazed at how much better you feel. Don't worry—one night of uninterrupted sleep won't set you back. In fact, you might even find yourself producing more milk after a good long rest.

## Take it One Day at a Time

Some days can seem to go on forever, and you may wonder how in the world you're going to make it through weeks and months (or even years) of breastfeeding. On days like these, it's hard to believe that these rough times will one day be behind you. It may even help to say to yourself, "I'll breastfeed just for today and wean tomorrow if I want to." Knowing that you *can* stop may provide a sense of control that helps you get through the day. And if you decide that today's that day? That's okay, too.

## Be Kind to Yourself

Sometimes we can be our own worst critic, as Bekki shared with us:

> *When Evelyn (my oldest) was a newborn, I was convinced that I would somehow work my way up to a full milk supply, and so I decided to save every single empty canister of formula that I had gone through. I stacked them on the counter as a visual reminder of how much formula she had taken, hoping that it would fuel my determination to keep going. In hindsight, building that mountain of formula cans that mocked me on a daily basis was one of the unhealthiest things I could have done to myself. So, I flipped that same strategy with my next baby when it came to nursing. I kept a little notebook and gave myself a tally mark for every time Coralie nursed. Because we had done some weighted feeds, I figured that she was transferring roughly an ounce every time she fed. So at the end of a week, month, etc., I would look back at my tally marks and see that in a month's time, she had received about 300oz just from me. Being able to visualize the sum of what she had gotten from me in any given time went a long way in my healing.*

Bekki's realization of the importance of being kind to herself in counting the positives rather than the negatives was a powerful, healing insight.

## Making Peace with Low Milk Supply

For some parents, just finding an explanation for their low supply brings a sense of relief and a measure of peace, regardless of how much could be remedied. For others, the emotional journey is full of ups and downs. Chantelle's key to peace started with revising her expectations: "My 'normal' was being able to offer the breast until each child wanted to wean . . . to supplement with donor milk and even sometimes formula." She also found catharsis in using her experience to help other parents. Michelle needed to take protective steps: therapy, focusing on her mental well-being, and avoiding emotional triggers by unfollowing "regular" breastfeeding groups on social media. Amanda found nursing her baby for 2½ years with the aid of an SNS (supplemental nutrition system) to be very healing.

Emily described the emotional tug-of-war she felt: "I'm currently feeding baby #6 with the Lact-Aid. There are some days I am grateful for the device, but there are other days where I hate that I have to use it. I am glad that the little plastic tube helps me feed the baby, but I also despise the need to have it at every feeding. It helps when I'm validated in my efforts and also when I realize that I'm not alone."

For Kristin, who now counsels low-supply parents, peace came with acceptance and rolling with the punches instead of fighting: "You don't have to focus on the amount of milk. You can just strap on that SNS and enjoy your baby at the breast. Many low-supply parents are so focused on the milk that they lose sight of the nursing relationship. They need 'permission' to let go of the pills, the pumping, the bottles. I'd rather see someone giving almost 100% formula at the breast than see them cuddling the pump and bottle-feeding the baby."

Laura's parenting journey was a rollercoaster of experiences and feelings as she worked her way to peace:

*After 6 long years of trying to conceive; we began to lose hope. While dealing with PCOS, infertility, foster care, and adoption issues, I also was struggling physically. I was very large breasted and dealt with back pain, awkwardness about my large breasts, and general dysphoria about my outward appearance. Desperate for relief, I had breast reduction surgery. Our first biological son, Benjamin, surprised us 3 years later. I was only able to pump drops of milk from each breast and was heartbroken that I didn't have a full supply. With baby losing weight, formula was pushed at me with no concern for my feelings or regard for other options. I felt like a failure as a mother. Thankfully, I had supportive family and friends. I came to realize that breastfeeding success looks different for every family. We nursed at the breast for Benjamin's "multivitamin," then bottle-fed donor milk and formula for the rest of his nutrition. Our nursing journey lasted 14 wonderful months.*

*Our second biological son was born 2 years later. While I produced a bit more milk, it still was not enough to fully feed Levi from my body. We fed him in a variety of ways: pumping for bottle, nursing first then the bottle, and a supplementer at breast. Levi was born with bilateral clubbed feet, and 2 weeks before he completed the hardest part of his care, he decided that nursing at the breast was just too hard, and he self-weaned around 6 months, which still brings tears to my eyes and a longing ache to my heart.*

*Was it worth it? Hands down, heart on my sleeve, absolutely. I fought so incredibly hard to feed my babies from my body. In the end, knowing I did all I could to provide what I believe is the best for my children, and knowing that the struggle, heartache,*

*devastation, but also bonding, nourishment, healthy attachment, and comfort it pro-*
*vided them will be something we will all live with for the rest of our lives. That, dear*
*friends, is something worth celebrating.*

Whatever form your own journey takes, you too have something to celebrate: your
love for your baby and the effort you have put in to provide the best of yourself. *That's* the
definition of success!

## To the Partners and Families of Those with Low Milk Supply

When a mother/parent struggles with low milk production, so do those closest to them.
We want to acknowledge the difficulty, the frustration, the helpless feelings, and the
unexpected extra work that no one signed up for. With all of the attention focused on
the person giving birth and nursing, you may feel overlooked, overwhelmed, or perhaps
even bewildered by what is being asked of you.

Although this may be more challenging than you had imagined, you play an important role in their breastfeeding journey. Research is clear that mothers/parents who feel
supported breastfeed longer and are more satisfied with their experience than those who
don't perceive support. They may or may not reach their original breastfeeding goals, but
knowing that you were behind them with love as well as emotional and practical support
will help them find balance and restore equilibrium.

As the supporting partner, family member, or friend, it's tempting to look for a quick
fix to the problem, but the suggestion to quit trying to breastfeed is rarely welcome and
can add to their pain and sense of isolation. If you're not sure what is being asked of you,
here are some thoughts from those in the trenches on what they need:

- Instead of saying, "As long as you're happy, I'm fine with formula," tell me, "I'm
  proud of any milk you can give our baby."
- If your loved one was training for a marathon and they had a bad day, you wouldn't
  tell them it was OK to quit, you would encourage them to keep up the good work,
  that they are doing a great job, that every baby step is worth the effort. Do the
  same thing with breastfeeding.
- Please tell me that every single drop of milk I provided is doing wonders for that
  beautiful little human.
- Tell me over and over that I'm doing a good job and that I am ENOUGH. Tell me
  how much you love me and how lucky the baby is that I'm her mom. Tell me I'm
  not broken.

- Every breastfeeding journey is different. Just because it was easy for you doesn't mean it's easy for me. Or just because you chose to stop trying when you struggled with low supply doesn't mean that I have to, too. Let me decide how I want to handle my own breastfeeding journey.
- Allow me to spend as much time as I need on trying to get it as right as possible. Please don't say things like, "You take up so much time pumping, etc., why don't you just switch to formula?" The effort we low-supply mothers put in is usually so monumental, and it's very disheartening to hear it's not appreciated or understood by the father or family.

What these mothers and parents are saying is that they need to work breastfeeding out for themselves, however it goes, and not be pushed to a premature conclusion. Nurit, who had low supply due to breast reduction surgery, shared how her partner stepped up to the plate with baby #2:

> . . . the biggest difference by far was how my husband and I approached this together. From the beginning, his attitude was, "What you are doing is amazing, but don't sacrifice your own mental health to do it." He was constantly helping me to get my pumping sessions in by taking care of our toddler, doing the supplemental feeds, bringing me water or snacks, etc., but also often let me know that it was okay to skip a session here and there if I really wanted to go to the movies, attend my daughter's play group, or anything else. He also sat by me as I pumped in the most public of places and carried my pump around for me wherever we went. Breastfeeding and pumping with low supply can feel so isolating, but having him there and hearing him say it was okay for me to go do other things helped me feel much less alone. This subtle shift has really helped me through this breastfeeding journey . . . which makes it easier to say goodbye to this stage in my son's life.

Beyond emotional support, there are practical things that you can do. Most important, make sure they aren't overly burdened with other responsibilities right now. Making milk for a baby is a full-time job, and help with the household can make all the difference. Encourage them to rest—if you're not available, can you find another supportive person to come over and help with the baby (or chores!) so they can nap? Limiting visitors to agreed-upon times may also be necessary to protect the time and space needed for feeding and pumping. And seeing to it that you both eat nutritious foods is important as well. These practical measures will free them to find their best path through the low milk supply maze.

Can you do this and survive the experience, too? How do *you* cope if this race turns into a marathon? It's important to attend to your own needs as well. Try to get out of the house for a little time to yourself here and there; taking the time rejuvenate yourself periodically is key to preventing resentment. Take a much-needed nap once the nursing couple is settled.

Communication is also crucial. When everyone can express their feelings, the door is open to finding a balance that addresses everyone's needs. If you just need to vent frustration, do it with a safe person who will keep confidentiality and provide nonjudgmental support. The low-supply journey is tough enough, and unsolicited undermining advice can be devastating to a family that is working so hard to provide for their baby.

On behalf of your loved one, we thank you for caring and supporting them. We know it's really hard right now, but this stage won't last forever and the remembrance of your care will be a cherished memory that helps deepen your bond as a couple and a family.

## CHAPTER 19

# What About Next Time?

When you've had challenges with milk supply and you're planning to have more children, the questions that naturally come to mind are, "What about next time . . . will this happen again? Is there anything I can do now to help with the next baby?" While there are no absolutes, we can tell you that most mothers/parents do make more milk with subsequent babies, though how much more depends on their individual circumstances. Having had a previous pregnancy and lactation helps because you will likely retain a little of the glandular growth and prolactin receptors, helping the milk-making tissue to be more responsive to the next pregnancy.[1] The time you've spent breastfeeding up to now is laying a foundation for making more milk in the future.

## A Proactive Approach

If you've made it through all of the chapters, you should have a more complete understanding of what happened or is still happening and what, if anything, can change that path. Working with the advantage of hindsight, more of the big picture should be evident now, and that puts you in a great position to become proactive. If this baby couldn't remove milk well, the next baby will be starting fresh with a clean slate. You'll know what pitfalls to avoid, and if you missed any windows of opportunity, you'll be ready and waiting for those as well. Whether you are thinking about another baby or already expecting one, a proactive approach will maximize your chances of making more milk the next time around.

## Planning for the Next Pregnancy

Now is the time to explore your options. For instance, if inverted nipples caused you problems, consider trying one of the therapies described in Chapter 10. Nipples are less sensitive when you're not pregnant, and more progress can be made when time is your friend, not your foe. Or maybe you're questioning your hormonal status for the first time. Now is the time to screen for hidden issues that can be addressed before the next pregnancy. Some doctors might dismiss your concerns with comments like, "Some people just can't breastfeed," but that's like saying, "Some people just can't get pregnant." You deserve to have professional assistance with investigating the why of your story, so don't give up easily. Lactation trouble may just be the first symptom of a future health problem. These answers are worth pursuing not only for the next baby but for your own long-term health.

### Address Hormonal or Structural Problems

Did you identify any hormonal problems that might be an issue for lactation? Not all can be easily remedied, but now is the time to see what can be done. And if answers don't come readily, it's also a good time to explore complementary or alternative remedies such as acupuncture. One mother took the dietary route to help rebalance her hormones and felt that nursing went better with the next baby. If you've had aches and pains due to an accident, postural issues, or other events, a visit to an osteopath or chiropractor might be worthwhile to make sure your nerves are communicating freely.

### Treat Insulin Resistance

As you've read, insulin resistance has emerged as one of the major underlying factors for lactation problems.[2] It occurs more commonly with a higher body mass index (BMI) or excessive weight gains in pregnancy, but you can also be thin and have insulin resistance. If you're wondering about this, ask to be tested and implement a treatment plan if necessary. For many, it will involve weight loss, diet changes, and exercise. For others, it will include medications or supplements. Metformin is one drug commonly used to treat people with insulin resistance and type 2 diabetes, and in some cases may correct enough underlying imbalances to allow for better mammary development during the next pregnancy. Myo-inositol is considered the natural alternative to metformin; you can add foods high in inositol to your diet or consider a supplement as discussed in Chapter 11. Anything that helps insulin resistance is going to improve your chances of making more milk the next time around.

## Lose Weight to Improve your Odds

We know that this is easier said than done and almost impossible for some. But excess body fat can contribute to insulin resistance, more androgens, hypertension, and poor mammary gland development, including fewer myoepithelial cells for the letdown reflex. What you take into pregnancy may influence breast changes and long-term breastfeeding. The good news is that research suggests that some of the negative effects on the breasts may be reversible—there's hope![3] And weight loss by itself may help rebalance hormones. A good place to start is reducing your carbohydrate intake and finding smart carbs to eat, which can help with insulin resistance and weight control. One highly successful, evidence-based program for weight loss is The Diabetes Prevention Program, now available through the YMCA (bit.ly/MMM-YMCA).

## Treat Polycystic Ovary Syndrome for the Long-Term

Often, the goal of PCOS treatment is to address symptoms such as irregular menstrual cycles, infertility, or hirsutism. But PCOS has real long-term health consequences, not to mention possible impacts on lactation. We don't have rock solid evidence directly linking PCOS and milk production, but we absolutely do have evidence that components of PCOS such as obesity, excess androgens, and insulin resistance can have a direct impact. There also is a strong theoretical basis for estrogen dominance and low progesterone affecting lactation as well.[4] Treating the underlying problems and not just the original concerns is more likely to improve hormone function. Herbs such as chasteberry and saw palmetto, which are sometimes used as natural treatments for PCOS, have reputations for balancing hormones as well as increasing breast tissue and may be useful between babies.

# Strategies for a Current Pregnancy

Every new season of pregnancy is a fresh opportunity. Staying on top of your health is key to getting the best start, including seeking help if you have structural problems such as pinched nerves or back pain. Consider a prenatal lactation appointment with an IBCLC to make sure you've covered all the bases. As a bonus, they will already be familiar with your story should you need help after birth.

## Treat Flat or Inverted Nipples

For low-risk pregnancies, it's not too late to try those cups to draw out tricky nipples. Nursing through a low-risk pregnancy is safe,[5] and passive suction cups are much less stimulating and should be safe to use at any time, though you'll still want to talk to your midwife or doctor. The more severe the inversion, the more time will be needed to make progress. Work up gradually to 8 hours daily or as tolerated. If the cups become uncomfortable or you experience more Braxton-Hicks contractions than usual, multiple shorter sessions should help. Covering the cups with a large breast shell helps them stay in place inside your bra. If colostrum leaks into the cups, you can freeze it for later use. Review Chapter 10 for more details.

## Watch Your Pregnancy Weight

Excessive weight gain during pregnancy is associated with shorter breastfeeding, especially for non-Hispanic white parents.[6] It's also a frequent cause of pregnancy-induced hypertension,[7] another risk factor for more trouble with milk production. If you began the pregnancy overweight, the effect is additive.[8] Eat as smart as you can, with more fruits and vegetables and whole grains and protein and minimal refined sugar and flour products. Your health care provider will tell you how much weight gain is healthy for you individually, and you can ask to see a dietitian if you need help with finding the right foods that you also like.

Interestingly, inadequate weight gain also carries risk for having more trouble getting breastfeeding going.[6,9] So be sure to eat enough healthy calories for appropriate weight gain.

## Keep an Eye on Those Hormones

### Progesterone

Katie had unexplained low milk supply with her first 2 children. Domperidone bumped up her production well, but she still had to supplement. She then experienced

## Institute of Medicine Gestational Weight Gain Guidelines (2009)[10]

| Prepregnancy BMI | Recommended Total Weight Gain at Term (40 wk) | Recommended Rate of Weight Gain in the 2nd and 3rd Trimesters, mean (range) of gain |
|---|---|---|
| Underweight (BMI less than 18.5) | 12.5-18 kg 28-40 lb | 0.51 (0.44-0.58) kg per week 1 (1-1.3) lb per week |
| Normal weight (BMI 18.5-24.9) | 11.5-16 kg 25-35 lb | 0.42 (0.35-0.5) kg per week 1 (0.8-1) lb per week |
| Overweight (BMI 25-29.9) | 7-11.5 kg 15-25 lb | 0.28 (0.23-0.33) kg per week 0.6 (0.5-0.7) lb per week |
| Obese (BMI over 30) | 5-9 kg 11-20 lb | 0.22 (0.17-0.27) kg per week 0.5 (0.4-0.6) lb per week |

three miscarriages. When her mainstream obstetrician was unable to find the root cause, she sought help from a physician trained in Natural Procreative Technology (NaPro), who checked her progesterone levels and found them low. *Bioidentical progesterone* (different from synthetic) was started at 4 weeks of pregnancy and continued to 38 weeks, with monitoring and adjustments throughout (bit.ly/MMM-PregProg). Katie's milk production started up slowly as with her other children, but once she started domperidone at 2 weeks, her milk production "skyrocketed," and she had to stop it after a few weeks because she was making too much, commenting, "I did not realize at the time the effect that progesterone supplementation would have on our breastfeeding relationship!"

If you have a history of infertility or miscarriages related to low progesterone, supplementation through the pregnancy might make a difference in mammary development. Progesterone treatment to prevent miscarriage traditionally is discontinued after the first trimester, but as in Katie's experience, therapy through most of the pregnancy may be more effective. She believes that using bioidentical instead of synthetic progesterone was significant for her body. We've also heard from a few mothers who believe that natural topical progesterone cream applied to their breasts during pregnancy helped them as well.

One important note: Progesterone needs to drop in order for labor to start, so any progesterone therapies should be stopped no later than 38 weeks or as otherwise directed by your health care provider.

### Insulin

When insulin is not working well at the time of delivery, milk production may start off sluggishly. Eat smart to maintain good blood sugar levels during pregnancy. If you develop gestational diabetes, work diligently to control it and try to avoid the use of insulin if at all possible because of the association with shorter lactation and immature infant sucking.

### Thyroid

If you have a history of thyroid problems or if they run in your family, consider having your thyroid checked at least each trimester. One mother even requested monthly testing because she knew her thyroid hormones were prone to swinging around. Also, be ready to request a check in the first few weeks after delivery if milk production doesn't start up normally—waiting until your 6-week check-up is way too long if there's a problem.

### Prolactin

If you had a history of low prolactin, are at risk for pituitary problems, or have a history of promising-looking breasts that just didn't produce as expected, it might be worth

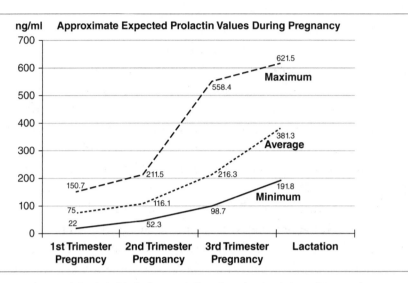

ng/ml   Approximate Expected Prolactin Values During Pregnancy

*Adapted from López M, Rodríguez J & García M (2013). Chapter 12: Physiological and Pathological Hyperprolactinemia: Can We Minimize Errors in the Clinical Practice? : InTech. Data from Tyson JE, Hwang P, Guyda H, Friesen Hg. Studies of prolactin secretion in human pregnancy. Am J Obstet Gynecol. 1972;113:14-20.*

checking your prolactin once or twice during the last half of pregnancy, as suggested by researchers. Mid to later 3rd trimester prolactin should hopefully be at least 150-250ng/ml (mcg/L).[11,12] If it's low, you'll be prepared and can discuss options with your lactation consultant and health care provider.

## Complementary and Alternative Therapies

It's not too late. Acupuncture, reflexology, chiropractics, naturopathy, etc. are viable options during pregnancy as well, though more care must be taken. If you have unaddressed issues, one of these might be worth exploring. At the very least, you'll have someone you know lined up for after delivery.

## Get a Head Start: Expressing Milk Before Your Baby Is Born

If expressing colostrum and milk after birth can accelerate the onset of milk production, what about expressing colostrum before birth, as mentioned in Chapter 5? This practice has been quietly happening for decades,[13] but Australian lactation consultant Sue Cox was the first to promote antenatal expression to the modern breastfeeding community, both for providing supplement for babies at risk of early supplementation and to get breastfeeding going faster after delivery.[14,15] Research conducted since our first edition supports this idea and has also shown that concerns of stimulating early labor in low-risk pregnancies are unfounded.[16] A study from India asked pregnant parents to express once daily for at least 5 minutes from 37 weeks of pregnancy until delivery; those who expressed established breastfeeding faster than those who did not express.[17]

Celine exclusively pumped for her third baby, who was very sick. After delivery, she had tried hand expressing colostrum but found it "very challenging." When she was pregnant with her fourth, she decided to express colostrum prior to birth as a safety net in case he ended up in the NICU as well: "It certainly helped my confidence and helped me feel like I had some sense of control." In a US study, nursing parents at risk for poor lactation due to pregnancy hypertension felt more confident even when the onset of milk production was delayed because they were able to provide prenatally expressed colostrum and more milk after delivery. Despite rocky starts, they all eventually reached full lactation. Expressing colostrum during pregnancy allows you to become more competent at this skill before crisis hits, and puts you ahead of the game if supplementation is needed.[18] A few pregnant parents are not able to express much, if anything, and although this may be discouraging, it does not necessarily predict future breastfeeding problems.

As long as your pregnancy is low risk, you can begin hand expressing for a few minutes daily starting at the 34th to 36th week of pregnancy, the full technique is described in Chapter 13. It's usually easiest when you're relaxed and warm, such as after taking a shower. Express any colostrum drops onto a spoon; then use a small periodontal or similar blunt-end syringe to draw it up. It's okay to refrigerate and reuse the same syringe for 48 hours, adding more colostrum as it is expressed, then freeze it in a small airtight container (Snappies® work great) for the hospital.

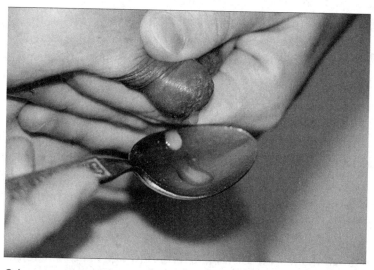

*Colostrum can be collected in a spoon and frozen for later use, if desired.*
*Photo by Amy Nansteel*

A variation on this idea is practiced in some traditional cultures. Young husbands are taught that it is their duty to suckle their wives' breasts during lovemaking in preparation for future babies. Lactation consultants report that these first-time mothers seem to experience early and abundant milk production. If your partner is so inclined, it may be worth trying.

## Think Through Your Birth Plan

As discussed earlier, there are many things about how labor and delivery are managed that affect the start-up of the milk factory. Continuous oxytocin for inductions or augmentation of labor can cause your body to stop releasing its own oxytocin and possibly alter receptor response as well. Both synthetic oxytocin and various labor drugs can affect your baby's suck at birth. Can you have an open discussion with your doctor or midwife about the research, your concerns, and how to minimize or avoid these medications? And if you're having a planned c-section, consider talking to them about the possibility of waiting until you go into labor so that you have the advantage of that natural oxytocin surge after birth. Finally, if you found the post-delivery care to be an obstacle to breastfeeding instead of helpful, talk to your doctor or midwife about what can be done to make sure that you and baby are kept together and interferences are kept to a bare minimum.

## Galactogogues During Pregnancy?

Animal lactation experts know that piglet growth is limited by the amount of milk the sow can produce—more milk, faster growth. In a novel experiment, they administered domperidone to first-time mama pigs during late pregnancy when the mammary tissue was growing and maturing. As they predicted, prolactin rose higher than normal and the milk-making cells grew larger. Piglets grew 20% faster because there was more milk.[19] When a Filipino researcher gave 35-week pregnant parents malunggay daily until they delivered, their milk came in stronger and the babies grew more than those who didn't take it.[20] Malunggay is known to stimulate prolactin and its status as a food makes it a great option when used moderately.

Alfalfa during pregnancy and goat's rue during the last trimester have both been credited by some parents with boosting breast growth. One mother, pregnant with her seventh child after a lapse of several years, was not experiencing the same breast changes as before. After consultation with her lactation consultant and physician at 36 weeks, she started taking goat's rue and began to experience new changes just a few days later, including leaking colostrum. (As a beneficial side effect, her blood sugar levels dropped, and her gestational diabetes resolved.) After a slow start and an additional month of herbs, she was able to exclusively nurse.

Red raspberry leaf is often recommended by midwives during the last few months of pregnancy to help tone the uterus for birth. As mentioned in Chapter 14, one study noticed that mothers taking red raspberry leaf during pregnancy seem to have their milk production increase sooner.[21] Definitely worth consideration!

It must be emphasized that many of these herbal applications are experimental and not backed by research. If you're interested but don't have expertise in herbs, consult an herbalist, naturopath, or doctor of Chinese medicine for guidance, and by all means keep your pregnancy health care provider in the loop.

## What About Hypoplasia?

True congenital mammary hypoplasia is considered irreversible but is also very rare. Acquired hypoplasia is a different matter. Some intriguing case studies demonstrate that insufficient glandular tissue may be reversible at times. Stein and Leventhal, the original researchers of PCOS, observed that some of the young women they treated, including a 22-year old, grew breast tissue where little was present before and went on to nurse successfully.[22] While you can't go back and change what happened during puberty, you *do* have the power to address health and hormonal problems (especially insulin resistance) now so that your breasts are able to respond to pregnancy and lactation hormones to the best of their ability.

### Beating the Odds

Miracles happen! Having insufficient glandular tissue can be discouraging, but some amazing things have happened for persistent parents. Angie described herself as "flat-chested" as a teenager, developing small breasts that were "pointy and conical" and less than an A cup size. Like many parents, she had heard that size doesn't matter and every woman can breastfeed, so her baby's serious weight loss was a wake-up call that all was not proceeding normally. After identifying hypoplasia and scant milk production, just 2-4oz (60-120ml) per day, Angie's LC set her up with a supplementer (SNS), but it wasn't easy. "The SNS saved our nursing relationship; I thought I couldn't last long. At the end of every week, I was saying, 'I'll do it another week, and if my supply doesn't increase, I will just give bottles.' . . . I got used to it and we used it every single day for 10 months!" Angie took domperidone for 6 weeks but pumped for 20 minutes after every feeding for the first 8 months, experiencing some breast growth and reaching a maximum production of 8oz per day. With her second baby, she pumped 12 times a day for the first 6 weeks; took domperidone, fenugreek, and alfalfa; and was able to make 50%

of her baby's needs while her breasts grew to a B cup size. Her daughter weaned from breastfeeding at 6 months, but Angie continued pumping 8 months longer, and to her amazement her breasts kept growing—to a D cup size! For her third baby, Angie took alfalfa at the end of pregnancy and experienced breast growth. She added fenugreek tea and barley drinks after birth and instituted pumping again. Miraculously, her breasts grew even further, and she actually developed oversupply! Angie believes all of the extra pumping made the difference (and we do, too) and that the galactogogues amplified her efforts.

Chana had asymmetrical breasts with especially severe hypoplasia on her right side; she experienced only slight enlargement and no tenderness during pregnancy. She struggled to make milk for her first baby with the aid of domperidone, supplementing at the breast for 2 years so she could have a breastfeeding relationship. With her second pregnancy, Chana again had slight enlargement and no tenderness. But this time she was diagnosed with hypothyroidism and began thyroid replacement therapy. After the birth, she nursed frequently, used breast compressions, kept her baby skin-to-skin, and pumped after every feeding with a hospital-grade pump. During the second week, she began using goat's rue, domperidone, and Lactation Blend capsules by Vitanica. She ate oatmeal every day and took a daily flaxseed supplement. Within 2 weeks, she noticed increased veining and enlargement. Although some supplementation was needed at first, she eventually achieved the exclusive nursing relationship she dreamed about. Chana doesn't attribute her success to any one thing in particular because she believes they all worked synergistically, but she does think that pumping and goat's rue had the biggest effect for her.

These intriguing stories suggest that some primary problems can be improved and sometimes even reversed with subsequent babies. You never know—it's always worth a try!

## Hope Is on the Horizon

Ten years ago, we wrote about potential breakthroughs on the horizon. Replacement prolactin is still on hold, and efforts to grow replacement or reparative breast tissue are progressing slowly. But we now have deeper insights into how metabolic health can affect lactation, and with that knowledge we have the opportunity to intervene earlier and change the course of lactation for some parents. One of the most promising ideas comes from a researcher who envisions testing milk to identify problem genes, paving the way for more targeted responses. There is much work to be done to make this a reality, but what a great vision for future breastfeeding families!

# References

## Introduction

**1.** Odom EC, Li R, Scanlon KS, Perrine CG, Grummer-Strawn L. Reasons for earlier than desired cessation of breastfeeding. *Pediatrics.* 2013;131(3):e726-732.

**2.** Porta F, Mussa A, Baldassarre G, et al. Genealogy of breastfeeding. *Eur J Pediatr.* 2016;175(1):105-112.

**3.** Bergmann RL, Bergmann KE, von Weizsacker K, Berns M, Henrich W, Dudenhausen JW. Breastfeeding is natural but not always easy: intervention for common medical problems of breastfeeding mothers—a review of the scientific evidence. *J Perinat Med.* 2014;42(1):9-18.

**4.** Lee S, Kelleher SL. Biological underpinnings of breastfeeding challenges: the role of genetics, diet, and environment on lactation physiology. *Am J Physiol Endocrinol Metab.* 2016;311(2):E405-E422.

**5.** Marasco LA. Unsolved mysteries of the human mammary gland: defining and redefining the critical questions from the lactation consultant's perspective. *J Mammary Gland Biol Neoplasia.* 2015;19(3-4):271-288.

**6.** Thomas EV. "Why even bother; they are not going to do it?" The structural roots of racism and discrimination in lactation care. *Qual Health Res.* 2018;28(7):1050-1064.

**7.** Farrow A. Lactation support and the LGBTQI community. *J Hum Lact.* 2015;31(1):26-28.

**8.** MacDonald T, Noel-Weiss J, West D, et al. Transmasculine individuals' experiences with lactation, chestfeeding, and gender identity: a qualitative study. *BMC Pregnancy Childbirth.* 2016;16:106-106.

**9.** Griswold MK, Crawford SL, Perry DJ, et al. Experiences of racism and breastfeeding initiation and duration among first-time mothers of the Black Women's Health Study. *J Racial Ethn Health Disparities.* 2018;5(6):1180-1191.

**10.** Merewood A, Bugg K, Burnham L, et al. Addressing racial inequities in breastfeeding in the Southern United States. *Pediatrics.* 2019;143(2). pii: e20181897. doi: 10.1542/peds.2018-1897. Epub 2019 Jan 18.

## Chapter 1

**1.** Stuebe AM. Enabling women to achieve their breastfeeding goals. *Obstet Gynecol.* 2014;123(3):643-652.

**2.** Morozova MG. [The significance of underdeveloped tissue of the mammary gland in the development of the so-called primary hypolactation.]. *Akush Ginekol (Mosk).* 1961;37:43-50.

**3.** Cox DB, Kent JC, Casey TM, Owens RA, Hartmann PE. Breast growth and the urinary excretion of lactose during human pregnancy and early lactation: endocrine relationships. *Exp Physiol.* 1999;84(2):421-434.

**4.** McGuire TM. Drugs affecting milk supply during lactation. *Aust Prescr.* 2018;41(1):7-9.

**5.** Pang WW, Hartmann P. Initiation of human lactation: secretory differentiation and secretory activation. *J Mammary Gland Biol Neoplasia.* 2007(12):211-221.

**6.** Boss M, Gardner H, Hartmann P. Normal human lactation: closing the gap. *F1000Res.* 2018;7(F1000 Faculty Rev):801.

**7.** Kent JC, Gardner H, Geddes DT. Breastmilk production in the first 4 weeks after birth of term infants. *Nutrients.* 2016;8(12).

**8.** Nommsen-Rivers LA, Thompson A, Ward L, Wagner E, Woo J. Metabolic syndrome severity score identifies persistently low milk output. *Breastfeed Med.* 2017;12(suppl 1):S22.

**9.** Kellams A, Harrel C, Omage S, Gregory C, Rosen-Carole C. ABM Clinical Protocol #3: Supplementary Feedings in the Healthy Term Breastfed Neonate, Revised 2017. *Breastfeed Med.* 2017;12:188-198.

**10.** Kent JC, Mitoulas LR, Cregan MD, Ramsay DT, Doherty DA, Hartmann PE. Volume and frequency of breastfeedings and fat content of breast milk throughout the day. *Pediatrics.* 2006;117(3):e387-e395.

**11.** Nielsen SB, Reilly JJ, Fewtrell MS, Eaton S, Grinham J, Wells JC. Adequacy of milk intake during exclusive breastfeeding: a longitudinal study. *Pediatrics.* 2011;128(4):e907-914.

**12.** Kent JC, Mitoulas L, Cox DB, Owens RA, Hartmann PE. Breast volume and milk production during extended lactation in women. *Exp Physiol.* 1999;84(2):435-447.

**13.** Neifert M, Bunik M. Overcoming clinical barriers to exclusive breastfeeding. *Pediatr Clin North Am.* 2013;60(1):115-145.

**14.** Gardner H, Kent JC, Prime DK, Lai CT, Hartmann PE, Geddes DT. Milk ejection patterns remain consistent during the first and second lactations. *Am J Hum Biol.* 2017;29(3).

**15.** Gardner H, Kent JC, Lai CT, et al. Milk ejection patterns: an intra-individual comparison of breastfeeding and pumping. *BMC Pregnancy Childbirth.* 2015;15:156.

**16.** De Carvalho M, Robertson S, Friedman A, Klaus M. Effect of frequent breastfeeding on early milk production and infant weight gain. *Pediatrics.* 1983;72(3):307-311.

**17.** Kim JY, Mizoguchi Y, Yamaguchi H, Enami J, Sakai S. Removal of milk by suckling acutely increases the prolactin receptor gene expression in the lactating mouse mammary gland. *Mol Cell Endocrinol.* 1997;131(1):31-38.

**18.** Trott JF, Schennink A, Petrie WK, Manjarin R, VanKlompenberg MK, Hovey RC. Triennial Lactation Symposium: prolactin: the multifaceted potentiator of mammary growth and function. *J Anim Sci.* 2012;90(5):1674-1686.

**19.** dos Santos CO, Dolzhenko E, Hodges E, Smith AD, Hannon GJ. An epigenetic memory of pregnancy in the mouse mammary gland. *Cell Rep.* 2015;11(7):1102-1109.

**20.** Kent J. How breastfeeding works. *J Midwifery Womens Health.* 2007;52(6):564-570.

**21.** Kent JC, Prime DK, Garbin CP. Principles for maintaining or increasing breast milk production. *J Obstet Gynecol Neonatal Nurs.* 2012;41(1):114-121.

**22.** Woolridge MW. Problems of establishing lactation. *Food Nutr Bull.* 1996;17(4):316-323.

# Chapter 2

**1.** Riddle SW, Nommsen-Rivers LA. Low milk supply and the pediatrician. *Curr Opin Pediatr.* 2017;29(2):249-256.

**2.** Stuebe AM. Enabling women to achieve their breastfeeding goals. *Obstet Gynecol.* 2014;123(3):643-652.

**3.** Smillie CM, Campbell SH, Iwinski S. Hyperlactation: how left-brained "rules" for breastfeeding can wreak havoc with a natural process. *Newborn Infant Nurs Reve.* 2005;5(1):49-58.

**4.** Genna W. *Supporting Sucking Skills in Breastfeeding Infants.* 3rd ed. Burlington, MA: Jones & Bartlett Learning; 2016.

**5.** Cregan MD, Mitoulas LR, Hartmann PE. Milk prolactin, feed volume and duration between feeds in women breastfeeding their full-term infants over a 24 h period. *Exp Physiol.* 2002;87(2):207-214.

**6.** Kent JC, Mitoulas LR, Cregan MD, Ramsay DT, Doherty DA, Hartmann PE. Volume and frequency of breastfeedings and fat content of breast milk throughout the day. *Pediatrics.* 2006;117(3):e387-e395.

7.  Yamada R, Rasmussen KM, Felice JP. "What is 'enough,' and how do I make it?": a qualitative examination of questions mothers ask on social media about pumping and providing an adequate amount of milk for their infants. *Breastfeed Med.* 2019;14(1):17-21.

8.  Dewey KG, Heinig MJ, Nommsen LA, Lonnerdal B. Maternal versus infant factors related to breast milk intake and residual milk volume: the DARLING study. *Pediatrics.* 1991;87(6):829-837.

## Chapter 3

1.  Sauer CW, Boutin MA, Kim JH. Wide variability in caloric density of expressed human milk can lead to major underestimation or overestimation of nutrient content. *J Hum Lact.* 2017;33(2):341-350.

2.  Kent JC, Mitoulas L, Cox DB, Owens RA, Hartmann PE. Breast volume and milk production during extended lactation in women. *Exp Physiol.* 1999;84(2):435-447.

3.  Paul IM, Schaefer EW, Miller JR, et al. Weight change nomograms for the first month after birth. *Pediatrics.* 2016;138(6).

4.  Samayam P, Ranganathan PK, Balasundaram R. Study of weight patterns in exclusively breast fed neonates—does the route of delivery have an impact? *J Clin Diagn Res.* 2016;10(1):Sc01-03.

5.  Deng X, McLaren M. Using 24-hour weight as reference for weight loss calculation reduces supplementation and promotes exclusive breastfeeding in infants born by cesarean section. *Breastfeed Med.* 2018;13(2):128-134.

6.  Noel-Weiss J, Woodend AK, Groll DL. Iatrogenic newborn weight loss: knowledge translation using a study protocol for your maternity setting. *Int Breastfeed J.* 2011;6(1):10.

7.  Riddle SW, Nommsen-Rivers LA. Low milk supply and the pediatrician. *Curr Opin Pediatr.* 2017;29(2):249-256.

8.  Camurdan AD, Beyazova U, Ozkan S, Tunc VT. Defecation patterns of the infants mainly breastfed from birth till the 12th month: prospective cohort study. *Turk J Gastroenterol.* 2014;25(suppl 1):1-5.

9.  Moretti E, Rakza T, Mestdagh B, Labreuche J, Turck D. The bowel movement characteristics of exclusively breastfed and exclusively formula fed infants differ during the first three months of life. *Acta Paediatr.* 2019;108(5):877-881.

10.  Eglash A, Leeper K, Hertz G. *The Little Green Book of Breastfeeding Management for Physicians and Other Health Care Providers.* 6th ed. Verona, WI: The Milk Mob; 2017.

11.  Kent JC, Mitoulas LR, Cregan MD, Ramsay DT, Doherty DA, Hartmann PE. Volume and frequency of breastfeedings and fat content of breast milk throughout the day. *Pediatrics.* 2006;117(3):e387-395.

**12.** Kent JC, Ramsay DT, Doherty D, Larsson M, Hartmann PE. Response of breasts to different stimulation patterns of an electric breast pump. *J Hum Lact*. 2003;19(2):179-186; quiz 187-178, 218.

**13.** Lai CT, Hale TW, Simmer K, Hartmann PE. Measuring milk synthesis in breast-feeding mothers. *Breastfeed Med*. 2010;5(3):103-107.

**14.** Kent J, Gardner H, Lai C-T, et al. Hourly breast expression to estimate the rate of synthesis of milk and fat. *Nutrients*. 2018;10(9):1144.

## Chapter 4

**1.** Kent JC, Mitoulas LR, Cregan MD, Ramsay DT, Doherty DA, Hartmann PE. Volume and frequency of breastfeedings and fat content of breast milk throughout the day. *Pediatrics*. 2006;117(3):e387-e395.

**2.** Hoover K, Marasco L. Low milk production and infant weight gain. In: Campbell SH; Lauwers J; Mannel R; Spencer B, ed. *Core Curriculum for Interdisciplinary Lactation Care*. Burlington, MA: Jones & Bartlett; 2018:343-366.

**3.** Kellams A, Harrel C, Omage S, Gregory C, Rosen-Carole C. ABM Clinical Protocol #3: Supplementary Feedings in the Healthy Term Breastfed Neonate, Revised 2017. *Breastfeed Med*. 2017;12:188-198.

**4.** Sriraman NK, Evans AE, Lawrence R. Academy of Breastfeeding Medicine's 2017 Policy Statement on Informal Milk Sharing. *Breastfeed Med*. 2017;12(9):547-547.

**5.** Akre JE, Gribble KD, Minchin M. Milk sharing: from private practice to public pursuit. *Int Breastfeed J*. 2011;6(1):8.

**6.** Walker S, Armstrong M. The four pillars of safe breast milk sharing. *Midwifery Today*. 2012(Spring):34-36.

**7.** Keim SA, Hogan JS, McNamara KA, et al. Microbial contamination of human milk purchased via the Internet. *Pediatrics*. 2013;132(5):e1227-1235.

**8.** Keim SA, Kulkarni MM, McNamara K, et al. Cow's milk contamination of human milk purchased via the Internet. *Pediatrics*. 2015;135(5):e1157-1162.

**9.** Smith WL, Erenberg A, Nowak A. Imaging evaluation of the human nipple during breast-feeding. *Am J Dis Child*. 1988;142(1):76-78.

**10.** Pados BF, Park J, Dodrill P. Know the flow: milk flow rates from bottle nipples used in the hospital and after discharge. *Adv Neonatal Care*. 2019;19(1):32-41.

**11.** Eglash A, Simon L. ABM Clinical Protocol #8: Human Milk Storage Information for Home Use for Full-Term Infants, Revised 2017. *Breastfeed Med*. 2017;12(7):390-395.

**12.** Fogleman AD, Meng T, Osborne J, Perrin MT, Jones F, Allen JC. Storage of unfed and leftover mothers' own milk. *Breastfeed Med*. 2018;13(1):42-49.

# Chapter 5

**1.** Capuco AV, Ellis SE, Hale SA, et al. Lactation persistency: insights from mammary cell proliferation studies. *J Anim Sci.* 2003;81(suppl 3):18-31.

**2.** Galipeau R, Goulet C, Chagnon M. Infant and maternal factors influencing breast-milk sodium among primiparous mothers. *Breastfeed Med.* 2012;7:290-294.

**3.** Forster DA, Moorhead AM, Jacobs SE, et al. Advising women with diabetes in pregnancy to express breastmilk in late pregnancy (Diabetes and Antenatal Milk Expressing [DAME]): a multicentre, unblinded, randomised controlled trial. *Lancet.* 2017;389(10085):2204-2213.

**4.** Tobolic TJ. Primum non nocere breastfeeding. *Breastfeed Med.* 2019;14(1):77-78.

**5.** Lamaze International. Position paper: promoting, supporting, and protecting normal birth. *J Perinat Educ.* 2007;16(3):11-15.

**6.** Spaeth A, Zemp E, Merten S, Dratva J. Baby-Friendly Hospital designation has a sustained impact on continued breastfeeding. *Matern Child Nutr.* 2018;14(1).

**7.** Barrera CM, Beauregard JL, Nelson JM, Perrine CG. Association of Maternity Care Practices and Policies with In-Hospital Exclusive Breastfeeding in the United States. *Breastfeed Med.* 2019;14(4):243-248.

**8.** Agudelo S, Gamboa O, Rodriguez F, et al. The effect of skin-to-skin contact at birth, early versus immediate, on the duration of exclusive human lactancy in full-term new-borns treated at the Clinica Universidad de La Sabana: study protocol for a randomized clinical trial. *Trials.* 2016;17(1):521.

**9.** Wagner DL, Lawrence S, Xu J, Melsom J. Retrospective chart review of skin-to-skin contact in the operating room and administration of analgesic and anxiolytic medication to women after cesarean birth. *Nurs Womens Health.* 2018;22(2):116-125.

**10.** Billner-Garcia R, Spilker A, Goyal D. Skin-to-skin contact: newborn temperature stability in the operating room. *MCN Am J Matern Child Nurs.* 2018;43(3):158-163.

**11.** Righard L, Alade MO. Effect of delivery room routines on success of first breast-feed. *Lancet.* 1990;336(8723):1105-1107.

**12.** Neczypor JL, Holley SL. Providing evidence-based care during the golden hour. *Nurs Womens Health.* 2017;21(6):462-472.

**13.** Varendi H, Porter RH, Winberg J. Attractiveness of amniotic fluid odor: evidence of prenatal olfactory learning? *Acta Paediatr.* 1996;85(10):1223-1227.

**14.** Dicioccio HC, Ady C, Bena JF, Albert NM. Initiative to improve exclusive breast-feeding by delaying the newborn bath. *J Obstet Gynecol Neonatal Nurs.* 2019;48(2):189-196.

**15.** Parker LA, Sullivan S, Krueger C, Mueller M. Association of timing of initiation of breastmilk expression on milk volume and timing of lactogenesis stage II among mothers of very low-birth-weight infants. *Breastfeed Med*. 2015;10(2):84-91.

**16.** Morton J. The importance of hands. *J Hum Lact*. 2012;28(3):276-277.

**17.** Walters M, Boggs K, Ludington-Hoe S, Price K, Morrison B. Kangaroo care at birth for full term infants. *MCN Am J Matern Child Nurs*. 2007;32(6):375-381.

**18.** Hurst NM, Valentine CJ, Renfro L, Burns P, Ferlic L. Skin-to-skin holding in the neonatal intensive care unit influences maternal milk volume. *J Perinatol*. 1997;17(3):213-217.

**19.** Raguindin P EUMDJ. Prolactin level and breast milk volume among mothers of low birth weight infants admitted to level II neonatal intensive care unit who underwent kangaroo mother care. *Breastfeed Med*. 2015;10(suppl):S4.

**20.** Marlier L, Schaal B, Soussignan R. Orientation responses to biological odours in the human newborn. Initial pattern and postnatal plasticity. *C R Acad Sci III*. 1997;320(12):999-1005.

**21.** Ohyama M, Watabe H, Hayasaka Y. Manual expression and electric breast pumping in the first 48 h after delivery. *Pediatr Int*. 2010;52(1):39-43.

**22.** Kellams A, Harrel C, Omage S, Gregory C, Rosen-Carole C. ABM Clinical Protocol #3: Supplementary Feedings in the Healthy Term Breastfed Neonate, Revised 2017. *Breastfeed Med*. 2017;12:188-198.

**23.** Witt AM, Bolman M, Kredit S. Mothers value and utilize early outpatient education on breast massage and hand-expression in their self-management of engorgement. *Breastfeed Med*. 2016;11:433-439.

**24.** Bowles BC. Breast massage: A "handy" multipurpose tool to promote breastfeeding success. *Clin Lact*. 2011;2(4):21-24.

**25.** Morton J, Hall JY, Wong RJ, Thairu L, Benitz WE, Rhine WD. Combining hand techniques with electric pumping increases milk production in mothers of preterm infants. *J Perinatol*. 2009;29(11):757-764.

**26.** Moore ER, Anderson GC, Bergman N, Dowswell T. Early skin-to-skin contact for mothers and their healthy newborn infants. *Cochrane Database Syst Rev*. 2012;5:Cd003519.

**27.** Neifert M, Bunik M. Overcoming clinical barriers to exclusive breastfeeding. *Pediatr Clin North Am*. 2013;60(1):115-145.

**28.** Freeman ME, Kanyicska B, Lerant A, Nagy G. Prolactin: structure, function, and regulation of secretion. *Physiol Rev*. 2000;80(4):1523-1631.

**29.** Stern JM, Reichlin S. Prolactin circadian rhythm persists throughout lactation in women. *Neuroendocrinology.* 1990;51(1):31-37.

**30.** Moon RY, Darnall A, Feldman-Winter L, Goodstein MH, Hauck FR. SIDS and Other Sleep-Related Infant Deaths: Updated 2016 Recommendations for a Safe Infant Sleeping Environment. *Pediatrics.* 2016;138(5).

**31.** Wiessinger D, West D, Smith L, Pitman T. *Sweet Sleep: Nighttime and Naptime Strategies for the Breastfeeding Family.* New York: Ballantine Books; 2014.

**32.** West D. Smart bedsharing gives breastfeeding mothers more sleep. *The Huffington Post.* https://www.huffingtonpost.com/diana-west/smart-bedsharing-gives-br_b_5662733.html.

## Chapter 6

**1.** Flaherman VJ, Maisels MJ, Academy of Breastfeeding Medicine. ABM Clinical Protocol #22: Guidelines for Management of Jaundice in the Breastfeeding Infant 35 Weeks or More of Gestation—Revised 2017. *Breastfeed Med.* 2017;12(5):250-257.

**2.** Iacovou M, Sevilla A. Infant feeding: the effects of scheduled vs. on-demand feeding on mothers' wellbeing and children's cognitive development. *Eur J Public Health.* 2012:cks012.

**3.** Deutsch Lash MW, N, Andrews G, Crane S. *The Stone Age Baby in a Techno Society.* CreateSpace Independent Publishing Platform; 2012.

**4.** Stern JM, Reichlin S. Prolactin circadian rhythm persists throughout lactation in women. *Neuroendocrinology.* 1990;51(1):31-37.

**5.** Anderson PO. Drugs that suppress lactation, part 2. *Breastfeed Med.* 2017;12(4):199-201.

**6.** Berens P, Labbok M. ABM Clinical Protocol #13: Contraception During Breastfeeding, Revised 2015. *Breastfeed Med.* 2015;10(1).

**7.** Lopez LM, Grey TW, Stuebe AM, Chen M, Truitt ST, Gallo MF. Combined hormonal versus nonhormonal versus progestin-only contraception in lactation. *Cochrane Database Syst Rev.* 2015(3):CD003988.

**8.** Pieh Holder KL. Contraception and breastfeeding. *Clin Obstet Gynecol.* 2015;58(4):928-935.

**9.** Sridhar A, Salcedo J. Optimizing maternal and neonatal outcomes with postpartum contraception: impact on breastfeeding and birth spacing. *Matern Health Neonatol Perinatol.* 2017;3:1.

**10.** Frew JR. Psychopharmacology of bipolar I disorder during lactation: a case report of the use of lithium and aripiprazole in a nursing mother. *Arch Womens Ment Health.* 2015;18(1):135-136.

**11.** Aljazaf K, Hale TW, Ilett KF, et al. Pseudoephedrine: effects on milk production in women and estimation of infant exposure via breastmilk. *Br J Clin Pharmacol.* 2003;56(1):18-24.

**12.** Marcus R. Suppression of lactation with high doses of pyridoxine. *South Afr Med J.* 1975;49(52):2155-2156.

**13.** Greentree LB. Inhibition of prolactin by pyridoxine. *Am J Obstet Gynecol.* 1979;135(2):280-281.

**14.** Haastrup MB, Pottegard A, Damkier P. Alcohol and breastfeeding. *Basic Clin Pharmacol Toxicol.* 2014;114(2):168-173.

**15.** Pepino MY, Steinmeyer AL, Mennella JA. Lactational state modifies alcohol pharmacokinetics in women. *Alcohol Clin Exp Res.* 2007;31(6):909-918.

**16.** Ho E, Collantes A, Kapur BM, Moretti M, Koren G. Alcohol and breast feeding: calculation of time to zero level in milk. *Biol Neonate.* 2001;80(3):219-222.

**17.** Koletzko B, Lehner F. Beer and breastfeeding. *Adv Exp Med Biol.* 2000;478:23-28.

**18.** Mennella JA, Pepino MY. Breastfeeding and prolactin levels in lactating women with a family history of alcoholism. *Pediatrics.* 2010;125(5):e1162-1170.

**19.** Anderson P. Cannabis. In: *Drugs and Lactation Database (LactMed).* Bethesda, MD: National Library of Medicine; 2018.

**20.** Mourh J, Rowe H. Marijuana and breastfeeding: applicability of the current literature to clinical practice. *Breastfeed Med.* 2017;12(10):582-596.

**21.** Crume TL, Juhl AL, Brooks-Russell A, Hall KE, Wymore E, Borgelt LM. Cannabis use during the perinatal period in a state with legalized recreational and medical marijuana: the association between maternal characteristics, breastfeeding patterns, and neonatal outcomes. *J Pediatr.* 2018;197:90-96.

**22.** Napierala M, Mazela J, Merritt TA, Florek E. Tobacco smoking and breastfeeding: effect on the lactation process, breast milk composition and infant development. A critical review. *Environ Res.* 2016;151:321-338.

**23.** Napierala M, Merritt TA, Mazela J, et al. The effect of tobacco smoke on oxytocin concentrations and selected oxidative stress parameters in plasma during pregnancy and post-partum—an experimental model. *Hum Exp Toxicol.* 2017;36(2):135-145.

**24.** Andersen AN, Lund-Andersen C, Larsen JF, et al. Suppressed prolactin but normal neurophysin levels in cigarette smoking breast-feeding women. *Clin Endocrinol (Oxf).* 1982;17(4):363-368.

**25.** Lok KYW, Wang MP, Chan VHS, Tarrant M. The Effect of Secondary Cigarette Smoke from Household Members on Breastfeeding Duration: A Prospective Cohort Study. *Breastfeed Med.* 2018;13(6):412-417.

**26.** Madarshahian F, Hassanabadi M. A comparative study of breastfeeding during pregnancy: impact on maternal and newborn outcomes. *J Nurs Res.* 2012;20(1):74-80.

**27.** Flowers H. Breastfeeding during pregnancy and tandem nursing: is it safe? Recent research. *Breastfeed Today.* 2016(34).

**28.** Moscone SR, Moore MJ. Breastfeeding during pregnancy. *J Hum Lact.* 1993;9(2):83-88.

**29.** Lopez-Fernandez G, Barrios M, Goberna-Tricas J, Gomez-Benito J. Breastfeeding during pregnancy: a systematic review. *Women Birth.* 2017;30(6):e292-e300.

**30.** Hartmann P. Personal communication, 2018.

## Chapter 7

**1.** Routh CHF. *Infant Feeding and Its Influence on Life, or, The Causes and Prevention of Infant Mortality.* London: William Wood & Co.; 1879.

**2.** Jelliffe DB, Jelliffe EF. The volume and composition of human milk in poorly nourished communities. A review. *Am J Clin Nutr.* 1978;31(3):492-515.

**3.** Jacobson H. *Mother Food: A Breastfeeding Diet Guide with Lactogenic Food and Herbs.* Ashland, OR: Rosalind Press; 2007.

**4.** Adams RS, Hutchinson LJ, Ishler VA. Trouble shooting problems with low milk production. *Penn State Dairy and Animal Science Fact Sheet 98-16.* 1998. http://extension.psu.edu/animals/dairy/health/nutrition/nutrition-and-feeding/troubleshooting-guides/troubleshooting-problems-with-low-milk-production/view.

**5.** Lee S, Kelleher SL. Biological underpinnings of breastfeeding challenges: the role of genetics, diet, and environment on lactation physiology. *Am J Physiol Endocrinol Metab.* 2016;311(2):E405-E422.

**6.** Butte NF, Garza C, Stuff JE, Smith EO, Nichols BL. Effect of maternal diet and body composition on lactational performance. *Am J Clin Nutr.* 1984;39(2):296-306.

**7.** Whichelow MJ. Breast feeding in Cambridge, England: factors affecting the mother's milk supply. *J Adv Nurs.* 1979;4(3):253-261.

**8.** Whichelow MJ. Letter: calorie requirements for successful breast feeding. *Arch Dis Child.* 1975;50(8):669.

**9.** Buntuchai G, Pavadhgul P, Kittipichai W, Satheannoppakao W. Traditional galactagogue foods and their connection to human milk volume in Thai breastfeeding mothers. *J Hum Lact.* 2017;33(3):552-559.

**10.** Mohammad MA, Sunehag AL, Haymond MW. Effect of dietary macronutrient composition under moderate hypocaloric intake on maternal adaptation during lactation. *Am J Clin Nutr.* 2009;89(6):1821-1827.

**11.** Torris C, Thune I, Emaus A, et al. Duration of lactation, maternal metabolic profile, and body composition in the Norwegian EBBA I-study. *Breastfeed Med.* 2013;8(1):8-15.

**12.** Achalapong J. Effect of egg and milk supplement on breast milk volume at 48 and 72 hours postpartum: a randomized-controlled trial. *Thai J Obstet Gynaecol.* 2016;24(1):20-25.

**13.** Edozien JC, Khan MAR, Waslien CI. Human protein deficiency: results of a Nigerian village study. *J Nutr.* 1976;106(3):312-328.

**14.** Dangat KD, Kale AA, Joshi SR. Maternal supplementation of omega 3 fatty acids to micronutrient-imbalanced diet improves lactation in rat. *Metabolism.* 2011;60(9):1318-1324.

**15.** Chubukov AS, Belentseva PN, Makarov EI. [Effect of vitamin B12 on lactation]. *Akush Ginekol (Mosk).* 1973;49(8):61-62.

**16.** Lamberts SW, Macleod RM. Regulation of prolactin secretion at the level of the lactotroph. *Physiol Rev.* 1990;70(2):279-318.

**17.** VanHouten J, Dann P, McGeoch G, et al. The calcium-sensing receptor regulates mammary gland parathyroid hormone-related protein production and calcium transport. *J Clin Invest.* 2004;113(4):598-608.

**18.** Weisstaub AR, Zeni S, de Portela ML, Ronayne de Ferrer PA. Influence of maternal dietary calcium levels on milk zinc, calcium and phosphorus contents and milk production in rats. *J Trace Elem Med Biol.* 2006;20(1):41-47.

**19.** Kolasa KM, Firnhaber G, Haven K. Diet for a healthy lactating woman. *Clin Obstet Gynecol.* 2015;58(4):893-901.

**20.** Muscogiuri G, Altieri B, de Angelis C, Palomba S, Pivonello R, Colao A, Orio F. Shedding new light on female fertility: the role of vitamin D. *Rev Endocr Metab Disord.* 2017;18(3):273-283.

**21.** Aranow C. Vitamin D and the immune system. J Investig Med. 2011;59(6): 881-886. doi:10.2310/JIM.0b013e31821b8755

**22.** Luk J, Torrealday S, Neal Perry G, Pal L. Relevance of vitamin D in reproduction. *Hum Reprod.* 2012;27(10): 3015-3027.

**23.** Hollis BW, Wagner CL. New insights into the vitamin D requirements during pregnancy. Bone Res. 2017;5:17030-17030. doi:10.1038/boneres.2017.30

**24.** NIH Office of Dietary Supplements. Vitamin D fact sheet for health professionals. National Institute of Health (2019). Retrieved from https://ods.od.nih.gov/factsheets/VitaminD-HealthProfessional/.

**25.** Hollis BW, Wagner CL, Howard CR, Ebeling M, Shary JR, Smith PG, . . . Hulsey TC. Maternal versus infant vitamin D supplementation during lactation: a randomized controlled trial. Pediatrics 2015;136(4):625-634. doi:10.1542/peds.2015

**26.** Rioux FM, Savoie N, Allard J. Is there a link between postpartum anemia and discontinuation of breastfeeding? *Can J Diet Pract Res.* 2006;67(2):72-76.

**27.** Mathur GP, Chitranshi S, Mathur S, Singh SB, Bhalla M. Lactation failure. *Indian Pediatr.* 1992;29(12):1541-1544.

**28.** Henly S, Anderson C, Avery M, Hills-Bonuyk S, Potter S, Duckett L. Anemia and insufficient milk in first-time mothers. *Birth.* 1995;22(2):87-92.

**29.** Salahudeen MS, Koshy AM, Sen S. A study of the factors affecting time to onset of lactogenesis-II after parturition. *J Pharm Res.* 2013;6(1):68-72.

**30.** Toppare MF, Kitapci F, Senses DA, Kaya IS, Dilmen U, Laleli Y. Lactational failure—study of risk factors in Turkish mothers. *Indian J Pediatr.* 1994;61(3):269-276.

**31.** O'Connor DL, Picciano MF, Sherman AR. Impact of maternal iron deficiency on quality and quantity of milk ingested by neonatal rats. *Br J Nutr.* 1988;60(3):477-485.

**32.** Lee S, Kelleher SL. Molecular regulation of lactation: the complex and requisite roles for zinc. *Arch Biochem Biophys.* 2016;611:86-92.

**33.** Dempsey C, McCormick NH, Croxford TP, Seo YA, Grider A, Kelleher SL. Marginal maternal zinc deficiency in lactating mice reduces secretory capacity and alters milk composition. *J Nutr.* 2012;142(4):655-660.

**34.** Scheplyagina LA. Impact of the mother's zinc deficiency on the woman's and newborn's health status. *J Trace Elem Med Biol.* 2005;19(1):29-35.

**35.** Lee S, Hennigar SR, Alam S, Nishida K, Kelleher SL. Essential role for zinc transporter 2 (ZnT2)-mediated zinc transport in mammary gland development and function during lactation. *J Biol Chem.* 2015;290(21):13064-13078.

**36.** Leung AM, Pearce EN, Braverman LE. Iodine nutrition in pregnancy and lactation. *Endocrinol Metab Clin North Am.* 2011;40(4):765-777.

**37.** Fisher W, Wang J, George NI, Gearhart JM, McLanahan ED. Dietary iodine sufficiency and moderate insufficiency in the lactating mother and nursing infant: a computational perspective. *PloS One.* 2016;11(3):e0149300.

**38.** Serrano-Nascimento C, Salgueiro RB, Vitzel KF, Pantaleao T, Correa da Costa VM, Nunes MT. Iodine excess exposure during pregnancy and lactation impairs maternal thyroid function in rats. *Endocr Connect.* 2017;6(7):510-521.

**39.** Miyai K, Tokushige T, Kondo M. Suppression of thyroid function during ingestion of seaweed "Kombu" (Laminaria japonoca) in normal Japanese adults. *Endocr J.* 2008;55(6):1103-1108.

**40.** Anderson NK, Beerman KA, McGuire MA, et al. Dietary fat type influences total milk fat content in lean women. *J Nutr.* 2005;135(3):416-421.

41. Bostanci Z, Mack RP Jr, Lee S, Soybel DI, Kelleher SL. Paradoxical zinc toxicity and oxidative stress in the mammary gland during marginal dietary zinc deficiency. *Reprod Toxicol.* 2015;54:84-92.

42. Thomas E, Zeps N, Rigby P, Hartmann P. Reactive oxygen species initiate luminal but not basal cell death in cultured human mammary alveolar structures: a potential regulator of involution. *Cell Death Dis.* 2011;2:e189.

43. Wallby T, Lagerberg D, Magnusson M. Relationship between breastfeeding and early childhood obesity: results of a prospective longitudinal study from birth to 4 years. *Breastfeed Med.* 2017;12:48-53.

44. Kuznetsov V. Clinical and pathogenetic aspects of hypogalactia in post-parturient women. *Bulletin of the Ukrainian Medical Stomatological Academy: Actual problems of modern medicine.* 2017;17(1 (57)):305-307.

45. Sebastiani G, Herranz Barbero A, Borras-Novell C, et al. The effects of vegetarian and vegan diet during pregnancy on the health of mothers and offspring. *Nutrients.* 2019;11(3).

46. Torgersen L, Ystrom E, Haugen M, et al. Breastfeeding practice in mothers with eating disorders. *Matern Child Nutr.* 2010;6(3):243-252.

47. Kimmel MC, Ferguson EH, Zerwas S, Bulik CM, Meltzer-Brody S. Obstetric and gynecologic problems associated with eating disorders. *Int J Eat Disord.* 2016;49(3):260-275.

48. Evans J, le Grange D. Body size and parenting in eating disorders: a comparative study of the attitudes of mothers towards their children. *Int J Eat Disord.* 1995;18(1):39-48.

49. Waugh E, Bulik CM. Offspring of women with eating disorders. *Int J Eat Disord.* 1999;25(2):123-133.

50. Javed A, Lteif A. Development of the human breast. *Semin Plast Surg.* 2013;27(1):5-12.

51. Lamb ML. Weight-loss surgery and breastfeeding. *Clin Lact.* 2011;2(3):17-21.

52. Kaska L, Kobiela J, Abacjew-Chmylko A, et al. Nutrition and pregnancy after bariatric surgery. *ISRN Obes.* 2013.

53. Stefanski J. Breastfeeding after bariatric surgery. *Today's Diet.* 2006(Jan):47-50.

54. Ndikom CM, Fawole B, Ilesanmi RE. Extra fluids for breastfeeding mothers for increasing milk production. *Cochrane Database Syst Rev.* 2014;6:Cd008758.

55. Olsen A. Nursing under conditions of thirst or excessive ingestion of fluids. *Acta Obstet Gynecol Scand.* 1940;20(4):313-343.

56. Illingworth RS, Kilpatrick B. Lactation and fluid intake. *Lancet.* 1953;2:1175-1177.

**57.** Dusdieker LB, Booth BM, Stumbo PJ, Eichenberger JM. Effect of supplemental fluids on human milk production. *J Pediatr.* 1985;106(2):207-211.

**58.** Marraccini ME, Gorman KS. exploring placentophagy in humans: problems and recommendations. *J Midwifery Womens Health.* 2015;60(4):371-379.

**59.** Young SM, Benyshek DC. In search of human placentophagy: a cross-cultural survey of human placenta consumption, disposal practices, and cultural beliefs. *Ecol Food Nutr.* 2010;49(6):467-484.

**60.** Selander J, Cantor A, Young SM, Benyshek DC. Human maternal placentophagy: a survey of self-reported motivations and experiences associated with placenta consumption. *Ecol Food Nutr.* 2013;52(2):93-115.

**61.** Brodribb W, Academy of Breastfeeding Medicine. ABM Clinical Protocol #9: Use of Galactogogues in Initiating or Augmenting Maternal Milk Production, Second Revision 2018. *Breastfeed Med.* 2018;13(5):307-314.

## Chapter 8

**1.** Bjelakovic L, Trajkovic T, Kocic G, et al. The association of prenatal tocolysis and breastfeeding duration. *Breastfeed Med.* 2016;11(10):561-563.

**2.** Anderson PO. Drugs that suppress lactation, part 1. *Breastfeed Med.* 2017;12(3):1-3.

**3.** Hernandez LL, Collier JL, Vomachka AJ, Collier RJ, Horseman ND. Suppression of lactation and acceleration of involution in the bovine mammary gland by a selective serotonin reuptake inhibitor. *J Endocrinol.* 2011;209(1):45-54.

**4.** Marshall AM, Nommsen-Rivers LA, Hernandez LL, et al. Serotonin transport and metabolism in the mammary gland modulates secretory activation and involution. *J Clin Endocrinol Metab.* 2010;95(2):837-846.

**5.** Everett M. Pyridoxine to suppress lactation. *JR Coll Gen Pract.* 1982;32(242):577-578.

**6.** AlSaad D, Awaisu A, Elsalem S, Abdulrouf PV, Thomas B, AlHail M. Is pyridoxine effective and safe for post-partum lactation inhibition? A systematic review. *J Clin Pharm Ther.* 2017;42(4):373-382.

**7.** LactMed. Doxylamine. In: *Drugs and Lactation Database (LactMed).* Bethesda, MD: National Library of Medicine; 2018.

**8.** Koren G, Clark S, Hankins GD, et al. Demonstration of early efficacy results of the delayed-release combination of doxylamine-pyridoxine for the treatment of nausea and vomiting of pregnancy. *BMC Pregnancy Childbirth.* 2016;16(1):371.

**9.** Leeners B, Rath W, Kuse S, Neumaier-Wagner P. Breast-feeding in women with hypertensive disorders in pregnancy. *J Perinat Med.* 2005;33(6):553-560.

**10.** Salahudeen MS, Koshy AM, Sen S. A study of the factors affecting time to onset of lactogenesis-II after parturition. *J Pharm Res.* 2013;6(1):68-72.

**11.** Demirci J, Schmella M, Glasser M, Bodnar L, Himes KP. Delayed Lactogenesis II and potential utility of antenatal milk expression in women developing late-onset pre-eclampsia: a case series. *BMC Pregnancy Childbirth.* 2018;18(1):68.

**12.** Nahar L, Nahar K, Hossain MI, Jahan S, Rahman MM. Placental changes in pregnancy induced hypertension. *Mymensingh Med J.* 2013;22(4):684-693.

**13.** Majumdar S, Dasgupta H, Bhattacharya K, Bhattacharya A. A Study of Placenta in Normal and Hypertensive Pregnancies. *J Anat Soc India.* 2005;54(2):7-12.

**14.** Wlodek M, Wescott K, Serruto A, et al. Impaired mammary function and parathyroid hormone-related protein during lactation in growth-restricted spontaneously hypertensive rats. *J Endocrinol.* 2003;178(2):233-245.

**15.** Cordero L, Valentine CJ, Samuels P, Giannone PJ, Nankervis CA. Breastfeeding in women with severe preeclampsia. *Breastfeed Med.* 2012;7:457-463.

**16.** Facchinetti F, Bizzarri M, Benvenga S, et al. Results from the International Consensus Conference on Myo-inositol and d-chiro-inositol in Obstetrics and Gynecology: the link between metabolic syndrome and PCOS. *Eur J Obstet Gynecol Reprod Biol.* 2015;195:72-76.

**17.** Yabes-Almirante C, Lim CHTN. Enhancement of breastfeeding among hypertensive mothers. Paper presented at Increasingly Safe and Successful Pregnancies, Manila, Philippines, 1996.

**18.** O'Dowd R, Kent J, Mosely J, Wlodek M. Effects of uteroplacental insufficiency and reducing litter size on maternal mammary function and postnatal offspring growth. *Am J Physiol Regul Integr Comp Physiol.* 2008;294(2):R539-R548.

**19.** O'Dowd R, Wlodek ME, Nicholas KR. Uteroplacental insufficiency alters the mammary gland response to lactogenic hormones in vitro. *Reprod Fertil Dev.* 2008;20(4):460-465.

**20.** Wlodek ME, Ceranic V, O'Dowd R, Westcott KT, Siebel AL. Maternal progesterone treatment rescues the mammary impairment following uteroplacental insufficiency and improves postnatal pup growth in the rat. *Reprod Sci.* 2009;16(4):380-390.

**21.** Dahl SK, Thomas MA, Williams DB, Robins JC. Maternal virilization due to luteoma associated with delayed lactation. *Fertil Steril.* 2008;90(5):2006 e2017-e2009.

**22.** Hoover KL, Barbalinardo LH, Platia MP. Delayed lactogenesis II secondary to gestational ovarian theca lutein cysts in two normal singleton pregnancies. *J Hum Lact.* 2002;18(3):264-268.

**23.** Betzold CM, Hoover KL, Snyder CL. Delayed lactogenesis II: a comparison of four cases. *J Midwifery Womens Health.* 2004;49(2):132-137.

**24.** Lind JN, Perrine CG, Li R. Relationship between use of labor pain medications and delayed onset of lactation. *J Hum Lact.* 2014;30(2):167-173.

**25.** French CA, Cong X, Chung KS. Labor epidural analgesia and breastfeeding: a systematic review. *J Hum Lact.* 2016;32(3):507-520.

**26.** Jordan S, Emery S, Watkins A, Evans JD, Storey M, Morgan G. Associations of drugs routinely given in labour with breastfeeding at 48 hours: analysis of the Cardiff Births Survey. *BJOG.* 2009;116(12):1622-1629; discussion 1630-1622.

**27.** Erickson EN, Emeis CL. Breastfeeding outcomes after oxytocin use during childbirth: an integrative review. *J Midwifery Womens Health.* 2017;62(4):397-417.

**28.** Garcia-Fortea P, Gonzalez-Mesa E, Blasco M, Cazorla O, Delgado-Rios M, Gonzalez-Valenzuela MJ. Oxytocin administered during labor and breast-feeding: a retrospective cohort study. *J Matern Fetal Neonatal Med.* 2014;27(15):1598-1603.

**29.** Robinson C, Schumann R, Zhang P, Young RC. Oxytocin-induced desensitization of the oxytocin receptor. *Am J Obstet Gynecol.* 2003;188(2):497-502.

**30.** Phaneuf S, Rodriguez Linares B, TambyRaja RL, MacKenzie IZ, Lopez Bernal A. Loss of myometrial oxytocin receptors during oxytocin-induced and oxytocin-augmented labour. *J Reprod Fertil.* 2000;120(1):91-97.

**31.** Odent MR. Synthetic oxytocin and breastfeeding: reasons for testing an hypothesis. *Med Hypotheses.* 2013;81(5):889-891.

**32.** Jonas W, Johansson LM, Nissen E, Ejdeback M, Ransjo-Arvidson AB, Uvnas-Moberg K. Effects of intrapartum oxytocin administration and epidural analgesia on the concentration of plasma oxytocin and prolactin, in response to suckling during the second day postpartum. *Breastfeed Med.* 2009;4(2):71-82.

**33.** Brimdyr K, Cadwell K, Widstrom AM, et al. The association between common labor drugs and suckling when skin-to-skin during the first hour after birth. *Birth.* 2015;42(4):319-328.

**34.** Dimitraki M, Tsikouras P, Manav B, et al. Evaluation of the effect of natural and emotional stress of labor on lactation and breast-feeding. *Arch Gynecol Obstet.* 2015;293(2):317-328.

**35.** Kong M-S, Bajorek B. Medications in pregnancy: impact on time to lactogenesis after parturition. *J Pharm Pract Res.* 2008;38(3):205-208.

**36.** Silva FV, Dias F, Costa G, Campos MD. Chamomile reveals to be a potent galactogogue: the unexpected effect. *J Matern Fetal Neonatal Med.* 2017:1-3.

**37.** Chapman DJ, Perez-Escamilla R. Identification of risk factors for delayed onset of lactation. *J Am Diet Assoc.* 1999;99(4):450-454; quiz 455-456.

**38.** Isik Y, Dag ZO, Tulmac OB, Pek E. Early postpartum lactation effects of cesarean and vaginal birth. *Ginekol Pol.* 2016;87(6):426-430.

**39.** Prior E, Santhakumaran S, Gale C, Philipps LH, Modi N, Hyde MJ. Breastfeeding after cesarean delivery: a systematic review and meta-analysis of world literature. *Am J Clin Nutr.* 2012;95(5):1113-1135.

**40.** Heller MM, Fullerton-Stone H, Murase JE. Caring for new mothers: diagnosis, management and treatment of nipple dermatitis in breastfeeding mothers. *Int J Dermatol.* 2012;51(10):1149-1161.

**41.** Zhang F, Xia H, Li X, et al. Intraoral vacuum of breast-feeding newborns within the first 24 hr: cesarean section versus vaginal delivery. *Biol Res Nurs.* 2016;18(4):445-453.

**42.** Kujawa-Myles S, Noel-Weiss J, Dunn S, Peterson WE, Cotterman KJ. Maternal intravenous fluids and postpartum breast changes: a pilot observational study. *Int Breastfeed J.* 2015;10:18.

**43.** Nommsen-Rivers LA, Chantry CJ, Peerson JM, Cohen RJ, Dewey KG. Delayed onset of lactogenesis among first-time mothers is related to maternal obesity and factors associated with ineffective breastfeeding. *Am J Clin Nutr.* 2010;92(3):574-584.

**44.** Willis CE, Livingstone V. Infant insufficient milk syndrome associated with maternal postpartum hemorrhage. *J Hum Lact.* 1995;11(2):123-126.

**45.** Thompson JF, Heal LJ, Roberts CL, Ellwood DA. Women's breastfeeding experiences following a significant primary postpartum haemorrhage: a multicentre cohort study. *Int Breastfeed J.* 2010;5:5.

**46.** Laway BA, Mir SA, Zargar AH. Recovery of prolactin function following spontaneous pregnancy in a woman with Sheehan's syndrome. *Indian J Endocrinol Metab.* 2013;17(suppl 3):S696-S699.

**47.** Shivaprasad C. Sheehan's syndrome: newer advances. *Indian J Endocrinol Met.* 2011;15(suppl 3):S203-S207.

# Chapter 9

**1.** Zhang F, Xia H, Shen M, et al. Are prolactin levels linked to suction pressure? *Breastfeed Med.* 2016;11(9):461-468.

**2.** Genna CW. Breastfeeding infants with congenital torticollis. *J Hum Lact.* 2015;31(2):216-220.

**3.** Genna CW. *Supporting Sucking Skills in Breastfeeding Infants.* Burlington, MA: Jones & Bartlett; 2016.

**4.** Francis DO, Chinnadurai S, Morad A, Epstein RA, Kohanim S, Krishnaswami S, Sathe NA, McPheeters ML. Treatments for ankyloglossia and ankyloglossia with concomitant lip-tie. In. *Comparative Effectiveness Review No. 149.* (Prepared by the Vanderbilt Evidence-based Practice Center under Contract No. 290-2012-00009-I.). Vol 20152015:284. Rockville, MD: Agency for Healthcare Research and Quality; 2015.

**5.** Geddes DT, Langton DB, Gollow I, Jacobs LA, Hartmann PE, Simmer K. Frenulotomy for breastfeeding infants with ankyloglossia: effect on milk removal and sucking mechanism as imaged by ultrasound. *Pediatrics.* 2008;122(1):e188-e194.

**6.** Pransky SM, Lago D, Hong P. Breastfeeding difficulties and oral cavity anomalies: the influence of posterior ankyloglossia and upper-lip ties. *Int J Pediatr Otorhinolaryngol.* 2015;79(10):1714-1717.

**7.** Siegel S. Aerophagia induced reflux associated with lip and tongue tie in breastfeeding infants. Paper presented at 2015 AAP National Conference and Exhibition; 2015.

**8.** Nakhash R, Wasserteil N, Mimouni FB, Kasirer YM, Hammerman C, Bin-Nun A. Upper lip tie and breastfeeding: a systematic review. *Breastfeed Med.* 2019;14(2):83-87.

**9.** Edmunds J, Miles SC, Fulbrook P. Tongue-tie and breastfeeding: a review of the literature. *Breastfeed Rev.* 2011;19(1):19-26.

**10.** Ferres-Amat E, Pastor-Vera T, Rodriguez-Alessi P, Ferres-Amat E, Mareque-Bueno J, Ferres-Padro E. Management of ankyloglossia and breastfeeding difficulties in the newborn: breastfeeding sessions, myofunctional therapy, and frenotomy. *Case Rep Pediatr.* 2016;2016:3010594.

**11.** Genna W. *Supporting Sucking Skills in Breastfeeding Infants.* 3rd ed. Burlington, MA: Jones & Bartlett Learning; 2016.

**12.** Edmunds JE, Fulbrook P, Miles S. Understanding the experiences of mothers who are breastfeeding an infant with tongue-tie: a phenomenological study. *J Hum Lact.* 2013;29(2):190-195.

**13.** Todd DA, Hogan MJ. Tongue-tie in the newborn: early diagnosis and division prevents poor breastfeeding outcomes. *Breastfeed Rev.* 2015;23(1):11-16.

**14.** Karabulut R, Sonmez K, Turkyilmaz Z, et al. Ankyloglossia and effects on breast-feeding, speech problems and mechanical/social issues in children. *B-ENT.* 2008;4(2):81-85.

**15.** Fernando C. *Tongue Tie: From Confusion to Clarity.* Sydney, Australia: Tandem Publications; 1998.

**16.** Macaluso M, Hockenbury D. Lingual and labial frenums. Early detection can prevent cascading health effects associated with tongue-tie. *RDHMAGcom.* 2015;35(12):2-5.

**17.** Ghaheri BA, Cole M, Mace JC. Revision lingual frenotomy improves patient-reported breastfeeding outcomes: a prospective cohort study. *J Hum Lact.* 2018;34(3):566-574.

**18.** Yamamoto I, Yamada Y, Ohira H, Ohtani S. Changes in sleep disorders after operation on the ankyloglossia with deviation of the epiglottis and larynx. *Bull Kanagawa Dent Coll.* 2005;33(2):106.

**19.** Elad D, Kozlovsky P, Blum O, et al. Biomechanics of milk extraction during breastfeeding. *Proc Natl Acad Sci U S A.* 2014;111(14):5230-5235.

**20.** Lambert JM, Watters NE. Breastfeeding the infant/child with a cardiac defect: an informal survey. *J Hum Lact.* 1998;14(2):151-155.

**21.** Marino BL, O'Brien P, LoRe H. Oxygen saturations during breast and bottle feedings in infants with congenital heart disease. *J Pediatr Nurs.* 1995;10(6):360-364.

**22.** Genna CW. *Sensory Integration and Breastfeeding.* Sudbury, MA: Jones and Bartlett; 2007.

**23.** Weiss-Salinas D, Williams N. Sensory defensiveness: a theory of its effect on breastfeeding. *J Hum Lact.* 2001;17(2):145-151.

**24.** Elster E. Sixteen infants with acid reflux and colic undergoing upper cervical chiropractic care to correct vertebral subluxation: a retrospective analysis of outcome. *J Pediatr Matern Fam Health Chiropract.* 2009;2:1-7.

**25.** Simons JP, Greenberg LL, Mehta DK, Fabio A, Maguire RC, Mandell DL. Laryngomalacia and swallowing function in children. *Laryngoscope.* 2016;126(2):478-484.

**26.** Alcantara J, Alcantara JD, Alcantara J. The chiropractic care of infants with breastfeeding difficulties. *Explore.* 2015;11(6):468-474.

**27.** Wescott N. The use of cranial osteopathy in the treatment of infants with breast feeding problems or sucking dysfunction. *Aust J Holist Nurs.* 2004;11(1):25-32.

## Chapter 10

**1.** Livingstone V. Breastfeeding kinetics: a problem-solving approach to breastfeeding difficulties. *World Rev Nutr Diet.* 1995;78:28-54.

**2.** Han S, Hong YG. The inverted nipple: its grading and surgical correction. *Plast Reconstr Surg.* 1999;104(2):389-395; discussion 396-387.

**3.** McGeorge DD. The "Niplette": an instrument for the non-surgical correction of inverted nipples. *Br J Plast Surg.* 1994;47(1):46-49.

**4.** Bouchet-Horwitz J. The use of supple cups for flat, retracting, and inverted nipples. *Clin Lact.* 2011;2-3:30-33.

**5.** Kesaree N. Treatment of inverted nipples using disposable syringe. *Indian Pediatr.* 1993;30(3):429-430.

**6.** Coentro V, Perella S, Tat Lai C, Geddes D. P-70. Effect of nipple shield use on milk removal in mothers experiencing nipple pain: preliminary findings of a mechanistic study. ISRHML Conference, Kanagawa, Japan, 2018.

**7.** Powers DC, Tapia VB. Clinical decision making when to consider using a nipple shield. *Clin Lact.* 2012;3(1):26-29.

**8.** Garbin CP, Deacon JP, Rowan MK, Hartmann PE, Geddes DT. Association of nipple piercing with abnormal milk production and breastfeeding. *JAMA.* 2009;301(24):2550-2551.

**9.** Huggins K, Petok E, Mireles O. Markers of lactation insufficiency: a study of 34 mothers. *Curr Iss Clin Lact.* 2000:25-35.

**10.** Winocour S, Lemaine V. Hypoplastic breast anomalies in the female adolescent breast. *Semin Plast Surg.* 2013;27(1):42-48.

**11.** Stuebe AM. Enabling women to achieve their breastfeeding goals. *Obstet Gynecol.* 2014;123(3):643-652.

**12.** Klinger M, Caviggioli F, Klinger F, Villani F, Arra E, Di Tommaso L. Tuberous breast: morphological study and overview of a borderline entity. *Can J Plast Surg.* 2011;19(2):42-44.

**13.** Neifert MR, Seacat JM, Jobe WE. Lactation failure due to insufficient glandular development of the breast. *Pediatrics.* 1985;76(5):823-828.

**14.** von Heimburg D, Exner K, Kruft S, Lemperle G. The tuberous breast deformity: classification and treatment. *Br J Plast Surg.* 1996;49(6):339-345.

**15.** Rosenberg CA, Derman GH, Grabb WC, Buda AJ. Hypomastia and mitral-valve prolapse. *N Engl J Med.* 1983;309(20):1230-1232.

**16.** Tsai FC, Hsieh MS, Liao CK, Wu ST. Correlation between scoliosis and breast asymmetries in women undergoing augmentation mammaplasty. *Aesthetic Plast Surg.* 2010;34(3):374-380.

**17.** Guillette EA, Conard C, Lares F, Aguilar MG, McLachlan J, Guillette LJ Jr. Altered breast development in young girls from an agricultural environment. *Environ Health Perspect.* 2006;114(3):471-475.

**18.** Hansen T. Pesticide exposure deprives Yaqui girls of breastfeeding—ever. *Indian Country Today.* 2010. http://www.indiancountrytoday.com/global/latin/85049497.html.

**19.** Goyal A, Mansel RE. Iatrogenic injury to the breast bud causing breast hypoplasia. *Postgrad Med J.* 2003;79(930):235-236.

**20.** Sadove AM, van Aalst JA. Congenital and acquired pediatric breast anomalies: a review of 20 years' experience. *Plast Reconstr Surg.* 2005;115(4):1039-1050.

**21.** Skalkeas G, Gogas J, Pavlatos F. Mammary hypoplasia following irradiation to an infant breast. Case report. *Acta Chir Plast.* 1972;14(4):240-243.

**22.** Haramis HT, Collins RE. Unilateral breast atrophy. *Plast Reconstr Surg.* 1995;95(5):916-919.

**23.** Velter C, Gronier C, Lipsker D. Small infantile haemangioma and breast hypoplasia. *J Eur Acad Dermatol Venereol.* 2017;31(8):e355-e356.

**24.** Theiler M, Hoffman WY, Frieden IJ. Breast hypoplasia as a complication of an untreated infantile hemangioma. *Pediatr Dermatol.* 2016;33(2):e129-e130.

**25.** Eser C, Temiz G, Dulgar AG, Gencel E, Yavuz M. Reconstruction of acquired breast hypoplasia by subcutaneous scar releasing and repeated fat grafting combination. *Plast Reconstr Surg Glob Open.* 2015;3(6):e408.

**26.** Hoon Jung J, Chan Kim Y, Joon Park H, Woo Cinn Y. Becker's nevus with ipsilateral breast hypoplasia: improvement with spironolactone. *J Dermatol.* 2003;30(2):154-156.

**27.** Hernandez-Quiceno S, Uribe-Bojanini E, Ramirez-Jimenez JJ, et al. Becker's nevus syndrome in a pediatric female patient. *Case Rep Pediatr.* 2016;2016:3856518.

**28.** McGuire E, Rowan M. PCOS, breast hypoplasia and low milk supply: a case study. *Breastfeed Rev.* 2015;23(3):29-32.

**29.** Burdina LM, Khdaib F, Smetnik VP, Volobuev AI. [State of the mammary glands in hypergonadotropic amenorrhea]. *Akush Ginekol (Mosk).* 1990(4):47-50.

**30.** Balcar V, Silinkova-Malkova E, Matys Z. Soft tissue radiography of the female breast and pelvic pneumoperitoneum in the Stein-Leventhal syndrome. *Acta Radiol Diagn (Stockh).* 1972;12(3):353-362.

**31.** Kasper N, Peterson KE, Zhang Z, et al. Association of bisphenol A exposure with breastfeeding and perceived insufficient milk supply in Mexican women. *Matern Child Health J.* 2016;20(8):1713-1719.

**32.** Arbour MW, Kessler JL. Mammary hypoplasia: not every breast can produce sufficient milk. *J Midwifery Womens Health.* 2013;58(4):457-461.

**33.** Gopalakrishnan K, Teitelbaum SL, Lambertini L, et al. Changes in mammary histology and transcriptome profiles by low-dose exposure to environmental phenols at critical windows of development. *Environ Res.* 2017;152:233-243.

**34.** Bever Babendure J, Reifsnider E, Mendias E, Moramarco MW, Davila YR. Reduced breastfeeding rates among obese mothers: a review of contributing factors, clinical considerations and future directions. *Int Breastfeed J.* 2015;10:21.

**35.** Cassar-Uhl D, Liberatos P. Association between maternal pre-pregnant BMI and breast markers for lactation insufficiency (poster presentation). Experimental Biology/American Society of Nutrition Annual Meeting, San Diego, CA, 2016.

**36.** Cassar-Uhl D. *Finding Sufficiency: Breastfeeding with Insufficient Glandular Tissue.* Amarillo, TX: Praeclarus Press; 2014.

**37.** Leal SC, Stuart SR, Carvalho Hde A. Breast irradiation and lactation: a review. *Exp Rev Anticancer Ther.* 2013;13(2):159-164.

**38.** Manservisi F, Gopalakrishnan K, Tibaldi E, et al. Effect of maternal exposure to endocrine disrupting chemicals on reproduction and mammary gland development in female Sprague-Dawley rats. *Reprod Toxicol.* 2015;54:110-119.

**39.** Jandacek RJ, Heubi JE, Buckley DD, et al. Reduction of the body burden of PCBs and DDE by dietary intervention in a randomized trial. *J Nutr Biochem.* 2014;25(4):483-488.

**40.** Redgrave TG, Wallace P, Jandacek RJ, Tso P. Treatment with a dietary fat substitute decreased Arochlor 1254 contamination in an obese diabetic male. *J Nutr Biochem.* 2005;16(6):383-384.

**41.** West DH, E;. *Breastfeeding After Breast and Nipple Procedures.* Amarillo, TX: Hale Publishing; 2008.

**42.** Ramsay D, Kent J, Hartmann R, Hartmann P. Anatomy of the lactating human breast redefined with ultrasound imaging. *J Anat.* 2005;206(6):525-534.

**43.** Schlenz I, Kuzbari R, Gruber H, Holle J. The sensitivity of the nipple-areola complex: an anatomic study. *Plast Reconstr Surg.* 2000;105(3):905-909.

**44.** Newman J. Breastfeeding after breast surgery (Part 1). In Vol 2019: Toronto, ON: International Breastfeeding Centre; 2017.

**45.** Cheng F, Dai S, Wang C, Zeng S, Chen J, Cen Y. Do breast implants influence breastfeeding? A meta-analysis of comparative studies. *J Hum Lact.* 2018;34(3): 424-432.

**46.** Filiciani S, Siemienczuk GF, Nardin JM, et al. Cohort study to assess the impact of breast implants on breastfeeding. *Plast Reconstr Surg.* 2016;138(6):1152-1159.

**47.** Mofid MM, Klatsky SA, Singh NK, Nahabedian MY. Nipple-areola complex sensitivity after primary breast augmentation: a comparison of periareolar and inframammary incision approaches. *Plast Reconstr Surg.* 2006;117(6):1694-1698.

**48.** Michalopoulos K. The effects of breast augmentation surgery on future ability to lactate. *Breast J.* 2007;13(1):62-67.

**49.** Schiff M, Algert CS, Ampt A, Sywak MS, Roberts CL. The impact of cosmetic breast implants on breastfeeding: a systematic review and meta-analysis. *Int Breastfeed J.* 2014;9:17-17.

**50.** Kraut RY, Brown E, Korownyk C, et al. The impact of breast reduction surgery on breastfeeding: systematic review of observational studies. *PloS One.* 2017;12(10):e0186591.

**51.** Walker M. Mammary dysbiosis. *Clin Lact.* 2018;9(3):130-136.

**52.** Jimenez E, Fernandez L, Maldonado A, et al. Oral administration of Lactobacillus strains isolated from breast milk as an alternative for the treatment of infectious mastitis during lactation. *Appl Environ Microbiol.* 2008;74(15):4650-4655.

**53.** Stopenski S, Aslam A, Zhang X, Cardonick E. After chemotherapy treatment for maternal cancer during pregnancy, is breastfeeding possible? *Breastfeed Med.* 2017;12:91-97.

**54.** Drake R, Vogl AW, Mitchell AW, Tibbitts R, Richardson P. *Gray's Atlas of Anatomy E-Book.* St. Louis, MO: Elsevier Health Sciences; 2014.

**55.** Halbert LA. Breastfeeding in the woman with a compromised nervous system. *J Hum Lact.* 1998;14(4):327-331.

**56.** Liu N, Krassioukov AV. Postpartum hypogalactia in a woman with Brown-Sequard-plus syndrome: a case report. *Spinal Cord.* 2013;51(10):794-796.

**57.** Holmgren T, Lee AHX, Hocaloski S, et al. The influence of spinal cord injury on breastfeeding ability and behavior. *J Hum Lact.* 2018;34(3):556-565.

**58.** Cowley KC. Psychogenic and pharmacologic induction of the let-down reflex can facilitate breastfeeding by tetraplegic women: a report of 3 cases. *Arch Phys Med Rehabil.* 2005;86(6):1261-1264.

# Chapter 11

**1.** Negro R, Schwartz A, Gismondi R, Tinelli A, Mangier IT, Stagnaro-Green A. Increased pregnancy loss rate in thyroid antibody negative women with TSH levels between 2.5 and 5.0 in the first trimester of pregnancy. *J Clin Endocrinol Metab.* 2010;95:E44-E48.

**2.** Moncayo R, Moncayo H. A post-publication analysis of the idealized upper reference value of 2.5 mIU/L for TSH: time to support the thyroid axis with magnesium and iron especially in the setting of reproduction medicine. *BBA Clin.* 2017;7:115-119.

**3.** Stuebe AM, Meltzer-Brody S, Pearson B, Pedersen C, Grewen K. Maternal neuroendocrine serum levels in exclusively breastfeeding mothers. *Breastfeed Med.* 2015;10(4):197-202.

**4.** Zuppa AA, Tornesello A, Papacci P, et al. Relationship between maternal parity, basal prolactin levels and neonatal breast milk intake. *Biol Neonate.* 1988;53(3):144-147.

**5.** Uvnas-Moberg K, Widstrom AM, Werner S, Matthiesen AS, Winberg J. Oxytocin and prolactin levels in breast-feeding women. Correlation with milk yield and duration of breast-feeding. *Acta Obstet Gynecol Scand.* 1990;69(4):301-306.

**6.** Ingram JC, Woolridge MW, Greenwood RJ, McGrath L. Maternal predictors of early breast milk output. *Acta Paediatr.* 1999;88(5):493-499.

**7.** Zhang F, Xia H, Shen M, et al. Are prolactin levels linked to suction pressure? *Breastfeed Med.* 2016;11(9):461-468.

**8.** Benson CT. Prolactin deficiency. In: Medscape; 2008: http://emedicine.medscape.com/article/124526-overview.

**9.** Callejas L, Berens P, Nader S. Breastfeeding failure secondary to idiopathic isolated prolactin deficiency: report of two cases. *Breastfeed Med.* 2015;10(3):183.

**10.** Marasco LA. Unsolved mysteries of the human mammary gland: defining and redefining the critical questions from the lactation consultant's perspective. *J Mammary Gland Biol Neoplasia.* 2015;19(3-4):271-288.

**11.** Johnston K, Vowels M, Carroll S, Neville K, Cohn R. Failure to lactate: a possible late effect of cranial radiation. *Pediatr Blood Cancer.* 2008;50(3):721-722.

**12.** Follin C, Link K, Wiebe T, Moell C, Bjork J, Erfurth EM. Prolactin insufficiency but normal thyroid hormone levels after cranial radiotherapy in long-term survivors of childhood leukaemia. *Clin Endocrinol (Oxf).* 2013;79(1):71-78.

**13.** Mennella JA, Pepino MY. Breastfeeding and prolactin levels in lactating women with a family history of alcoholism. *Pediatrics.* 2010;125(5):e1162-e1170.

**14.** Rasmussen K, Kjolhede C. Prepregnant overweight and obesity diminish the prolactin response to suckling. *Pediatrics.* 2004;113(5):1388.

**15.** Gei-Guardia O, Soto-Herrera E, Gei-Brealey A, Chen-Ku CH. Sheehan's syndrome in Costa Rica: clinical experience on 60 cases. *Endocr Pract.* 2011;17(3):337-344.

**16.** Powe CE, Allen M, Puopolo KM, et al. Recombinant human prolactin for the treatment of lactation insufficiency. *Clin Endocrinol.* 2010;73(5):645-653.

**17.** Welt C, Page-Wilson G, Smith P. Recombinant human prolactin is biologically active: potential treatment for lactation insufficiency. Paper presented at APHA, Boston, MA, November 4-8, 2006.

**18.** Palubska S, Adamiak-Godlewska A, Winkler I, Romanek-Piva K, Rechberger T, Gogacz M. Hyperprolactinaemia—a problem in patients from the reproductive period to the menopause. *Prz Menopauzalny.* 2017;16(1):1-7.

**19.** Batrinos ML, Panitsa-Faflia C, Anapliotou M, Pitoulis S. Prolactin and placental hormone levels during pregnancy in prolactinomas. *Int J Fertil.* 1981;26(2):77-85.

**20.** Wan EW, Davey K, Page-Sharp M, Hartmann PE, Simmer K, Ilett KF. Dose-effect study of domperidone as a galactagogue in preterm mothers with insufficient milk supply, and its transfer into milk. *Br J Clin Pharmacol.* 2008;66(2):283-289.

**21.** Nommsen-Rivers LA, Thompson A, Ward L, Wagner E, Woo J. Metabolic syndrome severity score identifies persistently low milk output. *Breastfeed Med.* 2017;12(suppl 1):S22.

**22.** Bever Babendure J, Reifsnider E, Mendias E, Moramarco MW, Davila YR. Reduced breastfeeding rates among obese mothers: a review of contributing factors, clinical considerations and future directions. *Int Breastfeed J.* 2015;10:21.

**23.** Rasmussen K. Association of maternal obesity before conception with poor lactation performance. *Ann Rev Nutr.* 2007(27):103-121.

**24.** Kamikawa A, Ichii O, Yamaji D, et al. Diet-induced obesity disrupts ductal development in the mammary glands of nonpregnant mice. *Dev Dyn.* 2009;238(5):1092-1099.

**25.** Chamberlin T, D'Amato JV, Arendt LM. Obesity reversibly depletes the basal cell population and enhances mammary epithelial cell estrogen receptor alpha expression and progenitor activity. *Breast Cancer Res.* 2017;19(1):128.

**26.** Vanky E, Nordskar J, Leithe H, Hjorth-Hansen A, Martinussen M, Carlsen S. Breast size increment during pregnancy and breastfeeding in mothers with polycystic ovary syndrome: a follow-up study of a randomised controlled trial on metformin versus placebo. 2012;19(11):1403-1409.

**27.** Buonfiglio DC, Ramos-Lobo AM, Freitas VM, et al. Obesity impairs lactation performance in mice by inducing prolactin resistance. *Sci Rep.* 2016;6:22421.

**28.** Nommsen-Rivers LA. Does insulin explain the relation between maternal obesity and poor lactation outcomes? An overview of the literature. *Adv Nutr.* 2016;7(2):407-414.

**29.** Carlsen SM, Jacobsen G, Vanky E. Mid-pregnancy androgen levels are negatively associated with breastfeeding. *Acta Obstet Gynecol Scand.* 2010;89(1):87-94.

**30.** Kair LR, Colaizy TT. Obese mothers have lower odds of experiencing pro-breastfeeding hospital practices than mothers of normal weight: CDC Pregnancy Risk Assessment Monitoring System (PRAMS), 2004-2008. *Matern Child Health J.* 2016;20(3):593-601.

**31.** Hartmann P, Cregan M. Lactogenesis and the effects of insulin-dependent diabetes mellitus and prematurity. *J Nutr.* 2001;131(11):3016S-3020S.

**32.** Sorkio S, Cuthbertson D, Barlund S, et al. Breastfeeding patterns of mothers with type 1 diabetes: results from an infant feeding trial. *Diabetes Metab Res Rev.* 2010;26(3):206-211.

**33.** Chevalier N, Fenichel P. Endocrine disruptors: new players in the pathophysiology of type 2 diabetes? *Diabetes Metab.* 2015;41(2):107-115.

**34.** Zdrojewicz Z, Popowicz E, Szyca M, Michalik T, Smieszniak B. TOFI phenotype—its effect on the occurrence of diabetes. *Pediatr Endocrinol Diabetes Metab.* 2017;23(2):96-100.

**35.** Lemay DG, Ballard OA, Hughes MA, Morrow AL, Horseman ND, Nommsen-Rivers LA. RNA Sequencing of the human milk fat layer transcriptome reveals distinct gene expression profiles at three stages of lactation. *PloS One.* 2013;8(7).

**36.** Nommsen-Rivers LA, Riddle SA, Thompson A, Ward L, Wagner E. Milk production in mothers with and without signs of insulin resistance. *FASEB J.* 2017;31:650.659.

**37.** Glover AV, Berry DC, Schwartz TA, Stuebe AM. The association of metabolic dysfunction with breastfeeding outcomes in gestational diabetes. *Am J Perinatol.* 2018;35(14):1339-1345.

**38.** Verd S, de Sotto D, Fernández C, Gutiérrez A. The effects of mild gestational hyperglycemia on exclusive breastfeeding cessation. *Nutrients.* 2016;8(11):742.

**39.** Herskin CW, Stage E, Barfred C, et al. Low prevalence of long-term breastfeeding among women with type 2 diabetes. *J Matern Fetal Neonatal Med.* 2015:1-6.

**40.** Nommsen-Rivers LA, Thompson A, Riddle S, Ward L, Wagner E, King E. A preliminary randomized trial of metformin to augment low supply (MALMS). *Breastfeed Med.* 2017;12(suppl):S22-S23.

**41.** Nommsen-Rivers L, Thompson A, Riddle S, Ward L, Wagner E, King E. Feasibility and acceptability of metformin to augment low milk supply: a pilot randomized controlled trial. *J Hum Lact.* 2019;35(2):261-271.

**42.** ACOG Committee on Practice Bulletins–Obstetrics. ACOG Practice Bulletin No. 190: Gestational Diabetes Mellitus. *Obstet Gynecol.* 2018;131(2):e49-e64.

**43.** Hale T, Kristensen J, Hackett L, Kohan R, Ilett K. Transfer of metformin into human milk. *Adv Exp Med Biol.* 2004;554:435-436.

**44.** Larner J, Brautigan DL, Thorner MO. D-chiro-inositol glycans in insulin signaling and insulin resistance. *Mol Med.* 2010;16(11-12):543.

**45.** Pintaudi B, Di Vieste G, Bonomo M. The effectiveness of myo-inositol and D-chiro inositol treatment in type 2 diabetes. *Int J Endocrinol.* 2016;2016:9132052.

**46.** Hajimonfarednejad M, Nimrouzi M, Heydari M, Zarshenas MM, Raee MJ, Jahromi BN. Insulin resistance improvement by cinnamon powder in polycystic ovary syndrome: a randomized double-blind placebo controlled clinical trial. *Phytother Res.* 2018;32(2):276-283.

**47.** Banaszewska B, Wrotynska-Barczynska J, Spaczynski RZ, Pawelczyk L, Duleba AJ. Effects of resveratrol on polycystic ovary syndrome: a double-blind, randomized, placebo-controlled trial. *J Clin Endocrinol Metab.* 2016;101(11):4322-4328.

**48.** Rodriguez-Moran M, Guerrero-Romero F. Oral magnesium supplementation improves insulin sensitivity and metabolic control in type 2 diabetic subjects: a randomized double-blind controlled trial. *Diabetes Care.* 2003;26(4):1147-1152.

**49.** Bindlish S, Shubrook Jr JH. Dietary and botanical supplement therapy in diabetes. *Osteopath Family Phys.* 2014;6(6).

**50.** Stuebe AM. Does breastfeeding prevent the metabolic syndrome, or does the metabolic syndrome prevent breastfeeding? *Semin Perinatol.* 2015;39(4):290-295.

**51.** Stuebe AM, Rich-Edwards JW. The reset hypothesis: lactation and maternal metabolism. *Am J Perinatol.* 2009;26(1):81-88.

**52.** Gunderson EP, Hurston SR, Ning X, et al. Lactation and progression to type 2 diabetes mellitus after gestational diabetes mellitus: a prospective cohort study. *Ann Intern Med.* 2015;163(12):889-898.

**53.** Cromi A, Serati M, Candeloro I, et al. Assisted reproductive technology and breastfeeding outcomes: a case-control study. *Fertil Steril.* 2015;103(1):89-94.

**54.** Wiffen J, Fetherston C. Relationships between assisted reproductive technologies and initiation of lactation: preliminary observations. *Breastfeed Rev.* 2016;24(1):21-27.

**55.** Joham AE, Teede HJ, Ranasinha S, Zoungas S, Boyle J. Prevalence of infertility and use of fertility treatment in women with polycystic ovary syndrome: data from a large community-based cohort study. *J Womens Health (Larchmt).* 2015;24(4):299-307.

**56.** Singla R, Gupta Y, Khemani M, Aggarwal S. Thyroid disorders and polycystic ovary syndrome: an emerging relationship. *Indian J Endocrinol Metab.* 2015;19(1):25-29.

**57.** Morgante G, Musacchio MC, Orvieto R, Massaro MG, De Leo V. Alterations in thyroid function among the different polycystic ovary syndrome phenotypes. *Gynecol Endocrinol.* 2013;29(11):967-969.

**58.** Sirmans SM, Pate KA. Epidemiology, diagnosis, and management of polycystic ovary syndrome. *Clin Epidemiol.* 2013;6:1-13.

**59.** Benson S, Hahn S, Tan S, et al. Prevalence and implications of anxiety in polycystic ovary syndrome: results of an internet-based survey in Germany. *Hum Reprod.* 2009;24(6):1446-1451.

**60.** Palomba S, Falbo A, Russo T, Tolino A, Orio F, Zullo F. Pregnancy in women with polycystic ovary syndrome: the effect of different phenotypes and features on obstetric and neonatal outcomes. *Fertil Steril.* 2010;94(5):1805-1811.

**61.** Marasco L, Marmet C, Shell E. Polycystic ovary syndrome: a connection to insufficient milk supply? *J Hum Lact.* 2000;16(2):143-148.

**62.** Balcar V, Silinkova-Malkova E, Matys Z. Soft tissue radiography of the female breast and pelvic pneumoperitoneum in the Stein-Leventhal syndrome. *Acta Radiol Diagn (Stockh).* 1972;12(3):353-362.

**63.** McGuire E, Rowan M. PCOS, breast hypoplasia and low milk supply: a case study. *Breastfeed Rev.* 2015;23(3):29-32.

**64.** Arbour MW, Kessler JL. Mammary hypoplasia: not every breast can produce sufficient milk. *J Midwifery Womens Health.* 2013;58(4):457-461.

**65.** Britz SP, Henry L. PCOS and breastfeeding: what's the issue? *J Obstet Gynecol Neonat Nurs.* 2011;40(s1).

**66.** Thatcher SS, Jackson EM. Pregnancy outcome in infertile patients with polycystic ovary syndrome who were treated with metformin. *Fertil Steril.* 2006;85(4):1002-1009.

**67.** Vanky E, Isaksen H, Moen MH, Carlsen SM. Breastfeeding in polycystic ovary syndrome. *Acta Obstet Gynecol Scand.* 2008;87(5):531-535.

**68.** Joham A, Nanayakkara N, Ranasinha S, et al. Obesity, polycystic ovary syndrome and breastfeeding: an observational Study. *Acta Obstet Gynecol Scand.* 2016;95:458-466.

**69.** Biloš LSK. Polycystic ovarian syndrome and low milk supply: is insulin resistance the missing link? *Endocr Oncol Metab.* 2017;3(2):49-55.

**70.** Harrison CL, Teede HJ, Joham AE, Moran LJ. Breastfeeding and obesity in PCOS. *Exp Rev Endocrinol Metab.* 2016;11(6):449-454.

**71.** Feng L, Lin XF, Wan ZH, Hu D, Du YK. Efficacy of metformin on pregnancy complications in women with polycystic ovary syndrome: a meta-analysis. *Gynecol Endocrinol.* 2015;31(11):833-839.

**72.** Zhao J, Liu X, Zhang W. The effect of metformin therapy for preventing gestational diabetes mellitus in women with polycystic ovary syndrome: a meta-analysis. *Exp Clin Endocrinol Diabetes.* 2018 Jun 11. doi: 10.1055/a-0603-3394. [Epub ahead of print].

**73.** Unfer V, Nestler JE, Kamenov ZA, Prapas N, Facchinetti F. Effects of inositol(s) in women with PCOS: a systematic review of randomized controlled trials. *Int J Endocrinol.* 2016;2016:1849162.

**74.** Nestler JE, Unfer V. Reflections on inositol(s) for PCOS therapy: steps toward success. *Gynecol Endocrinol.* 2015;31(7):501-505.

**75.** Wang Y, Fu X, Xu J, Wang Q, Kuang H. Systems pharmacology to investigate the interaction of berberine and other drugs in treating polycystic ovary syndrome. *Sci Rep.* 2016;6:28089.

**76.** Marasco L. The impact of thyroid dysfunction on lactation. *Breastfeed Abstr.* 2006;25(2):9, 11-12.

**77.** Fisher W, Wang J, George NI, Gearhart JM, McLanahan ED. Dietary iodine sufficiency and moderate insufficiency in the lactating mother and nursing infant: a computational perspective. *PloS One.* 2016;11(3):e0149300.

**78.** Talaei A, Ghorbani F, Asemi Z. The effects of vitamin d supplementation on thyroid function in hypothyroid patients: a randomized, double-blind, placebo-controlled trial. *Indian J Endocrinol Metab.* 2018;22(5):584-588.

**79.** Hapon MB, Simoncini M, Via G, Jahn GA. Effect of hypothyroidism on hormone profiles in virgin, pregnant and lactating rats, and on lactation. *Reproduction.* 2003;126(3):371-382.

**80.** Hapon MB, Varas SM, Jahn GA, Gimenez MS. Effects of hypothyroidism on mammary and liver lipid metabolism in virgin and late-pregnant rats. *J Lipid Res.* 2005;46(6):1320-1330.

**81.** Campo Verde Arbocco F, Persia FA, Hapon MB, Jahn GA. Hypothyroidism decreases JAK/STAT signaling pathway in lactating rat mammary gland. *Mol Cell Endocrinol.* 2017;450:14-23.

**82.** Campo Verde Arbocco F, Sasso CV, Actis EA, Caron RW, Hapon MB, Jahn GA. Hypothyroidism advances mammary involution in lactating rats through inhibition of PRL signaling and induction of LIF/STAT3 mRNAs. *Mol Cell Endocrinol.* 2016;419:18-28.

**83.** Taylor PN, Razvi S, Pearce SH, Dayan CM. A review of the clinical consequences of variation in thyroid function within the reference range. *J Clin Endocrinol Metab.* 2013;98(9):3562-3571.

**84.** Alexander EK, Pearce EN, Brent GA, et al. 2017 Guidelines of the American Thyroid Association for the diagnosis and management of thyroid disease during pregnancy and the postpartum. *Thyroid.* 2017;27(3):315-389.

**85.** Speller E, Brodribb W. Breastfeeding and thyroid disease: a literature review. *Breastfeed Rev.* 2012;20(2):41-47.

**86.** Lupoli R, Di Minno A, Tortora A, Ambrosino P, Lupoli GA, Di Minno MN. Effects of treatment with metformin on TSH levels: a meta-analysis of literature studies. *J Clin Endocrinol Metab.* 2014;99(1):E143-148.

**87.** Nordio M, Basciani S. Treatment with myo-inositol and selenium ensures euthyroidism in patients with autoimmune thyroiditis. *Int J Endocrinol.* 2017;2017:2549491.

**88.** Panda S, Tahiliani P, Kar A. Inhibition of triiodothyronine production by fenugreek seed extract in mice and rats. *Pharmacol Res.* 1999;40(5):405-409.

**89.** Tahiliani P, Kar A. Mitigation of thyroxine-induced hyperglycaemia by two plant extracts. *Phytother Res.* 2003;17(3):294-296.

**90.** Tahiliani P, Kar A. Role of Moringa oleifera leaf extract in the regulation of thyroid hormone status in adult male and female rats. *Pharmacol Res.* 2000;41(3):319-323.

91. Pennacchio GE, Neira FJ, Soaje M, Jahn GA, Valdez SR. Effect of hyperthyroidism on circulating prolactin and hypothalamic expression of tyrosine hydroxylase, prolactin signaling cascade members and estrogen and progesterone receptors during late pregnancy and lactation in the rat. *Mol Cell Endocrinol.* 2017;442:40-50.

92. Rosato RR, Gimenez MS, Jahn GA. Effects of chronic thyroid hormone administration on pregnancy, lactogenesis and lactation in the rat. *Acta Endocrinol (Copenh).* 1992;127(6):547-554.

93. Varas SM, Jahn GA, Gimenez MS. Hyperthyroidism affects lipid metabolism in lactating and suckling rats. *Lipids.* 2001;36(8):801-806.

94. Goldstein AL. New-onset Graves' disease in the postpartum period. *J Midwifery Womens Health.* 2013;58(2):211-214.

95. Trimeloni L, Spencer J. Diagnosis and management of breast milk oversupply. *J Am Board Fam Med.* 2016;29(1):139-142.

96. Akamizu T. Postpartum thyroiditis. In: De Groot LJ, Chrousos G, Dungan K, et al, eds. *Endotext.* South Dartmouth, MA: MDText.com; 2000.

97. Pereira K, Brown AJ. Postpartum thyroiditis: not just a worn out mom. *J Nurse Pract.* 2008;4(3):175-182.

98. Muscogiuri G, Palomba S, Caggiano M, Tafuri D, Colao A, Orio F. Low 25 (OH) vitamin D levels are associated with autoimmune thyroid disease in polycystic ovary syndrome. *Endocrine.* 2016;53(2):538-542.

99. Truchet S, Honvo-Houéto E. Physiology of milk secretion. *Best Pract Res Clin Endocrinol Metab.* 2017;31:367-384.

100. Hausman Kedem M, Mandel D, Domani KA, et al. The effect of advanced maternal age upon human milk fat content. *Breastfeed Med.* 2013;8(1):116-119.

101. Lubetzky R, Sever O, Mimouni FB, Mandel D. Human milk macronutrients content: effect of advanced maternal Age. *Breastfeed Med.* 2015;10(9):433-436.

102. Stuebe A, Meltzer-Brody, Grewen K. What is "normal" endocrine function during exclusive breastfeeding? *Acad Breastfeed Me.* 2011;6(suppl 1):S3.

103. Konkel L. Mother's milk and the environment: might chemical exposures impair lactation? *Environ Health Perspect.* 2017;125(1):A17-A23.

## Chapter 12

1. Gardner H, Kent JC, Hartmann PE, Geddes DT. Asynchronous milk ejection in human lactating breast: case series. *J Hum Lact.* 2015;31(2):254-259.

2. Leng G, Feng J. Modelling the milk-ejection reflex. *Comput Neuroendocrinol.* 2016:227.

**3.** Isbister C. A Clinical study of the draught reflex in human lactation. *Arch Dis Child.* 1954;29(143):66-72.

**4.** Yokoyama Y, Ueda T, Irahara M, Aono T. Releases of oxytocin and prolactin during breast massage and suckling in puerperal women. *Eur J Obstet Gynecol Reprod Biol.* 1994;53(1):17-20.

**5.** Sadovnikova A, Sanders I, Koehler S, Plott J. Systematic review of breast massage techniques around the world in databases and on YouTube. Paper presented at The Academy of Breastfeeding Medicine 20th Annual International Meeting, Los Angeles, 2015.

**6.** Patel U, Gedam D. Effect of back massage on lactation among postnatal mother. *Int J Med Res.* 2013;1(1): 5-13.

**7.** Asrani A, Varghese A, Sharma B, Jain AK. Assessment and comparison between effectiveness of techniques of improving lactation among postnatal mothers of new born babies. *Asian J Med Sci.* 2018;9(1):41-49.

**8.** Betts D. Postnatal acupuncture. *J Chinese Med.* 2005;77:5-15.

**9.** Stuebe AM, Grewen K, Meltzer-Brody S. Association between maternal mood and oxytocin response to breastfeeding. *J Womens Health.* 2013;22(4):352-361.

**10.** Kennett JE, McKee DT. Oxytocin: an emerging regulator of prolactin secretion in the female rat. *J Neuroendocrinol.* 2012;24(3):403-412.

**11.** Williams N. Maternal psychological issues in the experience of breastfeeding. *J Hum Lact.* 1997;13(1):57-60.

**12.** Niwayama R, Nishitani S, Takamura T, et al. Oxytocin mediates a calming effect on postpartum mood in primiparous mothers. *Breastfeed Med.* 2017;12:103-109.

**13.** Mezzacappa ES, Katkin ES. Breast-feeding is associated with reduced perceived stress and negative mood in mothers. *Health Psychol.* 2002;21:187-193.

**14.** Levine S, Muneyyirci-Delale O. Stress-induced hyperprolactinemia: pathophysiology and clinical approach. *Obstet Gynecol Int.* 2018;2018:9253083.

**15.** Ueda T, Yokoyama Y, Irahara M, Aono T. Influence of psychological stress on suckling-induced pulsatile oxytocin release. *Obstet Gynecol.* 1994;84(2):259-262.

**16.** Kitsantas P, Gaffney KF, Nirmalraj L, Sari M. The influence of maternal life stressors on breastfeeding outcomes: a U.S. population-based study. *J Matern Fetal Neonatal Med.* 2018:1-5.

**17.** Garfield L, Holditch-Davis D, Carter CS, et al. A pilot study of oxytocin in low-income women with a low birth-weight infant: is oxytocin related to posttraumatic stress? *Adv Neonatal Care.* 2019 Mar 19. doi: 10.1097/ANC.0000000000000601. [Epub ahead of print]

**18.** Soderquist J, Wijma B, Thorbert G, Wijma K. Risk factors in pregnancy for post-traumatic stress and depression after childbirth. *BJOG.* 2009;116(5):672-680.

**19.** Stramrood CA, Paarlberg KM, Huis In't Veld EM, et al. Posttraumatic stress following childbirth in homelike- and hospital settings. *J Psychosom Obstet Gynaecol.* 2011;32(2):88-97.

**20.** Beck CT, Gable RK, Sakala C, Declercq ER. Posttraumatic stress disorder in new mothers: results from a two-stage U.S. national survey. *Birth.* 2011;38(3):216-227.

**21.** Alcorn KL, O'Donovan A, Patrick JC, Creedy D, Devilly GJ. A prospective longitudinal study of the prevalence of post-traumatic stress disorder resulting from childbirth events. *Psychol Med.* 2010;40(11):1849-1859.

**22.** Kendall-Tackett K. Intervention for mothers who have experienced childbirth-related trauma and posttraumatic stress disorder. *Clin Lact.* 2014;5(2):56-61.

**23.** Perez-Blasco J, Viguer P, Rodrigo MF. Effects of a mindfulness-based intervention on psychological distress, well-being, and maternal self-efficacy in breast-feeding mothers: results of a pilot study. *Arch Womens Ment Health.* 2013;16(3):227-236.

**24.** Mohd Shukri N, Wells J, Fewtrell M. The effectiveness of interventions using relaxation therapy to improve breastfeeding outcomes: a systematic review. *Matern Child Nutr.* 2018;14(2):e12563.

**25.** Feher S, Berger L, Johnson J, Wilde J. Increasing breast milk production for premature infants with a relaxation/imagery audiotape. *Pediatrics.* 1989;83(1):57-60.

**26.** Yu J, Wells J, Wei Z, Fewtrell M. Randomized trial comparing the physiological and psychological effects of different relaxation interventions in Chinese women breastfeeding their healthy term infant. *Breastfeed Med.* 2019;14(1):33-38.

**27.** Ak J, Lakshmanagowda PB, G CMP, Goturu J. Impact of music therapy on breast milk secretion in mothers of premature newborns. *J Clin Diagnost Res.* 2015;9(4):Cc04-06.

**28.** Kittithanesuan Y, Chiarakul S, Poovorawan Y. Effect of music on immediately postpartum lactation by term mothers after giving birth: a randomized controlled trial. *J Med Assoc Thai.* 2017;100(8):834.

**29.** Keith DR, Weaver BS, Vogel RL. The effect of music-based listening interventions on the volume, fat content, and caloric content of breast milk-produced by mothers of premature and critically ill infants. *Adv Neonatal Care.* 2012;12(2):112-119.

**30.** Feijs L, Kierkels J, Schijndel NH, Lieshout M. Design for relaxation during milk expression using biofeedback. In: Marcus A, ed. *Design, User Experience, and Usability. User Experience in Novel Technological Environments*, Second International Conference, DUXU 2013, Held as Part of HCI International 2013, Las Vegas, NV, USA, July 21-26, 2013, Proceedings, Part III. Berlin, Heidelberg: Springer Berlin Heidelberg; 2013:494-503.

**31.** Cowley KC. Psychogenic and pharmacologic induction of the let-down reflex can facilitate breastfeeding by tetraplegic women: a report of 3 cases. *Arch Phys Med Rehabil.* 2005;86(6):1261-1264.

**32.** Porta F, Mussa A, Baldassarre G, et al. Genealogy of breastfeeding. *Eur J Pediatr.* 2016;175(1):105-112.

**33.** Kamikawa A, Ichii O, Yamaji D, et al. Diet-induced obesity disrupts ductal development in the mammary glands of nonpregnant mice. *Dev Dyn.* 2009;238(5):1092-1099.

**34.** Chamberlin T, D'Amato JV, Arendt LM. Obesity reversibly depletes the basal cell population and enhances mammary epithelial cell estrogen receptor alpha expression and progenitor activity. *Breast Cancer Res.* 2017;19(1):128.

**35.** Odent MR. Synthetic oxytocin and breastfeeding: reasons for testing an hypothesis. *Med Hypotheses.* 2013;81(5):889-891.

**36.** Erickson EN, Emeis CL. Breastfeeding outcomes after oxytocin use during childbirth: an integrative review. *J Midwifery Womens Health.* 2017;62(4):397-417.

**37.** Renfrew MJ, Lang S, Woolridge M. Oxytocin for promoting successful lactation. *Cochrane Database Syst Rev.* 2000(2):Cd000156.

**38.** Nice FJ. Oxytocin nasal spray. Personal communication to L. Marasco, 2018.

## Chapter 13

**1.** Riddle SW, Nommsen-Rivers LA. Low milk supply and the pediatrician. *Curr Opin Pediatr.* 2017;29(2):249-256.

**2.** Morton J. The importance of hands. *J Hum Lact.* 2012;28(3):276-277.

**3.** Mangel L, Ovental A, Batscha N, Arnon M, Yarkoni I, Dollberg S. Higher fat content in breastmilk expressed manually: a randomized trial. *Breastfeed Med.* 2015;10(7):352-354.

**4.** Eglash A, Malloy ML. Breastmilk expression and breast pump technology. *Clin Obstet Gynecol.* 2015;58(4):855-867.

**5.** Marcoux H. CDC's breast pump cleaning guidelines—what working mamas need to know. *Motherly.* 2018. https://www.mother.ly/news/dont-wash-your-breast-pump-in-the-sink-says-cdc-in-new-guidelines.

**6.** Jones E, Dimmock PW, Spencer SA. A randomised controlled trial to compare methods of milk expression after preterm delivery. *Arch Dis Child.* 2001;85(2):F91-F95.

**7.** Yigit F, Cigdem Z, Temizsoy E, et al. Does warming the breasts affect the amount of breastmilk production? *Breastfeed Med.* 2012;7(6):487-488.

**8.** Kent JC, Geddes DT, Hepworth AR, Hartmann PE. Effect of warm breastshields on breast milk pumping. *J Hum Lact.* 2011;27(4):331-338.

**9.** Zhang F, Xia H, Li X, et al. Intraoral vacuum of breast-feeding newborns within the first 24 hr: cesarean section versus vaginal delivery. *Biol Res Nurs.* 2016;18(4):445-453.

**10.** Ilyin VI, Alekseev NP, Troschkin MM, Uleziko VA. Comparative assessment of excretion of milk from two breast pumps with different vacuum strength and duration. *Breastfeed Med.* 2019;14(3):177-184.

**11.** Larkin T, Kiehn T, Murphy PK, Uhryniak J. Examining the use and outcomes of a new hospital-grade breast pump in exclusively pumping NICU mothers. *Adv Neonatal Care.* 2013;13(1):75-82.

**12.** Alekseev NP, Ilyin VI. The mechanics of breast pumping: compression stimuli increased milk ejection. *Breastfeed Med.* 2016;11:370-375.

**13.** Morton J, Hall JY, Wong RJ, Thairu L, Benitz WE, Rhine WD. Combining hand techniques with electric pumping increases milk production in mothers of preterm infants. *J Perinatol.* 2009;29(11):757-764.

**14.** McCue KF, Stulberger ML. Maternal satisfaction with parallel pumping technique. *Clin Lact.* 2019;10(2):68-73.

## Chapter 14

**1.** Mohanty I, Senapati M, Jena D, Behera P. Ethnoveterinary importance of herbal galactogogues—a review. *Vet World.* 2014;7(5):325-330.

**2.** Foong SC, Tan ML, Foong WC, Marasco LA, Ho JJ, Ong JH. Oral galactagogues for increasing breast-milk production in mothers of non-hospitalised term infants. *Cochrane Database Syst Rev.* 2015.

**3.** Anderson PO. Herbal use during breastfeeding. *Breastfeed Med.* 2017;12(9):507-509.

**4.** Travers MT, Barber MC, Tonner E, Quarrie L, Wilde CJ, Flint DJ. The role of prolactin and growth hormone in the regulation of casein gene expression and mammary cell survival: relationships to milk synthesis and secretion. *Endocrinology.* 1996;137(5):1530-1539.

**5.** Speroff L, Glass R, Kase N. *Clinical Gynecologic Endocrinology and Infertility.* 4th ed. Baltimore: Williams & Wilkins; 1989.

**6.** McGuire TM. Drugs affecting milk supply during lactation. *Aust Prescr.* 2018;41(1):7-9.

**7.** Haase B, Taylor SN, Mauldin J, Johnson TS, Wagner CL. Domperidone for treatment of low milk supply in breast pump–dependent mothers of hospitalized premature infants: a clinical protocol. *J Hum Lact.* 2016;32(2):373-381.

**8.** Kamala S, Gandhimathi M, Jeyagowri S. Role of herbal galactogogues in initiating and establishing milk secretion in lactating mothers. *Int J Nurs Educ Res.* 2015;3(3):335-336.

**9.** Grzeskowiak LE, Smithers LG, Amir LH, Grivell RM. Domperidone for increasing breast milk volume in mothers expressing breast milk for their preterm infants: a systematic review and meta-analysis. *BJOG.* 2018;125(11):1371-1378.

**10.** Bazzano AN, Hofer R, Thibeau S, Gillispie V, Jacobs M, Theall KP. A review of herbal and pharmaceutical galactagogues for breast-feeding. *Ochsner J.* 2016;16(4):511-524.

**11.** Asztalos EV, Kiss A, daSilva OP, Campbell-Yeo M, Ito S, Knoppert D. Evaluating the effect of a 14-day course of domperidone on breast milk production: a per-protocol analysis from the EMPOWER trial. *Breastfeed Med.* 2019;14(2):102-107.

**12.** Hale T, Rowe H. *Medications and Mothers' Milk.* 17th ed. New York: Springer; 2017.

**13.** Jones W, Breward S. Use of domperidone to enhance lactation: what is the evidence? *Community Pract.* 2011;84(6):35-37.

**14.** Papastergiou J, Abdallah M, Tran A, Folkins C. Domperidone withdrawal in a breastfeeding woman. *Can Pharm J (Ott).* 2013;146(4):210-212.

**15.** Grzeskowiak LE, Amir LH. Pharmacological management of low milk supply with domperidone: separating fact from fiction. *Med J Aust.* 2015;202(6):257-258.

**16.** Wan EW, Davey K, Page-Sharp M, Hartmann PE, Simmer K, Ilett KF. Dose-effect study of domperidone as a galactagogue in preterm mothers with insufficient milk supply, and its transfer into milk. *Br J Clin Pharmacol.* 2008;66(2):283-289.

**17.** Knoppert DC, Page A, Warren J, et al. The effect of two different domperidone doses on maternal milk production. *J Hum Lact.* 2013;29(1):38-44.

**18.** Paul C, Zenut M, Dorut A, et al. Use of domperidone as a galactagogue drug: a systematic review of the benefit-risk ratio. *J Hum Lact.* 2015;31(1):57-63.

**19.** Sewell CA, Chang CY, Chehab MM, Nguyen CP. Domperidone for lactation: what health care providers need to know. *Obstet Gynecol.* 2017;129(6):1054-1058.

**20.** Ingram J, Taylor H, Churchill C, Pike A, Greenwood R. Metoclopramide or domperidone for increasing maternal breast milk output: a randomised controlled trial. *Arch Dis Child Fetal Neonatal Ed.* 2012;97(4):F241-245.

**21.** Fisher AA, Davis MW. Serotonin syndrome caused by selective serotonin reuptake-inhibitors-metoclopramide interaction. *Ann Pharmacother.* 2002;36(1):67-71.

**22.** Hale TW, Kendall-Tackett P, Cong Z. domperidone versus metoclopramide: self-reported side effects in a large sample of breastfeeding mothers who used these medications to increase milk production. *Clin Lact.* 2018;9(1):10-17.

**23.** Forinash A, Yancey A, Barnes K, Myles T. The use of galactogogues in the breastfeeding mother (October). *Ann Pharmacother.* 2012;46(10):1392-404.

**24.** McGuire E, Rowan M. PCOS, breast hypoplasia and low milk supply: a case study. *Breastfeed Rev.* 2015;23(3):29-32.

**25.** Nommsen-Rivers L, Thompson A, Riddle S, Ward L, Wagner E, King E. Feasibility and acceptability of metformin to augment low milk supply: a pilot randomized controlled trial. *J Hum Lact.* 2019;35(2):261-271.

**26.** Nommsen-Rivers LA, Thompson A, Riddle S, Ward L, Wagner E, King E. A preliminary randomized trial of metformin to augment low supply (MALMS). *Breastfeed Med.* 2017;12(suppl):S22-S23.

**27.** Hale T, Kristensen J, Hackett L, Kohan R, Ilett K. Transfer of metformin into human milk. *Adv Exp Med Biol.* 2004;554:435-436.

**28.** Thaweekul P, Thaweekul Y, Sritipsukho P. The efficacy of hospital-based food program as galactogogues in early period of lactation. *J Med Assoc Thai.* 2014;97(5):478-482.

**29.** Torris C, Thune I, Emaus A, et al. Duration of lactation, maternal metabolic profile, and body composition in the Norwegian EBBA I-study. *Breastfeed Med.* 2013;8(1):8-15.

**30.** Ayala Macedo G. Consumption of quinoa in Peru. *Food Rev Int.* 2003;19(1-2):221-227.

**31.** Bnouham M. Medicinal plants with potential galactagogue activity used in the Moroccan pharmacopoeia. *J Complement Integr Med.* 2010;7(1):52.

**32.** Scott C, Jacobson H. A selection of international nutritional & herbal remedies for breastfeeding concerns. *Midwifery Today Int Midwife.* 2005;75:38-39.

**33.** Ergol S, Koc G, Kurtuncu M. A review of traditional knowledge on foods and plants supposed to increase lactation in pregnant women; a descriptive study. *Afr J Complement Altern Med.* 2016;13(3):27-32.

**34.** Monteban M. Maternal knowledge and use of galactagogues in Andean communities of Cusco, Peru. *Ethnobiol Lett.* 2017;8(1):81-89.

**35.** Humphrey S. Herbal therapies during lactation. In: Hale T, Hartmann P, eds. *Textbook of Human Lactation.* Amarillo TX: Hale Publishing; 2007.

**36.** Kingsbury S. Herbs for lactation. *J Am Herbalists Guild.* 2012;11(1):41-46.

**37.** Koletzko B, Lehner F. Beer and breastfeeding. *Adv Exp Med Biol.* 2000;478:23-28.

**38.** Bingel A, Farnsworth N. Higher plants as potential sources of galactogogues. *J Med Plant Res.* 1994;6:1-54.

**39.** Zeits R, Iliukhina M, Zefirov I. A method of complex treatment of secondary hypo-galactia. *Pediatriia.* 1990(1):97-98.

**40.** Winterfeld U, Meyer Y, Panchaud A, Einarson A. Management of deficient lacta-tion in Switzerland and Canada: a survey of midwives' current practices. *Breastfeed Med.* 2012;7:317-318.

**41.** Sayed N, Deo R, Mukundan U. Herbal remedies used by Warlis of Dahanu to induce lactation in nursing mothers. *Indian J Tradit Know.* 2007;6(4):602-605.

**42.** Goksugur SB, Karatas Z. Breastfeeding and galactogogues agents. *Acta Medica Anatolia.* 2014;2(3):113-118.

**43.** Mills E, Duguoa J, Perri D, Koren G. Herbal medicines in pregnancy and lactation: an evidence-based approach. Toronto: Taylor & Francis; 2006.

**44.** Nice F. *The Galactagogue Recipe Book.* Plano, TX: Hale Publishing; 2014.

**45.** Thurber MD, Fahey JW. Adoption of Moringa oleifera to combat under-nutri-tion viewed through the lens of the "Diffusion of Innovations" theory. *Ecol Food Nutr.* 2009;48(3):212-225.

**46.** King J RP, Dans L. Moringa oleifera as galactagogue for breastfeeding mothers: a systematic review and meta-analysis of randomized controlled trial. *Phillip J Pediatr.* 2013;61(2):34-42.

**47.** Raguindin PF, Dans LF, King JF. Moringa oleifera as a galactagogue. *Breastfeed Med.* 2014;9(6):323-324.

**48.** Briton-Medrano G, Perez L. The efficacy of malunggay (moringa oleifera) given to near term pregnant women in inducing early postpartum breast milk production—a double blind randomized clinical trial. Unpublished, 2004.

**49.** Fuglie L. Combating malnutrition with moringa. Paper presented at Development Potential for Moringa Products, Dar es Salaam, Tanzania, 2001.

**50.** Coppin J. A study of the nutritional and medicinal values of Moringa oleifera leaves from sub-Saharan Africa: Ghana, Rwanda, Senegal and Zambia. Rutgers University Graduate School, New Brunswick, 2008.

**51.** Buntuchai G, Pavadhgul P, Kittipichai W, Satheannoppakao W. Traditional galac-tagogue foods and their connection to human milk volume in Thai breastfeeding moth-ers. *J Hum Lact.* 2017;33(3):552-559.

**52.** Paritakul P, Ruangrongmorakot K, Laosooksathit W, Suksamarnwong M, Pua-pornpong P. The effect of ginger on breast milk volume in the early postpartum period: a randomized, double-blind controlled trial. *Breastfeed Med.* 2016;11(7):361-365.

**53.** Bumrungpert A, Somboonpanyakul P, Pavadhgul P, Thaninthranon S. Effects of fenugreek, ginger, and turmeric supplementation on human milk volume and nutrient content in breastfeeding mothers: a randomized double-blind controlled trial. *Breastfeed Med.* 2018;13(10).

**54.** El Sakka A, Salama M, Salama K. The effect of fenugreek herbal tea and palm dates on breast milk production and infant weight. *J Pediatr Sci.* 2014;6(e202).

**55.** Javan R, Javadi B, Feyzabadi Z. Breastfeeding: a review of its physiology and galactogogue plants in view of traditional Persian medicine. *Breastfeed Med.* 2017;12(7):401-409.

**56.** Cai B, Chen H, Sun H, et al. Lactogenic activity of an enzymatic hydrolysate from Octopus vulgaris and Carica papaya in SD rats. *J Med Food.* 2015;18(11):1262-1269.

**57.** Luo L-X, Wei G-Y, Huang F-X, et al. Study on lactation of parturient women separated from their infants regulated by regular intake of trotter and papaya soup. *Matern Child Health Care China.* 2011;33:5144-5146.

**58.** Damanik R, Wahlqvist ML, Wattanapenpaiboon N. Lactagogue effects of Torbangun, a Bataknese traditional cuisine. *Asia Pac J Clin Nutr.* 2006;15(2):267-274.

**59.** Tabares FP, Jaramillo JV, Ruiz-Cortés ZT. Pharmacological overview of galactogogues. *Vet Med Int.* 2014;2014:602894.

**60.** Tustanofskyj G. Medicinal herbs effect on lactation. *Farmacevtychnyj.* 1996;5-6:106-109.

**61.** Zava D, Dollbaum C, Blen M. Estrogen and progestin bioactivity of foods, herbs, and spices. *Proc Soc Exp Biol Med.* 1998;217(3):369-378.

**62.** Gardner Z, McGuffin M. *American Herbal Products Association's Botanical Safety Handbook.* Boca Raton, FL: CRC Press; 2013.

**63.** Saper RB, Phillips RS, Sehgal A, et al. Lead, mercury, and arsenic in U.S.- and Indian-manufactured Ayurvedic medicines sold via the Internet. *JAMA.* 2008;300(8):915-923.

**64.** Hale T. Personal communication, 2019.

**65.** Weed SS, Novet J. *Wise Woman Herbal for the Childbearing Years.* Woodstock, NY: Ash Tree Publishing; 1986.

**66.** Parks CG, de Souza Espindola Santos A, Barbhaiya M, Costenbader KH. Understanding the role of environmental factors in the development of systemic lupus erythematosus. *Best Pract Res Clin Rhematol.* 2017;31(3):306-320.

**67.** LactMed. Anise. In. *Drugs and Lactation Database.* Bethesda, MD: National Library of Medicine; 2006.

**68.** Hosseinzadeh H, Tafaghodi M, Abedzadeh S, Taghiabadi E. Effect of aqueous and ethanolic extracts of Pimpinella anisum L. seeds on milk production in rats. *J Acupunct Meridian Stud.* 2014;7(4):211-216.

**69.** Mayo JL. Black cohosh and chasteberry: herbs valued by women for centuries. *Target.* 1998;19:22-26.

**70.** Sharma AK, Basu I, Singh S. Efficacy and safety of Ashwagandha root extract in subclinical hypothyroid patients: a double-blind, randomized placebo-controlled trial. *J Altern Complement Med.* 2017;24(3):243-248.

**71.** McKenna DJ, Jones K, Humphrey S, Hughes K. Black cohosh: efficacy, safety, and use in clinical and preclinical applications. *Altern Ther Health Med.* 2001;7(3):93-100.

**72.** Grant P, Ramasamy S. An update on plant derived anti-androgens. *Int J Endocrinol Metab.* 2012;10(2):497-502.

**73.** Fugh-Berman A. "Bust enhancing" herbal products. *Obstet Gynecol.* 2003;101(6): 1345-1349.

**74.** Abu-Rabia A. Herbs as a food and medicine source in Palestine. *Asian Pac J Cancer Prevent.* 2005;6(3):404.

**75.** Yashmin S. Islamic and cultural practices in breastfeeding. *Aust Midwifery News.* 2017;17(1):49.

**76.** Abdel-Rahman H, Fathalla S, Assayed M, Masoad S, Nafeaa A. physiological studies on the effect of fenugreek on productive performance of white New-Zealand rabbit does. *Food Nutr Sci.* 2016;7:1276-1289.

**77.** Hosseinzadeh H, Tafaghodi M, Mosavi MJ, Taghiabadi E. Effect of aqueous and ethanolic extracts of Nigella sativa seeds on milk production in rats. *J Acupunct Meridian Stud.* 2013;6(1):18-23.

**78.** Westfall R. Galactagogogue herbs: a qualitative study and review. *Can J Midwifery Res Pract.* 2003;2(2):22-27.

**79.** Low Dog T. The use of botanicals during pregnancy and lactation. *Altern Ther Health Med.* 2009;15(1):54-58.

**80.** LactMed. Borage. In. *Drugs and Lactation Database.* Bethesda, MD: National Library of Medicine; 2006.

**81.** Mahboubi M. Caraway as important medicinal plants in management of diseases. *Nat Prod Bioprospect.* 2019;9(1):1-11.

**82.** Bruckner C. A survey on herbal galactogogues used in Europe. *Medicaments et Aliments: L'Approche Ethnopharmacologique.* Heidelberg; 1993.

**83.** Merz PG, Gorkow C, Schrodter A, et al. The effects of a special Agnus castus extract (BP1095E1) on prolactin secretion in healthy male subjects. *Exp Clin Endocrinol Diabetes.* 1996;104(6):447-453.

**84.** Humphrey S. *Nursing Mother's Herbal.* Minneapolis MN: Fairview Press; 2003.

**85.** Srinivasan K. Plant foods in the management of diabetes mellitus: spices as beneficial antidiabetic food adjuncts. *Int J Food Sci Nutr.* 2005;56(6):399-414.

**86.** Sultana A, ur Rahman K. Traditional Unani perspective of perceived insufficient milk (Qillatul Laban) and galactogogues: a literary research with recent studies. *TANG Hum Med.* 2014;4(3 e19):1-6.

**87.** Manjula S, Sultana A, Rahman K. Clinical efficacy of Gossypium herbaceum L. seeds in perceived insufficient milk (PIM) supply: a randomized single-blind placebo-controlled study. *Orient Pharm Exp Med.* 2014;14(1):77-85.

**88.** Agrawala IP, Achar MV, Boradkar RV, Roy N. Galactagogue action of Cuminum cyminum and Nigella sativa. *Indian J Med Res.* 1968;56(6):841-844.

**89.** Kaur GJ, Arora DS. Bioactive potential of Anethum graveolens, Foeniculum vulgare and Trachyspermum ammi belonging to the family Umbelliferae—current status. Journal of Medicinal Plants Research. 2010;4(2):87-94.

**90.** Javidnia K, Dastgheib L, Samani M, Nasiri A. Antihirsutism activity of fennel (fruits of Foeniculum vulgare) extract: a double-blind placebo controlled study. *Phytomedicine.* 2003(10):455-458.

**91.** Khan TM, Wu DB, Dolzhenko AV. Effectiveness of fenugreek as a galactagogue: a network meta-analysis. *Phytother Res.* 2018;32(3):402-412.

**92.** Lema MZ, Poornodai V, Adewale SS. The effect of fenugreek seed powder in augmenting expressed milk volume from mothers of preterm infants at Tikur Anbessa Neonatal Intensive Care Unit T. *Glob J Res Anal.* 2018;7(3):37-40.

**93.** LactMed. Fenugreek. In. *Drugs and Lactation Database.* Bethesda, MD: National Library of Medicine; 2006.

**94.** Tahiliani P, Kar A. Mitigation of thyroxine-induced hyperglycaemia by two plant extracts. *Phytother Res.* 2003;17(3):294-296.

**93.** LactMed. Goat's rue. In. *Drugs and Lactation Database.* Bethesda, MD: National Library of Medicine; 2006.

**96.** Rosengarten F Jr. A neglected Mayan galactagogue—ixbut (Euphorbia lancifolia). *J Ethnopharmacol.* 1982;5(1):91-112.

**97.** Pal A, Sharma PP, Pandya TN, et al. Phyto-chemical evaluation of dried aqueous extract of Jivanti [Leptadenia reticulata (Retz.) Wt. et Arn]. *Ayu.* 2012;33(4):557-560.

**98.** Rao P. Leptaden, a herbal drug useful in lactation and pregnancy, review of 20 clinical trials by 40 senior gynecologists. Paper presented at the 4th World Congress on human reproduction, November to December 1983.

**99.** Mehta A. Efficacy of Amino acids, vitamins, minerals, docosa-hexaenoic acid, galactagogue combination on lactation: a postmarketing surveillance study. *J South Asian Fed Obstet Gynaecol.* 2014;6(2):118-122.

**100.** Yarnell E, Abascal K. Botanical medicine for thyroid regulation. *Altern Complement Ther.* 2006;12(3):107-112.

**101.** Mortel M, Mehta SD. Systematic review of the efficacy of herbal galactogogues. *J Hum Lact.* 2013;29(2):154-162.

**102.** Wilinska M, Schleußner E. Galactogogues and breastfeeding. *Nutrafoods.* 2015;14(3):119-125.

**103.** Serrao F, Corsello M, Romagnoli C, D'Andrea V, Zecca E. The effect of a silymarin-phosphatidylserine and galega galactagogue on mothers of preterm infants milk production. *Breastfeed Med.* 2017.

**104.** Madej A, Persson E, Lundh T, Ridderstråle Y. Thyroid gland function in ovariectomized ewes exposed to phytoestrogens. *J Chromatogr B Analyt Technol Biomed Life Sci.* 2002;777(1-2):281-287.

**105.** Kong M-S, Bajorek B. Medications in pregnancy: impact on time to lactogenesis after parturition. *J Pharm Pract Res.* 2008;38(3):205-208.

**106.** Bulloch S. Phytotherapy for polycystic ovarian syndrome. *Mod Phytotherapist.* 2004;8(2):13-21.

**107.** Chalfoun C, McDaniel C, Motarjem P, Evans G. Breast-enhancing pills: myth and reality. *Plast Reconstr Surg.* 2004;114(5):1330-1333.

**108.** Gettel G. The history of saw palmetto. http://www.sawpalmetto.com/history.html.

**109.** Hoffman D. Saw palmetto: herbal medicine materia medica. http://www.healthy.net/Materia_Medica/Saw_Palmetto_Herbal_Materia_Medica/277.

**110.** Bennett B, Hicklin J. Uses of saw palmetto (Serenoa repens, Arecaceae) in Florida. *Econ Bot.* 1998;52(4):381-393.

**111.** Sabnis PB, Gaitonde BB, Jetmalani M. Effects of alcoholic extracts of Asparagus racemosus on mammary glands of rats. *Indian J Exp Biol.* 1968;6(1):55-57.

**112.** Sharma S, Ramji S, Kumari S, Bapna JS. Randomized controlled trial of Asparagus racemosus (Shatavari) as a lactogogue in lactational inadequacy. *Indian Pediatr.* 1996;33(8):675-677.

**113.** Gupta M, Shaw B. A double-blind randomized clinical trial for evaluation of galactogogue activity of Asparagus racemosus Willd. *Iran J Pharm Res.* 2011;10(1):167-172.

**114.** Garg R, Gupta V. A comparative study on galactogogue property of milk and aqueous decoction of Asparagus racemosus in rats. *J Pharmacogn Phytochem.* 2010;2(2):36-39.

**115.** Goyal RK, Singh J, Lal H. Asparagus racemosus—an update. *Indian J Med Sci.* 2003;57(9):408-414.

**116.** Goel RK, Prabha T, Kumar MM, Dorababu M, Prakash, Singh G. Teratogenicity of Asparagus racemosus Willd. root, a herbal medicine. *Indian J Exp Biol.* 2006;44(7):570-573.

**117.** Hatherly P. *The Homeopathic Physician's Guide to Lactation.* Chapel Hill, Australia: Luminoz Pty Ltd; 2004.

## Chapter 15

**1.** Neifert M, Bunik M. Overcoming clinical barriers to exclusive breastfeeding. *Pediatr Clin North Am.* 2013;60(1):115-145.

**2.** Robertson BD. Working and breastfeeding: practical ways you can support employed breastfeeding mothers. *Clin Lact.* 2014;5(4):137-140.

**3.** Mohrbacher N. The magic number and long-term milk production. *Clin Lact.* 2011;2(1):15-18.

**4.** Yamada R, Rasmussen KM, Felice JP. "What is 'enough,' and how do i make it?": a qualitative examination of questions mothers ask on social media about pumping and providing an adequate amount of milk for their infants. *Breastfeed Med.* 2019;14(1):17-21.

**5.** Eglash A, Simon L. ABM Clinical Protocol #8: Human Milk Storage Information for Home Use for Full-Term Infants, Revised 2017. *Breastfeed Med.* 2017;12(7):390-395.

**6.** Fogleman AD, Meng T, Osborne J, Perrin MT, Jones F, Allen JC. Storage of unfed and leftover mothers' own milk. *Breastfeed Med.* 2018;13(1):42-49.

## Chapter 16

**1.** Neifert M, Bunik M. Overcoming clinical barriers to exclusive breastfeeding. *Pediatr Clin North Am.* 2013;60(1):115-145.

**2.** Murase M, Nommsen-Rivers L, Morrow AL, et al. Predictors of low milk volume among mothers who delivered preterm. *J Hum Lact.* 2014;30(4):425-435.

**3.** Chatterton RT Jr, Hill PD, Aldag JC, Hodges KR, Belknap SM, Zinaman MJ. Relation of plasma oxytocin and prolactin concentrations to milk production in mothers of preterm infants: influence of stress. *J Clin Endocrinol Metab.* 2000;85(10):3661-3668.

**4.** Parker LA, Sullivan S, Krueger C, Mueller M. Association of timing of initiation of breastmilk expression on milk volume and timing of lactogenesis stage II among mothers of very low-birth-weight infants. *Breastfeed Med.* 2015;10(2):84-91.

**5.** Morton J, Hall JY, Wong RJ, Thairu L, Benitz WE, Rhine WD. Combining hand techniques with electric pumping increases milk production in mothers of preterm infants. *J Perinatol.* 2009;29(11):757-764.

**6.** Acuna-Muga J, Ureta-Velasco N, de la Cruz-Bertolo J, et al. Volume of milk obtained in relation to location and circumstances of expression in mothers of very low birth weight infants. *J Hum Lact.* 2014;30(1):41-46.

**7.** Spatz DL. The use of human milk and breastfeeding in the neonatal intensive care unit. In: Riordan KWaJ, ed. *Breastfeeding and Human Lactation.* 5th ed. Burlington, MA: Jones & Bartlett Learning; 2016:495-521.

**8.** Asztalos EV. Supporting mothers of very preterm infants and breast milk production: a review of the role of galactogogues. *Nutrients.* 2018;10(5).

**9.** Cregan MD, De Mello TR, Kershaw D, McDougall K, Hartmann PE. Initiation of lactation in women after preterm delivery. *Acta Obstet Gynecol Scand.* 2002;81(9):870-877.

**10.** Henderson J, Hartmann P, Newnham J, Simmer K. Effect of preterm birth and antenatal corticosteroid treatment on lactogenesis II in women. *Pediatrics.* 2008;121(1):192-100.

**11.** Meier PP, Patel AL, Hoban R, Engstrom JL. Which breast pump for which mother: an evidence-based approach to individualizing breast pump technology. *J Perinatol.* 2016;36(7):493-499.

**12.** Flidel-Rimon O, Shinwell ES. Breast feeding twins and high multiples. *Arch Dis Child Fetal Neonatal Ed.* 2006;91(5):F377-380.

**13.** Gromada KK, Spangler AK. Breastfeeding twins and higher-order multiples. *J Obstet Gynecol Neonatal Nurs.* 1998;27(4):441-449.

**14.** Hayden TJ, Thomas CR, Forsyth IA. Effect of number of young born (litter size) on milk yield of goats: role for placental lactogen. *J Dairy Sci.* 1979;62(1):53-63.

**15.** Knight CH, Sorensen A. Windows in early mammary development: critical or not? *Reproduction.* 2001;122(3):337-345.

**16.** Gromada KK. Breastfeeding more than one: multiples and tandem breastfeeding. *NAACOGS Clin Issu Perinat Womens Health Nurs.* 1992;3(4):656-666.

**17.** Hormann E, Savage F. Relactation: a review of experience and recommendations for practice. 1998.

**18.** Tomar RS. Initiation of relactation: an Army Hospital based study of 381 cases. *Int J Contemp Pediatr.* 2016;3(2):635-638.

**19.** Bose CL, D'Ercole AJ, Lester AG, Hunter RS, Barrett JR. Relactation by mothers of sick and premature infants. *Pediatrics.* 1981;67(4):565-569.

**20.** Banapurmath S, Banapurmath CR, Kesaree N. Initiation of lactation and establishing relactation in outpatients. *Indian Pediatr.* 2003;40(4):343-347.

**21.** Mehta A, Rathi AK, Kushwaha KP, Singh A. Relactation in lactation failure and low milk supply. *Sudan J Pediatr.* 2018;18(1):39-47.

**22.** Centuori S, Burmaz T, Ronfani L, et al. Nipple care, sore nipples, and breastfeeding: a randomized trial. *J Hum Lact.* 1999;15(2):125-130.

**23.** Astuti I. The effectiveness of nipple stimulation by providing supplementary food to successful breastfeeding back (relactation) to the breastfeeding mothers in Southern Tangerang 2016. Paper presented at the 4th International Conference on Health Science, Indonesia, 2017.

**24.** Agarwal A, Jain A. Early successful relactation in a case of prolonged lactation failure. *Indian J Pediatr.* 2010;77(2):214-215.

**25.** Kayhan-Tetik B, Baydar-Artantas A, Bozcuk-Guzeldemirci G, Ustu Y, Yilmaz G. A case report of successful relactation. *Turk J Pediatr.* 2013;55(6):641-644.

**26.** Dehkhoda N, Valizadeh S, Jodeiry B, Hosseini MB. The effects of an educational and supportive relactation program on weight gain of preterm infants. *J Caring Sci.* 2013;2(2):97-103.

**27.** Wittig SL, Spatz DL. Induced lactation: gaining a better understanding. *Am J Matern Child Nurs.* 2008;33(2):76.

**28.** Kulski JK, Hartmann PE, Saint WJ, Giles PF, Gutteridge DH. Changes in the milk composition of nonpuerperal women. *Am J Obstet Gynecol.* 1981;139(5):597-604.

**29.** Perrin MT, Wilson E, Chetwynd E, Fogleman A. A pilot study on the protein composition of induced nonpuerperal human milk. *J Hum Lact.* 2015;31(1):166-171.

**30.** Swaminathan N. Strange but true: males can lactate. *Sci Am.* 2007;6:558-563.

**31.** Goldfarb L. An assessment of the experiences of women who induced lactation [doctoral dissertation]. Cincinnati, OH, Union Institute and University, 2010.

**32.** Farhadi R, Philip RK. Induction of lactation in the biological mother after gestational surrogacy of twins: a novel approach and review of literature. *Breastfeed Med.* 2017;12(6):373-376.

**33.** Wahlert L, Fiester A. Induced lactation for the nongestating mother in a lesbian couple. *Virtual Mentor.* 2013;15(9):753.

**34.** Reisman T, Goldstein Z. Case report: induced lactation in a transgender woman. *Transgend Health.* 2018;3(1):24-26.

**35.** MacDonald T, Noel-Weiss J, West D, et al. Transmasculine individuals' experiences with lactation, chestfeeding, and gender identity: a qualitative study. *BMC Pregnancy Childbirth.* 2016;16:106.

## Chapter 17

**1.** Vallone S. The role of subluxation and chiropractic care in hypolactation. *J Clin Chiropract Pediatr.* 2007;8(1-2):518-524.

**2.** Neri I, Allais G, Vaccaro V, et al. Acupuncture treatment as breastfeeding support: preliminary data. *J Altern Complement Med.* 2011;17(2):133-137.

**3.** Wei L, Wang H, Han Y, Li C. Clinical observation on the effects of electroacupuncture at Shaoze (SI 1) in 46 cases of postpartum insufficient lactation. *J Tradit Chin Med.* 2008;28(3):168-172.

**4.** Clavey S. The use of acupuncture for the treatment of insufficient lactation (Que Ru). *Am J Acupunct.* 1996;24(1):35-46.

**5.** Esfahani MS, Berenji-Sooghe S, Valiani M, Ehsanpour S. Effect of acupressure on milk volume of breastfeeding mothers referring to selected health care centers in Tehran. *Iran J Nurs Midwifery Res.* 2015;20(1):7.

**6.** Zhou HY, Li L, Li D, et al. Clinical observation on the treatment of post-cesarean hypogalactia by auricular points sticking-pressing. *Chin J Integr Med.* 2009;15(2):117-120.

**7.** Danasu R. Effectiveness of reflex zone stimulation on initiation and maintenance of lactation among lactation failure mothers at SMVMCH, Kalitheerthalkuppam, Puducherry. *Asian J Nurs Educ Res.* 2015;5(4):505-512.

**8.** Mirzaie P, Mohammad-Alizadeh-Charandabi S, Goljarian S, Mirghafourvand M, Hoseinie MB. The effect of foot reflexology massage on breast milk volume of mothers with premature infants: a randomized controlled trial. *Eur J Integr Med.* 2018;17(suppl C): 72-78.

**9.** Mohammadpour A, Valiani M, Sadeghnia A, Talakoub S. Investigating the effect of reflexology on the breast milk volume of preterm infants' mothers. *Iran J Nurs Midwifery Res.* 2018;23(5):371-375.

**10.** Ahn S, Kim J, Cho J. [Effects of breast massage on breast pain, breast-milk sodium, and newborn suckling in early postpartum mothers]. *J Korean Acad Nurs.* 2011;41(4):451-459.

**11.** Chu JY, Zhang L, Zhang YJ, Yang MJ, Li XW, Sun LL. [The effect of breast massage at different time in the early period after cesarean section]. *Zhonghua Yu Fang Yi Xue Za Zhi.* 2017;51(11):1038-1040.

**12.** Kabir N, Tasnim S. Oketani lactation management: a new method to augment breast milk. *J Bangladesh Coll Phys Surg.* 2009;27(3):155.

**13.** Sadovnikova A, Sanders I, Koehler S, Plott J. Systematic review of breast massage techniques around the world in databases and on YouTube. Paper presented at the Academy of Breastfeeding Medicine 20th Annual International Meeting, Los Angeles, 2015.

**14.** Anderson L, Kynoch K, Kildea S. Effectiveness of breast massage in the treatment of women with breastfeeding problems: a systematic review protocol. *JBI Database System Rev Implement Rep.* 2016;14(8):19-25.

**15.** Valdez J, Lujan C, Valdez M. Effects of kinesio tape application on breast milk production [poster]. *Acad Breastfeed Med.* 2018;13(suppl 2):S36.

**16.** Kruger THC, Leeners B, Naegeli E, et al. Prolactin secretory rhythm in women: immediate and long-term alterations after sexual contact. *Hum Reprod.* 2012;27(4):1139-1143.

**17.** Menezes R. Is indulging in sexual activity a potential mode of treatment for hypogalactia? *Med hypotheses.* 2008;71:808-823.

**18.** Pincus L. How hypnosis can help increase breast milk production. *Medela Round-Up.* 1996;13(3):5.

**19.** Feher S, Berger L, Johnson J, Wilde J. Increasing breast milk production for premature infants with a relaxation/imagery audiotape. *Pediatrics.* 1989;83(1):57-60.

**20.** Jonas W, Nissen E, Ransjo-Arvidson AB, Matthiesen AS, Uvnas-Moberg K. Influence of oxytocin or epidural analgesia on personality profile in breastfeeding women: a comparative study. *Arch Womens Ment Health.* 2008;11(5-6):335-345.

**21.** Anuhgera DE, Kuncoro T, Sumarni S, Mardiyono M, Suwondo A. Hypnotherapy is more effective than acupressure in the production of prolactin hormone and breast milk among women having given birth with caesarean section. *Med Sci.* 2018;7(1):25-29.

**22.** Routh CHF. *Infant Feeding and Its Influence on Life, or, The Causes and Prevention of Infant Mortality.* London: William Wood & Co.; 1879.

**23.** El Taweel AYA, Hasanin M, Sabour A, Rashed M. Effect of low level laser therapy of the breasts on milk production and composition in supplement-dependent mothers. *Breastfeed Med.* 2017;12(suppl):S2-S3.

**24.** Wang Q, Qiao H, Bai J. [Low frequency ultrasound promotes lactation in lactating rats]. *Nan Fang Yi Ke Da Xue Xue Bao.* 2012;32(5):730-733.

## Chapter 18

**1.** Feder Ostrov B. Some ill adults use breast milk to fight disease. *Seattle Times.* 2004.

**2.** Cleveland Clinic. Research uncovers healing properties of breast milk. https://newsroom.clevelandclinic.org/2017/08/25/research-uncovers-healing-properties-of-breast-milk.

**3.** Snyder M. Breast milk: the next cancer treatment? In: *Research and Development.* 2017.

**4.** Kendall-Tackett K. It's not just milk—It's relationship: recent findings in neuroscience show breastfeeding's effects throughout the lifespan. 2014;5(2):37-40.

**5.** Ystrom E. Breastfeeding cessation and symptoms of anxiety and depression: a longitudinal cohort study. *BMC Pregnancy Childbirth.* 2012;12:36.

6. Hahn-Holbrook J, Haselton MG, Dunkel Schetter C, Glynn LM. Does breastfeeding offer protection against maternal depressive symptomatology? A prospective study from pregnancy to 2 years after birth. *Arch Womens Ment Health.* 2013;16(5):411-422.

7. Sriraman NK, Melvin K, Meltzer-Brody S. ABM Clinical Protocol #18: Use of Antidepressants in Breastfeeding Mothers. *Breastfeed Med.* 2015;10(6):290-299.

8. Zauderer C, Davis W. Treating postpartum depression and anxiety naturally. *Holist Nurs Pract.* 2012;26(4):203-209.

9. Kendall-Tackett KA. *Depression in New Mothers: Causes, Consequences, and Treatment Alternatives.* 3rd ed. London: Taylor & Francis; 2016.

10. Conrad P, Adams C. The effects of clinical aromatherapy for anxiety and depression in the high risk postpartum woman—a pilot study. *Complement Ther Clin Pract.* 2012;18(3):164-168.

11. Moon RD A, Feldman-Winter L, Goodstein MH, Hauck FR. SIDS and other sleep-related infant deaths: updated 2016 recommendations for a safe infant sleeping environment. *Pediatrics.* 2016;138(5).

## Chapter 19

1. dos Santos CO, Dolzhenko E, Hodges E, Smith AD, Hannon GJ. An epigenetic memory of pregnancy in the mouse mammary gland. *Cell Rep.* 2015;11(7):1102-1109.

2. Nommsen-Rivers LA. Does Insulin explain the relation between maternal obesity and poor lactation outcomes? An overview of the literature. *Adv Nutr.* 2016;7(2): 407-414.

3. Chamberlin T, D'Amato JV, Arendt LM. Obesity reversibly depletes the basal cell population and enhances mammary epithelial cell estrogen receptor alpha expression and progenitor activity. *Breast Cancer Res.* 2017;19(1):128.

4. Harrison CL, Teede HJ, Joham AE, Moran LJ. Breastfeeding and obesity in PCOS. *Exp Rev Endocrinol Metab.* 2016;11(6):449-454.

5. Madarshahian F, Hassanabadi M. A comparative study of breastfeeding during pregnancy: impact on maternal and newborn outcomes. *J Nurs Res.* 2012;20(1):74-80.

6. Haile ZT, Chavan BB, Teweldeberhan A, Chertok IR. Association between gestational weight gain and delayed onset of lactation: the moderating effects of race/ethnicity. *Breastfeed Med.* 2017;12:79-85.

7. Barton JR, Joy SD, Rhea DJ, Sibai AJ, Sibai BM. The influence of gestational weight gain on the development of gestational hypertension in obese women. *Am J Perinatol.* 2015;32(7):615-620.

**8.** Hilson JA, Rasmussen KM, Kjolhede CL. Excessive weight gain during pregnancy is associated with earlier termination of breast-feeding among White women. *J Nutr.* 2006;136(1):140-146.

**9.** Kominiarek MA, Peaceman AM. Gestational weight gain. *Am J Obstet Gynecol.* 2017;217(6):642-651.

**10.** Institute of Medicine. *Weight Gain During Pregnancy: Reexamining the Guidelines.* Washington, DC; 2009.

**11.** Benson CT. Prolactin deficiency. http://emedicine.medscape.com/article/124526-overview.

**12.** Batrinos ML, Panitsa-Faflia C, Anapliotou M, Pitoulis S. Prolactin and placental hormone levels during pregnancy in prolactinomas. *Int J Fertil.* 1981;26(2):77-85.

**13.** Chapman T, Pincombe J, Harris M. Antenatal breast expression: a critical review of the literature. *Midwifery.* 2013;29(3):203-210.

**14.** Cox S. Expressing and storing colostrum antenatally for use in the newborn period. *Breastfeed Rev.* 2006;14(3):5-8.

**15.** Singh G, Chouhan R, Kidhu K. Effect of antenatal expression of breast milk at term in reducing breast feeding failures. *Med J Armed Forces India.* 2009(65):131-133.

**16.** Forster DA, Moorhead AM, Jacobs SE, et al. Advising women with diabetes in pregnancy to express breastmilk in late pregnancy (Diabetes and Antenatal Milk Expressing [DAME]): a multicentre, unblinded, randomised controlled trial. *Lancet.* 2017;389(10085):2204-2213.

**17.** Lamba S, Chopra S, Negi M. Effect of antenatal breast milk expression at term pregnancy to improve post natal lactational performance. *J Obstet Gynaecol India.* 2016;66(1):30-34.

**18.** Demirci J, Schmella M, Glasser M, Bodnar L, Himes KP. Delayed lactogenesis II and potential utility of antenatal milk expression in women developing late-onset pre-eclampsia: a case series. *BMC Pregnancy Childbirth.* 2018;18(1):68.

**19.** Vanklompenberg MK, Manjarin R, Trott JF, McMicking HF, Hovey RC. Late gestational hyperprolactinemia accelerates mammary epithelial cell differentiation that leads to increased milk yield. *J Anim Sci.* 2013;91(3):1102-1111.

**20.** Briton-Medrano G, Perez L. The efficacy of malunggay (moringa oleifera) given to near term pregnant women in inducing early postpartum breast milk production—a double blind randomized clinical trial. Unpublished, 2004.

**21.** Kong M-S, Bajorek B. Medications in pregnancy: impact on time to lactogenesis after parturition. *J Pharm Pract Res.* 2008;38(3):205-208.

**22.** Stein I. Bilateral polycystic ovaries. *Am J Obstet Gynecol.* 1945;50:385–396.

# Index

**A**

Abuse
  sexual, 177–78
  spousal/partner, 178–79
Acupressure, 274–75
Acupuncture, 105, 274–75, 296, 300
Adopted children. *See* Induced lactation
Age, maternal, 155, 166–67
Airway problems, 120–21
Alcohol, 83
Alfalfa, 223, 224, 230, 233, 235, 245, 302, 303
Allergies, 18, 120, 222, 228
Almonds, 98, 218
Alternative therapies, 273, 300
Alveoli, 4–6, 10, 171
Ameda, 53, 194
  Baby Cup, 53
  Breastfeeding Aid, 53
  pumps, 194–95
American Academy of Pediatrics, 68, 288
Amniotic fluid, 62, 63
Androgens, 148, 159, 160, 167, 297
Anemia, 91, 101, 102, 108, 162, 237, 263
Aniseed/anise seed, 224, 239
Anji, Inc., 277
Ankyloglossia. *See* Tongue-tie
Anorexia, 95
Antidiuretic hormone (ADH), 106
Anti-galactogogues, 81
Ashwagandha, 224, 239
Asparagus, 232
At-breast supplementation, 42
  devices for, 45–47
  hypoplasia and, 133–34
  induced lactation and, 265
  Lact-Aid, 35, 42, 44, 45, 290
  relactation and, 263–64
Atole, 217
Augmentation surgery (implants), 140–41
Autocrine processes, 10
Autoimmune disorders, 224
Ayurvedic, 224
Ayurvedic medicine, 218, 224, 232

**B**

Babies
  behaviors, 16–23
  breastfeeding adopted, 265–66, 268, 278
  commonly misinterpreted feeding
    behaviors, 16–23
  crying after breastfeeding, 18
  delaying post-birth bathing, 62
  ducts, 5, 142
  ductules, 4, 24
  early proximity to mother, 66
  fussiness in, 19–20, 81, 90
  gender and milk production, 10
  influence on milk production, 14
  large for gestational age, 103, 261
  normal feeding behavior, 16
  premature, 23, 63, 100, 103, 111, 211
  significantly underfed, 18, 39
  small for gestational age, 103, 111, 261
Baby Cup, Ameda, 53
Barger, Jan, 84
Barley, 83, 98, 217
Bed sharing, 78–79, 252
Beer, 83, 217
Bell's palsy, 122
Berens, Pamela, 107
Beta human chorionic gonadotropin (b-hCG), 107
Betamethasone, 100
Bilirubin, 16, 75, 76
Biopsies, breast, 139
Birth
  drugs used during, 100, 102, 104
  trauma in, 175–77
Birth and breastfeeding resources, 61–62
Birth control, hormonal, 81, 82, 166, 267, 268, 270
Black cohosh, 236
Blackseed, 225
Blessed thistle, 223, 224, 225, 230, 235
Blood-brain barrier, 213
Blood clotting problems, 268
Blunt force trauma, breast, 146
Body mass index (BMI), 296
*Bond Like No Other, A* (CD), 277

Borage, 225
Bottles, 18, 41, 43, 45–52, 78, 79–80,
    121, 207
  appropriateness for breastfed baby, 45
  nipple preference, 53
  pacing of feeding, 49
  slow-flowing nipples, 48, 178
  tongue-tie and, 46, 60, 200
  unnecessary, 79
  when to offer, 49–51
  working and, 251, 252
BPA (Bisphenol A), 136
Breastfeeding. *See* Feedings
Breastfeeding After Reduction (BFAR),143
Breastfeeding Aid, Ameda, 53
*Breastfeeding Made Simple* (Mohrbacher and
    Kendall-Tackett), 37–38
*Breastfeeding Meditation* (Menelli), 179
Breast lift, 140
Breast refusal, 51, 251, 265
Breast(s), 127–46
  absence of pregnancy-related changes, 153
  anatomical variations in, 128–32
  anatomy, 5
  areola, 4, 5, 64, 65, 106, 128, 131–33, 135, 139, 141–43,
    171, 196
  asymmetrical, 120, 133, 304
  augmentation (implants), 140–41
  burn trauma, 146
  compression, 153, 183, 191, 198, 200, 202, 255
  development of, 4–6
  diagnostic procedures on, 139
  fibrocystic, 225
  hypoplasia of (see Hypoplasia, mammary)
  infections of, 19, 88, 93, 124, 132, 136, 138
  injuries to, 144–46
  lift, 140
  lobes, 4
  massage, 49, 65–66, 143, 171
  milk production differences by side, 12
  Montgomery glands, 4
  physiology, 4–11
  reduction surgery, 271, 290, 292
  resource efficiency of, 12
  softening of, 64, 128
  storage capacity of, 12–13
  structural issues, 120, 128, 132–37
  surgery on, 138–39, 140
  tenderness, 5, 63, 85, 232, 304
  tissue density of, 132
Brick dust urine, 29
Bromocriptine, 82
Brown, Jan Ellen, 204
Brown rice, 94, 216
Bubble palates, 118
Bulimia, 95
Bupropion, 82
Burn trauma (breast), 146
Busyness, 179

**C**
Cabbage, 106
Cabergoline, 82, 150
Cafix, 217
Calcium, 218–20, 229, 230
Calibration (milk production), 11, 13, 28, 66, 68, 248, 262
Caraway seed, 225, 240
Cardiac problems, 121
Caregivers, 107, 247, 252, 253, 254–256
Case studies
  Angie (second pregnancy), 303
  Chana (hypoplasia), 304
  Cindy (herbal galactogogue use), 235
  Emily (supplementation), 35
  Gina (perseverance), 279
  Janelle (breast shape), 187
  Jean (sexual abuse), 178
  Judy (grief and loss), 177
  Laura (older mother), 166
  Rocio (low milk production), 71
  Sylvia (confusing advice), 1
Cassar-Uhl, Diana, 136
Celery, 106
Centers for Disease Control and Prevention, CDC, US, 197
Cerebral palsy, 122
Cesarean delivery (C-section), 61, 105–106, 107, 108,
    111, 275
Chamomile, 105
Chasteberry, 161, 226, 236, 245, 297
Chicken soup, 98
Chickpeas, 98, 216
Chiropractics, 273–74, 300
Cholesterol, 152
Cleft lip, 119
Cleft palate, 119–120
  hard, 119
  soft, 119
  submucosal, 119
Cluster feeds, 16, 21
Coconut, 98, 196, 218, 267
Colic, 224, 227
Colostrum, 7, 16, 59, 62, 64, 85, 102, 103, 105, 143, 166,
    172, 190, 233, 259, 266, 283, 298, 300–302
Compression, breast, 20, 65, 77, 121, 133, 137, 139,
    165–66, 198, 200, 255, 304
  hypoplasia and, 133
  post-surgery, 138
  technique for, 65–66
Contractions, stimulation of, 100, 298. *See also*
    Premature labor
Coriander, 224, 226, 240, 245
Corticosteroids, 82
Cortisol, 6, 7, 148, 174
Co-sleeping, 69, 78–79
Cox, Sue, 300
Craig, Randall, 157
Craniosacral therapy (CST), 125
Criticism, 284–85
Cucumbers, 106

Cumin, 144, 225, 227, 239
Cups, for supplementing, 53, 94

**D**
Dairy foods, 90–91
Dancer hold, 122
Dandelion, 106, 218, 233, 241, 245
Dandy Blend, 217
DDE (dichlorodiphenyldichloroethylene), 136
Decongestants, 255
Depo-Provera, 82
Depression, 181, 213, 214, 286, 288
Deutsch-Lash, Margie, 236
DHA (docosahaexaenoic acid), 288
DHEAS (dehydroepiandrosterone sulfate), 160
Diabetes
  domperidone and, 151, 160, 166
  gestational, 100, 229, 299, 302
  goat's rue and, 136, 137, 304
  nettle and, 231
  type 1, 154–55, 164
  type 2, 155–56
Diaper charts, 29
Diaper output, 15, 17, 27, 55, 74, 262
  evaluating, 26–27
  supplementation and, 27
  wetness, 26
Dill seed, 227, 235, 241
Dioscorides, 226
Distraction, to help letdown, 180
Diuretics, 106, 218, 226, 227, 229–231, 233, 239
Doctors of Traditional Chinese Medicine (TCM), 172–73
Domperidone, 71, 151, 160, 166, 187, 212–15, 221, 227, 228, 232, 269, 270, 298, 299, 302–4
  dosage, 213, 215
  passage into milk, 215
  safety, 212
  shatavari as an alternative for, 232
  side effects, 269
Dopamine receptor agonists, 82
Dostinex, 82
Down syndrome, 122
Drugs. *See* Medications

**E**
Ear, nose, and throat (ENT) specialists, 117
Eating disorders, 95
Edema, 106, 231, 245
Endocrine processes, 10
Endometriosis, 159, 225
Engorgement, 12, 23, 103, 141
Environmental contaminants, 135
EPA (eicosapentaenoic acid), 288
Epidurals, 104
Ergot alkaloids, 82
Estrogen, 6, 81, 153, 159, 221, 267, 270, 297. *See also* Phytoestrogens
  estrogenic herbs, 221
  receptors, 82
Eyedroppers, for supplementing, 41

**F**
Facial abnormalities, 120
Feedings, 16–18. *See also* Milk intake choking, sputtering, and arching during,
  crying and taking bottle after, 18
  duration, impediments to, 75–77
  in the first hour after birth, 61, 105, 259
  frequency days, 16–18
  frequency of, 16–17, 38, 44, 203, 249
  intervals between, 17–18
  nighttime, 44, 68, 69, 78, 95, 252, 256, 285, 288
  nursing between, 18, 43
  pumping after, 23, 71, 83, 101, 111, 192, 204
  schedules, 75, 76, 78
  short, 18
Feelings
  anger, 282
  grief and loss, 177
  guilt, 282
  inadequacy, 221
  judgmental, 284
  loneliness, 285
  overwhelmed, 286
  painful, confronting, 105, 122, 123
  postpartum depression (PPD), 96, 286
  regret, 282
  rejection, 283, 264
  resentment, 282
  selfishness, 283
Feldman, Betsy, 179, 277
Fennel, 217, 224, 227, 233, 235, 236, 241, 270
Fenugreek seed, 217, 224, 227, 241
Fibrocystic breasts, 255
Finger-feeding, 52–53
"Finish at the Breast" supplementation method, 50–51
Flanges/shields, breast, 132, 192, 195, 196, 198, 199, 253, 258, 260
  correct fit, 258
Flaxseed, 304
Flow preference, 42, 53
Foley Cup Feeder, 53
Food and Drug Administration (FDA), US, 197, 212
Foods, lactogenic, 97, 102, 215–16
Foremilk, 9
Formula, choosing, 40, 41
Fourth intercostal nerve, 139
Frees, Robin, 179, 277
Frenotomy, 117
Frenulum, 71, 113, 118. *See also* Tongue-tie; Lip-tie
  labial, 114
  lingual, 113
Frequency days, 16–17, 97

**G**
Gabbay, Mona, 108
Galactogogues, 82, 85, 102, 108, 137, 139, 143, 150, 153, 158, 160, 165, 166, 209, 210, 211, 216, 220, 221, 222, 223, 231, 232, 233, 236, 237, 256, 258, 261, 265, 270, 274, 302
  after surgery, 139

Galactogogues (*Cont.*)
  anti-, 81
  capsules, 234
  discontinuing, 237–38
  food, 209–11
  herbal (*see* Herbal galactogogues)
  homeopathic, 236–37
  metformin, 213
  passage into milk
      domperidone, 187
      herbs, 150, 156, 158
      metoclopramide, 160
  pharmaceutical (medications), 211–15
  pituitary gland and, 149, 150
  polycystic ovary syndrome and, 297
  postpartum thyroiditis and, 161
  pumping and, 166
  relactation and, 263–65
  targeting to specific needs, 168–69
  teas, 222, 223, 224, 225, 228, 229, 231, 234, 235
Galegin, 158, 161, 214, 229
Gastric bypass surgery, 95
Gavage tubes, 42, 52
Genna, Cathy, 11, 203
GERD (gastroesophageal reflux disease), 125
Gestational diabetes, 111, 148, 155, 156, 157, 159, 160, 229
Gestational ovarian theca lutein cysts (GOTLC), 103–104
Gima, Patricia, 166
Ginger, 215, 219
GLA (gamma-linolenic acid), 225
Glucophage. *See* Metformin
Goat's rue, 136, 228, 229, 230, 233, 235, 242, 270, 302, 304
Goldfarb, Lenore, 268
Good, Cynthia, 175
Grams, Marilyn, 255
Graves' disease, 163
Gripe water, 227
Gromada, Karen, 263
Growth hormone, 6
Growth spurts, 17, 254–55

**H**
Hair
  excessive body and facial, 161, 231
  loss, 231
Hale, Thomas, 177, 212
Hand-expression, 190–91, 200, 201, 259, 260, 262, 266
Hartmann, Peter, 85
Hashimoto's disease, 162
Hatherly, Patricia, 237
Hazelbaker FingerFeeder, 52
HELLP syndrome, 102
Hemorrhage, postpartum, 108, 162
Herbal galactogogues, 85, 158, 165, 166, 220, 221, 222, 223, 233, 270, 272
  anti-, 81
  commercial, 233–34
  customizing blends, 234–35
  dosages, 223
  during pregnancy, 219, 224, 228, 229

effectiveness of, 221
  forms, 222
  how long to take, 222
  how to take, 223
  hypoplasia and, 304
  overview of key types, 224–33
  passage into milk, 209
  postpartum thyroiditis and, 164–65
  safety of, 221
  targeting to cause of problem, 223
  titration of dosage, 213
Herbalists, 211, 223, 229, 231, 234
Hindmilk, 9, 18
Homeopathy, 184, 236–237
Hoover, Kay, 33
Hops, 217, 235, 236, 242, 245
Hormone receptor, 6, 155, 170, 214, 302
  aging and, 166
  estrogen, 82
  insulin, 7, 154, 155, 214
  progesterone, 82
  prolactin, 7, 58, 81, 148
  resistance, 136, 148
  role and function of, 6
Hormone(s), 6–8, 10, 13, 33, 58, 81, 82, 85, 89, 100, 106, 107, 133, 134, 137, 138, 146, 147–68, 174, 178, 210, 218, 224, 228, 230, 231, 233, 267, 268–71, 297–99, 303
  complexity of, 147, 148
  conditions interacting with, 147, 161, 222–23
  lactogenesis and, 7
  simulation of pregnancy, 267–68
Human chorionic gonadotropin (hCG), 6
Human placental lactogen (hPL), 6, 154
Humphrey, Sheila, 222, 226
Hydration, 30
Hyoid bone, 118
Hyperinsulinemia, 155
Hyperlactation, 19, 164
Hypertension, 101–2, 159, 160, 162, 164, 297, 298, 301
  gestational, 101. (*see also* Pregnancy induced hypertension)
Hyperthyroidism, 100, 161, 163, 164, 165, 183
Hypertonia, 123
*Hypnosis for Making More Milk* (Frees), 179
Hypoplasia, mammary, 133, 134, 135, 136, 137, 153, 159, 215, 218, 229, 268, 303, 304
  causes and effects of, 133–35
  galactogogues and, 137
  metformin and, 214
Hypothalamus, 161
Hypothyroidism, 150, 152, 155, 159, 161, 162, 163, 164, 167, 228, 242, 304
Hypotonia, 122

**I**
IBCLC. *See* International Board Certified Lactation Consultant
Implants. *See* Augmentation surgery
Induced lactation, 265–68, 276
  menopause protocol, 268

Newman-Goldfarb protocols, 268
Induced lactation, 265–68
Infant oral motor function therapy, 125
Infections, 144
  in babies, 124
  breast, 19, 132, 136, 138
Infertility, 150, 157, 158–59, 226, 232, 261, 266, 290, 297, 299
Insensitive remarks, 284–85
Insulin, 7, 95, 100, 111, 148, 154–57, 299
  receptors, 7, 154, 155, 214
  resistance, 7, 95, 136, 148, 153, 155–61, 163, 167, 214, 215, 220, 229, 296, 297, 303
International Board Certified Lactation Consultant (IBCLC), 33, 60, 297, 357
International Lactation Consultant Association (ILCA), 33
Intrauterine devices (IUDs), 81
Intrauterine growth restricted (IUGR) babies, 261
Intravenous (IV) fluids, 61
Inverted nipples, 128–30, 296
Involution, 12, 93, 100, 103, 139, 162, 210, 264
Iron deficiency, 91, 101, 237

**J**
Jaundice, 16, 35, 60, 74–76
  physiologic jaundice, 75

**K**
Khalsa, Awtar Kaur, 276

**L**
Lact-Aid, 35, 42, 44, 45, 290
Lactare, 232
Lactation Blend, 304
Lactation consultants, 30, 45, 52, 60, 77, 84, 96, 102, 106, 110, 194, 196, 234, 286, 302. *See also* International Board Certified Lactation Consultant
Lactogenesis, 8
Lactogenesis I, 7
Lactogenesis II, 8, 101
Lactose, 10, 278
La Leche League, 79, 177, 272
Large for gestational age (LGA) babies, 111
Laryngomalacia, 121, 125
Latching, 21, 43, 48, 49, 52, 64, 65, 110, 117, 124, 130, 132, 139, 146, 178, 261, 265
  at-breast supplementation and, 42
  body language and, 21
  breast surgery and, 138–39
  clues to problems, 72
  hypotonia and, 122
  large nipples and, 132
  nipple inversion and, 131
  optimal, 63, 70
  sensory processing disorders and, 123–24
  suck problems and, 125, 182
  tongue-tie and, 46, 60, 113
Law of Similars, 236
Leaking, 23, 24, 47, 173, 302
Let down. *See* letdown

Let-Down Formula, 184
*Letting Down* (Wierzbicki and Feldman), 179, 277
Lettuce, 218
Liposuction, 140
Lip-tie, 116, 125
Lochia, 22
Low birth weight, 162
Lowdog, Tieraona, 230
Lupus, 224

**M**
Magnesium, 158, 166
Marshmallow root, 230, 235
Massage, breast, 65–66, 143, 153, 171–72
Mastitis, 93, 136, 144
Maternal Concepts Evert-It Nipple Enhancer, 130
Maternity leave, 174
Maxeran. *See* Metoclopramide
Meconium stools, 26
Medela, 193
  Baby Cup Feeder, 53
  BabyWeigh scale, 27, 28
  pumps, 193–94
  Supplemental Nursing System (SNS), 42
  Soft Feeder, 53
Medications, 21, 26, 40, 60, 61, 74, 75, 80–82, 90, 100, 101, 104, 107, 111, 125, 144, 149, 150, 152, 154–57, 162, 163, 177, 210–212, 214, 221–23, 255, 264, 266, 267, 268, 270, 286, 296, 302
  anti-depressant, 100
  anti-galactogogue, 81
  to decrease milk production, 80, 81
  to increase milk production, 212
  during labor, 60, 61
  passage into milk, 210–212, 221
  prenatal exposure to, 121–22
*Medications and Mothers' Milk* (Hale), 80, 177, 212, 286
Medicine droppers, 41, 53
Menelli, Sheri, 179, 277
Menopause, 268
Menstrual cycle, 6, 268, 297
Menstruation, 165–66
Metformin, 155–58, 160, 161, 163, 213–15, 226, 296
  passage into milk, 156
Methergine, 107
Methotrexate, 107
Methylergonovine maleate. *See* Methergine
Metoclopramide, 71, 160, 213, 214
  passage into milk, 160
Micrognathia, 120
Milk
  color of, 8, 24
  coming in of, 7, 8, 105
  drying up of, 80, 82
  excessive flow of, 9, 18, 20
  fat content of, 24, 91
  human donor, 102
  oversupply of, 257
  slow flow of, 48

Milk drunk expression, 22
Letdown, 9, 173, 183, 255, 261
  aids for, 44–45, 143, 190
  alcohol effect on, 83
  baby's inducement of, 265
  breast surgery and, 138–39
  chasteberry and, 226
  conditioning, 175
  dill seed and, 227
  fennel and, 227
  hyperthyroidism and, 163
  hypothyroidism and, 161
  inability to feel, 113
  mental stimulation of, 145, 180–82, 292
  overview of process, 5–6
  pharmaceutical aids, 211
  potential inhibitors of, 174–79
  red raspberry and, 231
  remedies for problems, 234, 236–37
  spinal cord injuries and, 145
Milk expression, 149, 195, 264, 265. *See also* Hand
    expression; Pumping
  after breastfeeding, 149
  during pregnancy, 149
  problems with, 149–50
Milk intake, 21, 27, 30, 31, 121. *See also* Feedings
  determining adequacy of, 32, 44
  using body language to gauge, 21–22, 51
Milk production,
  baby's influence on, 9–11
  body's decision-making in, 9–11, 12
  common inhibiting substances, 81–85
  commonly misinterpreted indicators of low, 16–24
  differences in breast size, 6, 12, 133
  four-hour test of, 32
  golden rule of, 12
  management problems, 75–80
  myths, truths, misunderstandings, 15, 80
  nutrition, role of in, 39, 41, 55, 59, 76, 87, 88, 93, 97,
    264, 290
  upper limit question, 13
Milk removal, 23, 42, 58, 65
Milk Supply Equation, 4
Milk thistle (blessed milk thistle; Lady's thistle; Mary's
    thistle), 230
Millet, 216
Mind-body connection, 173–82
  increasing milk via, 173–74, 182
  inhibiting factors, 174–79
Miscarriage, 159, 160, 165, 177, 299
Mohrbacher, Nancy, 250, 254
More Milk Plus, Motherlove Herbal Company, 187
More Milk Special Blend, Motherlove Herbal
    Company, 71
*Mothering Multiples* (Gromada), 263
Motherlove Herbal Company, 242
'Mothers Overcoming Breastfeeding Issues (MOBI),
    87, 285
Motherwort, 184
Motilium. *See* Domperidone

Multiples, 262–63
Muscular-skeletal problems, 146
Mushrooms, champignon, 172


**N**
Naps, 68, 203
Nature's Way, 79
Naturopaths, 211
Nerve damage, 120
Nervous system issues, 121–24
Nettle, 223, 231, 233, 235
Newman, Jack, 268
Nicotine, 84. *See also* Smoking
Niplette, Avent, 130
Nipple nudge technique, 130
Nipple(s), bottle, 45–46, 48
  confusion, 45–46
  slow-flowing, 48
Nipple(s), mother, 5, 9, 19, 21, 22, 31, 42, 45, 47, 52, 64,
    110, 128, 132
  inverted or flat, 128–32, 297
  inverted release surgery, 297
  large, 132
  piercings, 132
  soreness, 195. (*see also* Painful breastfeeding)
  unusually shaped, 132
Nipple shields, 265, 266
*Nursing Mother's Herbal, The* (Humphrey), 222
Nurturing, self, 177, 181
Nutrition affecting milk production, 54, 55, 59, 76, 87, 88,
    90, 95, 97, 216


**O**
Oatmeal, 216, 217, 304
Oat straw/oats, 233
Obesity, 96, 136, 152, 159, 160, 297
Obturators for cleft palate, 119
Omega-3 fatty acids, 288
Organic Partners, 182
Organochlorines, 136
Otolaryngologists. *See* Ear, nose, and throat (ENT)
    specialists
Outside interferences with feeding, 80
Ovarian cysts, 159
Overlying, 118
Oxytocin, 9, 10, 62, 83, 84, 104, 105, 106, 110, 139, 142,
    145, 148, 162, 170
  acupuncture and, 274
  emotional factors and, 145, 173
  fourth intercostal nerve and, 139
  herbal galactogogues and, 233
  hyperthyroidism and, 163
  hypothyroidism and, 161
  induced lactation and, 266
  nasal spray, 145, 164
  problems with, 148
  shatavari and, 232
  spinal cord injuries and, 145
  synthetic, 178, 302

**P**

Pacifiers, 67, 77–78

Painful breastfeeding, 23, 74, 123, 124, 281. *See also* Nipple(s), mother: soreness

Palatal variations, 118–120
  bubble palate, 118
  high palate, 118

Papaya, 219, 220

Parlodel, 82

Parsley, 84

Pasteurizing human milk, 40, 41

PCBs (polychlorinated biphenyls), 136

PCOS. *See* Polycystic ovary syndrome

Peppermint, 84

Periodontal syringe for supplementation, 130, 132

Pero, 217

Phenformin, 172

Phytoestrogens, 221, 224, 225, 227, 231

Pitocin, 104, 106

Pituitary
  gland, 7, 9, 10, 108, 149, 150, 161, 226
  insult, 108

Placenta, 6, 7, 96, 97, 102, 103, 106, 107, 111, 133, 162, 261, 262
  abruption, 162
  insufficiency, 133
  retention, 106–7

Polycystic ovary syndrome (PCOS), 71, 104, 152, 156–61, 165, 214, 226, 229, 232, 277, 290, 297, 303
  incidence of, 152, 156, 159
  symptoms of, 152–53, 159
  thyroid dysfunction and, 159, 160, 161
  treatment of, 160

Postpartum depression (PPD), 286

Postpartum thyroiditis/thyroid dysfunction (PPTD), 161, 164–65

Post-traumatic stress disorder (PTSD), 175–79

Preeclampsia, 1, 101, 102, 159, 162, 163. *See also* Pregnancy-induced hypertension

Pregnancy, 85, 100, 233, 297, 302
  breastfeeding during, 87–88
  herbal galactogogues during, 233
  milk expression during, 149
  planning for future, 296–97
  strategies for current, 297–301

Pregnancy-induced hypertension (PIH), 101, 160, 162, 298. *See also* Preeclampsia

Premature babies, 258–61

Premature delivery, 160, 163

Premature labor, 59, 85, 232. *See also* Contractions, stimulation of

Premenstrual syndrome, 225

Primary problems, 73, 304

Progesterone, 6, 7, 81, 82, 97, 103, 107, 226
  chasteberry and, 226
  polycystic ovary syndrome and, 297
  receptors, 82

Prolactin, 7, 10, 58, 68, 79, 82–84, 90, 92, 95, 101, 104, 105, 108, 110, 133, 139, 142, 145, 148–52, 153, 154, 163, 165, 166, 168, 174, 175, 197, 203, 210–13, 217, 219, 221, 224, 226, 232, 268, 270, 272, 274–78, 299, 302, 304
  acupuncture and, 105
  baseline, 10, 108, 149, 151, 212
  chasteberry and, 226
  diabetes and, 302
  domperidone and, 151
  emotional factors and, 145
  fenugreek and, 163
  fourth intercostal nerve and, 139
  galactogogues and, 270, 272
  gestational ovarian theca lutein cysts and, 103
  hyperthyroidism and, 163
  inhibitors of, 174–75
  measuring, 151
  medications stimulating, 150
  metoclopramide and, 213
  nighttime levels of, 95
  nutrition and, 95
  obesity and, 152
  polycystic ovary syndrome and, 161
  receptors, 81, 295
  replacement therapy, 150
  resistance, 153
  shatavari and, 232
  Sheehan's syndrome and, 108
  spinal cord injuries and, 145
  surge, 149–51, 163, 197

Protein requirements, 89, 90

Pseudoephedrine, 82

Puberty, 6, 13, 95, 133, 136, 137, 146, 153, 159, 303

Pumping, 9, 12, 13, 22, 23, 32, 40, 58, 60, 63, 64, 68, 71, 78, 80, 83, 101, 103, 105, 106, 107, 111, 119, 120, 121, 137, 139, 149, 150, 151, 158, 160, 166, 174, 182, 184, 192, 194
  after breast surgery, 139
  after feedings, 197, 202
  exclusive, 257–58
  between feedings, 202
  frequency of, 203–4, 255
  hypoplasia and, 137, 304
  induced lactation and, 265–66
  inverted nipples drawn out by, 128–30
  for multiples, 262–63
  during the night, 203
  power, 194, 203
  for premature babies, 258–59
  relactation and, 264
  taking a break from, 201
  techniques, 192

Pumpkin, 218

Pump(s)
  choosing, 192–94
  consumer-grade, 194, 253
  effectiveness of, 195, 196
  hospital-grade, 193, 267, 304
  manual, 192, 253
  used, 160

**R**

Receptors. *See* Hormone receptor
Red clover blossoms, 231
Red raspberry, 231, 233
Reduction surgery, 271, 290
Reflexology, 105, 300
Reflux, 124–25
Reglan. *See* Metoclopramide
Relactation, 263–65
Relaxation techniques, 179
Relaxing environment, 179
Rescue Remedy, 184
Reverse cycling, 255–56
Reverse pressure softening (RPS), 64, 128
Rice, 171, 216
Rice pudding, 218
RPS. *See* Reverse pressure softening

**S**

Sage, 84, 255
Santa Barbara County Breastfeeding Coalition, 79
Saw palmetto, 161, 231
Seaweed soup, 220
Secondary problems, 73
Selective serotonin reuptake inhibitors (SSRIs),
      100, 214
Self-talk, 181, 182
Sensory Processing Disorder Network, 123
Sensory processing disorders, 123–24
Sesame seeds, 218
Sexual abuse, 177–78
Shatavari, 223, 224, 230, 232, 244
Sheehan's syndrome (pituitary infarction), 108
Shiatsu. *See* Acupressure
Shields, breast. *See* Flanges/shields, breast
Side effects
      domperidone, 214
      herbal galactogogues, 221
      metformin, 90, 157
      metoclopramide, 214
Silymarin, 229
Skin-to-skin contact, 61, 63, 75, 102, 105, 124, 311
Sleep
      apnea, 118
      baby's, 165, 176, 249, 252, 255, 256, 287
      mother's, 203, 252
'Slings, 124
Small for gestational age (SGA) babies, 261
Smell, baby's sense of, 199, 266
Smillie, Tina, 50
Smoking, 24, 84, 164
Snoring, 118
Supplemental Nursing System (SNS)
      Medela, 42
Solids, 237, 256
Spinal cord injuries, 7, 35, 145–46
Spousal/partner abuse, 178–79
Star of anise, 224
Stinging nettle, 231

Stools, 19, 26, 231
      appearance of, 19, 26
      meconium, 26, 29
Storage capacity, 12, 250–51
Stretch marks, 133
Stridor, 121
Subluxation, 273
Sucking blisters, 113
Suck problems, 31, 46, 47, 52, 60, 110–11, 125, 182
Sudafed, 82
Sudden infant death syndrome (SIDS), 69, 288
Sunflower seeds, 218
Supplementation, 27, 37, 39, 42, 43, 45, 48, 50, 79,
      85, 89, 95, 102, 121, 157, 160, 207, 262, 299. *See
      also* At-breast supplementation; Bottles; Cups, for
      supplementing; Finger-feeding
      choosing, 210, 223
      determining amount of, 43
      devices for, 41–49
      for multiples, 262–63
      at night, 39, 51
      solids as, 55
      unnecessary, 79
      weaning from, 55, 95
      when to begin, 49–50
Support groups, 258, 285
Surgery, breast
      augmentation (implants), 140–41
      biopsies, 139
      lift, 140
      liposuction (reduction), 141
      pedicle (reduction), 142
      reduction, 141
Surgery to correct nipple inversion, 128, 138
Surrogate parenthood. *See* Induced lactation
Swaddling, 69, 123, 124
Syringes, 41, 43, 52

**T**

$T_3$. *See* Thyroid hormones: triiodothyronine
$T_4$. *See* Thyroid hormones: thyroxine
TCDD (tetrachlorodibenzo-p-dioxin), 136
Teas, as galactogogues, 222, 224, 225, 228, 229,
      231, 234
Testosterone, 81, 104, 160, 161, 167, 211, 271
Test weights, 30–32, 37, 55
Thyroid dysfunction, 161–65, 183
      fenugreek and, 163, 217, 219, 223–225, 227, 228
      Graves' disease, 163
      Hashimoto's disease, 162
      hyperthyroidism, 100, 161, 163–64, 165, 183
      hypothyroidism, 150, 152, 155, 159, 161–63, 183,
            228, 304
      nettle and, 223
      postpartum thyroiditis/thyroid dysfunction (PPTD),
            161, 164–65
      red clover blossoms and, 231
      subclinical hypothyroidism, 162
      testing for, 162, 164

Thyroid hormones, 6
    thyroid-releasing hormone (TRH), 161
    thyroid-stimulating hormone (TSH), 161, 165
    thyroxine (T₄), 145, 161, 163
    triiodothyronine (T₃), 145, 161, 167, 228, 231,
Tinctures, 71, 184, 187, 217, 218, 222, 223, 225, 228, 229,
    231, 234, 236
Tongue-tie, 46, 60, 111, 113–115, 117, 118, 120, 200, 277
Torticollis, 111
Touch, 113, 118, 123
Toxemia, 101. *See also* Pregnancy-induced hypertension
Tracheomalacia, 121
Traditional Chinese Medicine (TCM), 96, 172. *See also*
    Doctors of Traditional Chinese Medicine
Traditional Medicinals, 274
Trauma
    birth, 175–77
    to the breasts, 146
Travel, 253
Thyroid stimulating hormone (TSH)
Turner, Mechell, 184
Twins. *See* Multiples
Type 1 diabetes, 154–56, 164
Type 2 diabetes, 7, 100, 148, 155–59, 214, 296

**U**
Urinary tract infections, 124
Urine output, 29–30
Uvula, 119

**V**
Vegetarianism, 90, 94
Velopharyngeal insufficiency, 119
Vervain, 233, 236
Visitor syndrome, 67
Visualization, 180–81
Vitamin B₁₂, 90
Vitamin C, 92, 228
Vitanica, 304
Vitex. *See* Chasteberry

**W**
Warmth, applying, 171
Watermelon, 106
Weaning, 6, 55, 95, 136, 146, 156, 176, 212, 264, 286. *See also* Relactation
Weight conversions, 31
Weight gain (baby's), 15, 17–19, 27, 28, 33, 37–39, 55, 74,
    102, 113, 120, 124, 125, 152, 153, 162, 167, 183, 213,
    262, 267, 296, 298
    accurate measurement of, 28–29
    cleft palate and, 119
    excessive milk flow and, 18–19
    feeding test weights, 30
    frequency of measurement, 28
    gastroesophageal reflux and, 125
    infections and, 19, 124
    latch problems and, 74
    of multiples, 262
    supplementation and, 27, 37, 102
Weight loss (baby's), 26
Wellbutrin, 82
Wierzbicki, James, 277
Wine, 83
Women, Infants, and Children (WIC), US, 33
Working, 251–58
    advance maximization of milk production, 295,
        300, 303
    caregivers and, 247, 249, 252
    increasing milk supply, 255–56
    planning for breastfeeding, 60–61
    reasons for milk decrease, 252–53
    scheduling and, 249–51
World Health Organization, 27

**Y**
Yoga, 276

**Z**
Zinc, 88
Zyban, 82

# About the Authors

Lisa Marasco has worked with breastfeeding mothers for more than 35 years, first as a La Leche League Leader and then as an International Board Certified Lactation Consultant (IBCLC) since 1993. She holds a master's degree in human development with specialization in lactation consulting and was also designated a Fellow of ILCA. Recognized for her expertise in milk production issues, Lisa is a contributing author to the *Core Curriculum for Interdisciplinary Lactation Care* and is a Cochrane author and continues to research, write, and speak nationally and abroad as she pursues answers to milk supply mysteries. Lisa has 4 children and 7 grandchildren and lives with her husband Tom on the central coast of California, where she continues her clinical work with breastfeeding families through the Santa Barbara County Public Health Department Nutrition Services/WIC.

Diana West earned a bachelor's degree in psychology but discovered a passion for breastfeeding while struggling with low milk production for her first son. She was accredited as a volunteer La Leche League Leader in 1998 and became an IBCLC in 2002. She published her first book in 2001, *Defining Your Own Success: Breastfeeding After Breast Reduction Surgery*, and co-authored *Sweet Sleep: Nighttime and Naptime Strategies for the Breastfeeding Family*, *The Womanly Art of Breastfeeding* (8th ed), *The Clinician's Breastfeeding Triage Tool*, and *Breastfeeding After Breast and Nipple Procedures*. Diana is also co-author of a qualitative research study about trans men's experiences with birth and breastfeeding. She speaks at lactation conferences throughout the world and has published numerous breastfeeding articles for leading magazines. She has 3 grown sons and lives in the picturesque mountains of northwestern New Jersey while attending seminary to become a Unitarian Universalist minister.